AA TOWN PLANS

GW00717040

Editor Barry Francis
Designed by the Publications Production Unit
Compiled by the Publications Research Unit
Town Plans produced by the Cartographic Unit of the Automobile
Association and based upon Ordnance Survey maps with the sanction of
the controller of HM Stationery Office. Crown copyright reserved.

Typeset by: Turnergraphic Ltd
Printed by: Hazell Watson & Viney Ltd

Cover photographs reproduced by courtesy of the British Tourist
Authority, Bath City Council (Department of Leisure and Tourist
Services) and K S Reynolds, Sally Lunn's House, Bath.

Every effort has been made to ensure that the plans, including
one-way systems, were up to date at the time of going to press.
Recent changes may not have been included however: keep a careful
watch for signs.

*The contents of this publication are believed correct at the time of
printing, but the correct position may be checked through the AA.
While every effort is made to ensure that information appearing in
advertisements is correct, no responsibility can be accepted by
the AA for any inaccuracies.*

ISBN 0 86145 003 5   55686

Stop off in a Crest for a meal and a rest.

You'll have no trouble finding one. There are 29 EuroCrest Hotels and 20 Crest Motels within easy reach of motorways and major roads in Britain and Europe. And 27 CrestRest Hotels the length and breadth of the land.

Each offers excellent accommodation at very competitive rates — with even lower rates at weekends. And a superb choice of meals throughout the day. For your free copy of our map and tariff, ring today.

Crest Hotels Europe

Reservations/Information
London 01-903 6422
Coventry 0203 611813
Preston 0772 52682
Glasgow 041 812 0306

CONTENTS

LEGEND

Plans

AA Recommended route	
Other roads	
Restricted roads (Access only/ Buses only)	
Traffic roundabout	
One-way street	
Parking zone	
Official car park (open air)	P
Parking available on payment (open air)	P
Multi-storey car park	G
Convenience	C
Convenience with facilities for the disabled	C
Tourist Information Centre	i
Pedestrians only	
Shopping area	
Parks and open spaces	
AA Service Centre	AA
AA Road Service Centre	AA 83
Church/Cathedral	+
City Walls	
Post Office	HPO/GPO/PO
Public buildings and places of interest	10
Grid square letter	L
Map continuation	
The following symbols relate to advertisers:	

Text

Reference to the grid square and public buildings and places of interest is shown as a letter and number respectively. The letter comes first with the number following, in brackets.

Ancient Monument	(AM)
National Trust	(NT)
National Trust for Scotland	(NTS)

We have places in all the best places

In the heart of major towns and cities of Great Britain there is a Centre or Centrelink Hotel – each one observing the same high standards of service and value. You'll find a full range of facilities, modern comfortable bedrooms and an attractive choice of restaurants, bars and coffee shops, all at reasonable prices.

For reservations or further details ring any Centre or Centrelink Hotel or contact:

Centre Hotels
23 Newman Street, London W1P 3HA.
Tel: 01-637 5131 (Admin.)
01-580 3871 (Reservations)

† A Centrelink Hotel

LONDON
Bedford Corner Hotel	Tel: 01-580 7766
Bloomsbury Centre Hotel	Tel: 01-837 1200
Ivanhoe Hotel	Tel: 01-636 5601
Kenilworth Hotel	Tel: 01-636 3283
Regent Centre Hotel	Tel: 01-388 2300
St. James Hotel	Tel: 01-834 2360
West Centre Hotel	Tel: 01-385 1255

● **NAIRN** †Newton Hotel Tel: 066 75 31444

● **DUNDEE**
†Tay Hotel Tel: 0382 21641
†Royal Hotel Tel: 0382 24074
● **EDINBURGH** Grosvenor Centre Hotel Tel: 031-226 6001
● **PEEBLES** †Peebles Hotel Hydro Tel: 0721 20602

GLASGOW
Glasgow Centre Hotel
Tel: 041-248 2355

● **NEWCASTLE**
Newcastle Centre Hotel
Tel: 0632 26191

BOWNESS-ON-WINDERMERE
†Priory Hotel Tel: 09662 4377

†Imperial Hotel Tel: 0253 23971 **BLACKPOOL**

● **YORK** The White Swan Inn Tel: 0904 28851

†Prince of Wales Hotel Tel: 0704 36688 **SOUTHPORT**

● **HULL** Hull Centre Hotel Tel: 0482 26462

Liverpool Centre Hotel Tel: 051-709 7050 **LIVERPOOL**

CHESTER ●
†Blossoms Hotel Tel: 0244 23186

● **LEICESTER** Leicester Centre Hotel Tel: 0533 20471

NEWTOWN
†Bear Hotel
Tel: 0686 26964

BIRMINGHAM
Birmingham Centre Hotel
Tel: 021-643 2747
†Imperial Hotel
Tel: 021-643 6751

CAMBRIDGE
†University Arms Tel: 0223 51241

BASILDON Essex Centre Hotel
Tel: 0268 3955

CARDIFF
Cardiff Centre Hotel
Tel: 0222 388681

● **LONDON**

LONDON AIRPORT Heathrow
Centre Airport Hotel
Tel: 01-759 2400

GATWICK Centre Airport Hotel
Tel: 0293 29991

HASTINGS †Queen's Hotel
Tel: 0424 424167

BOURNEMOUTH †Kelvin Hotel Tel: 0202 292244

BRIGHTON/HOVE
†Imperial Hotel
Tel: 0273 731121

PLYMOUTH
Tel: Plymouth 20782
†Continental Hotel

PORTSMOUTH
Portsmouth Centre Hotel
Tel: 0705 27651

A Division of the Coral Leisure Group

4

Save money with an AA members personal loan

Specially arranged terms mean that, as an AA Member you can obtain a personal loan at a reduced rate of interest. And that means lower monthly instalments to pay. For full details fill in this coupon, cut out the complete page, then fold and post as shown overleaf. You don't need to find an envelope or a stamp.

P.T.O. for posting instructions

Please send AA Members Personal Loan details, current rate card, and application form to:–

Name

Address

County   Postcode

IMI Mercantile Credit   **AA**

77

Post now for the best route to a personal loan

(Remember to fill in the coupon overleaf first)

3. Fold here and tuck in.

NO
STAMP
REQUIRED

Mercantile Credit Co. Ltd.,
Marketing Administration,
FREEPOST,
London WC2B 5XA.

2. Fold here.

No stamp needed to get details of AA members loans

AA

1. Fold here.

How to post

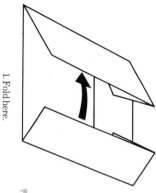

1. For full details of AA Members Loans complete coupon overleaf.

2. Detach complete page.

3. Fold and tuck in as indicated, and post. No stamp needed.

Anywhere in Britain you're never far from that THF smile of welcome

Trust Houses Forte have over 200 hotels in Britain.

They offer wonderful variety, quiet country inns, famous London hotels, seaside resort hotels, airport hotels and modern Post Houses. But at each of them you will find that certain smile of welcome, a friendly warmth, a desire to make you comfortable.

So when you need a hotel for holiday or business, for an overnight stay or a meal, choose a Trust Houses Forte Hotel.

Queen's Hotel Cheltenham

Albany Hotel Birmingham

Shakespeare Hotel Stratford-on-Avon

ABERDEEN

CENTRAL PLAN

F   **AA Service Centre** — Fanum House, 19 Golden Square *tel 51231*

G [i]   **Tourist Information Centre** — City Tourist Bureau, St Nicholas House, Broad Street *tel 23456* Monday to Friday; *24890/21814/21810* Saturdays and Bank Holidays

Public buildings and places of interest

G(1)   **Art Gallery, War Memorial and Cowdray Hall**
The Art Gallery contains works of art of the Scottish school from the 16thC to the present day, the French Impressionists and post-Impressionists and the Modern English school; sculpture, lithography, and the decorative arts.
James Dun's House is an 18th-C building now used as a museum for children.

H(2)   **Civic Arts Centre**

G(3)   **East and West Churches of St Nicholas**
These churches were divided into their separate parts at the Reformation. Notable features include the tapestries by Mary Jamesone, daughter of the Scottish artist George Jamesone, St Mary's Chapel (15th-C) and the fine Gothic roof.

L(4)   **Fish Market**

G(5)   **Gordon's College** Founded in 1739 by Robert Gordon.

L(6)   **Harbour Offices**

G(7)   **James Dun's House**

F(8)   **Library**

G(9)   **Marischal College** Founded in 1593 and since 1860 part of the University of Aberdeen. The building has an impressive frontage of white Kemnay granite of 1906, and houses the University's Anthropological Museum.

H(10)   **Mercat Cross** Dating from 1668, with relief portraits of Scottish kings.

G(11)   **Municipal Buildings** City of Aberdeen District Council

J(12)   **Music Hall** Two adjoining halls built in the 19thC in Classic style.

H(13)   **Provost Ross's House (NTS)** Built in 1593.

G(14)   **Provost Skene's House** A 17th-C house restored as a museum of local history and social life.

E(15)   **Rubislaw Academy (Grammar School) and Byron Statue**

H(16)   **St Andrew's Episcopal Cathedral** Built in 1816 and elevated to Cathedral status in 1914, it is the mother church of the Episcopal Communion in America.

J(17)   **St Mary of the Assumption Cathedral (RC)** Built in 1860 and raised to cathedral status in 1878.

H(18)   **Tolbooth** The tower and spire remain of the 14th-C tolbooth, outside which public executions took place until 1857.

H(19)   **Town House** A medieval Gothic building of 1868-74 with a fine collection of portraits in the Council Chamber.

G(20)   **Union Bridge** One of the widest single-span granite arches in Britain.

Hospitals

F   **Aberdeen Royal Infirmary** (Out-patients Department), *tel 23423*

M   **Fonthill Maternity Home,** 62 Fonthill Road *tel 23423*

E   **Queen's Cross Maternity Home,** 70 Carden Place *tel 23423*

Sport and Recreation

C   **ABC Tenpin Bowling Alley,** George Street

I   **Bon Accord Swimming Pool,** Justice Mill Lane

C   **Ice Rink,** Spring Garden

Theatres and Cinemas

H   **ABC Cinema,** Shiprow *tel 51477*

J   **Capitol Cinema,** 431 Union Street *tel 23141*

C   **Grand Central Picture House,** 286 George Street *tel 22826*

F   **His Majesty's Theatre,** Rosemount Viaduct *tel 28080*

I   **Odeon Cinema,** Justice Mill Lane *tel 26050*

G   **Queen's Cinema,** 120 Union Street *tel 23688*

Department Stores

Arnotts, 143 George Street
Co-operative (Northern), 88-154 George Street
Esslemont and MacIntosh Ltd, 30 Union Street
Frasers, 65 Union Street
Lawson's Ltd, 190 George Street
Marks and Spencer Ltd, 68 Netherkirkgate
Talbots Ltd, 32 Market Street
Early closing day Wednesday or Saturday

Markets

L(4)   **Fish Market** (see also public buildings and places of interest)

G   **Green Market,** Market Street (Open-air) (Friday)

H   **Justice Market,** Castle Street (Open-air) (Friday)

Advertisers

M   **Mercantile Credit**

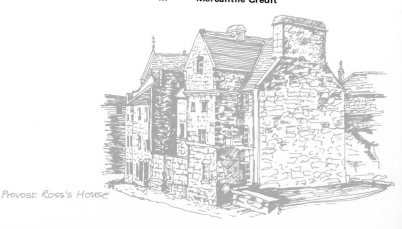

Provost Ross's House

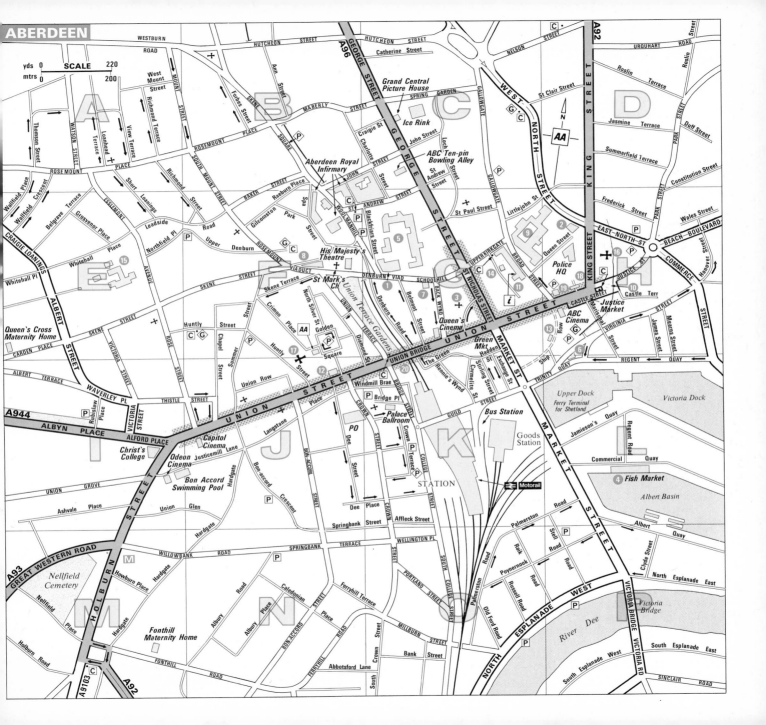

DISTRICT PLAN
Public buildings and places of interest

B(21) **Auld Brig o'Balgownie.** This single-span Gothic bridge with great buttresses and pointed arch, dates back to the 14thC.

H(22) **Bridge of Dee** A notable seven-arched structure of 1520-27.

B(23) **Cruikshank Botanical Gardens**

F(24) **Girdleness Lighthouse** Dating from 1833, this lighthouse is approximately 150ft high

D(25) **Gordon Highlanders' Regimental Museum** Medals, uniforms etc.

B(26) **King's College** Founded in 1494, and part of the University since it was created in 1860. It is the oldest school of medicine in Great Britain. The chapel, with a rare 'crown' spire, and the library of 1885 are particularly notable.

B(27) **St Machar's Cathedral** The present structure, which dates from 1357, is a fine example of a fortified church. Features include a beautiful 16th-C heraldic ceiling, ancient records, 15th-C effigies and modern stained glass.

B(28) **Wallace Tower** A fine example of a Scottish Z-plan tower, built in 1616, and resited following a city centre redevelopment scheme.

Hazlehead Park Contains a collection of British indigenous animals, free-flying aviary and walk-through parrot house, maze and three golf courses. (D)

Hospitals

D **Aberdeen Royal Infirmary,** Forresterhill *tel 23423*

F **City Hospital,** Urquhart Road *tel 22242*

D **Morningfield Hospital,** King's Gate *tel 23423*

D **Royal Aberdeen Children's Hospital,** Cornhill Road *tel 23423*

E **Royal Cornhill Hospital,** 26 Cornhill Road *tel 52411*

D **Summerfield Maternity Hospital,** *tel 23423*

Auld Brig o'Don

Sport and Recreation

B **Aberdeen Football Club,** Pittodrie Park
G **Aberdeenshire Cricket Club,** Mannofield
F **Balnagask Golf Course**
D **Hazlehead Park Golf Courses**

C **Royal Aberdeen Golf Course,** Bridge of Don
B **Sports Stadium,** Linksfield Road
C **The Links Golf Course**

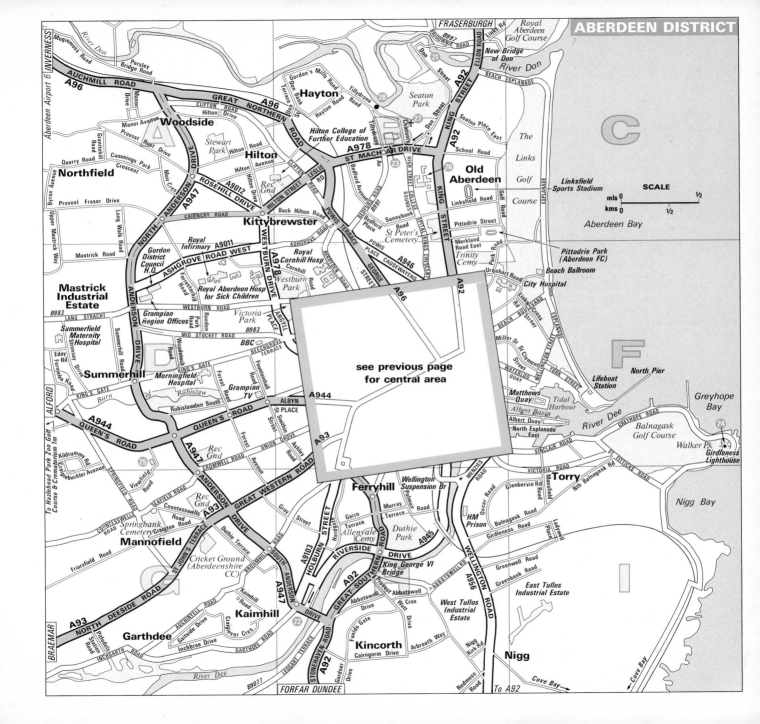

ABERDEEN DISTRICT

J **AA Road Service Centre** (2) Park Avenue tel 4801

F  **Welsh Tourist Board Information Centre** — Promenade tel 612125 (Whitsun to September)

J(3) **Information Bureau** — Ceredigion District Council Amenities and Tourism Department, Park Avenue tel 617911 (open all year except weekends)

Public buildings and places of interest

I(1) **Castle** Remains of 12th- to 13th-C Castle on the promontory.

I(2) **Ceredigion Museum** A museum illustrating aspects of life and history in the district of Ceredigion (formerly the county of Cardigan).

J(3) **Information Bureau**

L(4) **National Library of Wales** Founded by Royal Charter in 1907, the Library is a national storehouse of printed, manuscript and graphic material relating to Wales. It is one of Britain's six copyright libraries. The library is open to any responsible person who obtains a reader's ticket.

F(5) **Town Hall**

I(6) **University College of Wales** Established in 1872, the original building is scheduled as a building of historic and architectural interest and is open to members of the public. The new campus is located on the south side of the A487 Machynlleth Road adjacent to the National Library. The campus also houses the Arts Centre which consists of the Great Hall, an art gallery and the Theatre y Werin. The complex is open to the public for most of the year and presents a wide range of concerts, exhibitions and theatrical performances.

J(7) **Vale of Rheidol Railway** This famous narrow-gauge railway, British Rail's only steam-operated line, climbs to 680ft in the course of its 12-mile route to Devil's Bridge along the very attractive Rheidol Valley.

Hospitals

H **Bronglais General Hospital** tel 3131

Sport and Recreation

I **Castle Grounds** — crazy golf and putting green

F **Queens Road Recreation Ground** — putting green, bowling green and tennis courts

C **Aberystwyth Golf Club**, Bryn-y-mor Road

N **Aberystwyth Football Ground**, off Park Avenue

P **Plas Crug Avenue** — indoor swimming pool

Theatres and Cinemas

F **Commodore Cinema and Conference Centre** tel 612421

F **Kings Hall**, Marine Terrace tel 617911

H **Theatre y Werin**, University Campus, Penglais tel 4277

Shopping

Early closing day Wednesday

Markets

J **Cattle Market**, Park Avenue (Monday)

Advertisers

F **Crest** Belle Vue Royal Hotel

Castle ruins

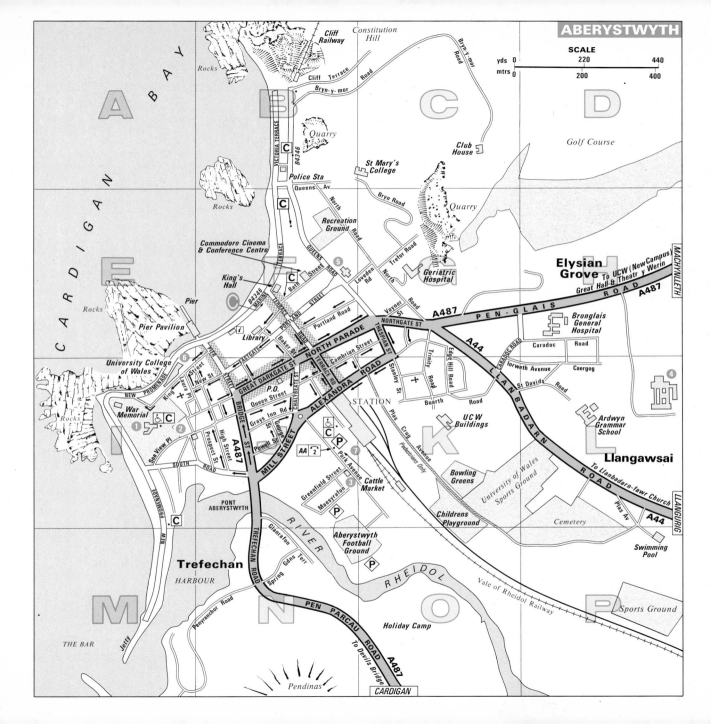

CARDIGAN BAY

A

B

C

D

E

F

G

H

I

J

K

L

M

N

O

P

SCALE
yds 0   220   440
mtrs 0   200   400

Constitution Hill
Cliff Railway
Rocks
Rocks
Rocks
Cliff Terrace
Bryn-y-mor Road
Bryn-y-mor Road
Victoria Terrace
B4346
Quarry
Police Sta
Queens Av
Commodore Cinema & Conference Centre
King's Hall
B4346
MARINE TERRACE
C
C
C
North Road
Recreation Ground
St Mary's College
Bryn Road
Trefor Road
North Road
Quarry
Club House
Geriatric Hospital

Golf Course

Elysian Grove
To UCW (New Campus)
Great Hall & Theatr y Werin
A487
MACHYNLLETH
A487
PEN - GLAIS ROAD
A44
CARADOC ROAD
LLANBADARN ROAD
Bronglais General Hospital
Caradoc Road
Iorweth Avenue
St Davids Road
Caergog

Pier
Pier Pavilion
i
Library
C
Baker St
Portland Road
Portland Road
Portland St
Queen's Road
Bath Street
North Parade
Terrace Rd
Thespian St
Northgate St
NORTHGATE ST
Vaynor St
A487
A44

University College of Wales
Rocks
PROMENADE
NEW
Pier Street
King Street
New St
Laura Pl
EASTGATE
GREAT DARKGATE ST
CHALYBEATE ST
P.O.
Queen Street
Greys Inn Rd
NORTH PARADE
Cambrian Street
ALEXANDRA ROAD
Stanley St
Trinity Road
Edge Hill Road
Caradoc Road
Caergog
Ardwyn Grammar School

War Memorial
C
Sea View Pl
High Street
Prospect St
Powell St
BRIDGE ST
MILL STREET
A487
Greenfield Street
Maesyrafon
AA 2
P
Park Avenue
STATION
Pedestrians Only
Plas Crug Avenue
Buarth
Road
UCW Buildings
University of Wales Sports Ground
Llangawsai
To Llanbadarn-fawr Church
Plas Av
A44
Cemetery
LLANGURIG

SOUTH ROAD
PONT ABERYSTWYTH
C
Cattle Market
Bowling Greens
Childrens Playground
Swimming Pool

TREFECHAN ROAD
RIVER
Glantafon
Spring Gdns Terr
Aberystwyth Football Ground
P
P

Trefechan
HARBOUR
Penyranchor Road
Jetty
THE BAR
RHEIDOL
PEN PARCAU ROAD
A487
To Devils Bridge
Holiday Camp
Vale of Rheidol Railway
Sports Ground
Pendinas
CARDIGAN

1
2
3
4
5
6
7

CENTRAL PLAN

J [i] **Tourist Information Centre** — 30 Miller Road *tel 68077*

Public buildings and places of interest

F(1) **Academy** Founded in the 13th C, and now occupying a striking building.

F(2) **Auld Brig** Probably 13th-C, and for 500 years the only bridge over the river at Ayr, it was renovated in 1910. Burns' poem *The Twa Brigs* refers to it.

J(3) **Auld Kirk** Erected in 1655 after Cromwell despoiled the Kirk of St John. The churchyard contains a tombstone commemorating the Covenanting Martyrs.

N(4) **Burns' Statue** By Lawson in 1891.

F(5) **Carnegie Library, Museum and Art Gallery** Local history and monthly changing art exhibitions.

I(6) **Strathclyde Regional Offices, Ayr Division** On the site of the old county prison.

F(7) **Loudoun Hall** Restored house of c1500, now the oldest building in the town.

J(8) **McAdam's Monument** Erected 1936 in memory of the inventor of the 'Macadam' road-making process, who was born nearby.

F(9) **St John's Tower** This 13th-C tower, a splendid viewpoint, was part of the 12th-C Kirk of St John absorbed by Cromwell's Citadel, of which remains of the walls can be seen nearby.

J(10) **Tam o'Shanter Museum** This thatched inn associated with Burns' poem, is now a museum of Burns' relics.

K(11) **Technical College**

F(12) **Town Buildings** Including the Town Hall and featuring a fine steeple.

J(13) **Wallace Tower** 113ft-high, built in 1832 with a small statue of Sir William Wallace in a niche halfway up.

Hospitals

O **Ayr County Hospital,** Holmston Road *tel 66991*

Sport and Recreation

E **Ayr Baths,** South Beach Road

H **Ayr Racecourse**

C **Ayr United Football and Athletic Club,** Somerset Park

P **Indoor Bowling Green,** off Holmston Road

Theatres and Cinemas

K **Civic Theatre,** Craigie Road *tel 63755*

J **Gaiety Theatre,** Carrick Street *tel 64639*

N **Odeon Cinema,** Burns Statue Square *tel 64049*

F **Orient Cinema,** Main Street *tel 63419*

Department Stores

Arnotts, 39 Alloway Street
Marks and Spencer Ltd, High Street
Early closing day Wednesday

Markets

O **Cattle Market** (Tuesday)

Advertisers

F **Mercantile Credit**

Auld Brig

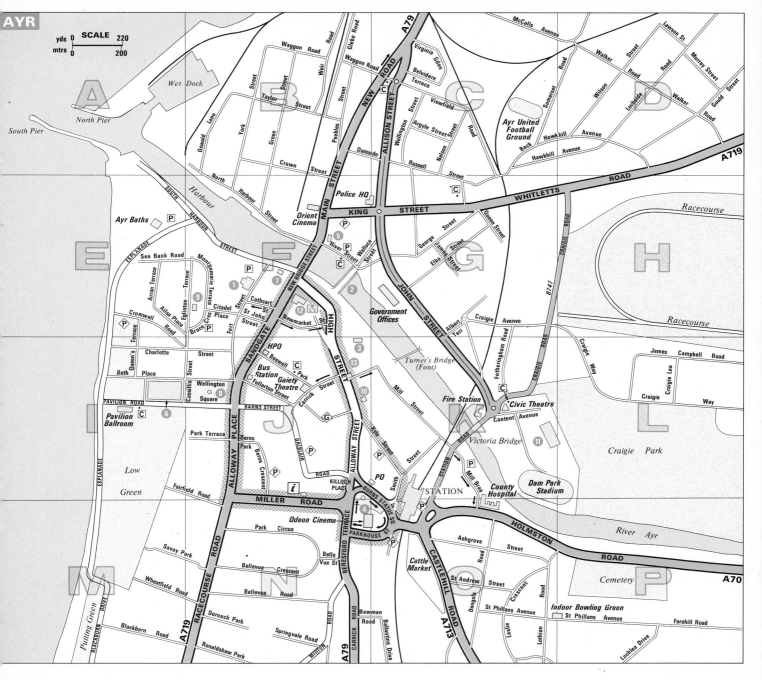

AYR

SCALE

yds 0   220
mtrs 0   200

Wet Dock

North Pier

South Pier

South Harbour

Harbour

Waggon Road

Weir Street

Taylor Street

Oswald Lane

York Street

Green Street

Crown Street

North Harbour Street

Peebles Street

Glebe Road

Waggon Road

MAIN STREET

NEW ROAD

A79

Virginia Gdns

Belvidere Terrace

Viewfield

ALLISON STREET

Wellington Street

Argyle Street

Nelson Street

Russell Street

Damside

McCalls Avenue

Somerset Road

Walker Road

Wilson Road

Lochside Road

Walker Road

Murray Street

Gould Street

Lawson St

Ayr United Football Ground

Back Hawkhill Avenue

Hawkhill Avenue

WHITLETTS ROAD

A719

Police HQ

Orient Cinema

KING STREET

George Street

Queen Street

James Street

Elba Street

CRAIGIE ROAD

B747

Racecourse

Racecourse

Ayr Baths

P

ESPLANADE

Sea Bank Road

Arran Terrace

Montgomerie Terrace

Eglinton Terrace

RIVER STREET

NEW BRIDGE STREET

Wallace Street

C

⑤ P

②

JOHN STREET

Government Offices

H

Cromwell Road

Ailsa Place

Citadel Place

Bruce Cres

Fort Street

St John St

Cathcart St

Newmarket St

⑫ M

HIGH STREET

③

Turner's Bridge (Foot)

Albert Terr

Craigie Avenve

Fotheringham Road

Craigie Way

Craigie Way

James Campbell Road

Craigie Lea

Queen's Terrace

Charlotte Street

Bath Place

Cassillis Street

SANDGATE

HPO

Boswell Park

Gaiety Theatre

Fullarton Street

Carrick Street

⑬

⑩

Mill Street

Fire Station

Civic Theatre

C

Content Avenue

⑪

Craigie Park

Pavilion Ballroom

C

⑥

Wellington Square

⑧

BARNS STREET

ALLOWAY PLACE

Barns Street

DALBLAIR ROAD

Kyle Street

Smith Street

Victoria Bridge

STATION ROAD

Mill Brae

Indoor Bowling Green

Park Terrace

Barns Park

Barns Crescent

P

STATION

Dam Park Stadium

Esplanade

Low Green

Fairfield Road

KILLOCH PLACE

i

MILLER ROAD

BURNS STATUE SQ

PO

PARKHOUSE ST

BERESFORD TERRACE

④

P

County Hospital

P

HOLMSTON ROAD

River Ayr

Putting Green

BLACKBURN DRIVE

RACECOURSE ROAD

A719

Savoy Park

Wheatfield Road

Dornoch Park

Blackburn Road

Springvale Road

Ronaldshaw Park

Park Circus

Bellevue Crescent

Bellevue Road

Belle Vue St

Odeon Cinema

CARRICK ROAD

MIDTON ROAD

Bowman Road

A79

Ballantine Drive

Cattle Market

CASTLEHILL ROAD

A713

St Andrew Street

Dongola Road

St Phillans Avenue

Ashgrove Road

Leslie Road

Lothian Road

St Phillans Avenue

Crescent

Cemetery

P

Forehill Road

Lochlea Drive

A70

15

DISTRICT PLAN

D   **AA Road Service Centre (78)** — On the Ayr by-pass, ½m S of junction A77/A719 *tel 77789*

A *i*   **Tourist Information Centre** — Municipal Buildings, Station Road, Prestwick *tel 79234*

Public buildings and places of interest

E(14)   **Alloway Auld Kirk (Ruins)** It was here that Tam o'Shanter was reputed to have witnessed the witches' orgy described so vividly by Burns in his poem, *Tam o'Shanter.* In the churchyard is the grave of Burns' father.

E(15)   **Auld Brig o'Doon** A single-arched bridge, dating probably from the 13thC, which is referred to in Burns' poem *Tam o'Shanter.*

E(16)   **Burns' Cottage** Birthplace of the poet in 1759, with a museum of Burns' relics adjoining.

E(17)   **Burns' Monument** Built 1823 to a design of Thomas Hamilton Junior, it contains a number of Burns' relics including bibles belonging to Burns and his 'Highland Mary'.

E(18)   **Land o'Burns Centre,** Alloway Audio/visual theatre, exhibition area, gardens and picnic area.

E   **Belleisle Estate** 220 acres of parkland, with beautiful gardens, an aviary and a deer park.

E   **Rozelle Estate and Nature Trail** 96 acres, given to the town in 1968, of woodland, ponds and gardens.

Hospitals

F   **Ailsa Hospital** *tel 65136*
B   **Biggart Hospital** *tel Prestwick 70611*
C   **Heathfield Hospital** *tel 68621*
E   **Seafield Sick Children's Hospital** *tel 65161*

Sport and Recreation

E   **Ayr Cricket Club,** Cambusdoon
C   **Ayr Ice Rink,** 9 Limekiln Road
E   **Ayr Rugby Football Club,** Cambusdoon
E   **Belleisle Golf Course**
D   **Dalmilling Golf Course**
A   **Prestwick Indoor Bowling Club**
D   **Prestwick St Cuthbert Golf Course**
C   **Prestwick St Nicholas Golf Course**
A   **Royal Troon Golf Club**
E   **Seafield Golf Course**

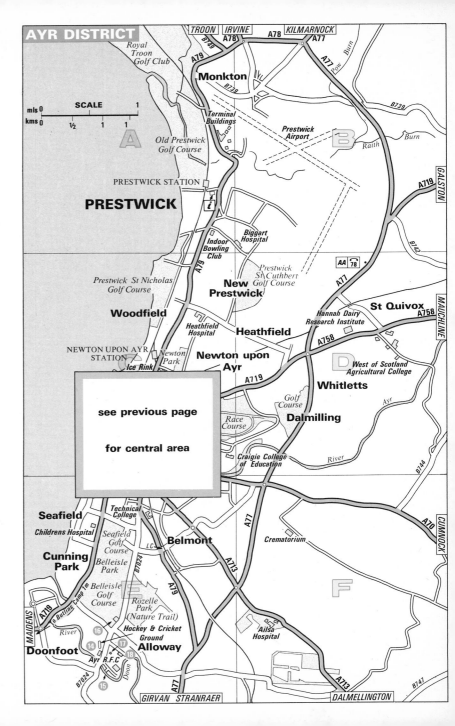

motor accidents don't just happen – they are caused

BATH

N   **AA Road Service Centre** — Avon Street Car Park tel 24731

J i   **Tourist Information Centre** — 8 Abbey Churchyard tel 62831

Public buildings and places of interest

K(1)   **Abbey Church** A splendid example of Perpendicular Gothic, notable for its fine tower, with façade portraying the ladder dream of Bishop Oliver King, which led to his rebuilding of the Abbey 1495-1503. It was again restored in the late 16th to early 17thC after suffering much damage after its dissolution in 1539. Also of interest are the fan-vaulted chancel, the Prior Bird's chantry and the enormous clerestory windows.

F(2)   **Assembly Rooms** Built c1771 to a design by John Wood the younger. Now fully restored (NT) after severe Second World War damage. They contain the Museum of Costume with displays illustrating fashion through the ages.

N(3)   **Beechen Cliff** Affords a fine view over the city.

F(4)   **Costume and Fashion Research Centre** An extension of the museum of costume, with a library and study collection. It is housed in No. 4 The Circus. The Circus is considered to be John Wood the elder's greatest work.

J(5)   **Grand Pump Room and Roman Baths** The Grand Pump Room was designed by Baldwin and Palmer and built 1798-99. The Roman Baths of Aquae Sulis are England's most impressive survival from the Roman period. Excavations have taken place over the past two centuries. The impressive Great Bath was re-discovered in 1880. There is also a museum.

K(6)   **Guildhall and Municipal Buildings** The Guildhall, built 1766-75, is the work of Baldwin and contains a notable banqueting room, a masterpiece of late 18th-C interior decoration.

H(7)   **Holburne of Menstrie Museum** A collection of paintings, silver, porcelain, glass, and furniture housed in a building of 1796

J(8)   **New Royal Baths and Treatment Centre** The mineral water springs which feed the baths and treatment centre are Britain's only natural hot water springs.

G(9)   **Pulteney Bridge** An Adam design, built in 1770 by Sir William Pulteney. It is lined on both sides by shops.

F(10)   **Reference Library and Exhibition Rooms** These house the Charles Moore Geological collection and a varied programme of temporary exhibitions.

A(11)   **Royal Crescent** Perhaps Bath's most imposing 18th-C crescent, designed in 1767-74 by John Wood the younger. No. 1 Royal Crescent has been restored with furniture and fittings of this period.

J(12)   **Theatre Royal**

K(13)   **Victoria Art Gallery and Library** Contains a permanent collection of paintings and applied arts including English and Bohemian glass, coins of Bath mint, ceramics and watches.

American Museum in Britain, Claverton Manor. A museum of American decorative arts, and domestic life of the late 17th to mid 19thC, housed in a building of 1820 by Sir Jeffry Wyatville. 1¾m E via George Street (L)

Botanical Gardens, Victoria Park. Over 5,000 species of plants from all over the world. ¼m W via Weston Road (A)

Hospitals

J   **Royal National Hospital for Rheumatic Diseases**, Upper Borough Walls tel 27341

Sport and Recreation

A   **Approach Golf Course**, Victoria Park

K   **Bath Cricket Club**, North Parade Cricket Ground

K   **County Cricket and Rugby Football Ground**

K   **Sport and Leisure Centre** — varied facilities including a swimming pool

Bath City Association Football Club, Twerton Park. 1m W via Lower Bristol Road, A36 (I)

Bath Racecourse, Lansdown. 2m N via Lansdown Road (B)

Theatres and Cinemas

J   **ABC Beau Nash Cinema**, 22 Westgate Street tel 4330

J   **Gemini Cinemas 1 & 2**, St Johns Place tel 61506

J   **Little Theatre (Cinema)**, St Michael's Place tel 66822

J(12)   **Theatre Royal**, Sawclose tel 66700

Department Stores

Jollys, Milsom Street

Marks and Spencer Ltd, 16 Stall Street

Owen Owen Ltd, Union Street

Early closing day Thursday, but most stores are open six days a week.

Markets

Market day Wednesday

K   **Market**, Guinea Lane

G   **Cattle Market**, Walcot Street (Monday)

Advertisers

O   **Berni** Royal

F   **Berni** The Oliver

K   **Mercantile Credit**

J   **THF** Francis Hotel

Sally Lunn's House

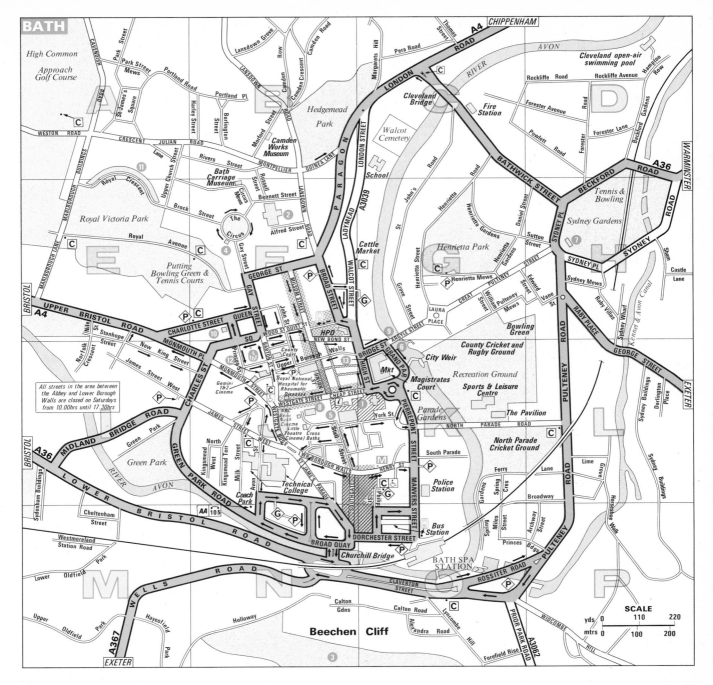

CENTRAL PLAN

M   **AA Service Centre** — 134 New Street *tel 021-550 4858*

M ⓘ   **Tourist Information Centres** — 110 Colmore Row *tel 021-235 3411* (Regional)

M ⓘ   **Birmingham Art Shop**, City Arcade *tel 021-643 2514* (Specialised)

Public buildings and places of interest

L(1)   **British Waterways Information Centre**

L(2)   **Central Public Library and School of Music** Includes Shakespeare Memorial Library.

L(3)   **Civic Centre** (Baskerville House)

L(4)   **College of Food and Domestic Arts**

M(5)   **Council House, City Museum and Art Gallery** The Council House is a 19th-C building in Italian Renaissance style. The museum contains important archaeological, ethnographical, natural and local history collections. The art gallery is noted for its fine collection of pre-Raphaelite paintings, and its collections of Old Masters and 17th-C Italian paintings.

L(6)   **Engineering and Building Centre**

L(7)   **Hall of Memory (War Memorial)** Contains illuminated Roll of Honour of Citizens of Birmingham who died in the two World Wars.

L(8)   **Midland Institute and Birmingham Library**

L(9)   **Museum of Science and Industry** An interesting museum with exhibits including machinery, veteran cars and motor bikes and the *City of Birmingham* locomotive.

S(10)   **Old Crown House** This inn, the oldest building in the city centre, is a splendid timber-framed structure of 1368, partially rebuilt in 1830.

L(11)   **Repertory Theatre** A magnificent building of 1972.

H(12)   **St Chad's Cathedral (RC)** Built 1839-41 to a design by A W Pugin. Of particular interest are the 15th-C Flemish pulpit, throne, canon's stalls and statue of Our Lady.

M(13)   **St Martin's Church** Rebuilt in Gothic style in 1873 and contains De Bermingham tombs and a Burne-Jones window.

M(14)   **St Philip's Cathedral** The 18th-C baroque-style church of St Philip, begun in 1711 to a design by Thomas Archer and raised to cathedral status in 1905. Notable features are four magnificent Burne-Jones stained-glass windows, a fine organ case of 1715 and a wrought iron screen.

M(15)   **School of Art**

X(16)   **Stratford House** An old house dating from 1601.

L(17)   **Town Hall** A building of 1834-50 designed by Joseph Hansom, best known for 'hansom cabs'. There is a notable organ in the large hall.

I(18)   **University of Aston in Birmingham and College of Art and Commerce**

H(19)   **West Midlands County Hall**

Hospitals

A   **All Saints Hospital**, Lodge Road *tel 021-523 5151*

Q   **Birmingham Accident Hospital**, Bath Row *tel 021-643 7041*

M   **Birmingham and Midland Ear, Nose and Throat Hospital**, Edmund Street *tel 021-236 6576*

M   **Birmingham and Midland Eye Hospital**, Church Street *tel 021-236 4911*

L   **Chest Clinic**, 151 Great Charles Street *tel 021-236 8791*

P   **Children's Hospital**, Ladywood Road *tel 021-454 4851*

H   **Dental Hospital**, St Chad's Queensway *tel 021-236 8611*

H   **General Hospital**, Steelhouse Lane *tel 021-236 8611*

V   **Midland Nerve Hospital**, Elvetham Road *tel 021-440 3206*

Q   **Royal Orthopaedic Hospital**, 80 Broad Street *tel 021-643 3804*

V   **Skin Hospital**, (in patients) 35 George Road *tel 021-455 7444*

M   **Skin Hospital**, (out patients) John Bright Street *tel 021-643 5921*

Sport and Recreation

C   **Aston Swimming Baths**, Newtown Shopping Centre

T   **Birmingham City Football Club**, St Andrew's Ground

K   **Monument Road Swimming Baths**, Ladywood Middleway

R   **Silver Blades Ice Rink**, Pershore Street

Theatres and Cinemas

M   **ABC Cinemas**, New Street *tel 021-643 4549*

W   **ABC Cinemas 1, 2 & 3**, Bristol Road *tel 021-440 1904*

R   **Alexandra Theatre**, Suffolk Street Queensway *tel 021-236 1231*

L(11)   **Birmingham Repertory Theatre**, Broad Street *tel 021-236 4455* (see also public buildings and places of interest).

L   **Crescent Theatre**, Cumberland Street *tel 021-643 5858*

M   **Futurist Cinema**, John Bright Street *tel 021-643 0292*

M   **Gaumont Cinerama**, Colmore Circus, Queensway *tel 021-236 1488*

R   **Hippodrome Theatre**, Hurst Street *tel 021-622 2576*

M   **Jacey News Cinema**, Station Street *tel 021-643 1556*

M   **Odeon Cinema**, New Street *tel 021-643 6101*

R   **Odeon Queensway Cinema**, Holloway Circus, Queensway *tel 021-643 2418*

W   **Pakistani Film Theatre**, 125 Balsall Heath Road *tel 021-440 2008*

L(17)   **Town Hall Concert Hall** *tel 021-236 2392* (see also public buildings and places of interest)

Department Stores

Bini Beca, 120 Corporation Street
Debenhams, Bull Street
Lewis's Ltd, Bull Street
Marks and Spencer Ltd, High Street
Rackhams (Harrods) Ltd, 35 Temple Row
Early closing day Wednesday

Markets

M   **Open Market**, Bull Ring Centre (Monday to Saturday)

M   **Covered Market**, Bull Ring Centre (Monday to Saturday except Wednesday afternoon)

Advertisers

DISTRICT PLAN

M   **AA Service Centre and Midland Region Headquarters** — Fanum House, Dogkennel Lane, Halesowen *tel 021-550 4858*

B   **AA Vehicle Inspection Centre**, West Bromwich

Public buildings and places of interest

J(20)   **Aston Hall** A magnificent Jacobean mansion of 1618-35, with fine oak staircase, panelled long gallery, marble chimney pieces and intricate plaster ceilings. It is now a museum.

O(21)   **Barber Institute of Fine Arts** Superb art collection including masterpieces by Degas, Botticelli, Rembrandt, Goya and Rubens.

Q(22)   **Birmingham Railway Museum** Tyseley steam locomotive preservation centre covering 125 years of railway history, with exhibits including locomotives, reproductions of historic coaches and former working machinery.

Q(23)   **Blakesley Hall**, Yardley. A half-timbered 16th-C yeoman's house, furnished in 17th-C style and now a museum of local history and rural crafts.

O(24)   **Botanical Gardens**, Edgbaston. Founded over 140 years ago, these gardens contain a wide variety of trees, flowering shrubs and other plants.

O(25)   **Cannon Hill Nature Reserve and Museum** This centre is concerned with the appreciation and preservation of nature. Animals, birds, freshwater fish and insects are shown in their natural surroundings.

O(26)   **King Edward VI School** Founded originally in 1552.

O(27)   **Midland Arts Centre**

B(28)   **Oak House**, West Bromwich. A 16th-C house furnished in the Jacobean style.

O(29)   **Oratory** Home of the Congregation of the Oratory established by Cardinal Newman in 1847.

O(30)   **Queen Elizabeth Medical Centre**

V(31)   **Sarehole Mill**, Hall Green. A restored 18th-C watermill containing exhibits on agricultural history and rural crafts.

U(32)   **Selly Manor House and Minworth Greaves**, Bournville. Two 13th- and 14th-C timbered houses (rebuilt), now museums containing old furniture and domestic equipment.

O(33)   **University of Birmingham**

N(34)   **Weoley Castle**, Selly Oak. Remains of a 13th-C fortified manor house, with small site museum displaying finds from excavations.

Hospitals

P   **Birmingham and Midland Hospital for Women**, Showell Green Lane *tel 021-772 1101*

I   **Dudley Road Hospital** *tel 021-554 3801*

K   **East Birmingham Hospital**, Bordesley Green Road *tel 021-772 4311*

B   **Hallam Hospital**, Hallam Street, West Bromwich *tel 021-553 1831*

E   **Jaffrey Hospital**, Erdington *tel 021-373 1428*

H   **Midland Centre for Neurosurgery and Neurology**, Smethwick *tel 021-558 3232*

V   **Monyhull Hospital**, Monyhull Hall Road *tel 021-444 2271*

P   **Moseley Hall Hospital**, Alcester Road *tel 021-449 5201*

O(30)   **Queen Elizabeth Medical Centre**, Edgbaston, *tel 021-472 1377* (see also public buildings and places of interest)

O   **St Chad's Hospital**, 213 Hagley Road *tel 021-454 4151*

U   **Selly Oak Hospital**, Raddlebarn Road *tel 021-472 5313*

X   **Solihull Hospital**, Lode Lane *tel 021-705 6741*

P   **Sorrento Maternity Hospital**, 15 Wake Green Road *tel 021-449 4242*

I   **Summerfield Hospital**, Western Road *tel 021-554 3801*

V   **Uffculme Hospital**, Queensbridge Road *tel 021-449 4011*

B   **West Bromwich and District General Hospital**, Edward Street *tel 021-553 3021*

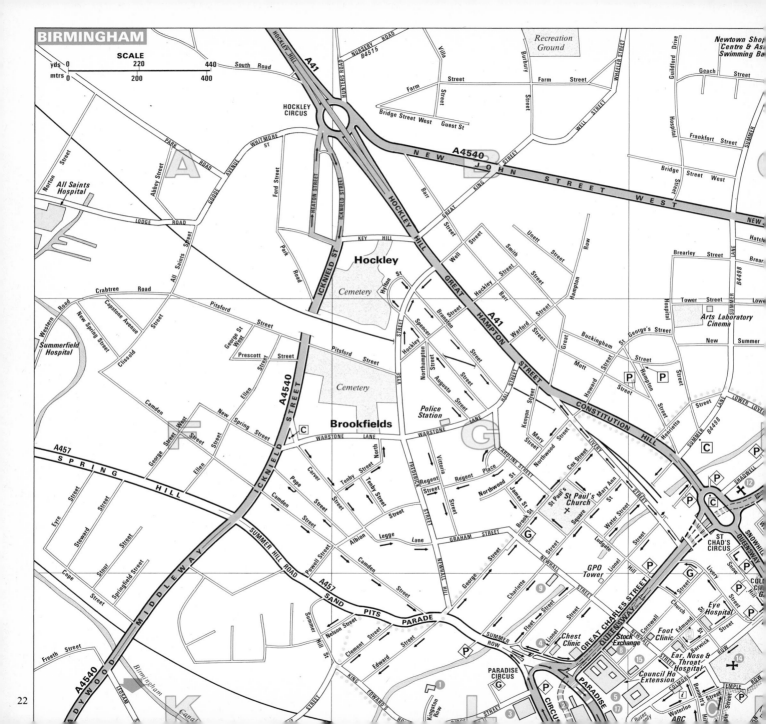

23

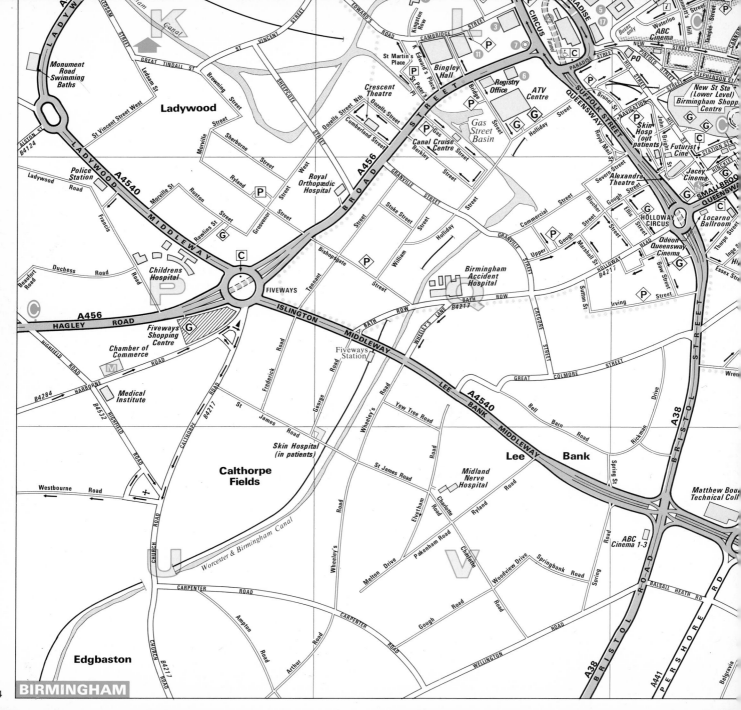

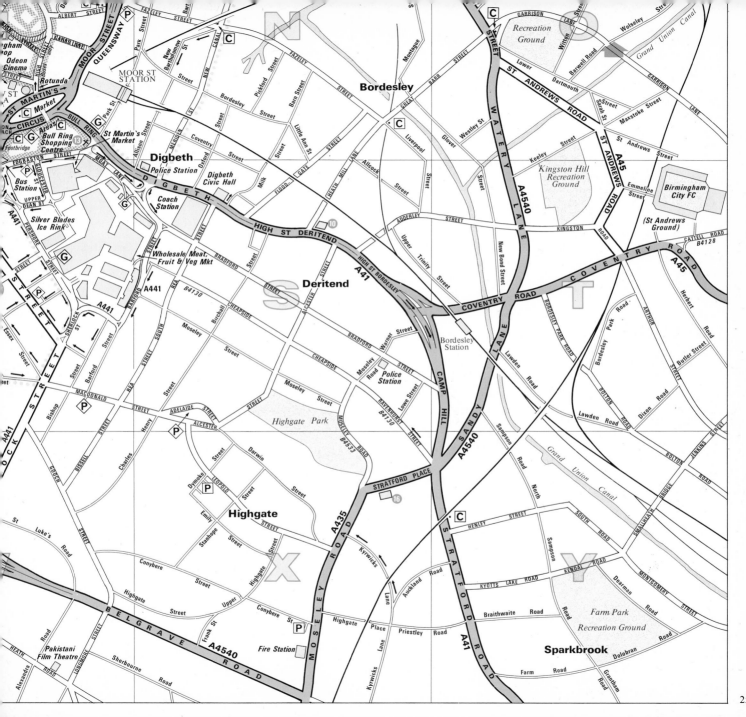

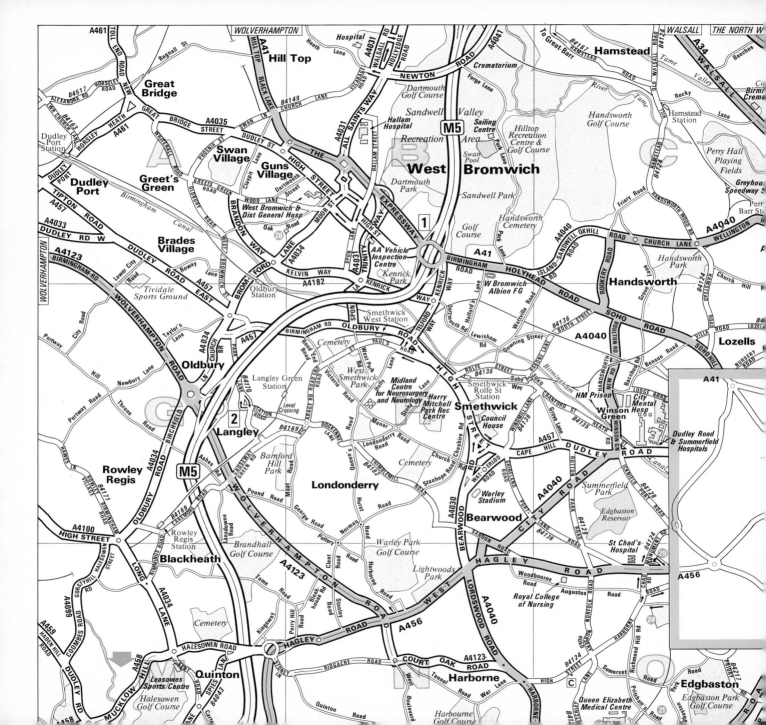

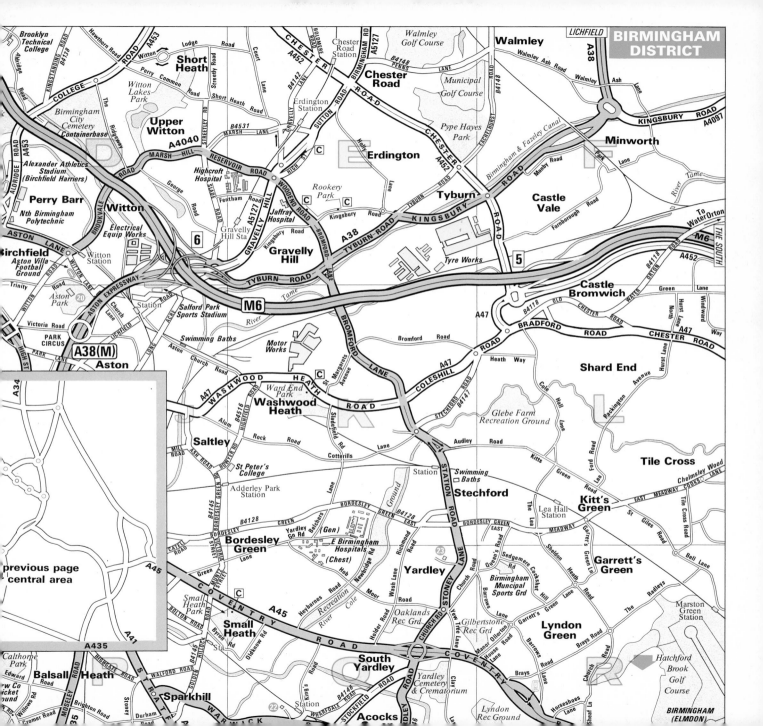

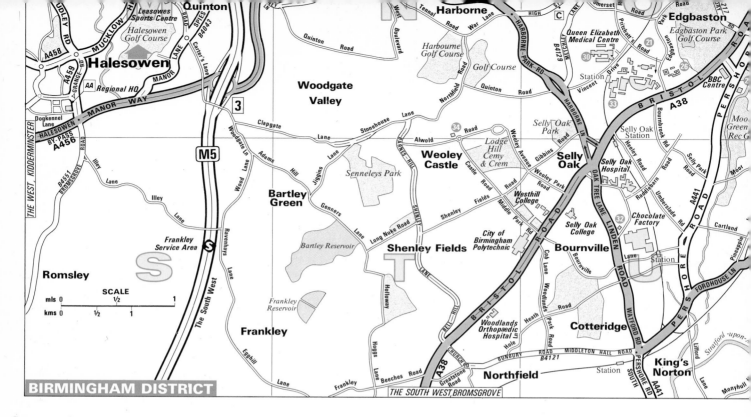

BIRMINGHAM DISTRICT

Sport and Recreation

D	**Aston Villa Football Club**, Villa Park
R	**Birmingham Municipal Sports Ground**, Queens Road
M	**Brandhall Golf Course**, Heron Road, Oldbury
V	**Cocks Moors Woods Golf Course**
B	**Dartmouth Golf Club**, Churchfields, Stonecross
O	**Edgbaston Golf Club**, Edgbaston Park
M	**Halesowen Golf Club**, The Leasowes, Leasowes Lane, Halesowen
W	**Hall Green Stadium**, York Road — greyhound racing
N	**Harborne Golf Club**, Tennal Road
H	**Harry Mitchell Recreational Centre**
R	**Hatchford Brook Golf Course**, Coventry Road
R	**Ice Rink**, Hobs Moat Road, Solihull
V	**Moseley Golf Club**, Springfield Road
P	**Moseley Rugby Football Club**, The Reddings, Reddings Road
W	**Old Edwardians Rugby Football Club**, Streetsbrook Road
X	**Olton Golf Club**, Mirfield Road, Solihull
C	**Perry Barr Stadium**, Walsall Road — greyhound racing and speedway
E	**Pype Hayes Golf Course**, Ashfield
W	**Robin Hood Golf Club**, St Bernards Road, Solihull
B	**Sandwell Park Golf Club**, Birmingham Road, West Bromwich
X	**Solihull Rugby Club**, Sharmans Cross Road
A	**Tividale Sports Ground**, Lower City Road
H	**Warley Stadium**, Waterloo Road, Smethwick
P	**Warwickshire County Cricket Club**, County Ground, Edgbaston
B	**West Bromwich Albion Football Club**, Hawthorns, Birmingham Road, West Bromwich

Department Stores

Barretts of Feckenham, 146 High Street, Solihull
Beattie James Ltd, 700 Warwick Road, Solihull
Owen Owen (Erdington) Ltd, 224 High Street

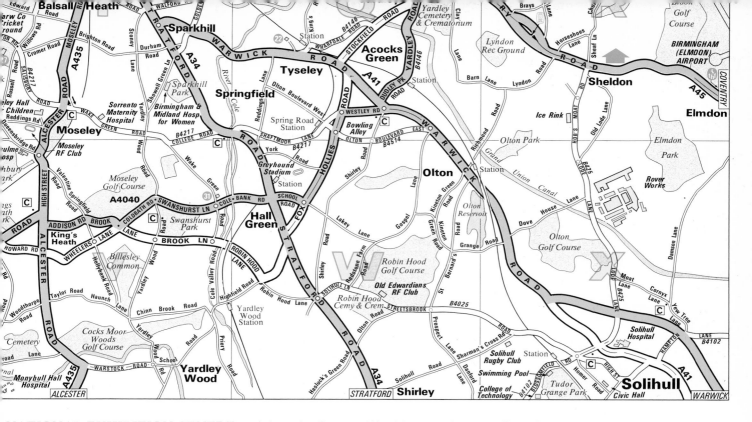

NATIONAL EXHIBITION CENTRE

See plan on page 30

The new Exhibition Centre was opened by HM the Queen in February 1976. It is situated some 8 miles east of Birmingham City Centre on the main A45 road to Coventry, and adjacent to the junction of the M6 and M42 Motorways. A network of road, rail and air services provides the centre with excellent transport facilities. It is located at the hub of Britain's motorway system and alongside the complex is Birmingham International Station which is on the main line between London and Birmingham. Close by is Birmingham Airport (1 mile to west).
The six exhibition halls have a gross interior area of 962,510 square feet and when the Centre is fully developed it will cover 310 acres including the man-made Pendigo Lake. The central feature of the complex — the Piazza — houses shops, banks, medical and visitor services. There is also a Tourist

Information Centre and Hotel Accommodation Bureau, and special provisions have been made to serve the disabled visitor. Catering services range from snack kiosks to an international restaurant with full à la carte menu. Two new hotels, the Warwick and Metropole, have been built within the complex; the latter providing conference and banqueting facilities.

Parking

Extensive parking facilities have been provided for 15,000 cars in four main parking areas. In addition there is parking space for 1,000 coaches. A fee is charged for car parking; this is variable for each exhibition. Payment is made by purchasing a ticket from special kiosks located inside the Piazza. A vehicle cannot be removed from a car park until this payment ticket is produced at the exit barriers. A free shuttle bus services operates between the car parks and the main entrance of the exhibition buildings.

Public Transport

By rail — to Birmingham International Station which is adjacent to the centre, and connected to the main building by a covered walkway.
By air — to Birmingham Airport then by taxi or bus to the centre (2½ miles).
By bus — the West Midlands Passenger Transport Executive operate regular services from Birmingham and Coventry centres to either the National Exhibition Centre or Birmingham International Station.
By taxi — a taxi rank is provided outside the Piazza canopy and also the forecourt of Birmingham International Station.

Exhibitions

Details of shows and exhibitions can be obtained from the National Exhibition Centre Ltd, Birmingham B40 1NT. *Tel 021-780-4141*

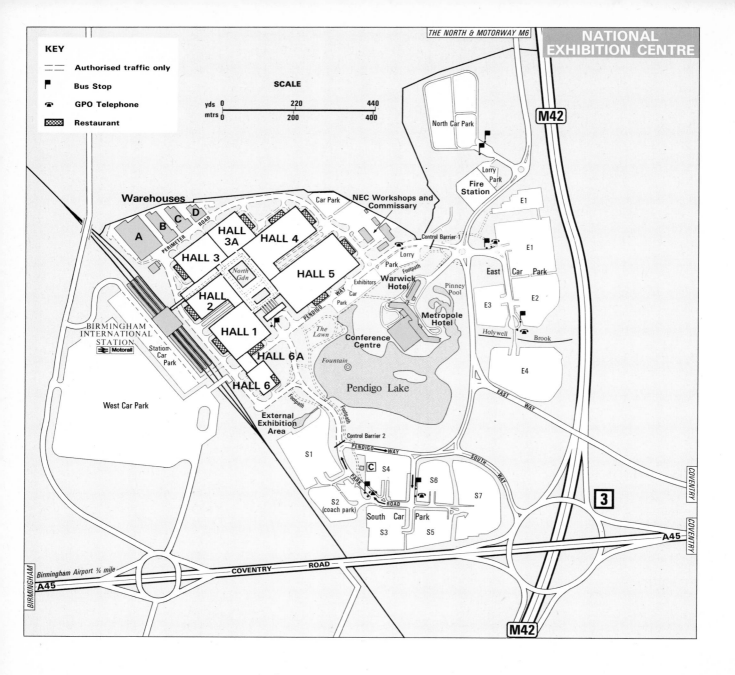

KEY

- − − Authorised traffic only
- ▐ Bus Stop
- ☎ GPO Telephone
- ▨ Restaurant

SCALE

| yds | 0 | 220 | 440 |
| mtrs | 0 | 200 | 400 |

THE NORTH & MOTORWAY M6

M42

North Car Park

Lorry Park

Fire Station

E1

E1

E2

E3

East Car Park

E4

Warehouses

A B C D

PERIMETER ROAD

Car Park

NEC Workshops and Commissary

Control Barrier 1

Lorry Park

Footpath

HALL 3A

HALL 4

HALL 3

North Gdn

HALL 5

Exhibitors Car Park

Warwick Hotel

Pinney Pool

Metropole Hotel

Holywell Brook

PENDIGO WAY

HALL 2

HALL 1

The Lawn

Conference Centre

Fountain

Pendigo Lake

EAST WAY

BIRMINGHAM INTERNATIONAL STATION

Motorail

Station Car Park

HALL 6A

HALL 6

West Car Park

External Exhibition Area

Footpath

Footpath

Control Barrier 2

PENDIGO WAY

S1

PARK ROAD

C S4

S6

S7

SOUTH WAY

S2 (coach park)

South Car Park

S3

S5

3

COVENTRY

COVENTRY

A45

Birmingham Airport ¾ mile

BIRMINGHAM A45

COVENTRY ROAD

M42

Now you can book any holiday at your own AA Travel Agencies.

AA Travel Agencies now offer one of the most comprehensive ranges of inclusive holidays in the world, with all the dependability and experience of the AA behind them. You can book with confidence in the security of the world's largest motoring organization.

What you can buy: Virtually anything to do with holidays and air travel. Inclusive air holidays to Europe and beyond. Cruising, Villa and apartment holidays. East African safari and beach holidays. Barbados sun holidays. USA Big Adventure holidays. The lot!

Where? Check your town plan for the exact location of your own local AA Travel Agency.

Aberdeen
Belfast
*Birmingham
Bournemouth
*Bristol
Cambridge
*Cardiff
Cheadle Hulme
Chelmsford
Colchester
Coventry
Dundee

Edinburgh
Exeter
*Glasgow
Guildford
Halesowen
Hull
Leeds
London
   King William Street,
   EC4R 9AN
   New Coventry Street,
   W1V 8HT

Leicester
Liverpool
*Manchester
*Newcastle-Upon-Tyne
Norwich
*Northampton
Nottingham
Plymouth
*Reading
Sheffield
Southampton
*Stanmore

Stoke-on-Trent
Teddington
Truro
Wolverhampton
York

*These offices are trading as Arena World Travel

You can depend on it

BLACKPOOL

AA Road Service Centre (6) — Squires Gate Lane
tel 44947 3m S via Promenade A584 (G)
A [i]   **Tourist Information Centre** — Central
Promenade *tel 21623*

Public buildings and places of interest

A(1) **Grundy Art Gallery and Central Library** Established 1911, this gallery exhibits a permanent collection of paintings and drawings by 19th- and 20th-C British artists. Also temporary exhibitions.

D(2) **Louis Tussaud's Waxworks** Lifelike models of famous people. Chamber of Horrors, many tableaux, including Robin Hood and his Merry Men and Bernadette of Lourdes, and educational exhibition of anatomy.

F(3) **Model Village, Stanley Park** An accurate and realistic representation of a real-life village.

G(4) **Platform 3 Model Railway,** South Shore Station. The largest electronically-controlled 00 Gauge System in Britain.

C(6) **Stanley Park** 256 acres of formal gardens including rose and Italian gardens, conservatories, lake and recreational facilities.

A(7) **Tower Buildings and Circus** The tower stands 518ft high. The buildings at its base contain a spacious ballroom, Ocean room, cabaret lounge, Apollo playground, zoo and aquarium, and the Tower Circus.

A(8) **Town Hall**

C(9) **Zoopark** Over 400 different species of animals and birds, in natural landscaped setting. Also free flight bird hall, with over 200 tropical and sub-tropical birds; children's corner and miniature railway.

Seafront Tramway Operating along the seafront between Squires Gate (Blackpool) and Fleetwood and is Britain's only electric tram service.

Hospitals

C **Victoria Hospital** *tel 34111*
Devonshire Road Hospital *tel 32121* ¾m N via Talbot Road A586 (A) or Devonshire Road A587 (B)

Sport and Recreation

C **Blackpool Cricket Club,** Stanley Park
D **Blackpool Football Club,** Bloomfield Road
D **Blackpool Rugby League Ground and Greyhound Stadium,** Princess Street
G **Lido Pool**
G **Open Air Baths,** South Shore
C **Stanley Park Golf Course**
Go-Karting and Canoeing, Starr Gate, South Shore 3m S via Promenade A584 (G)
Ice-Drome, South Shore 1¾m S via Promenade A584 (G)
North Shore Golf Course 2m N via Talbot Road A586 (A) then Devonshire Road A587

Theatres and Cinemas

A **ABC Theatre** (Cinema), Church Street *tel 24233*
D **Central Pier Theatre** *tel 20423*
A **North Pier Theatre** *tel 20980*
A **Odeon Cinema,** Dickson Road *tel 23565*
G **Palladium Cinema,** Waterloo Road *tel 420223*
D **Royal Pavilion Cinema,** Rigby Road *tel 25313*
G **South Pier Theatre** *tel 43096*
A **Studios 1, 2, 3 and 4,** Star Entertainment Centre, The Promenade *tel 25957*
A **Tivoli Cinema,** Clifton Street *tel 20508*
A **Winter Gardens Theatre and Opera House** *tel 25252*
Ice Drome, Pleasure Beach *tel 41707* 1¾m S via Promenade A584 (G)

Department Stores

Hills R H O (Blackpool) Ltd, Bank Hey Street
Hincks D S, 175 Central Drive
Lewis's Ltd, 50 The Promenade
Marks and Spencer Ltd, 78 Bank Hey Street
Marks and Spencer Ltd, 51 Church Street
Early closing day Wednesday

Blackpool Tower

BLACKPOOL

A Golden Rail Resort

A GOLDEN MILE AHEAD!

Britain's top entertainment holiday resort. New Golden Mile, Super Shows, Circus, Cabarets and Casinos. Three Piers and Magic Coast.

THE BIG FULL-COLOUR HOLIDAY GUIDE SEND NOW–IT'S FREE!

To:- Dept. 37   Town Hall, Blackpool FY1 1LY.

Name_____

Address_____

Use
your headlights when visibility
Is Poor!

In Bournemouth
Telephone 20696
for loans at special reduced rates exclusive to AA members

Personal loans for cars, caravans, boats, holidays, home improvements etc – a personal cheque to shop around with all the advantages of a cash buyer.

MMI Mercantile Credit
128 Old Christchurch Road, Bournemouth BH1 1NS.

and over 100 branches throughout the country.

BOURNEMOUTH

I **AA Service Centre** — Fanum House, 47 Richmond Hill *tel 25751*

O ⓘ **Tourist Information Centres** — Tourism Department, Westover Road, Bournemouth *tel 291715*

L(4) **Information Bureau**, Royal Arcade, Boscombe *tel 35561*
ⓘ

Public buildings and places of interest

I(1) **Big Four Railway Museum**, Dalkieth Hall. A large collection of railway relics and models. There are also film shows and lectures.

D(2) **British Typewriter Museum**

O(3) **Ice Rink**

L(4) **Information Bureaux:** Boscombe

O(5) **Lower Gardens and Rock Gardens**

J(6) **Poole and Bournemouth Further Education College and Library**

O(7) **Pavilion and Pavilion Theatre**

O(8) **Rothesay Museum** Contains collections including early Italian paintings; pottery; china; 17th-C furniture; an armoury room; a marine room; and butterflies and moths.

P(9) **Russell-Cotes Art Gallery and Museum** Housed in East Cliff Hall, a building of 1894 and containing 17th- to 20th-C paintings, period rooms, Oriental art, the Henry Irving Theatrical collection, and an aquarium. Outside is a geological terrace of about 200 rocks, building stones and ores covering 2,600 million years of history.

L(10) **St John's Church**, Boscombe. A Victorian church of flint and stone.

O(11) **St Peter's Church** This church by Street, dates from 1879.

I(12) **St Stephen's Church** A late Victorian church by Pearson, perhaps the finest in town.

O(13) **Swimming Pool**

I(14) **Town Hall**

O(15) **Winter Gardens**

Compton Acres Gardens, Canford Cliffs. Seven distinct gardens: Japanese, Italian, Roman, English, Rock, Heather, and Palm Court covering an area of 15 acres. 3¾m SW via the Avenue B3065 (M)

Hospitals

F **Royal Victoria Hospital**, Shelley Road, Boscombe *tel 35201*

H **Royal Victoria Hospital** (Eye, Ear, Nose and Throat Unit), Poole Road *tel 761332*

Sport and Recreation

F **AFC Bournemouth**, Dean Court Ground

J **County Cricket Ground**, Dean Park

F **King's Park Athletic Centre**

B **Meyrick Park Golf Course**

O(13) **Pier Approach Baths** (see also public buildings and places of interest)

O(3) **Westover Ice Rink**, Westover Road (see also public buildings and places of interest)

Theatres and Cinemas

O **ABC Film Centre**, Westover Road *tel 28433*

O **Playhouse Theatre and Galaxy Cinema**, Westover Road *tel 23277*

O **Gaumont Twin Cinema** *tel 22402*

O(7) **Pavilion Theatre** *tel 25861* (see also public buildings and places of interest)

O(13) **Pier Approach Baths** (Aqua Show) *tel 24393* (see also public buildings and places of interest)

O **Pier Theatre**, Bournemouth Pier *tel 20250*

O **Playhouse Theatre**, Westover Road *tel 23275*

O(3) **Westover Ice Rink** (Ice Follies) *tel 22611* (see also public buildings and places of interest)

O(15) **Winter Gardens** *tel 26446* (see also public buildings and places of interest)

Department Stores

Beales, Old Christchurch Road
Bealesons, Commercial Road
Debenhams Ltd, The Square
Dingles, Old Christchurch Road
Marks and Spencer Ltd, 23 Commercial Road
Marks and Spencer Ltd, 603 Christchurch Road, Boscombe
Early closing day Wednesday or Saturday but most stores open 6 days a week

Advertisers

I **Mercantile Credit**

K **Centrelink** Kelvin Hotel

Bournemouth Pier

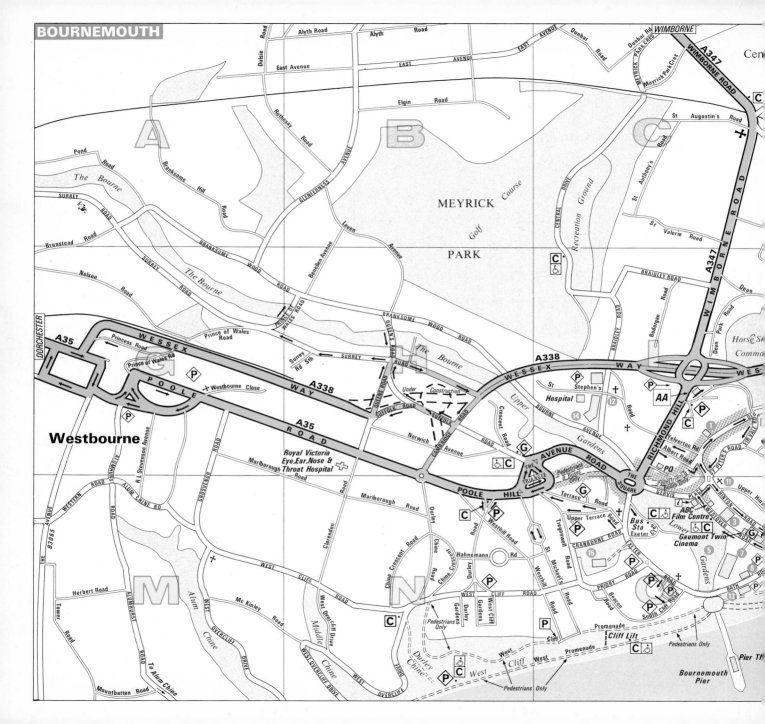

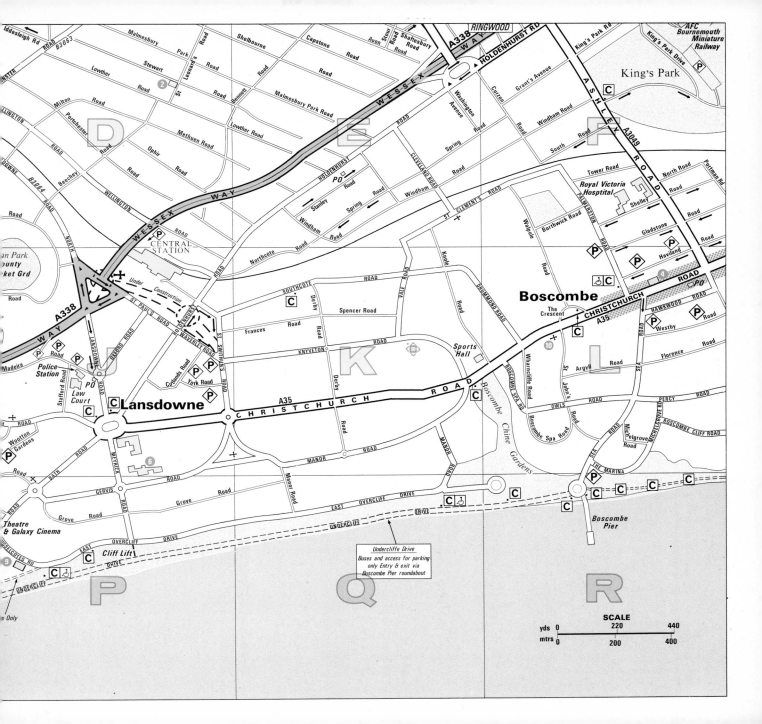

BRADFORD

CENTRAL PLAN

G   AA Road Service Centre (99) — Hall Ings Car Park *tel 24703*

J(2) ⓘ   Tourist Information Centre — Central Library, Princes Way *tel 33081 ext 45* (Regional)

Public buildings and places of interest

G(1)   **Cathedral** Formerly the parish church which was raised to cathedral status in 1919. It is mainly 15th-C, notably the Bowling Chapel and typical Yorkshire four-square tower, but also includes modern extensions of 1951-63. Features of note are the 15th-C font cover, a stone, (probably of Saxon origin) in the north wall, and a sculpture by Flaxman.

J(2)   **Central Library, Theatre and Tourist Information Centre** A modern building opened in 1967.

J(3)   **City Hall** Dates from 1873. The 220ft tower is styled on the campanile of the Palazzo Vecchio in Florence.

G(4)   **Exchange** Opened in 1867, the Wool Exchange is a reminder of Bradford's importance in the wool trade. The clock tower is 150ft high and beneath it are statues of Bishop Blaize and Edward IV.

K(5)   **St George's Hall** One of the main centres of northern musical tradition. Today the setting for great orchestral and choral works.

Sport and Recreation

J   **Wardley Entertainment Centre** — Ice Rink and Swimming Pool

J   **Windsor Swimming Pool**, Morley Street

Theatres and Cinemas

G   **ABC 1, 2 & 3 Cinemas**, Broadway *tel 28689*

J   **Alhambra Theatre**, Morley Street *tel 27007*

H   **Bradford Playhouse and Film Theatre**, Chapel Street *tel 20329*

G   **Cinecenta**, 12/16 Cheapside *tel 23177*

J(2)   **Library Theatre** *tel 23975* (see also public buildings and places of interest)

J   **Majestic Cinema**, Morley Street *tel 33943*

J   **Odeon Twin 1 & 2 Cinemas**, Princes Way *tel 26716*

K(5)   **St George's Hall**, Hall Ings (Concerts) *tel 32513* (see also public buildings and places of interest)

Department Stores

Brown Muff and Co Ltd, 26 Market Street
Debenhams Ltd, Manningham Lane
Marks and Spencer Ltd, 16 Darley Street
Early closing day Wednesday

Markets

F   **James Street Market** (Daily)

F   **John Street Open Market** (Thursday, Friday and Saturday)

F   **Kirkgate Market** (Daily) (Arndale Centre)

F   **Rawson Place Market** (Daily)

P   **St James's Wholesale Market** (Daily)

Advertisers

F   **Berni** The Grosvenor

B   **Mercantile Credit**

K   **THF** Victoria Hotel

DISTRICT PLAN

K(6)   **Bolling Hall** A fine 14th- to 18th-C house, now a museum of social history, with well-furnished period rooms.

B(7)   **Cartwright Hall, Art Gallery and Museum**, Lister Park. It was built as a memorial to Edward Cartwright, inventor of the power loom. It now houses Bradford's permanent art collection and temporary exhibitions on natural history, geology and archaeology.

D(8)   **Moorside Mills Industrial Museum**, Moorside Road. Housed in an old textile mill and illustrating the history and development of the worsted and woollen industry. Also included are sections on dyeing and printing, and a transport section featuring the last trolley bus to run in this country.

Hospitals

O   **Bierley Hall Hospital**, Bierley Lane *tel 682837*

B   **Bradford Children's Hospital**, St Mary's Road *tel 45324*

A   **Bradford Royal Infirmary**, Duckworth Lane *tel 42200*

D   **Calverley Hospital**, Thornbury *tel 662692*

G   **Leeds Road Hospital** *tel 29661*

N   **Northern View Hospital**, Rooley Avenue *tel 29130*

J   **St Luke's Hospital**, Little Horton Lane *tel 34744*

B   **Waddilove's Hospital**, Queen's Road *tel 44397*

Sport and Recreation

B   **Bradford City Association Football Club**

J   **Bradford Cricket Club**, Park Avenue

C   **Bradford Moor Golf Club**

N   **Bradford Northern Rugby League Football Club**, Odsall Stadium

E   **Bradford Rugby Union Football Club**

I   **Clayton Golf Club**

P   **East Bierley Golf Club**

B   **Lister Park Open-air Swimming Pool**

N   **Richard Dunn Sports Centre**

N   **South Bradford Golf Club**, Taylor Road

O   **West Bowling Golf Club**

Cinemas

B   **Sangeet Cinema**, Ambler Street *tel 492626*

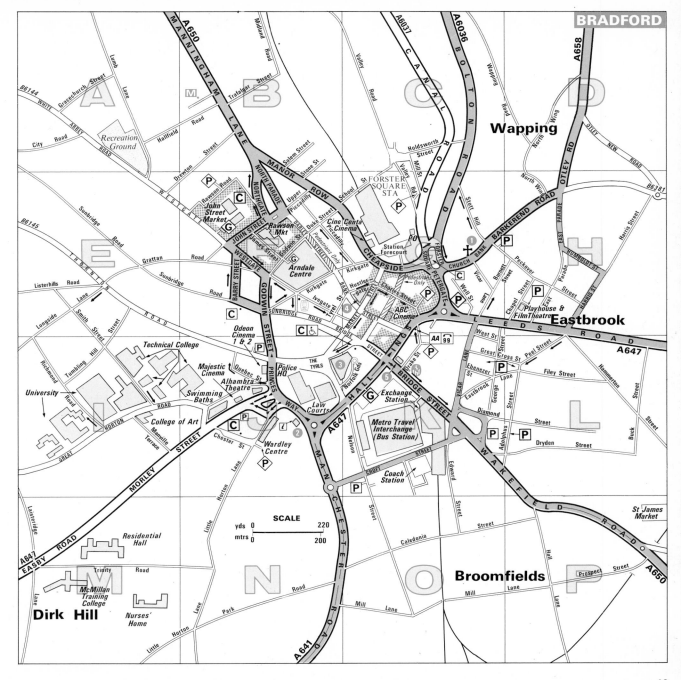

Wapping

B6144
Gracechurch Street
Lumb Lane
A650
MANNINGHAM LANE
Midland Road
A6037
A6036 BOLTON ROAD
Wapping Road
A658
D

City Road
Recreation Ground
Halfield Road
Drewton Street
Trafalgar Street
Salem Street
Stone St
Holdsworth Street
North Wing
OTLEY RD
NEW ROAD
B6381

ABBEY ROAD
WESTGATE ROAD
Sunbridge Road
Rawson Road
NORTHGATE
MANOR ROW
Upper Piccadilly
School Street
Valley St
Mill St
FORSTER SQUARE STA
North Parade
East Parade
Harris Street
H

B6145
THORNTON ROAD
Sunbridge Road
Grattan Road
JOHN STREET
John Street Market
Rawson Mkt
James Street
Duke Street
Cine Centa Piccadilly
Cinema
Station Forecourt
PO
FORSTER SQUARE
CHURCH
Well St
Vicar Lane
Burnett Street
Peckover Street
Chapel Street
Playhouse & Film Theatre
Eastbrook

Listerhills Road
Smith Street
WESTGATE
BARRY STREET
GODWIN STREET
Arndale Centre
Kirkgate
Kirkgate
Ivegate
Hustlergate
Charles Street
ABC Cinema
Pedestrians Only
SQUARE PETERGATE
Burnett Street
LEEDS ROAD
A647

Longside Lane
Richmond Road
Tumbling Hill Street
SUNBRIDGE ROAD
Odeon Cinema 1 & 2
BRIDGE STREET
MARKET STREET
West St
Cross St
Peel Street
Filey Street
Hammerton Street

University Road
Technical College
Quebec St
PRINCES WAY
Police HQ
THE TYRLS
Norfolk Gds
HALL INGS
Drake St
Ebenezer St
Great
George
Street
Eastbrook
Diamond Street
Buck Street

Majestic Cinema
Alhambra Theatre
Swimming Baths
College of Art
Manville Terrace
A647
Law Courts
Nelson Street
Exchange Station
Metro Travel Interchange (Bus Station)
Adolphus
Dryden Street

GREAT HORTON ROAD
MORLEY STREET
Chester St
Horton Lane
Wardley Centre
MANCHESTER ROAD
BRIDGE STREET
VICAR LANE
Coach Station
CROFT STREET
Edward Street
WAKEFIELD ROAD
St James Market

A647
EASBY ROAD
Residential Hall
Trinity Road
McMillan Training College
Nurses' Home
Little Horton Lane
Park Road
Caledonia Street
Mill Lane
Mill Lane
Hall Lane
Prospect Street
A650

Dirk Hill
Laisteridge Lane
A641
A647

Broomfields
A650

SCALE
yds 0 ———— 220
mtrs 0 ———— 200

39

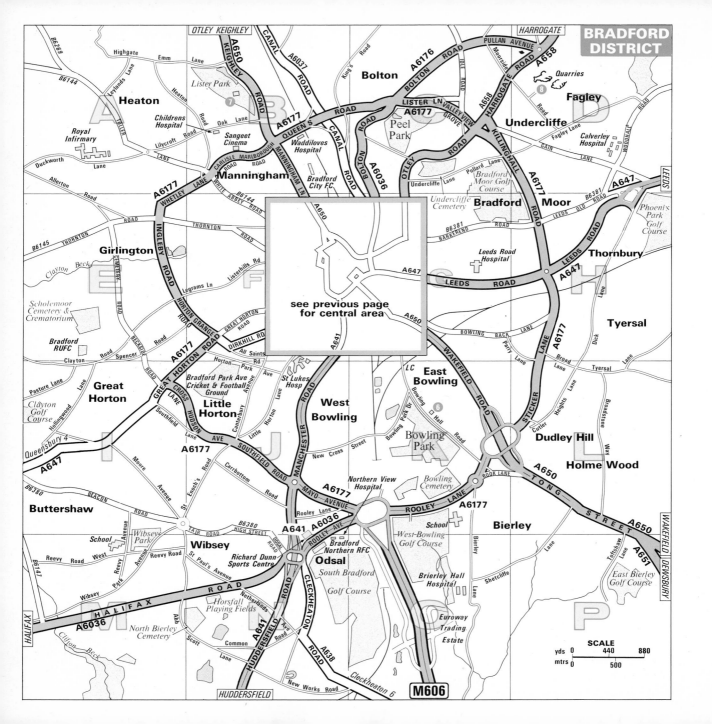

BRADFORD DISTRICT

see previous page for central area

SCALE
yds 0 — 440 — 880
mtrs 0 — 500

M606

BRIGHTON

CENTRAL PLAN

N   **AA Service Centre** — 10 Churchill Square *tel 24933*

D(5)   **Tourist Information Centres** — Marlborough House, 54 Old Steine *tel 23755* (weekends *tel 26450*) (see also public buildings and places of interest)

N   Seafront *tel 26450* (summer only)

Public buildings and places of interest

D(1)   **Aquarium and Dolphinarium** Thousands of tropical and freshwater fish, sea lions, turtles, seals and performing dolphins.

N(2)   **Dolls' Museum** A unique display of over 300 dolls displayed in a wonderland setting.

K(3)   **Dome** A 2,100-seat concert and conference hall, housed in former Royal stables of the Royal Pavilion.

D(4)   **Louis Tussaud's Waxworks** Famous and infamous characters of the past and present presented in wax.

D(5)   **Marlborough House** Designed by Robert Adam in 1786, and now housing the Tourist Information Centre.

K(6)   **Museum, Art Gallery and Library** Housed in part of former Royal stables. Collections include Old Master paintings, watercolours, Sussex archaeology and folk life, ethnography, natural history, musical instruments, the Willet collection of pottery and porcelain and displays of 20th-C fine and applied art.

K(7)   **Royal Pavilion** A marine residence built for the Prince Regent, later George IV. It was begun in 1787 by Henry Holland and completed in the style of the Moghul palaces of India by John Nash. The interior contains some fantastic Chinoiserie decorations and is furnished in its original style.

F(8)   **St Bartholomew's Church** Built between 1872 and 1874 and has a nave 135ft high.

J(9)   **St Nicholas Church** Dates from the 14thC and preserves a Norman font.

G(10)   **St Peter's Church** The parish Church of Brighton, built in 1824 to a design by Sir Charles Barry.

O(11)   **The Lanes** These quaint old lanes of 17th-C fishermen's cottages now form a paradise for seekers of all kinds of antiques and curios.

O(12)   **Town Hall**

P(13)   **Volks Railway** This delightful relic of the Victorian era was the first public electric railway in Great Britain, opened in 1883.

N   **Brighton Centre** Opened during 1977, the Centre is one of Britain's largest entertainment, conference and exhibition centres.

Hospitals

I   **New Sussex Hospital**, Windlesham Road *tel 736255*

I   **Royal Alexandra Children's Hospital**, Dyke Road *tel 28145*

J   **Sussex Throat and Ear Hospital**, Church Street *tel 202911*

Sport and Recreation

K   **North Road Swimming Baths**

J   **Sussex Sports Centre**, 11 Queen Square

Theatres and Cinemas

O   **ABC Cinema**, East Street *tel 27010*

J   **Brighton Film Theatre**, 64 North Street *tel 29563*

I   **Classic Cinema**, Western Road *tel 29414*

K(3)   **Dome**, Church Street *tel 682127* (see also public buildings and places of interest)

B   **Duke of York's Theatre** (cinema), Preston Circus *tel 62503*

M   **Embassy Cinema**, 1 Western Road, Hove *tel 735124*

N   **Odeon Film Centre**, Kingswest Centre, West Street *tel 23317*

K   **Pavilion Theatre**, New Road

K   **Theatre Royal**, New Road *tel 28488*

Department Stores

Co-operative, 92 London Road
Debenhams, 95 Western Road
Hannington's Ltd, North Street and East Street
Marks and Spencer Ltd, 195 Western Road
Marks and Spencer Ltd, 5 London Road
Owen Owen, 188 Western Road
Vokins, North Street
Early closing day — Wednesday — St James' Street; Thursday — London Road and Western Road; Saturday — North Street area

Markets

K   **Fruit and Vegetable Market**

G   **Open Market**

Advertisers

K   **Mercantile Credit**

M   **THF** Hotel Curzon

Royal Pavilion

DISTRICT PLAN

J(17) **Tourist Information Centre** — Hove Town
Hall, Church Road *tel 775400* (see also
public buildings and places of interest)

Public buildings and places of interest

F(14) **Booth Museum of Natural History**
Contains a comprehensive collection of
birds displayed in their natural
habitat, a notable butterfly collection
and an evolution gallery.

G(15) **College of Technology**

J(16) **Hove Museum of Art** Contains paintings
and prints, particularly of the 18th
to 19thCs, a fine collection of
ceramics, period furniture and other
valuable items.

J(17) **Hove Town Hall** A modern building,
opened 1974.

F(18) **Preston Park and Preston Manor** A
Georgian house (with Edwardian
additions) showing a fine collection
of period furniture including the
Maquoid bequest, pictures, china
and silver.

D(19) **University of Sussex**

Hospitals

H **Bevendean Hospital**, Bear Road *tel 67091*

H **Brighton General Hospital**, Elm Grove *tel
66444*

J **Hove General Hospital**, Sackville Road
tel 735244

I **Lady Chichester Hospital**, Aldrington
House, New Church Road, Hove *tel 778383*

L **Royal Sussex County Hospital**, Eastern
Road *tel 66611*

L **Sussex Eye Hospital**, Eastern Road *tel
66126*

Sport and Recreation

L **Black Rock Swimming Pool**

J **Brighton and Hove Albion Football Club**,
Goldstone Ground, Hove

E **Brighton and Hove Golf Course**, Dyke Road

B **Brighton Rugby Club**, Pavilion,
Recreation Ground, Vale Avenue

F **Brighton Sports Arena**, Tongdean Lane

F **Greyhound Stadium**, Nevill Road, Hove

C **Hollingbury Park Golf Course**, Ditchling
Road

F **Hove Rugby Football Club**, New Pavilion,
Hove Park

J **King Alfred Sports Centre**, Kingsway,
Hove — tenpin bowling and swimming
baths.

L **Marina**, Designed to provide moorings for
over 2,000 boats. The scheme also includes
commercial and leisure facilities.

J **Sussex County Cricket Club**, County
Ground, Eaton Road, Hove

A **Waterhall Golf Club**, Mill Road

I **West Hove Golf Course**, Old Shoreham Road,
Portslade

Theatres and Cinemas

L **Continentale Cinema**, Sudeley Place *tel
681348*

D **Gardner Arts Centre**, Sussex University

Department Stores

Hills of Hove, Western Road, Hove
Chiesmans Ltd, 141 Church Road, Hove
Early closing day Wednesday — Hove

Advertisers

J **Centrelink** Imperial Hotel

J **THF** Dudley Hotel

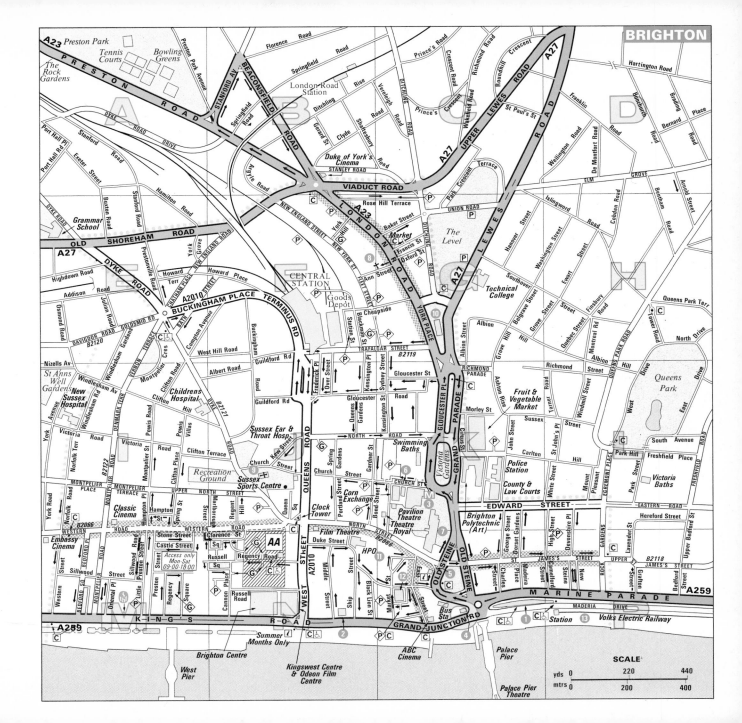

BRIGHTON

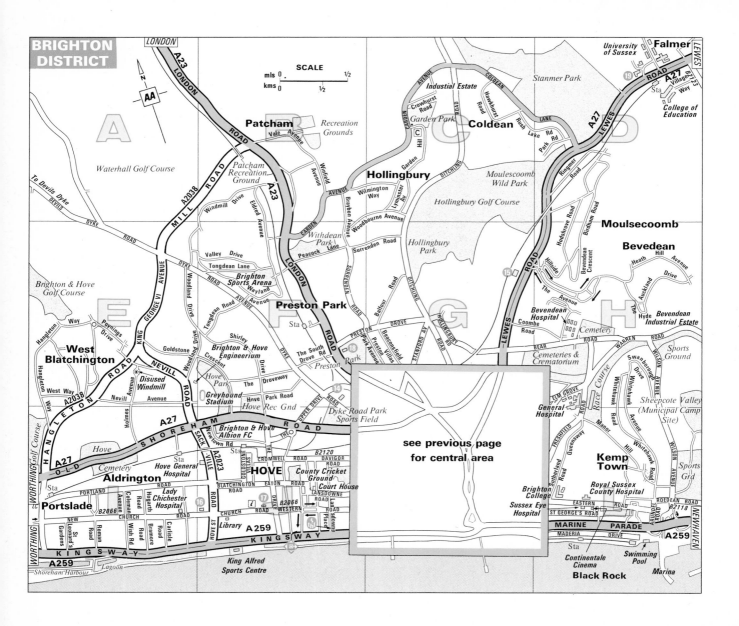

BRIGHTON DISTRICT

LONDON

A23 LONDON ROAD

SCALE
mls 0 ½
kms 0 ½

N
AA

A

B

C

D

University of Sussex

Falmer

LEWES ROAD

B2123 Village Way

Coldean

Industrial Estate

Crowhurst Road

Garden Park

Stanmer Park

College of Education

19 Sta

A27 LEWES

Patcham
Vale Avenue

Recreation Grounds

Winfield Avenue

CARDEN AVENUE

Coldean Lane

Rush Lake Rd

Park Rd

Waterhall Golf Course

A2038 MILL ROAD

A23 ROAD

Patcham Recreation Ground

AVENUE

Hollingbury

Wilmington Way

Lynmister Av

Braybon Avenue

DITCHLING

Moulescoomb Wild Park

Hollingbury Golf Course

Rimmer Road

Moulsecoomb

To Devils Dyke

DYKE ROAD

Windmill Drive

Eldred Avenue

Woodbourne Avenue

Withdean Park

CARDEN Lane

Peacock Lane

Surrenden Road

Hollingbury Park

Hollingbury

Hodshrove Road

Birdham Road

Bevedean

Heath Hill

Avenue

Brighton & Hove Golf Course

Valley Drive

Tongdean Lane

KING GEORGE VI AVENUE

Brighton Sports Arena

Wayfield Avenue

DYKE ROAD AVENUE

Tongdean Road

Woodland Drive

SURRENDEN ROAD

Balfour Road

DITCHLING ROAD

HOLLINGBURY RD

STAFFORD AV

15

LEWES ROAD

Hillside

The Avenue

Bevendean Crescent

Auckland Drive

The Hyde

Bevendean Industrial Estate

E

F

Preston Park

Sta

Beaconsfield Villas

Preston Park Avenue

DROVE

Bevendean Hospital

Coombe Road

Cemetery

Bear Road

West Blatchington

Hangleton Way

Paynings Drive

Goldstone Crescent

Shirley Drive

Brighton & Hove Engineerium

The South Drive

Preston Park

The Droveway

Rd

18

Park Road

14

Dyke Road Park Sports Field

see previous page for central area

Cemeteries & Crematorium

General Hospital

ELM GROVE

Race Course

Sheepcote Valley (Municipal Camp Site)

Swanborough Drive

Whitehawk Road

Whitehawk Avenue

Manor Hill

WILSON AVENUE

Sports Ground

G

H

Hove Park

Disused Windmill

Nevill Avenue

Holmes Avenue

Greyhound Stadium

Hove Rec Gnd

Hnve Park Road

UPPER DRIVE

THE

Brighton & Hove Albion FC

A27 OLD SHOREHAM ROAD

NEVILL ROAD

WORTHING Golf Course

HANGLETON ROAD

A2038

West Way

A27

Hove

Cemetery

Aldrington

Newtown Rd

Sta

Sta

CROMWELL ROAD

DAVIGOR ROAD

B2120

County Cricket Ground

Court House

EATON ROAD

LANSDOWNE ROAD

Sutherland Road

Queensway

FRESHFIELD ROAD

Brighton College

Sussex Eye Hospital

Kemp Town

Royal Sussex County Hospital

Sports Grd

Worthing

A27

Hove General Hospital

Portslade

B2066

St Leonard's Gardens

New Road

Roman Road

Coleman Road

Hogarth Road

Bramore Road

Carlisle Road

A2023

SACKVILLE ROAD

GOLDSTONE VILLAS

HOVE ST

BLATCHINGTON ROAD

CHURCH ROAD

Library

A259

Lady Chichester Hospital

16

17

WESTERN ROAD

Sackville Place

CHURCH ROAD

B2066

Hove

KINGSWAY

A259

Shoreham Harbour

Lagoon

King Alfred Sports Centre

ST GEORGE'S ROAD

EASTERN ROAD

MARINE PARADE

MADERIA DRIVE

Sta

Continentale Cinema

Black Rock

ROEDEAN ROAD

B2118

A259

NEWHAVEN

Swimming Pool

Marina

44

C   **AA Service Centre** — Fanum House, Park Row *tel 298531*

CENTRAL PLAN

D ⓘ   **Tourist Information Centre** — City Information Centre, Colston House *tel 293891*

Public buildings and places of interest

C(1)   **Cabot Tower** A 150-ft-high tower on the summit of Brandon Hill. Built 1897-98 on the four hundreth anniversary of John Cabot's discovery of the mainland of North America at Labrador.

J(2)   **Cathedral** Founded as an Augustinian monastery in 1140, it has developed continuously over the past 800 years, with examples of Norman, Early English, Gothic and Victorian architecture.

B(3)   **Cathedral (RC)**

K(4)   **Chatterton House** The birthplace of Thomas Chatterton (1752-70), famous boy poet.

C(5)   **City Museum and Art Gallery** Collections of archaeological, geological, natural history, scientific and transport exhibits.

A(6)   **Clifton Observatory** Situated on a hill above the Avon Gorge, with a large camera obscura on the summit of the tower. A passage below the tower leads to Giant's Cave.

A(7)   **Clifton Suspension Bridge** Designed by Isambard Kingdom Brunel in 1836, the bridge carries the toll road from Bristol towards Portishead 254ft above the Avon Gorge.

D(8)   **Colston Hall** One of the finest concert halls in the country.

D(9)   **The Exchange** In front of the building (1743) are four bronze pillars known as 'Nails' which were at one time used by merchants to complete cash transactions.

I(10)   **Council House**

D(11)   **Foster Almshouses** A 19th-C building on 15th-C foundations. Adjacent is the chapel of the Three Kings of Cologne (1504), and Christmas Steps (1669).

C(12)   **The Georgian House** With 18th-C furniture and fittings.

D(13)   **Guildhall** Now used as the Court House.

E(14)   **Quakers Friars** Once a Dominican Friary, part of the building now houses the Bristol Register Office and the Permanent Planning Exhibition.

D(15)   **Red Lodge** The 16th-C house, altered in the early 18th-C with oak carvings and furnishings of both periods.

C(16)   **Royal Fort House** An 18th-C merchant's house with decorated plaster work on both ceilings and walls, now part of the University of Bristol.

C(17)   **Royal West of England Academy**

I(18)   **SS Great Britain** Built in Bristol by Isambard Kingdom Brunel in 1843, it was the largest iron ship of its time. It was shipwrecked in the Falkland Islands and finally raised and towed back to Bristol in 1970.

D(19)   **St John's Church and Old City Gate** The small 14th-C church is built above the gate which has statues of Brennus and Belinus, mythical figures of the founders of Bristol.

Demoiselle Crane, Clifton Zoo

J(20)   **St Marks** The Lord Mayor's Chapel is noted for its monuments and vestry. Founded in 1220 and restored in 1889.

K(21)   **St Mary Redcliffe Church** A magnificent church of the 13th-15thCs, one of the largest in England. It has a large 13th-C tower with a 285ft spire. The hexagonal north porch dates from 1290.

D(22)   **St Nicholas Church and City Museum** Contains the history of Bristol from its beginnings until the Reformation including Bristol church art. There are also displays of watercolours and drawings.

D(23)   **St Stephen's Church** A 15th-C church with several interesting monuments.

K(24)   **Temple Church** A ruined 15th-C church with a leaning tower.

C(25)   **University**

E(26)   **Wesley's Chapel** Dating from 1739, it is the oldest Methodist Chapel in the world and was built by John Wesley whose statue is outside.

J   **Bristol Exhibition Centre**

Hospitals

D   **Bristol Eye Hospital,** Lower Maudlin Street *tel 27988*

J   **Bristol General Hospital,** Guinea Street *tel 25001*

D   **Bristol Royal Infirmary,** 2 Marlborough Street *tel 22041*

B   **Chesterfield Hospital,** Clifton *tel 30391*

D   **Dental Hospital,** Lower Maudlin Street *tel 23385*

C   **St Mary's Private Hospital,** Up Byron Place *tel 23186*

Sport and Recreation

H   **Baltic Wharf Leisure Centre,** Cumberland Wharf

N   **Bristol City Football Club,** Ashton Gate

D   **Bristol Ski School,** Bryant's Outdoor Centre, Colston Street

P   **Bristol South Swimming Baths,** Dean Lane

E   **Broad Weir Baths,** Stratton Street

C   **Clifton Pool,** Southleigh Road, Clifton

D   **Silver Blades Ice Rink,** New Bristol Centre, Frogmore Street

Theatres and Cinemas

D **ABC Cinema,** New Bristol Centre, Frogmore Street *tel 22848*

E **Europa Cinemas,** adj Holiday Inn, Lower Castle Street *tel 291810*

D **Gaumont Cinema,** Baldwin Street *tel 25882*

J **The Hippodrome,** St Augustines Parade *tel 239444*

D(8) **Little Theatre,** Colston Hall, Colston Street *tel 291182* (see also public buildings and places of interest)

E **Odeon Film Centre,** Broadmead *tel 26141*

D **Studios 1, 2, 3** and Pithay Centre, 9 All Saints Street *tel 25069*

J **Theatre Royal and New Vic Theatre,** King Street *tel 24388*

Department Stores

The Co-operative, Fairfax House, Fairfax Street, Newgate

Debenhams Ltd, 1 St James Barton

Dingles, House of Fraser, Queens Road

Lewis's Ltd, 2 The Haymarket

B Maggs and Co, Queens Road

Marks and Spencer Ltd, 78 Broadmead

Primark Stores, 82 The Horsefair

Early closing day Wednesday and Saturday (many shops in the main shopping area are open six days a week)

Markets

D **St Nicholas Market,** (general — Monday to Saturday)

M **Bristol City Football Club Car Park,** Ashton Gate (Sunday morning)

Advertisers

J **Berni** Tavern
C **Berni** Hawthorns Hotel
J **Berni** Hole in the Wall
D **Berni** Hort's Restaurant
J **Berni** Llandoger Trow
B **Berni** Marco's Tavern
C **Berni** Marco's Trattoria
D **Berni** The Rummer
D **Mercantile Credit**

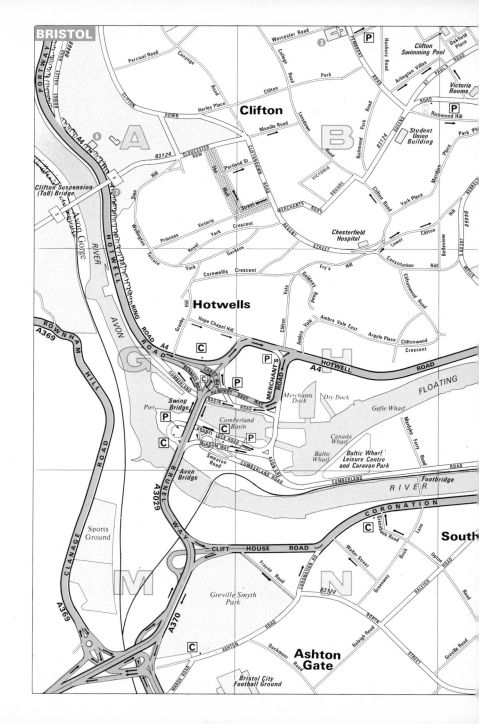

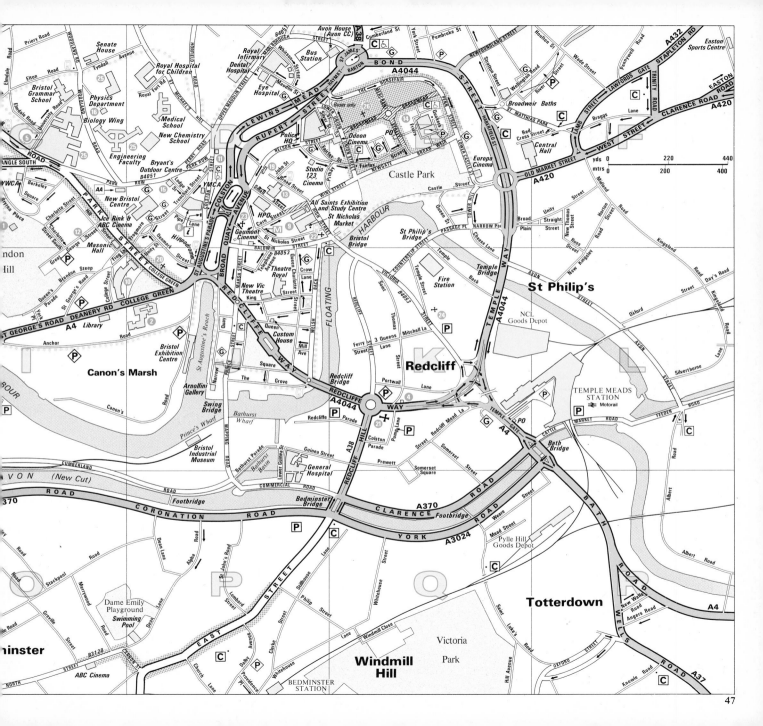

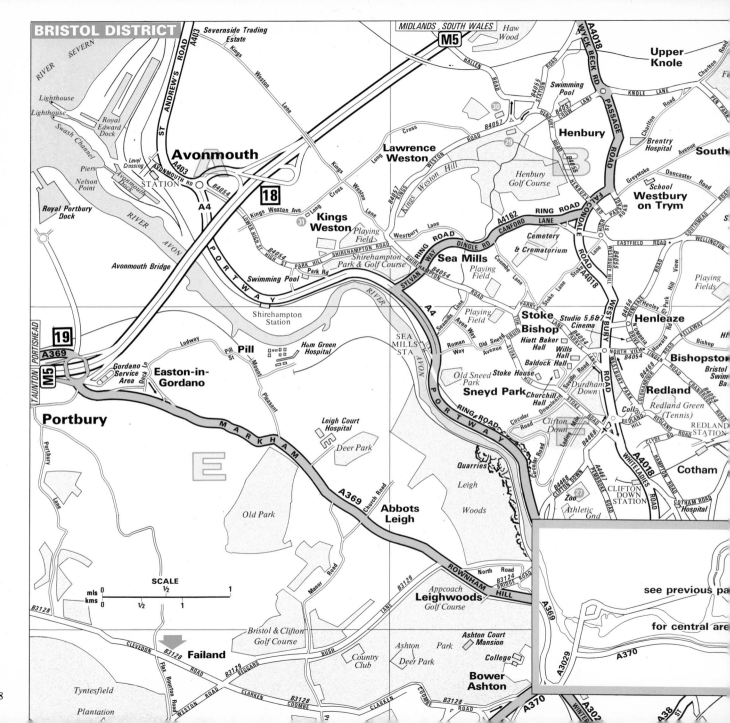

49

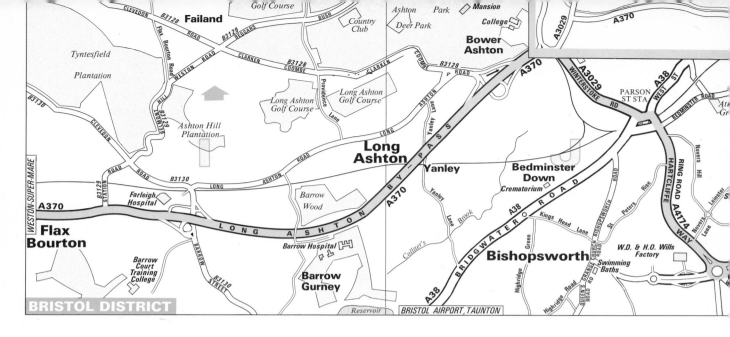

DISTRICT PLAN
Public buildings and places of interest

F(27) **Clifton Zoo** Extensive gardens and varied collection of animals, reptiles and fish.

L(28) **Bitton Station** Bristol Suburban Railway

B(29) **Blaise Castle House** An 18th-C mansion, now a folk museum. The extensive grounds contain a thatched dairy and a watermill.

B(30) **Blaise Castle Hamlet (NT)**

A(31) **Kings Weston Roman Villa** Mosaics and walls of a Roman villa occupied between AD270 and AD370.

Hospitals

I **Barrow Hospital,** Barrow Gurney *tel Long Ashton 3162*

B **Brentry Hospital,** Charlton Road, Westbury-on-Trym *tel 623443*

C **Burden Neurological Hospital,** *tel 567444*

F **Bristol Homeopathic Hospital,** 6 Cotham Hill *tel 312231*

H **Cossham Memorial Hospital,** Kingswood *tel 671661*

I **Farleigh Hospital,** Flax Bourton *tel Flax Bourton 3275*

D **Frenchay Hospital** *tel 565656*

G **Glenside Hospital,** Blackberry Hill, Stapleton *tel 653285*

E **Ham Green Hospital,** Pill *tel Pill 2661*

L **Hanham Hospital** *tel 677871*

E **Leigh Court Hospital,** Pill *tel Pill 2109*

G **Manor Park Hospital,** Manor Road, Fishponds *tel 656061*

G **Meadowsweet Hospital,** Blackberry Hill *tel 653294*

G **Purdown Hospital,** Bell Hill *tel 653554*

B **Southmead General Hospital,** Westbury-on-Trym *tel 622821*

Sport and Recreation

I **Long Ashton Golf Course,** Clarken Coombe Road off B3128

I **Bristol and Clifton Golf Course,** off Beggars Bush Lane B3129

F **Bristol North Swimming Baths,** Gloucester Road

G **Bristol Rovers Football Club, Greyhound and Speedway Stadium,** Eastville

C **Bristol Rugby Club,** Memorial Ground, Horfield

B **Henbury Golf Course,** off Henbury Road B4055

B **Filton Golf Course,** off Charlton Road

K **Filwood Swimming Baths,** Filwood Broadway

G **Gloucester County Cricket Club,** Ashley Down

B **Henbury Pool,** Crow Lane, Henbury

K **Jubilee Swimming Baths,** Jubilee Road

F **Redland Green,** Redland — tennis

A **Shirehampton Swimming Baths,** Park Road, Shirehampton

G **Speedwell Swimming Baths,** Whitefield Road

K **Whitchurch Sports Centre,** Bamfield — badminton, squash, football, volleyball, tennis, basketball, netball and athletic track.

Markets

G **Bristol Stadium,** Stapleton Road, Eastville (Friday and Sunday)

Advertisers

C **Crest** Euro Crest Hotel

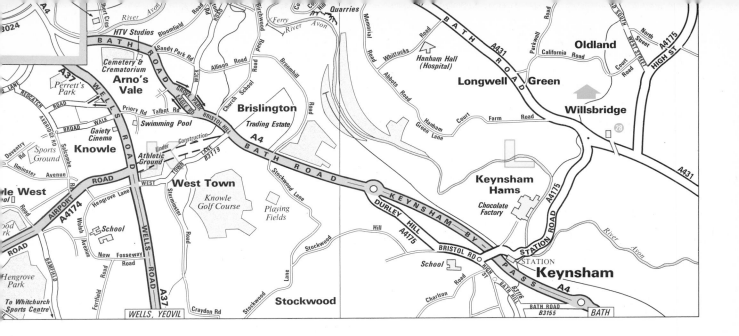

CAMBRIDGE

CENTRAL PLAN

K   **AA Service Centre** — Janus House, 46-48 St Andrew's Street *tel 63101*

K ⓘ   **Tourist Information Centre** — 4 Bene't Street *tel 58977*

K ⓘ   Information Kiosk, Market Square (summer only)

Public buildings and places of interest

COLLEGES

K(1)   **Christ's College (1505)** The main gate bears the statue and insignia of the foundress, Lady Margaret Beaufort.

A(2)   **Churchill College (1960)**

J(3)   **Clare College (1326)** The present buildings date from 1638.

I(4)   **Clare Hall**

K(5)   **Corpus Christi College (1352)** The old court (14th-C) is the earliest complete court in Cambridge. The new court in Gothic style dates from 1827-32. The library contains a fine collection of Anglo-Saxon and medieval manuscripts.

N(6)   **Darwin College (1964)**

O(7)   **Downing College (1749)**

K(8)   **Emmanuel College (1584)** The chapel of 1666 was designed by Sir Christopher Wren.

A(9)   **Fitzwilliam College (1869)**

J(10)   **Gonville (1348) & Caius College (1557)** Notable features are the 'Honour' and 'Virtue' gates.

P(11)   **Hughes Hall (Teachers' Training) (1885)**

G(12)   **Jesus College (1496)** Founded in buildings of former nunnery of St Radegund. The chapel, the former church of the nunnery, contains ceiling and windows by William Morris and Burne-Jones.

J(13)   **Kings College and Chapel (1441)** The magnificent chapel is the only completed medieval part of this college built 1441-1515 in Perpendicular style. It retains all its original stained glass and contains Rubens' *Adoration of the Magi*. Other buildings are mainly 19th-C with the exception of the Fellows Building by Gibbs, a fine classical addition of 1723-9.

A(14)   **Lucy Cavendish Collegiate Society**

F(15)   **Magdalene College (1542)** The library of Samuel Pepys is housed here.

A(16)   **New Hall (1954)** The third women's college.

M(17)   **Newnham College (1871)** The second women's college.

K(18)   **Pembroke College (1347)** The chapel built in 1663-6 is the first completed building designed by Wren.

O(19)   **Peterhouse College (1284)** The 13th-C Hall, which was greatly restored in the 19thC, now features a tiled fireplace by William Morris and windows by Ford Madox-Brown and Burne-Jones.

J(20)   **Queens' College (1448 & 1465)** Founded by the Queens of Henry VI and Edward IV.

N(21)   **Ridley Hall Theological**

I(58)   **Robinson College**

J(22)   **St Catherine's College (1473)**

A(23)   **St Edmund's House**

F(24)   **St John's College (1511)** Consists of three red-brick courts with a fine gate tower and chapel of the 1860s designed by Sir George Gilbert Scott.

M(25)   **Selwyn College (1882)**

G(26)   **Sidney Sussex College (1596)** Has associations with Cromwell.

F(27)   **Trinity College (1546)** The Great Court is the largest of its kind in the world completed in 1676-90 by the addition of a library designed by Sir Christopher Wren. Statues of many famous men of the college, including Newton and Tennyson are to be found in the ante-chapel.

J(28)   **Trinity Hall (1350)**

G(29)   **Wesley House Theological**

G(30)   **Westcott House Theological**

F(31)   **Westminster College Theological and Cheshunt College** A fine red-brick building of 1889 in Tudor-style.

M(32)   **Wolfson College (1964-65)**

CHURCHES

K(33)   **Great St Mary's** The University church (1478-1514) in Perpendicular Gothic style with a fine tower and some Georgian screenwork.

G(34)   **Holy Sepulchre, Round Church** Dates from 1104 and is the oldest surviving round church in England. Mainly Norman, it has been extensively restored.

O(35)   **Little St Mary's** Mostly 14thC, in decorated style.

K(36)   **St Bene't's** Retains a notable early 11th-C Saxon tower, the oldest building in Cambridge.

MUSEUMS

F(37)   **Cambridge and County Folk Museum** Exhibits include domestic items, agricultural tools and trade equipment illustrating the life of Cambridgeshire people since medieval times.

O(38)   **Fitzwilliam Museum** Contains Egyptian Greek and Roman antiquities, paintings manuscripts, ceramics, textiles, Medieval and Renaissance objets d'art, an armoury and a library.

N(39)   **Museum of Classical Archaeology** Houses casts of Greek and Roman statues.

P(40)   **Scott Polar Research Institute** Includes sections on former polar expeditions, current research and the geography and geology of the Antarctic.

K(41)   **Sedgwick Museum of Geology** Display of fossils of all ages and subordinate display of building and ornamental stones.

K(42)   **University Museum of Archaeology and Ethnology** Comprises archaeogical collections from the Old Stone Age in Africa and the Near East; from prehistoric to medieval times in Britain and prehistoric America; and ethnological collections from Africa, the Americas, Asia and the Pacific.

K(43)   **University New Museums' Site** includes Museum of Zoology, with sections on marine life, birds, insects, mammals and fossil specimens of extinct animals. Also Whipple Science Museum, a collection of scientific instruments and books, mainly from the 16th-17thC.

OTHER PLACES OF INTEREST

K(45)   **Arts Theatre**

K(47)   **Guildhall and Central Library**

I(48)   **History Faculty**

O(49)   **Hobson's Conduit** Dates from 1614 and was transferred here from Market Hill in 1855.

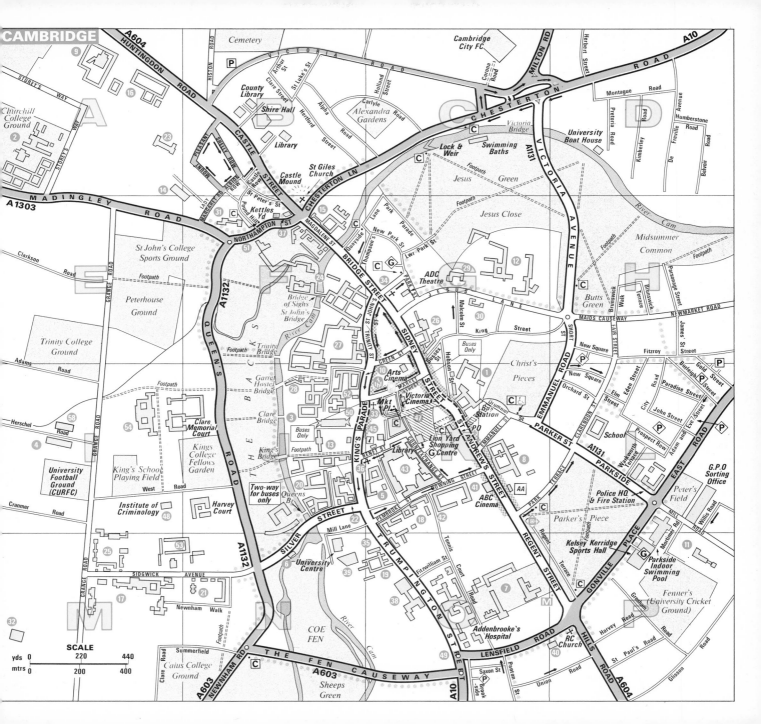

J(50) **Old Schools** These date from the 14thC and house the University's central administration.

F(51) **School of Pythagoras** An old house dating back in part to the 12thC.

J(52) **Senate House** A fine building of 1722-30 by James Gibb, noted for its wood and plasterwork.

M(53) **University Arts Faculty**

I(54) **University Library** An impressive design of 1931-34 by Sir George Gilbert Scott with a tower of 160ft.

B **Castle Mound** All that remains of Cambridge's Norman Castle.

Hospitals

O **Addenbrookes Hospital,** Trumpington Street *tel 55671*

Sport and Recreation

C **Cambridge City Football and Sports Club,** Milton Road

I **Cambridge University Rugby Football Club,** The Ground, Grange Road

P **Fenner's** (university Cricket Ground) Gresham Road

C **Jesus Green Open-air Swimming Pool**

P **Kelsey Kerridge Sports Hall,** Gonville Place

P **Parkside Indoor Swimming Pool,** Mill Road

Theatres and Cinemas

K **ABC 1 & 2,** 37 St Andrews Street *tel 54572*

G **ADC Theatre,** Park Street *tel 59547*

K **Arts Cinema,** Market Passage *tel 52001*

K(45) **Arts Theatre,** Peas Hill *tel 52000* (see also public buildings and places of interest)

K **Victoria Cinemas 1 & 2,** 6 Market Hill *tel 52677*

Department Stores

Co-operative, Burleigh Street
Joshua Taylor Ltd, Sidney Street and Bridge Street
Marks and Spencer Ltd, Sidney Street
Robert Sayle, 12/17 St Andrews Street
W Eaden and Lilly, Market Street
Early closing day Thursday, but some shops close all day Monday

Markets

K **Market Place** (daily but main market day Saturday)

Advertisers

P **Mercantile Credit**
K **Berni** Steak Bar
K **Centrelink** University Arms
K **THF** Blue Boar Hotel

DISTRICT PLAN
Public buildings and places of interest

A(55) **Girton College (1869)** The first college for women.

O(56) **Homerton College** Teachers' training

K(57) **University Botanic Gardens** Lawns, flower beds, a notable rockery, scented garden and greenhouses containing many rare and exotic plants.

Hospitals

O **Addenbrookes Hospital,** Hill's Road *tel 45151*

L **Brookfields Geriatric Hospital,** 351 Mill Road *tel 45926*

C **Chesterton Hospital,** 29 Union Lane *tel 63415*

Sport and Recreation

H **Cambridge United Football Club,** Newmarket Road

Girton Golf Course, Dodford Lane, Girton 3½m NW via Girton Road (A)

Gog Magog Golf Course, Babraham Road 4m SE via Hills Road A604 (P)

Markets

K **Cattle Market** (Monday)

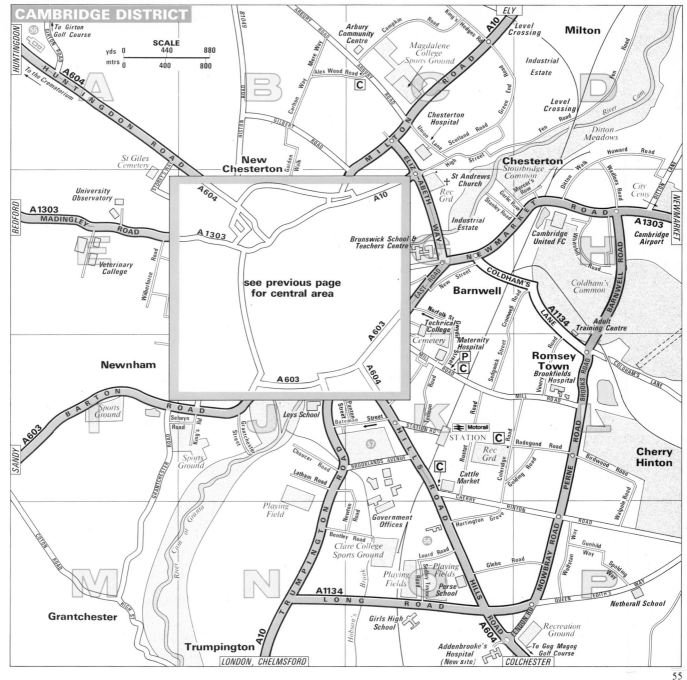

CAMBRIDGE DISTRICT

see previous page for central area

SCALE

yds 0 440 880
mtrs 0 400 800

To Girton Golf Course

GIRTON ROAD

HUNTINGDON

To the Crematorium

A604 HUNTINGDON ROAD

St Giles Cemetery

STOREY'S WAY

New Chesterton

B1049

BRISTOW

GILBERT ROAD

Carlton Way
Mere Way
Alex Wood Road

Garden Walk

C

Arbury Community Centre
ARBURY ROAD

Campkin

Magdalene College Sports Ground

King's Hedges Rd

A10 ELY

Level Crossing

Milton

Road

Road

Industrial Estate

Level Crossing

River Cam

Fen

Ditton Meadows

Chesterton Hospital

Union Lane

Scotland Road

High Street

Green End Road

Fen Road

Howard Road

Ditton Walk

Chesterton

Stourbridge Common
Mercer's Row

St Andrews Church

Garlic Row

Stanley Road

MILTON ROAD

ELIZABETH WAY

Rec Grd

Industrial Estate

NEWMARKET ROAD

NEW Street

EAST ROAD

Brunswick School & Teachers Centre

COLDHAM'S

Waddelos Road

City Cemy

DITTON

NEWMARKET

A1303

Cambridge Airport

Cambridge United FC

Whitehill Road

BARNWELL ROAD

Coldham's Common

COLDHAM'S LANE

Barnwell

A1134 LANE

Adult Training Centre

Romsey Town

Brookfields Hospital

University Observatory

Veterinary College

Wilberforce Road

A1303

BEDFORD

MADINGLEY ROAD

Road

Newnham

Norfolk St
Technical College

Cemetery

Maternity Hospital

P C

BROOKS ROAD

PERNE ROAD

Cherry Hinton

BARTON ROAD

Sports Ground

Selwyn Road

King's Rd

Grantchester Street

Leys School

Panton Street

Bateman Street

STATION RD

Motorail

STATION

C

Rustat Road

Rec Grd

Radegund Road

Coleridge Road

Birdwood Road

Walpole Road

Cattle Market

Golding Road

CHERRY

HINTON ROAD

Hartington Grove

Glebe Road

A603

SANDY

Sports Ground

Chaucer Road

Latham Road

Playing Field

River Cam or Granta

COTON ROAD

HIGH ST

Grantchester

Trumpington

A10

TRUMPINGTON ROAD

57

BROOKLANDS AVENUE

Newton Road

Bentley Road

Clare College Sports Ground

Government Offices

56

Luard Road

Sedley Taylor Rd

Playing Fields

Perse School

HILLS ROAD

Playing Fields

A1134 LONG ROAD

Hobson's Brook

Girls High School

Addenbrooke's Hospital (New site)

LONDON, CHELMSFORD

Wulfstan Way

Gunhild Way

Spalding Way

EDITH'S WAY

QUEEN EDITH'S WAY

Mowbray Road

Netherall School

FENDON RD

A604

COLCHESTER

Recreation Ground

To Gog Magog Golf Course

55

CANTERBURY

F ⓘ **Tourist Information Centre,** Sidney Cooper Centre, St Peters Street *tel 66567*

Public buildings and places of interest

F(1) **Beaney Institute, Royal Museum, Art Gallery and Public Library** The museum displays the archaeology, including a hoard of Roman silver spoons and other finds, natural history and geology of the East Kent region.

F(2) **Black Friars Refectory** The refectory dates from c1300.

J(3) **Castle** The castle keep, one of the largest in the country, dates back to c1175.

G(4) **Cathedral** Founded in 602 by St Augustine. The present Cathedral, however, is a beautiful 15th-C edifice, where Thomas a Becket was murdered in 1170. Of particular interest are the Trinity Chapel; the 12th-C choir; the 'Corona' or Becket's Crown; the old glass; the Norman crypt; and the 15th-C Angel Steeple.

G(5) **Chequers of Hope** A few roof-beams of the famous old hostelry which stood here are still to be seen at the tobacconists'. There are associations with Chaucer.

G(6) **Christ Church Gateway** A Tudor structure of 1507-17 with 17th-C gates.

H(7) **Christ Church Teachers' Training College** A modern building.

J(8) **Dane John Fortifications, Gardens and City Walls** The Dane John, an 80ft-high tumulus, has pleasant gardens partly enclosed by a dry moat. There are remains of the old city walls nearby.

F(9) **Grey Friars Monastery** Oldest Franciscan settlement in England of which one building, restored in 1920, remains. It has associations with the Royalist poet, Richard Lovelace.

F(10) **Holy Cross Church** Contains a notable font cover of the 15thC.

G(12) **King's School** Founded originally in the 7thC and placed here as a grammar school by Henry VIII. The unique exterior Norman staircase is notable.

F(13) **Marlowe Theatre**
J(14) **Municipal Buildings**
F(15) **Poor Priests' Hospital and Buffs' Museum** The much altered buildings of the Hospital are of 14th-C date, and house a clinic and the Regimental Museum of the Buffs containing weapons, medals, uniforms, trophies, and pictures illustrating the history of the regiment.

F(16) **Queen Elizabeth's Guest Chamber** An old house dating back to 1573.

G(17) **Roman Pavement** Here are the remains of two mosaic floors, a hypocaust and other Roman relics.

A(18) **Roper Gateway** An elaborate 16th-C brick structure which once led to the home of Sir Thomas More's daughter.

F(19) **St Alphege's Church** A church of very old foundation, preserving some interesting brasses.

G(20) **St Augustine's Abbey and St Pancras Church** The restored abbey gateway of 1300 is impressive, and the nearby remains of St Pancras Church incorporates Roman brickwork.

G(21) **St Augustine's College** A college of the Anglican church founded in 1848 which incorporates some remains of the former abbey.

E(22) **St Dunstan's Church** Saxon work is preserved here, and in the vault is the head of Sir Thomas More, executed in 1535.

G(23) **St George's Church** Only the tower survives from this church where Marlowe was baptised.

C(24) **St John's Hospital** A foundation of 1074, with an old gatehouse and chapel.

H(25) **St Martin's Church** Probably England's oldest church still in use, preserving early Saxon work, notably the font.

J(26) **St Mildred's Church** The 13th-C church in which Izaak Walton was married.

F(27) **St Peter's Church** Possibly of Saxon origin and preserving a massive Norman font.

F(28) **St Thomas (or Eastbridge) Hospital** This was re-established in 1342 and preserves a Norman hall and crypt with two chapels.

F(29) **Weavers** Picturesque gabled 15th-C houses with bay windows overlooking the River Stour.

F(30) **West Gate** Of 14th-C date and considered to be the finest city gate in England. It houses an armoury relating to its former use as city gaol.

University of Kent at Canterbury A modern university which opened in 1965. 2m NW via Whitstable Road A290 (A)

Hospitals

P **Kent at Canterbury Hospital,** Ethelbert Road *tel 66877*

O **Nunnery Fields Hospital,** *tel 66877*

Sport and Recreation

C **Canterbury City Football Club,** Kingsmead Stadium

P **Kent County Cricket Club,** St Lawrence Ground, Old Dover Road

C **Kingsmead Indoor Swimming Pool**

C **Speedway,** Kingsmead Stadium

Canterbury Golf Club, Littlebourne Road 1½m E via St Martins Hill A257 (H)

Theatres and Cinemas

K **ABC Cinema,** 43 St George's Place *tel 62022*

A **Gulbenkian Theatre,** at the University of Kent at Canterbury, Giles Lane *tel 69075*

F(13) **Marlowe Theatre,** St Margarets Street *tel 64747* (see also public buildings and places of interest)

F **Odeon Cinema,** The Friars *tel 62480*

Department Stores

Debenhams, Guildhall Street
Marks and Spencer Ltd, 4 St George's Street
Ricemans (Canterbury) Ltd, St George's Lane

Markets

B **General Market** (Wednesday)
B **Cattle Market** (Monday)

Advertisers

G **Berni** Tudor Tavern
G **Mercantile Credit**
G **THF** Chaucer Hotel

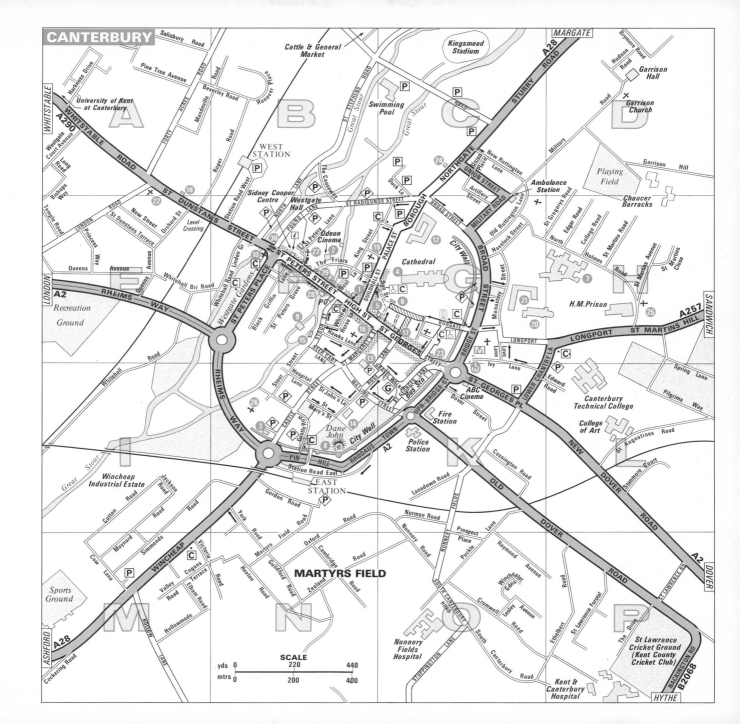

CARDIFF

CARDIFF

Blackweir

Roath

Aberdare
Hall

County
Cricket
Ground

Nursery

Sophia
Gardens

Bute

Park

Mansion
House

Cardiff
Royal
Infirmary

Pavilion

River

Taff

Cathays   Park

Police HQ

Pavilion

Mansion
House

St David's
Hospital
A4161

BOULEVARD – DE – NANTES

DUMFRIES LANE

Greyfriars

The Friary

Road

Greyfriars

Queen St
STATION

St David's
Hospital
A4161

Riverside

Cardiff
Bridge

Cardiff
Rugby Club

Cardiff
Arms Park

National
Rugby Stadium

HPO

AA

Church

Public
Library

Shopping Centre
(Under Const'n)

Central
Fire Station

Central
Fire Station

H.M.
Prison

NCL
Goods
Depot

Level
Crossing

Empire
Swimming Pool

Bus
Station

CENTRAL
STATION

Motorail

Bute East
Dock

SCALE

yds 0   220   440

mtrs 0   200   400

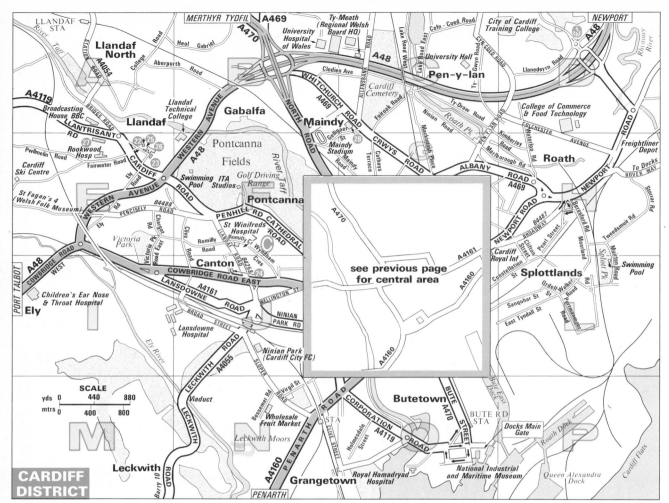

CARDIFF DISTRICT

DISTRICT PLAN
Public buildings and places of interest

E(22)   **Bell Tower** Remains of Llandaf Cathedral's 13th-C bell tower.

E(23)   **Bishops' Castle Gatehouse** The 14th-C gatehouse of the former Bishops' Castle which was sacked in 1402 by Owain Glyndwr.

J(24)   **Chapter Arts Centre**

E(25)   **City Cross**

E(26)   **Llandaf Cathedral** The Cathedral which dates from the 13thC has been restored after severe war damage.

E(27)   **South Wales Gwent Training College of the Domestic Arts**

C(28)   **Welsh Regiment Museum, Maindy Barracks**

Hospitals

I   **Children's Ear, Nose and Throat Hospital,** Cowbridge Road West *tel 561371*

J   **Lansdowne Hospital,** Sanatorium Road *tel 33651*

E   **Rookwood Hospital,** Fairwater Road, Llandaf *tel 566281*

O   **Royal Hamadryad Hospital,** Cardiff *tel 24895*

F   **St Winifred's Private Hospital,** Romilly Crescent *tel 28784*

Docks *tel 24895*

B   **University Hospital Of Wales,** Heath Park *tel 755944*

Sport and Recreation

J   **Cardiff City Association Football Club,**

F   **Llandaf Fields Open-air Swimming Poo**

F   **Pontcanna Fields Driving Range**

L   **Splott Park Swimming Baths**

Cardiff Golf Course, Sherbourne Avenue 3¾m N Allesbank Road (C)

Advertisers

F   **Crest** Beverley Hotel

D   **THF** Post House

Use your headlights when visibility Is Poor!

CHELTENHAM

G(6) Tourist Information Centre — Municipal Offices, The Promenade *tel 22878* (see also public buildings and places of interest)

Public buildings and places of interest

O(1) Cheltenham College A well-known boys' public school, with a fine chapel, founded in 1841.

G(2) Holst Museum A Regency house where the composer Gustav Holst was born, with period rooms, paintings and Holst memorabilia.

J(3) Ladies College A well-known girls' school founded in 1835.

G(4) Library, Art Gallery and Museum The library houses the historic archives of the borough. The art gallery is rich in 17th-C Dutch and Flemish paintings and 19th- and 20th-C British art. The museum displays English ceramics, Chinese porcelain, Cotswold bygones and furniture, and local geology.

J(5) Montpellier Gardens Nearby stands the Rotunda, a fine building of the Regency period, partly by Papworth. In Montpellier Walk, which adjoins, the shops are spaced between replicas of the Erectheon Caryatids.

G(6) Municipal Buildings Housed in a typical Regency terrace.

F(7) St Gregory's Church (RC)

G(8) St Mary's Church This 14th- to 15th-C church, which bears traces of an earlier building of the 12thC, is the town's oldest building. A rare and beautiful example of a rose window is to be seen in the north transept.

N(9) St Mary's College

B(10) St Paul's College

K(11) Town Hall and Spa

Pittville Pump Rooms, Pittville Park. A masterpiece of the Greek revival, built between 1825 and 1830 by Forbes and Papworth and restored after the war. Notable colonnaded façades, portico and pillared balcony and hall. It is situated in the Pittville Gardens off the Evesham road north of the town centre (C).

Hospitals

K Cheltenham General Eye, Ear and Throat Hospital, Sandford Road *tel 21344*

B St Paul's Hospital (Maternity), Swindon Road *tel 56291*

Sport and Recreation

C Approach Golf Course, Pittville Park

H Cheltenham Cricket Club, Victoria Ground

P Cheltenham Croquet Club Old Bath Road

H Cheltenham Rugby Football Club, Athletic Ground

D Cheltenham Town Football Club, Robbin Whaddon Road

B Pittville Swimming Pool, Tommy Taylors Lane

K Sandford Park Open-Air Swimming Pool

Cheltenham Racecourse, Prestbury Park 1½m N via Evesham Road A435 (C)

Lilleybrook Golf Club, Charlton Kings 2m SE via A40 and Cirencester Road A435 (P)

Theatres and Cinemas

G ABC Cinema, The Promenade *tel 52603*

K Cheltenham Playhouse Theatre, Bath Road *tel 22852*

G Everyman Theatre, Regent Street *tel 25544*

G Odeon Film Centre, Winchcombe Street *tel 24081*

Department Stores

Cavendish House, Cambray Galleries
Habitat Designs Ltd, 108 The Promenade
Marks and Spencer Ltd, 179 High Street
Shirers and Lances Ltd, The Promenade
Early closing day Wednesday but most shops are open six days a week

Markets

F Open Market (Thursday)

G Indoor Market (Thursday, Friday and Saturday)

Advertisers

J Berni Montpellier Grill

G Berni The Star

F THF George Hotel

J THF Queen's Hotel

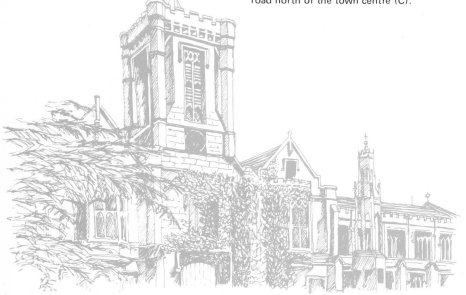

Cheltenham College

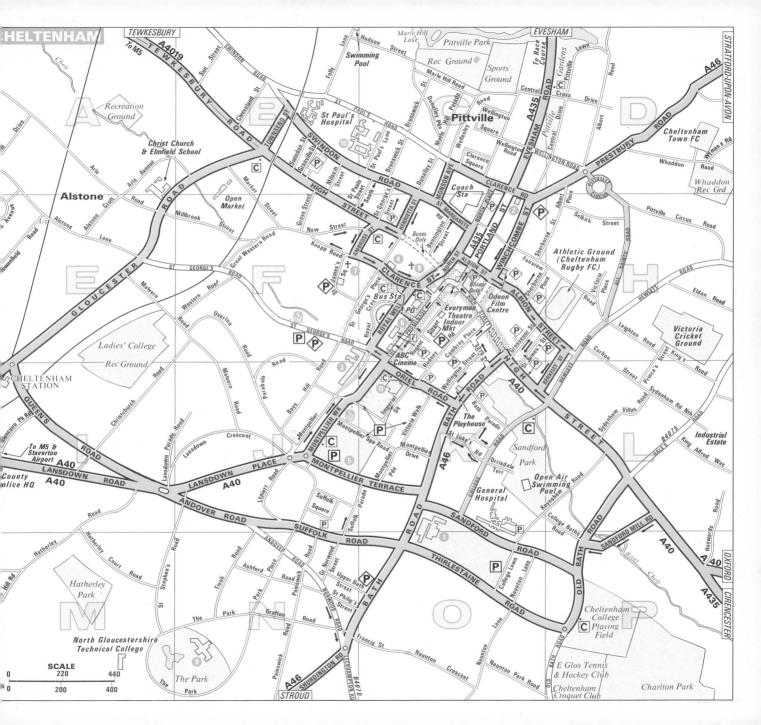

CHESTER

G **AA Service Centre** — Mercia Square, Frodsham Street *tel 20438* (07.00-23.00hrs)

F(26) **Tourist Information Centre** — Town Hall
[i] *tel 40144* (see also public buildings and places of interest)

Public buildings and places of interest

F(1) **Bishop Lloyd's House** One of the city's finest half-timbered houses dating from 1615, with a richly-carved, panelled front showing scenes from sacred history and series of animals.

F(2) **Boneswaldesthorne Tower** Situated at the north-west corner of the City walls and linked to the Water Tower by an embattled spur wall.

K(3) **Bridgegate** Built 1782, this gate replaced an earlier medieval structure.

G(4) **British Heritage Centre** An audio-visual programme with an exhibition craft shop and a replica of the 'Rows' with a 'sight and smell' feature.

J(5) **Castle** Mainly 19thC, but the square Agricola Tower dates back to the 13thC and contains an old chapel and the Regimental Museum of the Cheshire Regiment, with relics, photographs, plans and maps covering over 250 years of service.

G(6) **Cathedral** A mainly 14th-C red sandstone structure, which prior to its dissolution in 1540 was an abbey of ancient foundation. Of particular interest are the monastic remains, including cloisters, chapter house and refectory; the shrine of St Werburgh in the Lady Chapel; the choir stalls with carved misericords of 1380 and the only example of an old consistory court (1636) to be found in England.

G(7) **Chester Heritage Centre** St Michael's Church Exhibition of Chester's architectural and conservation heritage including 20-minute audio-visual shows.

K(8) **County Hall** Modern administrative offices, opened in 1957.

G(9) **East Gate** A gateway of 1769, replacing earlier Roman and medieval structures, which is surmounted by a clock tower erected in 1897 to commemorate Queen Victoria's Jubilee.

F(10) **God's Providence House** A timbered house of 1652 in the Rows. Altered in 1862.

J(11) **Grosvenor Museum** Well-known for its collection of Roman antiquities but also contains natural history and art galleries and in an adjacent house, period rooms and displays of furniture, costume and folk-life.

F(12) **Guildhall Museum** Documents, regalia, records and silver of 23 city companies dating from the 14thC.

F(13) **High Cross** The original High Cross, destroyed in 1646, has now been restored and re-erected in its original position near the south door of St Peter's Church.

C(14) **King Charles or Phoenix Tower** Although much restored in 1613 and 1658, it retains its medieval appearance. It contains a Civil War Exhibition.

G(15) **New Gate** Opened in 1938 to provide a wider entranceway to the city than was previously afforded by the Wolfe Gate of 1768, which stands immediately to the north.

G(16) **Nine Houses** An unusual terraced group of timber-framed buildings of the 17thC, restored in 1969.

B(17) **North Gate** An early 19thC structure, once used as a prison.

F(18) **Pemberton's Parlour** Known also as the Goblin Tower, this was rebuilt in 1894.

G(19) **Roman Amphitheatre** This is the site of the largest Roman building to have been excavated in Britain (1939). Later excavations have revealed large granaries.

G(20) **Roman Garden** Contains a collection of Roman columns which have been re-erected here along with other architectural fragments.

G(21) **St John's Church** A partly-ruined church which preserves a fine Norman nave.

J(22) **St Mary-on-the-Hill** Mainly of the 15th and 16thCs and preserving a splendid medieval timber roof in the nave.

K(23) **St Mary-without-the-Walls** A church of 1887 in Perpendicular style.

F(24) **St Peter's Church** The principal city church which occupies the site of the headquarters of the Roman fortress.

F(25) **Stanley Palace** A gabled and timbered former 16thC home of the Earls of Derby, which has been much restored and is now the local headquarters of the English-speaking Union.

F(26) **Town Hall** A Gothic-style building opened in 1869.

E(27) **Water Tower** This outwork dates from 1322 and was once washed by the River Dee. It contains an exhibition on medieval Chester.

J **Grosvenor Bridge** A single stone span of 200ft built in 1832.

K **Old Dee Bridge** Dating from the 13thC, it was until 1832, the only bridge crossing the Dee at Chester.

F **The City Walls** These encircle the town for a distance of two miles and provide a splendid example of a fortified medieval town. Fine views can be obtained from a stroll around the walls on their raised rampart walk.

G **The Rows** Unique in England, these are continuous arcades or galleries running along the first floor of houses in Eastgate Street, Watergate Street and Bridge Street, and may be compared with somewhat similar examples in the Swiss town of Thun.

Zoological Gardens Interesting collection of animals displayed in natural surroundings, amid fine gardens. Tropical house, aquarium and walk-through aviary. 3m N via Liverpool Road A5116 (B)

Hospitals

F **Chester Royal Infirmary**, St Martins Fields *tel 28261*

Sport and Recreation

E **Chester Golf Course**, Curzon Park
J **Chester Racecourse**, Roodee
H **Swimming Baths**, Union Street
Chester Football Club, Sealand Road 1m NW via Sealand Road A548B (A)
Greyhound Racing Track, Sealand Road 1¼m NW via Sealand Road A548B (A)

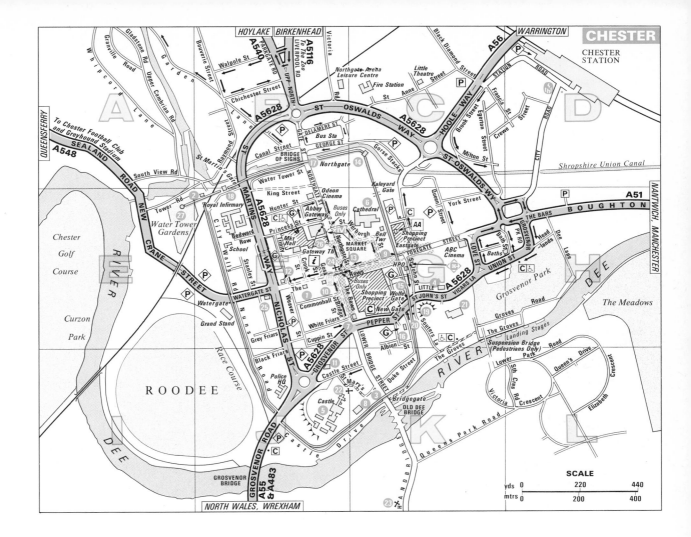

Theatres and Cinemas

G **ABC Cinema,** Foregate Street *tel 22931*
C **Chester Theatre Club,** Little Theatre, Gloucester Street *tel 22674*
E **Gateway Theatre,** Hamilton Place *tel 40393*
E **Odeon Theatre,** Northgate Street *tel 24930*

Department Stores

Army and Navy Stores (Coates), Mercia Square
Browns of Chester Ltd, Eastgate Street
Burrells Ltd, 28 & 30 Foregate Street
Famous Army Stores, 102 Northgate Street
King L and Co (Chester) Ltd, 20 Handbridge
Marks and Spencer Ltd, 22 Foregate Street
Owen Owen Ltd, Eastgate Street
Early closing day Wednesday

Markets

F **Public Market,** Market Hall (at rear of Town Hall) (daily)
Cattle Market, Bumpers Lane (Tuesday and Thursday) 1m NW via Sealand Road A548B (A)

Advertisers

F **Berni** The Criterion
G **Centrelink** Blossoms Hotel
G **Mercantile Credit**
D **THF** Queen Hotel

AA Road Service Centre (7) — 1m E via Westhampnett Road at junction of A285 and A27 (H) *tel 783111*

J(4) ⓘ **Tourist Information Centre** — (summer) Council House, North Street *tel 82226* (see also public buildings and places of interest)

J(5) ⓘ **Tourist Information Centre** — (winter) District Council Offices, Greyfriars, North Street *tel 842555*

Public buildings and places of interest

J(1) **Canon Gate** A 16th-C gateway leading from South Street into the Cathedral precincts along Canon Lane. To the south of Canon Lane is the Chantry with its 13th-C Hall and Chapel.

J(2) **Cathedral** Norman and later, with the only example in England of a detached bell-tower. Two 12th-C sculptures and the retrochoir are of particular note. Close to the Cathedral are the Bishop's Palace, Chapel and 14th-C Palace Gatehouse.

M(3) **College of Further Education**

J(4) **Council House, Assembly Rooms and Tourist Information Centre,** An interesting 17th- and 18th-C town hall containing the City Council Chamber. Preserved at the front of the building is the Roman Neptune and Minerva Stone discovered in 1723.

J(5) **District Council Offices and Tourist Information Centre**

F(6) **Festival Theatre** Opened in 1962, its summer season has acquired an international reputation.

J(7) **Library**

J(8) **Market Cross** Restored and renovated 16th-C cross which is arguably the finest example of its type in the country.

J(9) **Museum** Local relics and a display of material from the Royal Sussex Regiment are housed in this 18th-C building.

J(10) **Priory Park** In the park stands the Early English Choir of Greyfriars Church, later used as a Guildhall and now housing pottery and other archaeological material from the City museum.

K(11) **Roman Amphitheatre Site** This was the ampitheatre of the Roman town of Regnum.

J(12) **St Andrew's Church** A 15th-C structure built above a Roman pavement. Although now in an unsafe condition, its situation shows how valuable building space was wisely used in medieval times.

K(13) **St John's Church** Completed in 1813, the church contains a three-decker pulpit.

J(14) **St Mary's Hospital and St Martin's Square** The almshouses, refounded c1240, preserve a fine hall, with a wagon roof and an interesting Chapel screen. In St Martin's Square are some attractive Georgian houses.

J(15) **St Olave's Church** A partly-Norman Church, converted into a bookshop. It rests on Roman foundations and has an elaborate piscina in the North wall.

N(16) **St Richard's Church (RC)** A recent building which contains some notable modern French stained glass.

Fishbourne Roman Palace One of the major archaeological finds of this century in Britain. Mosaic-floored rooms, a museum and formal gardens are on display. 2m W via Westgate A259 and A27(I)

Hospitals

C **Graylingwell (Mental) Hospital,** College Lane *tel 85171*

G **St Richard's Hospital (Royal West Sussex),** Spitalfield Lane *tel 88122*

Sport and Recreation

F **Chichester City Football Club,** Oaklands Park *tel 82517*

F **Chichester Rugby Football Club,** Oaklands Park *tel 85545*

K **Swimming Pool,** Eastgate Square *tel 86587*

Theatres and Cinemas

F(6) **Festival Theatre** *tel 86333*

J **Granada Cinema,** East Street *tel 82407*

Department Stores

Marks and Spencer Ltd, 16 East Street
Morants (Army & Navy Stores), West Street
Portsea Island Mutual Co-operative, North Street
Early closing day Thursday

Markets

K **Cattle Market,** Market Road (Wednesdays)

Advertisers

J **THF** Dolphin and Anchor Hotel

Chichester Cathedral bell-tower

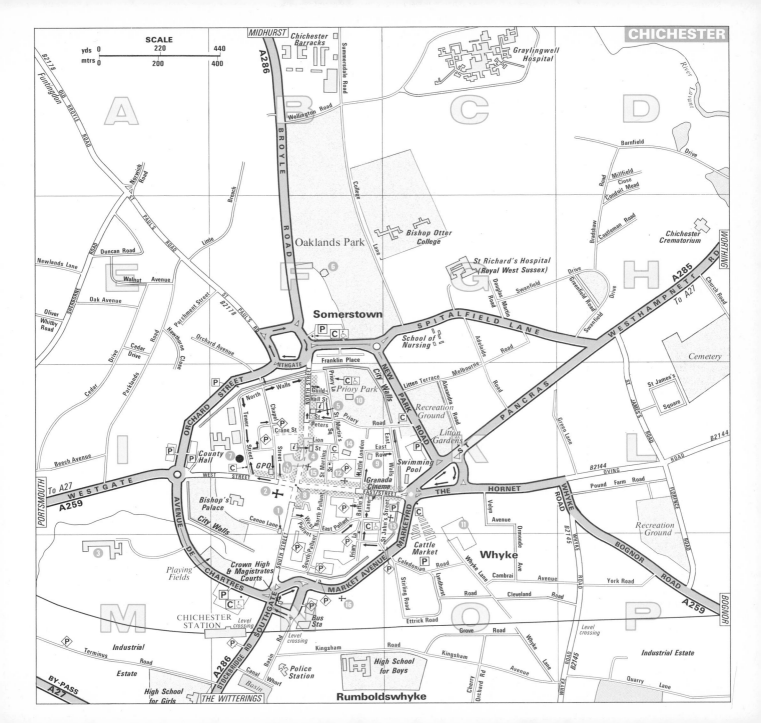

CHICHESTER

SCALE
yds 0   220   440
mtrs 0   200   400

MIDHURST
A286

Chichester Barracks

Graylingwell Hospital

River Lavant

Summersdale Road

Wellington Road

Barnfield

Drive

Millfield Close
Conduit Mead
Road

Bradshaw
Castleman Road

Chichester Crematorium

WORTHING RD

College Lane

Bishop Otter College

St Richard's Hospital
(Royal West Sussex)

Oaklands Park

Douglas Martin Road

Swanfield

Greenfield Road

Drive

Drive

Swanfield

A285
To A27

Newlands Lane

Duncan Road

Walnut Avenue

Oak Avenue

Oliver Road
Whitby Road

Cedar Drive
Hawthorne Close

Orchard Avenue

Parchment Street

St PAUL'S RD
B2178

Somerstown

Spitalfield Lane

School of Nursing

Adelaide Road

Melbourne Road

ST PANCRAS

Cemetery

St James's Square

St JAMES'S ROAD

B2144

Franklin Place

NORTHGATE

North Walls

Priory La
Priory Park

Litten Terrace

Alexandra Road

Recreation Ground

Green Lane

OVING

B2144

Beech Avenue

ORCHARD STREET

Tower Street

Chapel St

Crane St

Guild Hall St

St Martin's St

Priory Road

Litton Gardens

Lion St

St Martins
Little London

East Row

East Walls

Swimming Pool

County Hall

GPO

St John's Street

Granada Cinema

EAST STREET

THE HORNET

B2144

B2145

Recreation Ground

FLORENCE ROAD

WESTGATE
WEST STREET

Bishop's Palace

City Walls

Canon Lane

West Pallant
North Pallant
East Pallant
South Pallant

Baffins Lane

MARKET RD

Cattle Market

Whyke

Velyn Avenue

Ormonde Avenue

Pound Farm Road

Whyke Lane

Cambrai Avenue

WHYKE ROAD

BOGNOR ROAD
A259

BOGNOR

To A27
A259
PORTSMOUTH

AVENUE DE CHARTRES

Crown High & Magistrates Courts

Playing Fields

South Street

Friary Lane

MARKET AVENUE

Caledonian Road

Stirling Road

Lyndhurst Road

Whyke Road

Cleveland Road

York Road

A259

BOGNOR

CHICHESTER STATION

Bus Sta

SOUTHGATE

STOCKBRIDGE RD

Level crossing

Basin Rd

Kingsham Road

Ettrick Road

Grove Road

Whyke Lane

Kingsham Avenue

Level crossing

Industrial Estate

Terminus Road

Industrial Estate

A286

Canal
Basin

Police Station

Wharf

High School for Boys

Cherry Orchard Rd

WHYKE ROAD B2145

Quarry Lane

BY-PASS
A27

High School for Girls

THE WITTERINGS

Rumboldswhyke

COVENTRY

Public buildings and places of interest

F(1)   **Belgrade Theatre** Opened in 1958 and incorporating softwood from Yugoslavia in its construction.

F(2)   **Bond's Hospital and Bablake Old School** An enchanting Tudor almshouse, with half-timbered and stone façade and nearby the picturesque old school building.

F(3)   **Broadgate** Here are the Lady Godiva statue and New Clock Tower, with figures of Lady Godiva and Peeping Tom.

L(4)   **Charter House** There are slight remains of these buildings, founded in 1381.

J(5)   **Cheylesmore Manor House (Registry Office)** Dates back originally to 1230 and is built over a lane.

J(6)   **Christ Church** Noted for its tall, restored 14th-C spire, which survived the bombing of 1940.

G(7)   **City Walls and Gate** Slight remains of the 14th-C walls, together with two gates, are still to be seen.

J(8)   **Council House**

G(9)   **Coventry Theatre**

J(10)   **Ford's Hospital** A half-timbered almshouse with interior courtyard considered to be an exceptional example of 16th-C domestic architecture.

G(11)   **'Golden Cross Inn'** A gabled and restored half-timbered inn, probably dating from the 17th-C.

K(12)   **Herbert Museum and Art Gallery** The museum contains a collection of old motor vehicles, particularly of Coventry manufacture; a Warwickshire natural history section; a full-scale working loom; Stevengraphs (silk pictures); and silk woven bookmarks. The art gallery's permanent collection relates to British life and landscape, in particular of Warwickshire.

G(13)   **Holy Trinity Church** A 15th-C church with a 231ft-high spire. The 15th-C brass eagle lectern and west window of 1955 are notable.

G(14)   **Lanchester Polytechnic**

K(15)   **Martyrs' Memorial** This memorial of 1910 is in memory of the Coventry martyrs of the 16thC.

F(16)   **St John's Church** A restored 14th-to 15th-C church.

F(17)   **St John's Hospital** Mainly 14th-C and formerly a school, with a fine hall. It has now been restored.

G(18)   **St Mary's Guildhall** A building of 1340 and later, with restored Great Hall adorned with much fine, stained glass, in particular the North Wall window; portraits and a 15th-C Arras tapestry, minstrel's gallery, and 13th-C Caesar's watch-tower, rebuilt after bomb damage.

G(19)   **St Michael's Cathedral** Only the walls, the 303ft-high, 15th-C tower and spire of the medieval Cathedral survived the bombing of 1940. The new cathedral by Sir Basil Spence was completed in 1962 and is in a striking, modern style, incorporating richly-coloured glass, Epstein sculptures, an engraved glass screen by John Hutton and a vast Aubusson altar tapestry of *Christ in Glory* by Graham Sutherland.

F(20)   **Spon Street** An attempt is being made to create a medieval street by rebuilding here ancient buildings from other parts of the town.

K(21)   **Whitefriars Monastery and Museum** A beautifully restored, old sandstone building housing an archaeological collection of the Coventry area with exhibits dating from the Stone Age.

Bond's Hospital

Hospitals

G   **Coventry and Warwickshire Hospital**
    tel 24055
K   **Gulson Hospital** *tel 28331*

Sport and Recreation

G   **Coventry Baths,** Fairfax Street
H   **Coventry City Football Club,** Highfield
    Road
E   **Coventry Rugby Football Club,** Coundon
    Road
H   **Primrose Hill Baths,** Coronation Road

Theatres and Cinemas

F   **ABC Cinema,** Hertford Street *tel 23600*
F(1) **Belgrade Theatre,** Corporation Street
      tel 20205 (see also public buildings
      and places of interest)
G(9) **Coventry Theatre,** Hales Street *tel
      23141* (see also public buildings and
      places of interest)
K   **Odeon Cinema,** Jordan Wall *tel 22042*
K   **Paris Cinema,** Far Gosford Street *tel
      26526*
G   **Theatre One Cinema,** Ford Street *tel
      24301*

Department Stores

Co-operative, Lower Precinct
Marks and Spencer Ltd, The Precinct
Owen Owen Ltd, Broadgate
Early closing day Thursday, but most shops
remain open six days

Markets

J   **Coventry Market** (Wednesday, Friday and
    Saturday)
D   **Coventry Wholesale Market,** Barras Heath

Advertisers

J   **Mercantile Credit**

70

DISTRICT PLAN

Public buildings and places of interest

O(22) **Lunt Roman Fort** Reconstruction of
       Roman Fort, which stood on this site
       AD71-75, with interpretive centre
       housed in reconstructed granary.
M(23) **University of Warwick**
O(24) **Zoo** Covers a wide representation of
       the animal kingdom.

Hospitals

E   **Paybody Hospital** *tel 20455*
H   **Walsgrave Hospital** *tel 613232*
K   **Whitley Hospital** *tel 20455*

Sport and Recreation

P   **Brandon Wood Golf Course,** Brandon
    Lane

N   **Coventry Golf Club,** Finham Park
K   **Grange Golf Course**
L   **Greyhound and Speedway Stadium,**
    Brandon
J   **Hearsall Golf Club,** Beechwood Avenue
K   **Humber Bowling Centre,** Forum Bowl,
    Longfellow Road
F   **Livingstone Road Baths**

Markets

K   **Coventry Wholesale Market,** Barras Heath

Advertisers

F   **Berni** Shepherd and Shepherdess
O   **Crest** Coventry Crest Motel
H   **Crest** Euro Crest Hotel
E   **THF** The Post House

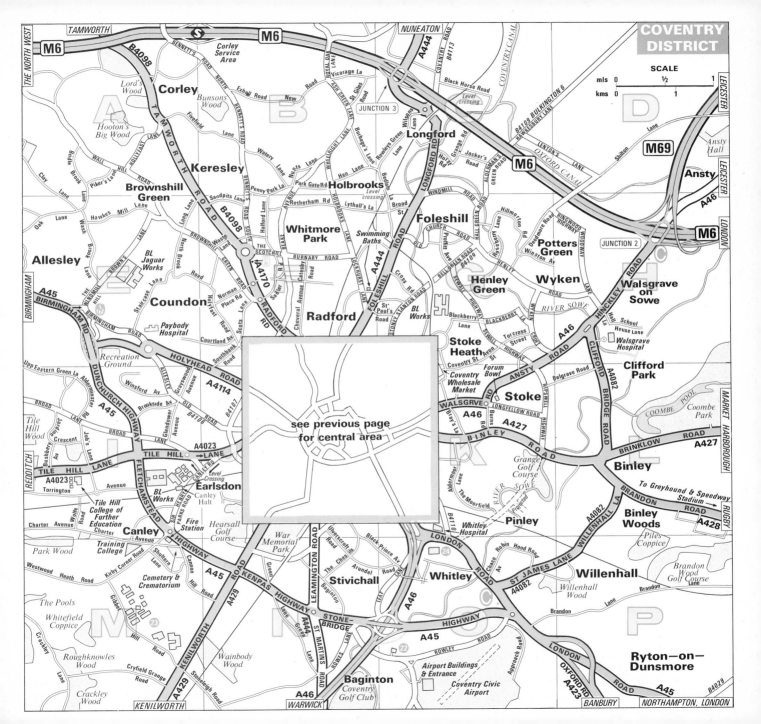

DERBY

CENTRAL PLAN

F(1) **Tourist Information Centre** — The Reference Library, Central Library, The Wardwick *tel 31111 ext 2185/6* (see also public buildings and places of interest)

Public buildings and places of interest

F(1) **Art Gallery, Museum and Central Library** Contains antiquities, local and social history and natural history collections, Derby porcelain, costumes, militaria, 'Bonnie Prince Charlie' room (1745 rebellion), a scaled working layout of the former Midland Railway and paintings by Joseph Wright of Derby (1734-97).

B(2) **Art School** St Helen's House, 18th-C.

F(3) **Assembly Rooms**

B(4) **Brigg Chapel** A restored 14th-C chapel situated on the 18th-C bridge spanning the River Derwent.

F(5) **Cathedral** Formerly the Parish Church until 1927. It was rebuilt by James Gibbs in 1725 and is noted for its 16th-C western tower, an 18th-C wrought iron screen by Robert Bakewell and modern windows by Ceri Richards executed by Patrick Reynteins.

F(6) **County Hall** The notable façade dates from 1660.

F(7) **Guildhall and Market Hall**

K(8) **New Market Hall**, Eagle Centre

K(9) **New Playhouse Theatre**, Eagle Centre

O(10) **Royal Crown Derby Porcelain Company** Factory tours on written application.

B(11) **St Mary's Church (RC)** A building by the famous 19th-C architect Pugin.

F(12) **St Michael's Church** Rebuilt in the 19th C.

J(13) **St Peter's Church** This church has preserved a fine Flemish chest.

F(14) **St Werburgh's Church** Dr Johnson was married in this church.

F(15) **Silk Mill, Industrial Museum and Art Gallery** Housed in an early 17th-C silk mill which was substantially rebuilt in 1910, this museum contains a Rolls Royce aero engine collection, exhibitions on the history of aviation from the Wright Brothers to the present day and 'An Introduction to Derbyshire Industries'.

Hospitals

J **Derby Chest Clinic,** Green Lane *tel 40366*

B **Derbyshire Children's Hospital,** North Street *tel 47141*

E **Derbyshire Hospital for Women,** Friar Gate *tel 47141*

O **Derbyshire Royal Infirmary,** London Road *tel 47141*

O **Nightingale Maternity Home,** London Road *tel 47141*

Sport and Recreation

D **County Cricket Ground**

F **Queen Street Swimming Baths**

Theatres and Cinemas

K **ABC Cinema,** East Street *tel 43964*

K(9) **New Playhouse Theatre,** Eagle Centre *tel 363275* (see also public buildings and places of interest)

K **Odeon Cinema,** London Road *tel 40139*

Department Stores

Debenhams Departmental Store, 17 Victoria Street

Marks and Spencer Ltd, 11 St Peter's Street *Early closing day* Wednesday, but most shops are open six days a week

Markets

F(7) **Market Hall** (General retail, meat, poultry, fish — daily) (see also public buildings and places of interest)

K(8) **New Market Hall,** Eagle Centre (daily) (see also public buildings and places of interest)

Advertisers

F **Berni** Iron Gates Tavern

F **Mercantile Credit**

DISTRICT PLAN

F **AA Road Service Centre (25)** — On A52 at junction with A38 *tel 41496*

Public buildings and places of interest

B(16) **Darley Abbey** (ruins)

A(17) **Kedleston Hall** Outstanding Robert Adam mansion, with unique marble hall, state room and collection of fine pictures, which stands in a lake-watered, 500-acre park.

Hospitals

I **Derby City Hospital,** Uttoxeter Road *tel 40131*

G **Derwent Hospital,** Mansfield Road *tel 47141*

I **Kingsway Hospital,** Kingsway *tel 362221*

I **Manor Hospital,** Uttoxeter Road *tel 49694*

I **Pastures Hospital,** Mickleover *tel 513921*

M **Rykneld Hospital** *tel 53656*

F **Queen Mary Maternity Home,** Duffield Road *tel 47141*

Sport and Recreation

B **Allestree Park Golf Course**

K **Derby County Football Association**

N **Derby Golf Course,** Sinfin

B **Derby Rugby Football Club,** Pavilion, Kedleston Road

F **Greyhound Stadium,** Vernon Street

A **Kedleston Park Golf Course**

I **Mickleover Golf Course,** Uttoxeter Road

O **Municipal Sports and Athletic Stadium,** Moor Lane, Osmaston Park Road

K **Reginald Street Baths**

O **Regional Swimming Pool,** Municipal Sport Ground, Moor Lane, Allenton

Cinemas

H **Lucky Seven Film Centre,** Nottingham Road, Chaddesden *tel 674161*

Markets

O **Allenton Open Market** (Friday and Saturday)

G **Cattle and Wholesale Markets,** Chequers Road (daily, except cattle — Tuesday and Saturday)

Advertisers

I **Crest** Derby Crest Motel

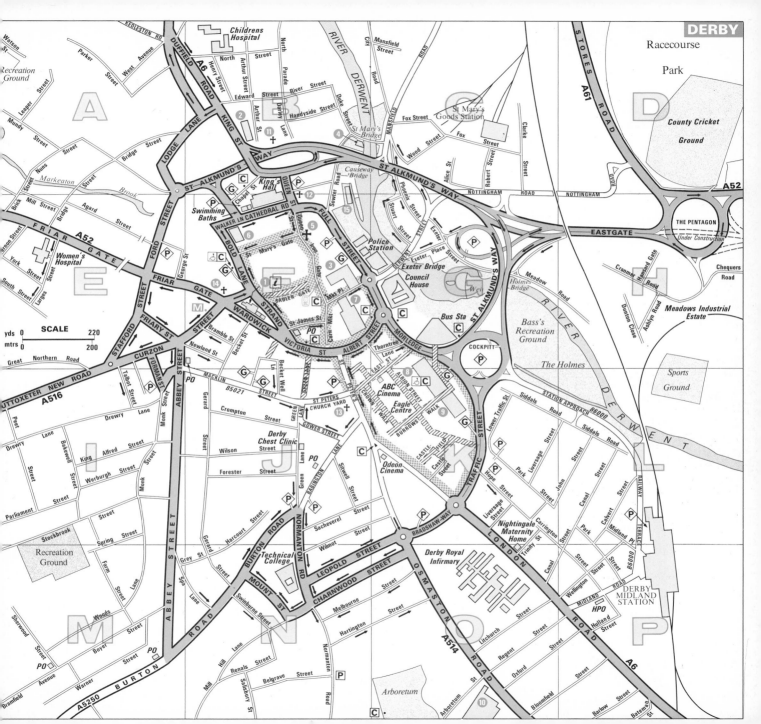

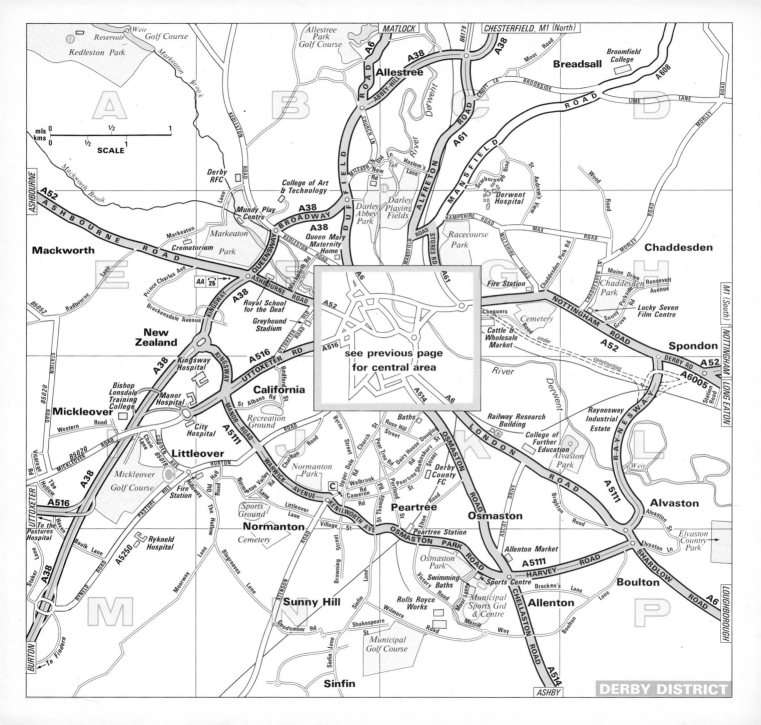

DRIVE
DRIVE
DRIVE

If you're a motorist you daren't go without it.

Now six times a year. From any newsagent.

DOVER

D   **AA Port Service Centre** — Terminal Building, Eastern Docks *tel 208122*

M   **AA Port Service Centre** — Seaspeed Hovercraft Terminal, Western Docks *tel 208122*

H   **Tourist Information Centre** — Townwall Street *tel 205108*

Public buildings and places of interest

D(1)   **Bleriot Memorial** A granite aeroplane commemorates Louis Bleriot's epic flight across the English Channel in 1909.

D(2)   **Castle, St Mary de Castra Church and Roman Lighthouse** The impressive Norman Castle, the 'Key to England' overlooks the Channel. The Keep dates from 1181. The Church of St Mary de Castra is a pre-Conquest structure of the 10th or 11thC and has been used as the garrison church since the restoration by Scott in 1860-62. Nearby stands the Roman 'pharos' or lighthouse.

G(3)   **Dover College** The College preserves portions of the monastery of St Martin of the New Wark, often called Dover Priory.

G(4)   **Library** This is housed in the attractive 17th-C building, Maison Dieu House, a former pilgrim's hostel.

H(5)   **St Edmund's Chapel** This was consecrated by St Richard of Chichester in 1253 and fell into disuse as a chapel in 1544. It has now been restored and was reconsecrated in 1968.

H(6)   **St Mary's Church** Retains a Norman Tower, much of the structure having been rebuilt in 1843.

G(7)   **Town Hall, Museum, Information Bureau and Magistrates Court** The building includes the 13th-C Hall of Maison Dieu. The museum contains exhibits on local history, diorama, early furniture, textiles, pictures, ceramics, ships, etc.

Hospitals

F   **Buckland Hospital**, Coombe Valley Road *tel 201624*

F   **Eye Hospital**, Noah's Ark Road *tel 201624*

G   **Royal Victoria Hospital**, High Street *tel 204508*

Sport and Recreation

G   **Maison Dieu Gardens** — bowls

H   **Sports Centre**, Townwall Street

Theatres and Cinemas

H   **ABC Cinema**, Castle Street *tel 206750*

Department Stores

The Co-operative, Biggin Street
Marks and Spencer Ltd, 28 Biggin Street
Early closing day Wednesday

The Roman 'pharos'

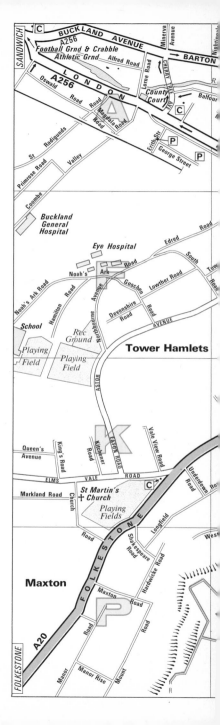

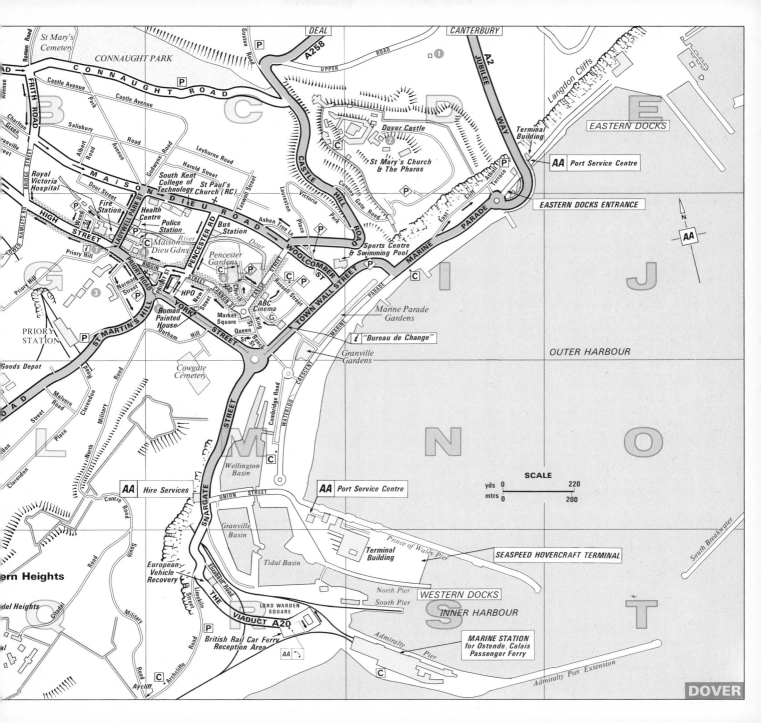

DOVER

DUNDEE

CENTRAL PLAN

F   **AA Service Centre** — 124 Overgate *tel 25585*

G [i]   **Tourist Information Centre** — 16 City Square *tel 27723*

Public buildings and places of interest

F(1)   **Barrack Street Museum** Contains shipping and industrial exhibits relating to the City.

G(2)   **Caird Hall** Built 1914-23, comprises the city hall and council chambers.

G(3)   **City Museum, Art Gallery and Library** Housed in the Albert Institute it covers local archaeology, history, natural history, geology and botany; a display on the life and works of Mary Slessor, the missionary, and works of art by principal British and European masters.

C(4)   **Cowgate Port** The only surviving gate of the old town walls. George Wishart is said to have preached from the gate during the plague of 1544.

A(5)   **Dudhope Castle** A restored 13th-C castle, now used as a meeting place for clubs and societies.

G(6)   **HMS Unicorn** The oldest floating warship, it was completed in the early 19thC.

F(7)   **Mercat Cross** A replica of 1874 of the original cross that stood in Seagate.

F(8)   **St Andrew's Cathedral (RC)**

F(9)   **St Mary's Tower** A 15th-C steeple or bell-tower, 160ft-high, which is part of the three City churches. A small museum displaying the history of the churches is housed here.

G(10)   **St Paul's Cathedral** Designed by Sir Giles Gilbert Scott and completed in 1853, it stands on the site of the old Dundee Castle.

G(11)   **Tayside House** Regional Council HQ

E(12)   **University**

F   **The Howff** Old burial ground founded by charter of Mary, Queen of Scots in 1564 and used until 1878. Also formerly used as a meeting place for local craftsmen until 1778.

Hospitals

F   **Dundee Eye Institution,** 138 Nethergate *tel 23639*

B   **Dundee Royal Infirmary,** Barrack Road *tel 23125*

Sport and Recreation

K   **Swimming and Leisure Centre**

Theatres and Cinemas

G   **ABC Cinema,** Seagate *tel 26865*

A   **Dundee Repertory Theatre,** 113 Lochee Road *tel 23530*

C   **Little Theatre,** 58 Victoria Road *tel 25835*

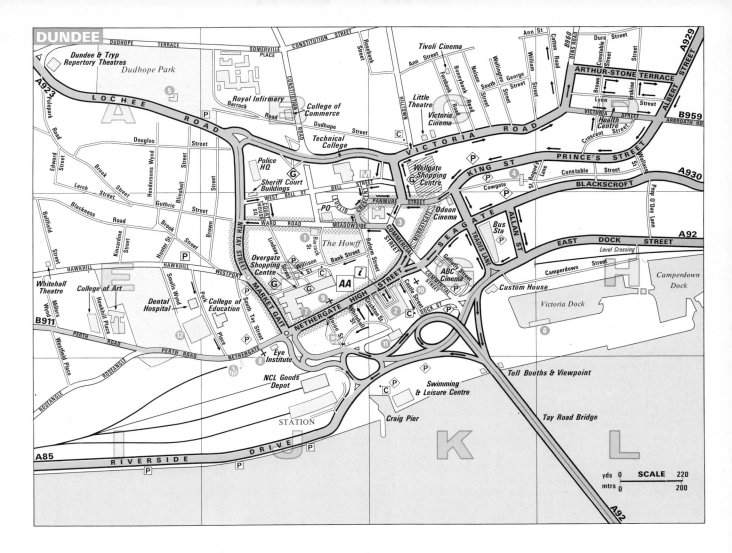

G	**Odeon Cinema,** Cowgate *tel 26767*
C	**Tivoli Cinema,** Bonnybank Road *tel 24258*
A	**Tryp Repertory Theatre,** 113 Lochee Road *tel 24532*
C	**Victoria Cinema,** Victoria Road *tel 26186*
E	**Whitehall Theatre,** Bellfield Street *tel 22200*

Lawsons Ltd, Whitehall Crescent
McGill Brothers Ltd, 5 Victoria Road
Marks and Spencer Ltd, 41 Murraygate
Robertsons, Barrack Street
Smith Alex (Stores) Ltd, 100 Commercial Street

Early closing day Wednesday

Advertisers

C	**Mercantile** Credit
J	**THF** Queen's Hotel
F	**Centre** Tay Centre Hotel
F	**Centre** Royal Centre Hotel

Department Stores

Arnotts, 80 High Street
Draffens, Nethergate

Markets

G	**City Arcade,** Caird Hall Buildings, Shore Terrace (daily)

DISTRICT PLAN
Public buildings and places of interest

C(13)   **Dundee Law** A 571ft-high viewpoint.

C(14)   **Mains of Fintry Castle** Ruins of a late 16th-C castle standing in Caird Park.

F(15)   **Mills Observatory** Stands in Balgay Park and can be visited.

A(16)   **Spalding Golf Museum,** Camperdown Park. This museum portrays the history of golf through three centuries and includes an iron club of c1680. It is housed in Camperdown House, a classical mansion of 1824-28. The park also contains a children's zoo and aviary.

H(17)   **The Tay Road Bridge** This bridge carries dual two-lane carriageways each 22ft wide, and there is a 10ft-wide central reservation for pedestrians. The toll booths are on the Dundee side. Situated two miles downstream from the Tay railway bridge, it is 7,365ft (1.4 miles) long. Begun in May 1963, the Tay road bridge was opened by HM The Queen Mother on 18 August 1966. It consists of 42 spans with twin concrete columns of an unusual developing parabolic shape, and the deck rises from 32ft to 125ft above mean water level. There are two public viewing platforms; one above the tollbooths, and one above the navigation span, half a mile from the Fife shore.

K(18)   **The Tay Railway Bridge** A double track structure 11,653ft (2.2 miles) long, and opened in 1887. It was built to replace the single line bridge opened in 1878, part of which collapsed during a great storm in December 1879 with the loss of a train and 75 passengers. The remains of the old piers can be seen alongside the present bridge.

Hospitals

E   **Ninewells Hospital** *tel 60111*

C   **Kings Cross Hospital,** West Clepington Road *tel 85241*

F   **Royal Victoria Hospital,** Jedburgh Road *tel 66246*

Sport and Recreation

C   **Caird Park Golf Course**

A   **Camperdown Golf Course,** Camperdown Park

B   **Dundee-Angus Ice Rink,** Kingsway West

C   **Dundee Football Club,** Dens Park, Sandeman Street

C   **Dundee United Football Club,** Tannadice Street

B   **Downfield Golf Club**

B   **Swimming Baths,** High Street, Lochee

Markets

D   **Cattle Market,** Broughty Ferry Road (Tuesday; general agricultural sales Friday and Saturday)

C   **Dens Road Market,** 39 Dens Road (Tuesday mornings)

B   **Lorne Street Market,** Lochee

Mains of Fintry Castle

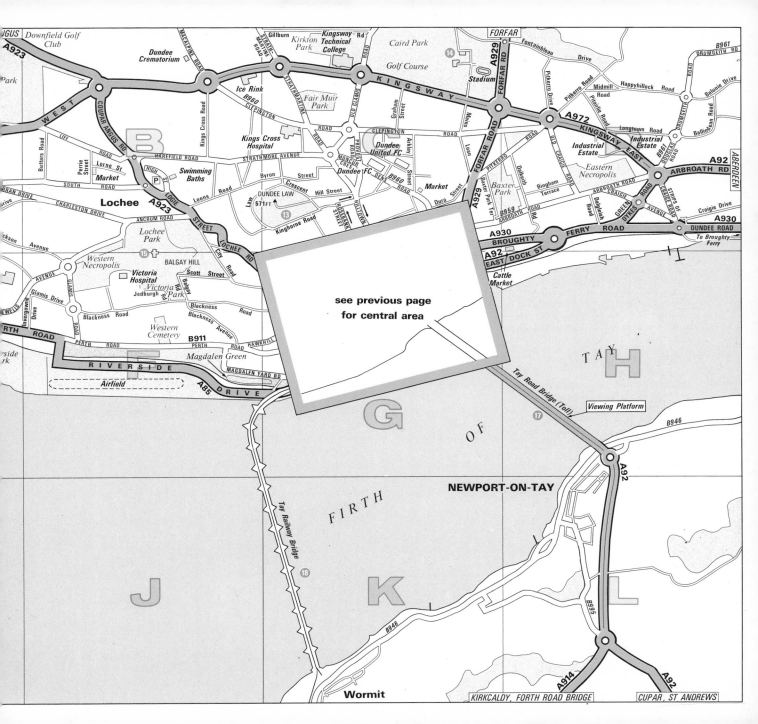

Downfield Golf Club

A923

Park

WEST

COUPAR ANGUS RD

Dundee Crematorium

MACALPINE ROAD

STRATHMORE RD

Gillburn

Kirkton Park

Kingsway Technical College

KINGSWAY RD

Caird Park Golf Course

14

FORFAR

FORFAR RD

A929

Stadium

Fontainbleau

Drive

B961

DRUMGEITH RD

Pitkerro Drive

Midmill Road

Happyhillock Road

Balunie Drive

Ballindean Road

Ice Rink

B960

Kings Cross Road

STRATHMARTINE

OLD GLAMIS

CLEPINGTON

Fair Muir Park

ROAD

KINGSWAY

A929

FORFAR ROAD

A972

KINGSWAY EAST

Longtown Road

Pitkerro Road

Prairie Road

Industrial Estate

B961

DOUGLAS ROAD

Industrial Estate

DRUMGEITH

ARBROATH RD

A92

ABERDEEN

B

LIFF

Buttars Road

Perrie Street

Lorne St

Market

SOUTH ROAD

HIGH

P

Swimming Baths

ROAD

Kings Cross Hospital

STRATHMORE AVENUE

Byron Street

Crescent

Hill Street

Dundee United FC

MONCUR CRES

PROVOST ROAD

CLEPINGTON

Dundee FC

B960

DENS ROAD

Arklay Street

Graham Street

Market

Dura Street

Mains Loan

Loan

FORFAR ROAD

A929

Baxter Park

Dalkeith

Bingham Terrace

B959

ARBROATH

ROAD

Eastern Necropolis

ARBROATH CRAIGIE ROAD

GREEN

DYKES ROAD

STRIPS OF CRAIGIE ROAD

Craigie Drive

A930

Lochee

LOGIE STREET

A923

HAREFIELD ROAD

Loons Road

Law

Dundee Law 571FT

13

Kinghorne Road

ROSEBANK STREET

HALLTOWN

Dalgleish Road

CRAIGIE AVENUE

A930

CHARLESTON DRIVE

ANCRUM ROAD

Lochee Park

City Road

LOCHEE RD

Scott Street

Balgay Rd

BALGAY HILL

Victoria Park

A930

BROUGHTY FERRY ROAD

A92

EAST DOCK ST

Cattle Market

To Broughty Ferry

RRAN DRIVE

Dickson Avenue

AVENUE

Western Necropolis

15

Victoria Hospital

GLAMIS

Glamis Drive

Jedburgh Rd

Blackness Road

Blackness Avenue

Scott Street

Blackness Road

Western Cemetery

B911

PERTH ROAD

HAWKHILL

Magdalen Green

FEWELLS

Invergowrie Drive

RTH ROAD

PERTH ROAD

RIVERSIDE

DRIVE

A85

MAGDALEN YARD RD

Airfield

rside Park

TAY

H

see previous page for central area

G

Tay Road Bridge (Toll)

17

Viewing Platform

B946

Tay Railway Bridge

FIRTH

OF

NEWPORT-ON-TAY

18

J

K

L

A92

B996

B946

Wormit

KIRKCALDY, FORTH ROAD BRIDGE

A914

A92

CUPAR, ST ANDREWS

DURHAM

AA Road Service Centre (18) — *tel 62894*
2½m E at Carville via A690 (H)
G ⓘ **Tourist Information Centre** — 13 Claypath
tel 3720

Public buildings and places of interest

L(1) **Assize Courts**
K(2) **Castle** A fine, mainly 12th- to 14th-C
building with a notable hall and 11th-C
chapel. It is now used by Durham
University.
K(3) **Cathedral and Monastic Buildings**
A splendidly-situated cathedral dating
from the Norman period and later. It is
famous for the great Norman piers of
the nave; the Galilee Porch containing
Bede's tomb; the 13th-C chapel of the
Nine Altars; the Sanctuary Knocker;
and the Neville Screen of 1380. There
are considerable remains of the
Monastic buildings.
O(4) **College** A peaceful close containing
dwellings of the Cathedral dignitaries.
B(5) **County Hall**
K(6) **Dunelm House, Student Union**
C(7) **Durham Light Infantry Museum and Arts
Centre** Collection of military relics,
exhibitions, recitals and lectures.
K(8) **Elvet Bridge** A 12th-C bridge widened
in 1805.
K(9) **Framwelgate Bridge** The bridge dating
from c1128 was rebuilt 1388-1405.
R(10) **Gulbenkian Museum of Oriental Art**
The only museum in the country devoted
entirely to Oriental art and
archaeology.
I(11) **Neville's Cross** The ruined cross
commemorates a battle of 1346 when the
Scots were defeated.
O(12) **Prebends Bridge** (no cars). A bridge
of the late 18thC.
K(13) **Public Library**
H(14) **St Giles' Church** Partly Norman,
containing a wooden effigy of 1591.
O(15) **St Oswald's Church** A 12th- to 15th-C
building.
G(16) **Town Hall**
K(17) **University Library**

Hospitals

F **County Hospital** *tel 64911*
J **St Margaret's Hospital** *tel 64911*

Sport and Recreation

D **Durham City Association Football Club,**
Ferens Park
L **Durham City Rugby Football Club,** Green
Lane
G **Durham Ice Rink,** Freemans Place
L **Durham Swimming Pool,** Elvet Waterside

Theatres and Cinemas

K **Classic Cinema,** North Road *tel 3184*

Department Stores

Marks and Spencer Ltd, Silver Street
Early closing day Wednesday

Markets

G **Market Place** (Saturday — covered and
open)
Note
Framwelgate Bridge, Silver Street and Elvet Bridge
are closed to traffic from 10.00 hrs. They are open
at night and early morning for access only.
Saddler Street access only, all times. North Road
access only, vehicles travelling in a westerly direction
Eastbound lane of North Road is restricted to buses
only.

Cathedral

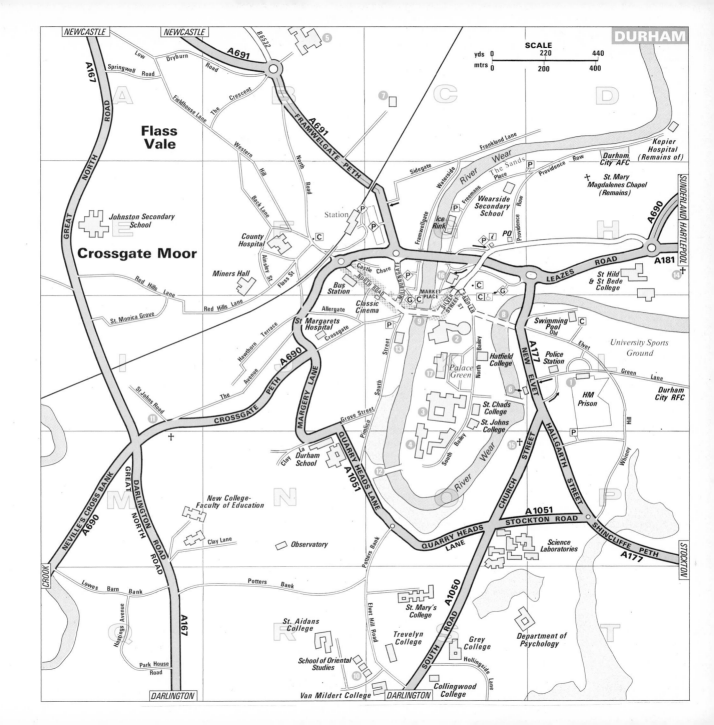

EDINBURGH

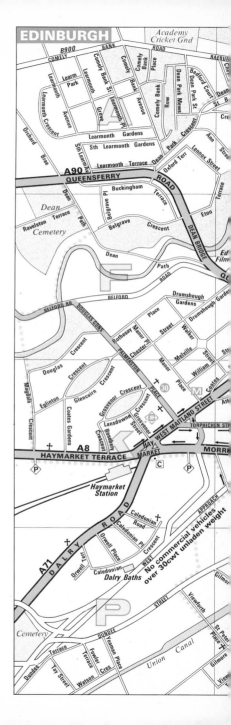

G   AA Service Centre — Fanum House, 18-22 Melville Street *tel 031-225 8464*

CENTRAL PLAN

H 33   Tourist Information Offices — 5 Waverley
ⓘ   Bridge *tel 031-226-6591* (City) and
031-332-2433 (Scottish Tourist Board)
(see also public buildings and places
of interest)

Public buildings and places of interest

I(1)   **Acheson House** The headquarters of the Scottish Craft Centre is housed in this 17th-C mansion.
H(2)   **Assembly Rooms and Music Hall**
M(3)   **Castle and Scottish National War Memorial** The historical castle on its commanding site has many Royal associations. The Norman St Margaret's Chapel is Scotland's oldest ecclesiastical building still in use. The Scottish National War Memorial was opened in 1927.
I(4)   **City Chambers** Originally erected in 1753 as the Royal Exchange.
I(5)   **Canongate Tolbooth** Once a prison and courthouse dating back to 1591. It has a curious projecting clock.
H(6)   **Edinburgh Festival Office**
H(7)   **Floral Clock** This is the oldest floral clock in the world. It dates from 1903.
G(8)   **Freemasons' Hall**
M(9)   **George Heriot's School** Dates from 1628 and was founded by George Heriot.
H(10)   **Gladstone's Land** Built in 1620 it preserves Edinburgh's last arcaded ground floor.
M(11)   **Greyfriars Church and Greyfriars Bobby Statue** The church dates from 1612 and is famous for the signing of the National Covenant in 1638. There is also a memorial to the Covenanters. The statue recalls an Edinburgh dog who watched over his master's grave from 1858 to 1872.
J(12)   **Holyroodhouse and Abbey** The Palace of Holyroodhouse dates from 1500 and is noted for its historical apartments, state rooms and picture gallery. There are associations with Mary., Queen of Scots, and Prince Charles Edward. The Abbey (now in ruins) was founded in 1128.

I(13)   **Huntly House** Dating from 1570, Huntly House now houses the City Museum of local history.
I(14)   **John Knox's House** A 15th-C house preserving wooden galleries. Built by the goldsmith to Mary, Queen of Scots, and probably lived in by John Knox.
H(15)   **Lady Stair's House** A restored house built in 1622. It is now a literary museum.
I(16)   **Museum of Childhood** Contains an extremely large collection of items relating to childhood in the past.
H(17)   **National Gallery of Scotland** Contains a comprehensive collection of paintings of a number of schools.
M(18)   **National Library Of Scotland** Contains a large collection of books and manuscripts.
I(19)   **National Monument and Nelson Monument** Commenced in 1822 but left unfinished. It commemorates the Scottish dead in the Napoleonic Wars and forms a notable viewpoint. The nearby Nelson Monument is 108-ft high.
C(20)   **National Portrait Gallery and Museum of Antiquities** The Portrait Gallery was founded in 1882 and contains a collection of portraits of famous Scots. The museum contains a representative collection of history and everyday life of Scotland from the Stone Age to modern times.
N(21)   **New University**
N(22)   **Old University** A Robert Adam design of 1789 with 19th-C additions.
M(23)   **Outlook Tower** This tower contains a fine camera obscura, which has been in use since 1892.
N(24)   **Parliament House** Built 1633-40 but now masked by later buildings. The Hall has a fine hammer-beam roof.
I(25)   **Register House** Built between 1774-89 from designs by Robert Adam. It houses the Archives of Scotland.
H(26)   **Royal Scottish Academy** Founded in 1826 to promote Fine Arts in Scotland.
N(27)   **Royal Scottish Museum** Opened in 1866, it contains the United Kingdom's largest display of the decorative arts, natural history, geology and technology under one roof.

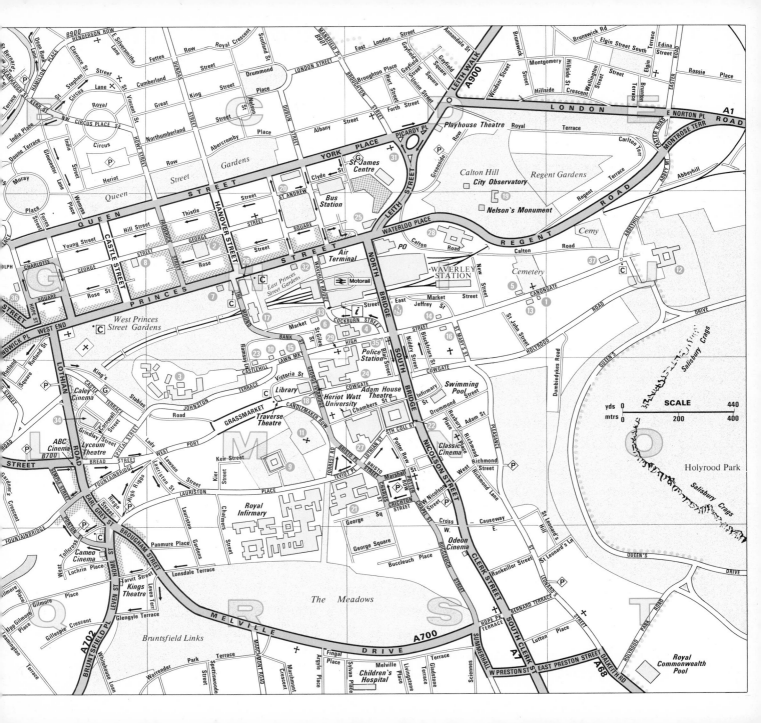

I(28) **St Andrew's House**
Government Offices.

H(29) **St Giles Cathedral and Mercat Cross**
The Cathedral is an imposing and lofty
Gothic building. The tower is the
oldest part and is surmounted by the
famous 'Crown' steeple. The ornate
Thistle Chapel dates from 1911. The
Mercat Cross, which incorporates the
original shaft, was erected in 1885 by
Gladstone.

K(30) **St Mary's Episcopal Cathedral** Designed
by Sir Giles Gilbert Scott and completed
in 1917.

D(31) **St Mary's Cathedral (RC)**

H(32) **Scott Monument** A 19th-C memorial to Sir
Walter Scott, designed by George Kemp.

H(33) **Scottish Tourist Board Offices and Tourist
Information Centre**

L(34) **Usher Hall**

I(35) **Wax Museum** The museum contains an
interesting collection of over 100 wax
figures from the 11thC to the present
day.

G(36) **West Register House** The former St
George's Church is now an annexe of the
Record Office.

J(37) **White Horse Close** An original coaching
terminus.

Hospitals

S **Royal Hospital for Sick Children,**
Sciennes Road *tel 031-667 6811*

M **Royal Infirmary of Edinburgh,** Lauriston
Place *tel 031-229 2477*

Sport and Recreation

P **Dalry Baths,** Caledonian Crescent
N **Swimming Pool,** Infirmary Street
T **Royal Commonwealth Pool,** Dalkeith
Road

Theatres and Cinemas

L **ABC Film Theatre,** Lothian Road *tel 031-
229 3030*

N **Adam House Theatre,** Chambers Street *tel
031-225 3744*

L **Caley Cinema,** 31 Lothian Road *tel
031-229 7670*

Q **Cameo Cinema,** 138 Home Street,
Tollcross *tel 031-229 6822*

N **Classic Cinema,** Nicolson Street
tel 031-667 1839

G **Edinburgh Film Theatre,** Randolph
Crescent *tel 031-225 1671*

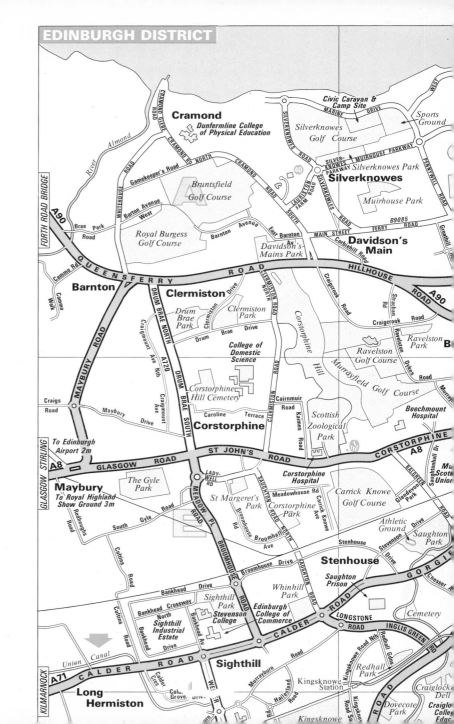

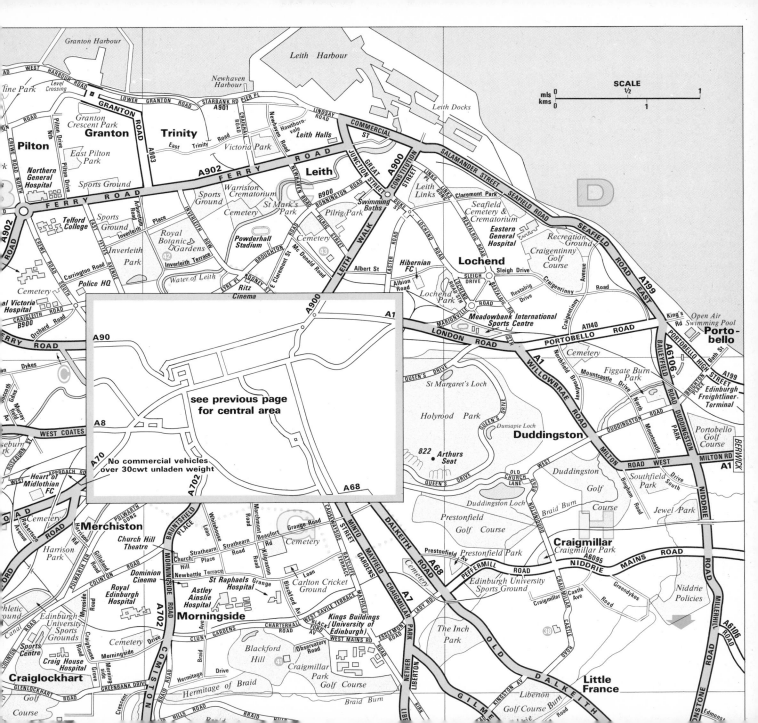

EDINBURGH continued

Q   **King's Theatre,** Leven Street, Tollcross *tel 031-229 1201*
S   **Odeon Cinema,** 7 Clerk Street *tel 031-667 3805*
D   **Playhouse Theatre,** Greenside Place *tel 031-556 7226*
L   **Royal Lyceum Theatre,** Grindlay Street *tel 031-229 4353*
M   **Traverse Theatre Club,** 112 West Bow *tel 031-226 2633*

Department Stores

Arnotts, 15 North Bridge
R W Forsyth Ltd, Princes Street
Frasers Ltd, Princes Street
A Goldberg and Sons Ltd, Tollcross
Jenners, Princes Street, St David Street
J Lewis and Son, St James Centre
Marks and Spencer Ltd, 53 Princes Street
Early closing day various parts of the town close Tuesday, Wednesday and Saturday

Advertisers

K   **Mercantile Credit**
K   **Centre** Grosvenor Centre Hotel
I   **THF** Carlton Hotel

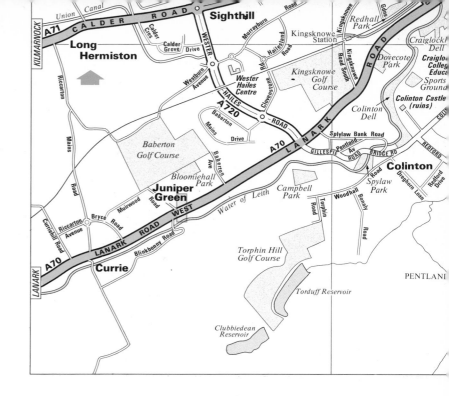

Canongate Tolbooth

DISTRICT PLAN
Public buildings and places of interest

H(38) **Craigmillar Castle** (ruins). A 14th-C stronghold associated with Mary, Queen of Scots, and the Earl of Mar. Notable 16th-and 17th-C apartments.

K(39) **Hillend Ski Centre** Situated south of the city on the Pentland Hills the 400-metre artificial ski slope is the largest in Britain.

A(40) **Lauriston Castle** A late 16th-C mansion with furniture and antiques displaying English and French styles. Associated with John Law, the early 18th-C broker.

G(41) **Royal Observatory** The Royal Observatory was moved from Calton Hill to Blackford Hill at the end of the 19thC, and is now a research establishment of the Science Research Council.

C(42) **Scottish National Gallery of Modern Art** A modern building set in the surrounds of the Royal Botanic Gardens. Contains a large collection of paintings of various important schools.

C(43) **Transport Museum** Contains several old trams and buses, a collection of old uniforms and model exhibits which together illustrate the trend of transport in Edinburgh over the centuries.

E **Zoo** Set in 80 acres of grounds, the zoo is one of the finest in Europe. Also magnificent views of Edinburgh and the surrounding countryside.

Hospitals

G **Astley Ainslie Hospital,** Grange Loan *tel 031-447 3399*
F **Beechmount Hospital,** 102 Corstorphine Road *tel 031-337 2888*
J **City Hospital,** Greenbank Drive *tel 031-447 1075*
E **Corstorphine Hospital,** 136 Corstorphine Road *tel 031-334 4952*
F **Craig House Hospital,** Craig House Road *tel 031-447 2011*
D **Eastern General Hospital,** Seafield Street *tel 031-554 2266*

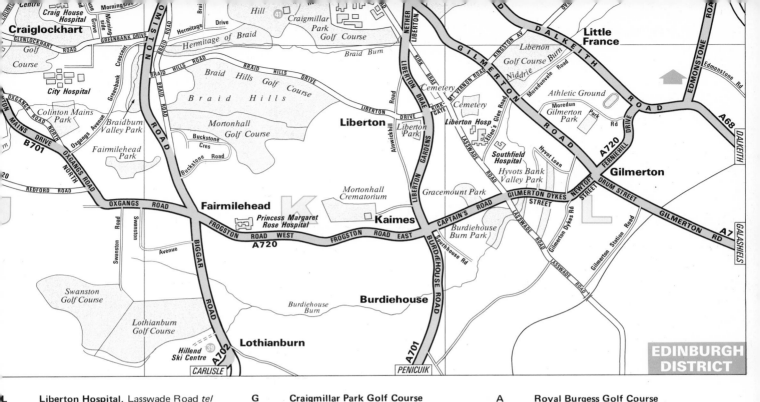

L	Liberton Hospital, Lasswade Road *tel* 031-664 4997	G	Craigmillar Park Golf Course	A	Royal Burgess Golf Course

L **Liberton Hospital,** Lasswade Road *tel* 031-664 4997

B **Northern General Hospital,** Ferry Road *tel* 031-332 2511

K **Princess Margaret Hospital,** Fairmilehead *tel 031-445 2007*

F **Royal Edinburgh Hospital,** Morningside *tel 031-447 2011*

B **Royal Victoria Hospital,** Craigleith Road, Comeley Bank *tel 031-332 1221*

G **St Raphael's Hospital,** 6 Blackford Avenue *tel 031-667 3604*

L **Southfield Hospital,** Lasswade Road *tel* 031-664 1788

B **Western General Hospital,** Crewe Road South *tel* 031-332 2525

Sport and Recreation

I **Baberton Golf Course**
K **Braid Hills Golf Courses**
A **Bruntsfield Golf Course**
F **Carrick Knowe Golf Course**
F **Craiglockhart Sports Centre,** Colinton Road
D **Craigentinny Golf Course**
J **Craiglockhart Golf Course**

G **Craigmillar Park Golf Course**
H **Duddingston Golf Course**
F **Heart of Midlothian Football Club,** Tynecastle Park
C **Hibernian Football Club,** Easter Road Park
K(39) **Hillend Ski Centre** (see also public buildings and places of interest)
I **Kingsknowe Golf Course**
C **Leith Baths,** Junction Place
L **Liberton Golf Course**
K **Lothianburn Golf Course**
D **Meadowbank International Sports Centre,** London Road
D **Meadowbank Thistle Football Club,** Meadowbank International Sports Centre
K **Mortonhall Golf Course**
F **Murrayfield Golf Course**
F **Murrayfield Ice Rink**
D **Open air Swimming Pool,** Rosebank Lane
H **Portobello Golf Course**
C **Powderhall Greyhound Stadium,** off Broughton Road
H **Prestonfield Golf Course**
B **Ravelston Golf Course**

A **Royal Burgess Golf Course**
F **Scottish Rugby Union Football Ground,** Murrayfield
A **Silverknowes Golf Course**
J **Swanston Golf Course**
I **Torphin Hill Golf Course**

Department Stores

Asda, Milton Road
Presto Discount Centre, Wester Hailes Centre

Advertisers

B **Crest** Edinburgh Euro Crest Hotel
F **THF** The Post House

J   **AA Service Centre** — Fanum House, Bedford Street *tel 32121*

K(4)   **Tourist Information Centre** — Civic Centre, Paris Street *tel 77888 ext 2297/8* (see also public buildings and places of interest)

Public buildings and places of interest

F(1)   **Albert Memorial Museum and Art Gallery** Founded in 1865. It contains natural history, ethnographical, industrial and technological displays; collections of English water colours, oil paintings and silverware.

J(2)   **Cathedral** A Norman to Decorated structure. Points of interest are the twin Norman transeptal towers, minstrel's gallery, carved-stone screen, clock (originally constructed in the 14thC), wood carvings and a wealth of carved roof bosses.

J(3)   **City Walls** Roman Wall with medieval buttresses, of which the best remains are seen in Southernhay and from Northernhay and Bartholomew Street.

K(4)   **Civic Centre**

N(5)   **Custom House** A fine Georgian quayside house.

J(6)   **Guildhall** A picturesque building dated 1330, and altered in 1446 and 1593; regarded as the oldest municipal building in the United Kingdom.

N(7)   **Maritime Museum** Over 70 sail and steam vessels from all over the world, in a setting of quays and old warehouses.

J(8)   **Mol's Coffee House** A tall, late 16th-C house with an oak-panelled room. Now an art dealers.

F(9)   **Rougemont Castle Grounds, Museum, Public Library and Northernhay Park** The grounds contain the scanty remains of the Norman Castle (keep and gateway), a Saxon tower (Athelstan's) and portions of the city walls.
Rougemont House Museum (late 18thC) contains exhibits on the archaeology of Devon and Exeter since the Ice Ages.

J(10)   **St Mary Arches Church** A mainly 12th-C structure but with some Saxon work. The double Norman arcade, c1130, is the only example in Devon.

J(11)   **St Mary Steps Church** In this church are a Norman font, a good screen and a curious old clock.

J(12)   **St Nicholas' Priory** A restored Norman to Tudor building.

J(13)   **Tucker's Hall** An old hall, used as a guild house since 1471, with a wagon roof and panelling dated 1634.

F(14)   **Underground Passages** The entrance to these medieval aqueducts, of which the earliest channel dates from the 14thC, is in Eastgate. Open to the public at certain times (organised parties on application to the Town Clerk's Office).

B(15)   **University**

K(16)   **Wynard's Almshouses** Founded in 1436 and has a restored chapel.

Hospitals

P   **Exe Vale Hospital (Wonford)**, Dryden Road *tel 77358*

P   **Princess Elizabeth Orthopaedic Hospital**, Barrack Road *tel 54217*

L   **Royal Devon and Exeter Hospital**, Heavitree *tel 77991*

P   **Royal Devon and Exeter Hospital**, Wonford *tel 77833*

K   **West of England Eye Infirmary**, Magdalen Street *tel 77833*

Sport and Recreation

H   **Clifton Hill Athletic Ground and Ski Slope**

K   **Corporation Baths**, Heavitree Road

C   **Exeter City Football and Athletic Club**, St James Park

B   **Exeter Cricket Club**, Prince of Wales Road

M   **Exeter Rugby Football Ground and Greyhound Stadium**, County Ground, Church Road, St Thomas

Theatres and Cinemas

F   **ABC Cinema**, New North Road *tel 75274*

K   **Barnfield Theatre**, Barnfield Road *tel 70891/71808*

B   **Northcott Theatre**, Stocker Road *tel 54853*

G   **Odeon Cinema**, Sidwell Street *tel 54057*

Department Stores

Debenhams Ltd, 123 Sidwell Street
Dingles, High Street
Marks and Spencer Ltd, 247 High Street

Markets

J   **Corn Exchange,** St George's Hall (Friday)

J   **Market,** Fore Street (Daily)

Advertisers

F   **Berni** Hole in the Wall
J   **Berni** White Lion
O   **Crest** Buckerell Lodge Hotel
G   **Mercantile Credit**
A   **THF** Great Western Hotel

Maritime Museum

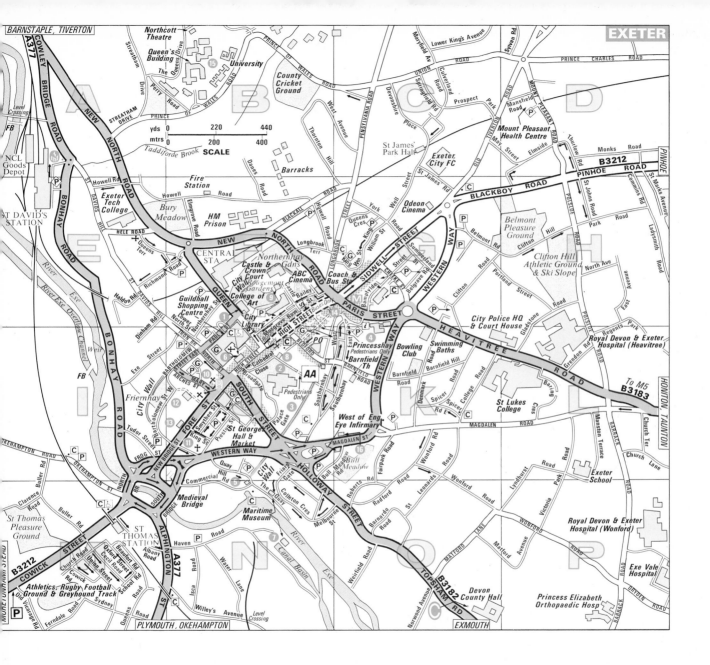

EXETER

GLASGOW

CENTRAL PLAN

H   **AA Service Centre** — 269 Argyle Street *tel 041-812 0101*

H [i]   **Tourist Information Centre** — Municipal Information Bureau, George Square *tel 041-221 7371 and 6136*

Public buildings and places of interest

A(1)   **Art Gallery and Museum** The art gallery's collection of Italian, Flemish, Dutch, French and British paintings constitutes Britain's finest civic art collection. The museum contains sections on armour, archaeology and history, technology, ethnography and natural history.

N(2)   **Cathedral** This 12th- to 15th-C structure is considered to be a perfect example of pre-Reformation Gothic architecture. The fan vaulting over the tomb of St Mungo in the crypt is notable.

(3)   **City Chambers** This fine building of 1883-8 by William Young in Italian Renaissance style has a rich and lavish interior including a marble staircase and notable banqueting hall.

(4)   **City Hall** A concert hall built in 1841, now refurbished to house the Scottish National Orchestra.

(5)   **George Square** Contains statues of many famous people, including Sir Walter Scott, Queen Victoria, Prince Albert, Robert Burns, James Watt, William E Gladstone and Sir Robert Peel.

N(6)   **Mercat Cross** Erected in 1929, it is a replica of the medieval cross.

N(7)   **Merchants Hall Steeple** The only remaining part of the old Merchants House which was built in 1651-9 and is now surrounded by the old fish market. The tower is noted for its effect of diminishing storeys.

B(8)   **Mitchell Library** Founded in 1874 and contains numerous rare books including a valuable Burns collection.

B(9)   **Museum of the Royal Highland Fusiliers** Housed in the Regiment's headquarters is a chronological display showing the histories of the Royal Scots Fusiliers and The Highland Light Infantry from their foundation to amalgamation in 1959.

N(10)   **People's Palace** Incorporates the Old Glasgow Museum which displays a visual record of the history of the City.

I(11)   **Provands Lordship** Built in 1471 it is the oldest house in the City. It now houses a museum, mainly of domestic articles and 17th- and 18th-C furniture.

M(12)   **St Andrew's Cathedral (RC)**

G(13)   **St Vincent Street Church** A striking design of 1857-59 by 'Greek' Thomson.

I(14)   **Sheriff Court Buildings** Built in 1842 and enlarged in 1874. They were once the Municipal Buildings.

H(15)   **Stirling's Library** Contains special collections of books on music and pictorial arts and is housed in the Royal Exchange Building, originally a suburban residence built in 1780.

C(16)   **Stow College**

I(17)   **Strathclyde University** One of the leading institutions in the field of applied science.

N(18)   **Tolbooth Steeple** The surviving portion of the tolbooth of 1626. It is surmounted by a 'Crown' somewhat similar to examples in Edinburgh and Aberdeen.

N(19)   **Tron Steeple** This forms an arch over the footpath and is all that remains of St Mary's Church dating from 1637 which was burnt down in 1793 by the Hellfire Club.

A(20)   **Glasgow University** The university, founded in 1450, occupies buildings dating from 1868-70 which were designed by Sir George Gilbert Scott. The Bute Hall is an addition of 1882, and the Pearce Lodge is built of stones from the former structure. The Hunterian Museum and Library are outstanding.

Hospitals

J   **Duke Street Hospital,** Duke Street *tel 041-554 1221*

B   **Glasgow Dental Hospital,** 378 Sauchiehall Street *tel 041-332 7020*

G   **Glasgow Ear, Nose and Throat Hospital,** 306 St Vincent Street *tel 041-221 7921*

A   **Glasgow Eye Infirmary,** 3 Sandyford Place *tel 041-221 7464;* Orthoptic Department, *tel 041-248 5363*

B   **Royal Beatson Memorial Hospital,** 132 Hill Street *tel 041-332 0286*

J   **Royal Infirmary,** Castle Street *tel 041-552 3535*

I   **Royal Maternity Hospital,** Rottenrow *tel 041-552 4513*

Sport and Recreation

C   **North Woodside Baths,** 10 Moncrieff Street

Theatres and Cinemas

C   **ABC 1 & 2 Cinemas,** Sauchiehall Street *tel 041-332 1592 & 9513*

M   **Citizens Theatre,** 119 Gorbals Street *tel 041-429 0022*

I(4)   **City Hall,** Candleriggs *tel 041-552 1850*

H   **Classic Cinemas Ltd,** 15 Renfield Street *tel 041-221 3400*

H   **Classic Grand Cinema,** 18 Jamaica Street *tel 041-248 4620*

M   **Coliseum Cinema,** Eglinton Street *tel 041-429 1500*

C   **Glasgow Film Theatre,** 12 Rose Street *tel 041-332 6535*

B   **King's Theatre,** Bath Street *tel 041-248 5153*

C   **Scala Cinemas,** 155 Sauchiehall Street *tel 041-332 1228*

H   **Odeon Film Centre,** 56 Renfield Street *tel 041-322 8701*

C   **Pavilion Theatre,** Renfield Street *tel 041-332 0478*

H   **Regent Cinema,** 72 Renfield Street *tel 041-332 3303*

C   **Theatre Royal,** Hope Street *tel 041-331 1234*

Department Stores

Arnotts, 193 Argyle Street
Arnotts, 83 Sauchiehall Street Centre
Bremner and Co Ltd, 44 Glassford Street
Campbells and Stewart and McDonald Ltd, 137 Ingram Street
Daly's, Sauchiehall Street Centre
Frasers, Buchanan Street
Goldberg A and Sons, Candleriggs
Holbourne (Granite House) Ltd, Trongate
Lewis's Ltd, Argyle Street

Marks and Spencer Ltd, 12 Argyle Street
Marks and Spencer Ltd, 172 Sauchiehall Street
Paisley's, Jamaica Street
Treron Ltd, 254 Sauchiehall Street
Wilson John and Son (Belfast) Ltd, 219
Sauchiehall Street
*Shops in the City Centre are open
six days a week.*

Markets

O	**Cattle and Meat Market,** Gallowgate
N/O	**The Barrows — General** (Saturday and Sunday)

Advertisers

H	**Berni** The Berni Inn
H	**Centre** Glasgow Centre Hotel
B	**Mercantile Credit**
G	**THF** Albany Hotel

DISTRICT PLAN
Public buildings and places of interest

B(21) **Botanic Gardens** 42 acres of grounds with glasshouses, including notable collections of orchids and begonias, and Kibble Palace with its unique collection of tree ferns and plants from temperate areas.

I(23) **Crookston Castle** Probably 13th-C with an earlier defensive ditch. Visited by Mary, Queen of Scots and Darnley in 1565.

J(24) **Haggs Castle** A new museum of history for children.

F(25) **Kelvin Hall and Arena** Rebuilt in 1926, it is the largest hall in Scotland and is used for exhibitions and concerts.

J(26) **Langside Monument** This memorial at Queen's Park, recalls the battle of 1568, which was fatal to the cause of Mary, Queen of Scots.

J(27) **Pollok House** This building of 1752 was designed by William Adam and stands in extensive wooded grounds. It houses the famous Stirling-Maxwell Collection of Spanish and other paintings, as well as some fine furniture, silver and porcelain.

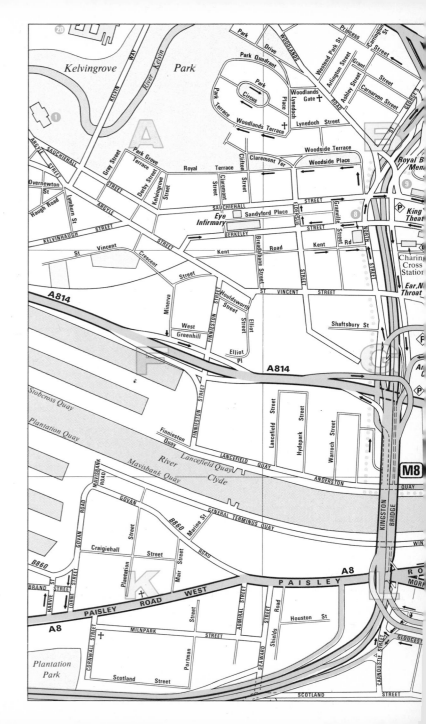

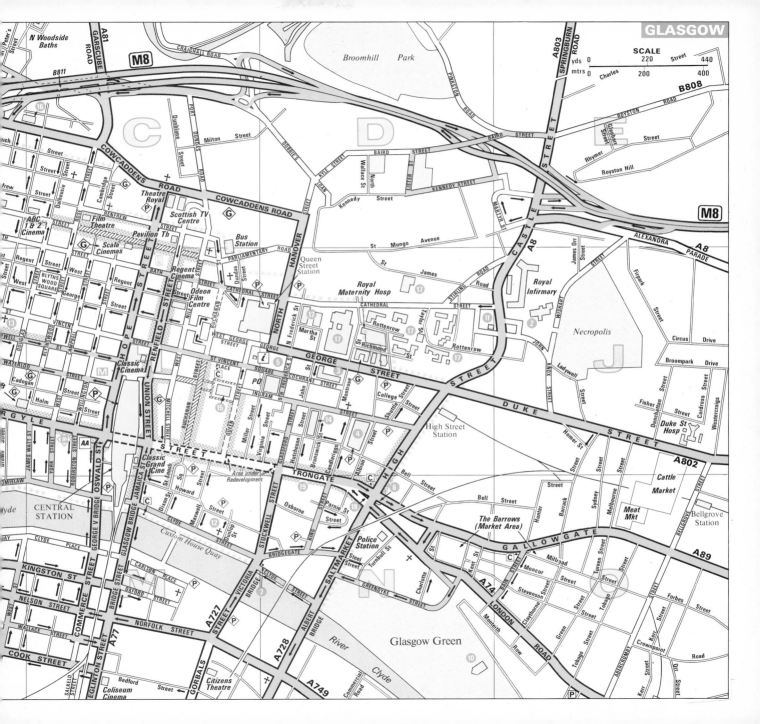

GLASGOW

SCALE

yds 0   220   440
mtrs 0   200   400

J(29) **Transport Museum** A museum displaying the development of the bicycle, horse-drawn vehicles, tram cars, Scottish motor cars from vintage to the present day, and a collection of railway locomotives and ship models.

A(30) **Victoria Park** The park contains the best-known fossilized tree stumps of the prehistoric Coal Age period; they were discovered in 1887 and are housed in the Fossil Grove Building.

Calderpark Zoo, Uddingston. A variety of birds, mammals, fish and reptiles housed in spacious new enclosures and buildings. 6m ESE off A74 (L)

Provan Hall 15th-C house, formerly the mansion of the lairds of Provan. Well-restored and considered the most perfect example of a simple pre-Reformation house remaining in Scotland. 5m E via A8 (H), then Bartiebeith Road and Auchinlea Road.

Hospitals

H **Belvidere Hospital**, London Road *tel 041-554 1855*

A **Blawarthill Hospital**, Holehouse Drive *tel 041-959 1864*

I **Cowglen Hospital**, Boydstone Road *tel 041-632 9106*

C **Foresthall Hospital**, Petershill Road *tel 041-558 5684*

B **Gartnavel General Hospital**, 1055 Great Western Road *tel 041-334 8122*

B **Gartnavel Royal Hospital**, 1055 Great Western Road *tel 041-334 6241*

B **Glasgow Homeopathic Hospital**, 1000 Great Western Road *tel 041-339 0382*

A **Knightswood Hospital** *tel 041-954 9641*

I **Leverndale Hospital**, 510 Crookston Road *tel 041-882 6255*

H **Lightburn Hospital**, Carntyne Road *tel 041-774 5102*

F **Queen Mother's Maternity Hospital and Royal Hospital for Sick Children**, Yorkhill *tel 041-339 8888*

K **Royal Samaritan Hospital for Women**, Coplaw Street *tel 041-423 3033*

C **Ruchill Hospital**, Bilsland Drive *tel 041-946 7120*

F **St Francis Maternity Home**, Merryland Street *tel 041-445 1118*

E **Southern General Hospital**, 1345 Govan Road *tel 041-445 2466*

C **Stobhill Hospital**, Springburn *tel 041-558 0111*

J **Victoria Infirmary**, Langside *tel 041-649 4545*

B **Western Infirmary**, Dumbarton Road *tel 041-339 8822*

Sport and Recreation

C **Ashfield Stadium**, 404 Hawthorn Street — greyhound racing

E **Bellahouston Sports Centre**, Bellahouston Drive

L **Cambuslang Golf Club**, Western Green

G **Celtic Football and Athletic Club**, Celtic Park, 95 Kerrydale Street

J **Clydesdale Cricket Club**,

K **Clyde Football Club**, Shawfield Park

I **Cowglen Golf Club**, Pollokshaws

J **Crossmyloof Ice Rink**, Titwood Road

J **Haggs Castle Golf Club**, Dumbreck Road

A **Knightswood Park Golf Course**

C **Littlehill Golf Course**

D **Lethamhill Golf Course**

B **Partick Thistle Football Club**, Firhill Road

J **Poloc Cricket Club**

I **Pollok Golf Club**, 90 Barrhead Road

K **Queen's Park Football Club**, Hampden Park

E **Ralston Golf Club**

F **Rangers Football Club**, Ibrox Stadium

H **Sandyhills Golf Club**

K **Shawfield Stadium** — greyhound racing

B **West of Scotland Cricket Club**, Peel Street

Markets

G **Fruit, Vegetable and Fish Market**, Blochairn Road

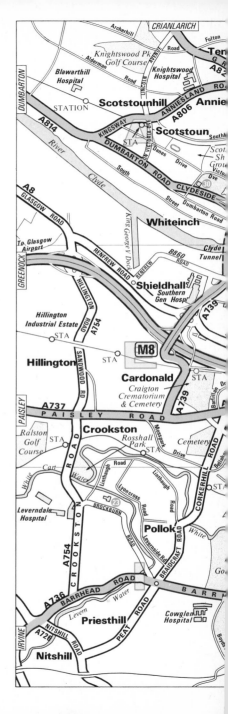

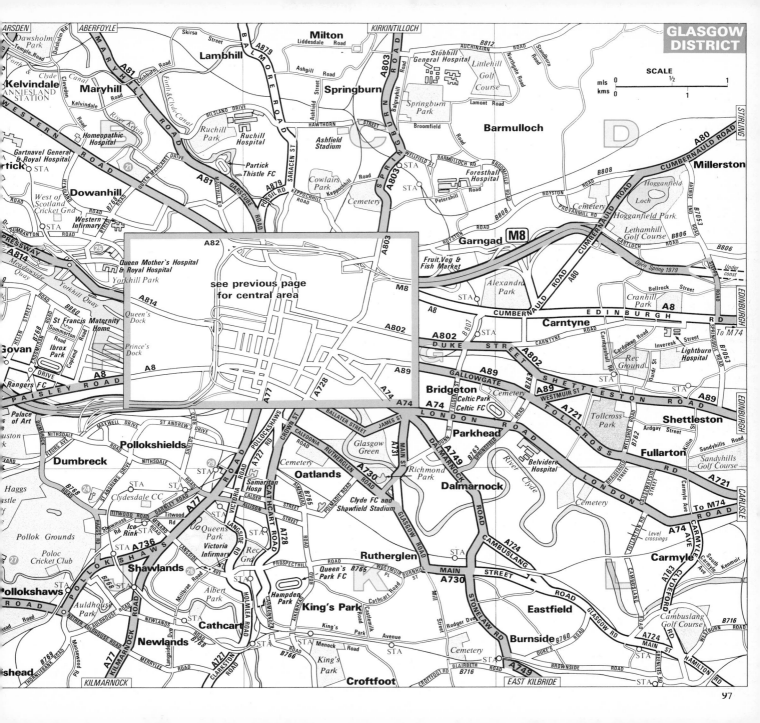

SCALE

mls 0   ½   1
kms 0   1

ARSDEN   **ABERFOYLE**   **KIRKINTILLOCH**

Milton

Lambhill

Kelvindale
ANNIESLAND
STATION

Maryhill

Springburn

Stobhill
General Hospital

Littlehill
Golf
Course

Springburn
Park

Barmulloch

Homeopathic
Hospital

Ruchill
Park

Ruchill
Hospital

Ashfield
Stadium

Foresthall
Hospital

Millerston

Gartnavel General
& Royal Hospital

STA

Dowanhill

Partick
Thistle FC

Cowlairs
Park

Cemetery

Hogganfield
Loch

Hogganfield Park

West of
Scotland
Cricket Gnd

Western
Infirmary

Petershill

Lethamhill
Golf Course

PRESSWAY

Cemetery

Garngad

M8

Open Spring 1979

Under
const

Queen Mother's Hospital
& Royal Hospital

see previous page
for central area

Fruit, Veg &
Fish Market

Alexandra
Park

STA

Bellrock
Street

Cranhill
Park

A8

Queen's
Dock

St Francis Maternity
Home

Carntyne

Prince's
Dock

Govan

DUKE
STREET

STA

Rec
Ground

Lightburn
Hospital

Ibrox
Park

GALLOWGATE

To M74

Rangers FC

Bridgeton

Celtic Park
Celtic FC

Parkhead

Cemetery

Shettleston

Palace
of Art

Tollcross
Park

Fullarton

Sandyhills
Golf Course

Pollokshields

Glasgow
Green

Belvidere
Hospital

Sandyhills Road

Dumbreck

Cemetery

Samaritan
Hosp

Oatlands

Richmond
Park

Dalmarnock

Cemetery

To M74

Haggs

Clydesdale CC

Pollok
Grounds

Ice
Rink

Queens
Park

Victoria
Infirmary

Clyde FC and
Shawfield Stadium

Carmyle

Poloc
Cricket Club

Rutherglen

Cambuslang
Golf Course

Shawlands

Rec
Grd

Queen's
Park FC

Eastfield

Pollokshaws

Auldhouse
Park

Albert
Park

Hampden
Park

King's Park

Cathcart

Cambuslang

Burnside

Newlands

King's
Park

Cemetery

KILMARNOCK   **Croftfoot**   **EAST KILBRIDE**

GLOUCESTER

AA Road Service Centre (21) — *tel 23278* 2¼m NE on Cheltenham Road A40 at its junction with the B4063 (D)

J(6) ⓘ **Tourist Information Centre** — The Gloucester Leisure Centre, Station Road *tel 36788* (see also public buildings and places of interest)

Public buildings and places of interest

I(1) **Blackfriars Priory** The Priory remains include some early library buildings and an Early English church vestry.

F(2) **Cathedral** A magnificent Norman to Perpendicular building especially notable for the imposing central tower, the 14th-C east window, the choir stalls and the beautiful cloisters.

J(3) **City Museum, Art Gallery and Central Library** Collections include local archaeology, geology and natural history, period furnishings, silver, glass, clocks and watches. Temporary art exhibitions are held.

E(4) **Bishop Hooper's Lodging — Folk Life and Regimental Museum** Housed in three timber-framed buildings of the 15th to 17thCs, one of which is supposed to be the place where the Protestant Bishop Hooper spent the night before he was martyred in 1555.
Collections include the history and agriculture of Gloucester and the surrounding countryside, Civil War relics and the Gloucestershire Regiment.

J(5) **Guildhall** A handsome building of 1890 with large assembly hall which is the headquarters of the City's administration.

J(6) **Leisure Centre and Tourist Information Centre**

I(7) **Llanthony Priory** There are slight remains of this 12th-C priory near the river.

F(8) **'New Inn'** An exceptionally picturesque, open-galleried pilgrim's inn dating back to the 15thC.

F(9) **Parliament House** A well-restored, timbered, 15th-C building on the site where a parliament was held in 1378.

J(10) **Raikes' House** A 16th-C, timber-framed house associated with Robert Raikes, often held to have been the founder of Sunday schools.

J(11) **St Mary-de-la-Crypt Church** Dating from the 12thC, but with tower, nave and chancel of the 15thC, this church contains the tomb of Robert Raikes.

E(12) **St Mary-de-la-Lode Church** This church which rests on Roman foundations features a late Norman tower and Early English vaulted chancel.

E(13) **St Nicholas Church** A Norman to Perpendicular style church with 15th-C spire, which was shortened and topped with a pinnacled cap in 1783.

F(14) **St Oswald's Priory** The Norman and Early English north nave arcade incorporates an arch which may derive from the priory church begun in 909.

F(15) **St Peter's Church (RC)**

E(16) **Shire Hall** Built in 1814 to the designs of Sir Robert Smirke RA, with extensive additions and reconstructions in recent years.

G(17) **United Hospitals Almshouses** These include the partly-Norman Chapel of St Mary Magdalene and also the remains of St Margaret's Chapel.

I **The Docks** The canal basin which opened in 1827, retains several of its old warehouses.

Hospitals

G **Gloucestershire Royal Hospital,** Great Western Road *tel 28555*

G **Horton Road Hospital,** Horton Road *tel 20324*

Sport and Recreation

L **Gloucester City Association Football Club,** Sports Stadium, Horton Road

N **Gloucester City Cricket Club,** Spa Pleasure Ground

J(6) **Gloucester Leisure Centre,** Station Road — bowls, sports hall, remedial facilities, swimming pools etc.

B **Gloucester Rugby Football Club,** Kingsholm Road

E **Gloucester Squash Club,** St Oswolds Road

Winget Sports Ground (for Gloucester County cricket matches), Tuffley Avenue. 1¼m S via Bristol Road A430 (M)

Greyhound Racing Track, Cheltenham Road 2m NE via Cheltenham Road A40 (D)

Theatres and Cinemas

F **ABC Film Centre,** St Aldate Street *tel 223*

J(6) **Cambridge Theatre,** Leisure Centre *tel 36788*

J **Gloucester Operatic and Dramatic Society,** Olympus, Kingsbarton Street *tel 25917*

Department Stores

Debenhams Ltd, King's Square

Marks and Spencer Ltd, 13 Northgate Street

Early closing day Thursday

Markets

B **Cattle Market,** St Oswald's Road (Monday and Thursday; open market Saturday)

J **New Eastgate Retail Market,** Bell Walk (Daily)

Advertisers

F **Berni** Steak Bar

F **Berni** New Inn

F **Mercantile Credit**

New Inn

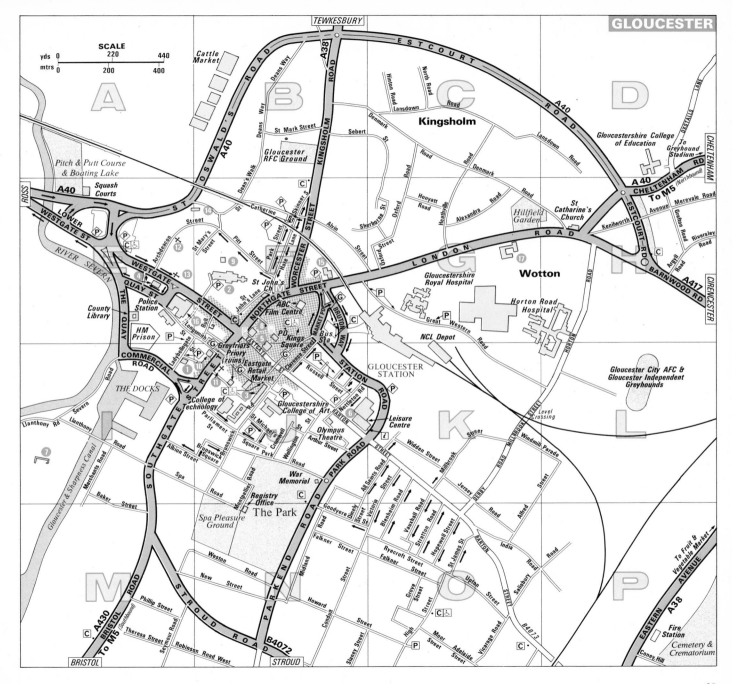

GLOUCESTER

SCALE
yds 0   220   440
mtrs 0   200   400

TEWKESBURY

ESTCOURT

A38

A40 ROAD

Cattle Market

Kingsholm

Hinton Road
North Road
Lansdown Road
Denmark Road
Sebert Street
Denmark Road
Lansdown Road

Gloucestershire College of Education

To Greyhound Stadium

OXSTALLS LANE

CHELTENHAM

Pitch & Putt Course & Boating Lake

Squash Courts

A40

ST OSWALD'S ROAD

KINGSHOLM ROAD

Deans Way
Deans Way
Dean's Walk
St Mark Street
St Mark Street

Gloucester RFC Ground

Skinner St

Catherine Street

Oxford Road
Honyatt Road
Sherborne St
Oxford Street
Alexandra Road
Heathville Road
Denmark Road

Hillfield Garden

St Catharine's Church

A40 CHELTENHAM RD (Northbound)
To M5

Merevale Road
Avenue
Grafton Road
Riversley Road
Argyll Road

Kenilworth Road

BARNWOOD RD

A417 CIRENCESTER

ROSS

A40

LOWER WESTGATE ST

RIVER SEVERN

WESTGATE STREET

QUAY ST

THE QUAY

County Library

Police Station

HM Prison

COMMERCIAL ROAD

THE DOCKS

Gloucester & Sharpness Canal

Llanthony Rd
Llanthony Road
Severn Road
Baker Street

Merchants Road

St Mary's Street
Archdeacon St
Pitt Street
Park Street
Hare Lane
Alvin Street

St Catherine Street

Park Road

WORCESTER STREET

NORTHGATE STREET

St John's Ch
St John's Lane
St John's Lane
ABC Film Centre
Market Parade
Russell Street

LONDON ROAD

Gloucestershire Royal Hospital

Wotton

Horton Road Hospital

Great Western Road

NCL Depot

HORTON ROAD

MILLBROOK STREET

Level Crossing

Gloucester City AFC & Gloucester Independent Greyhounds

SOUTHGATE STREET

College of Technology

Parliament St
Brunswick Square
Albion Street
Spa Road
Weston Road
New Street

St Michael's Square
Cromwell Street
Wellington Road

Brunswick Square

Gloucestershire College of Art

Olympus Theatre
Arthur Street

War Memorial

Registry Office

The Park

Spa Pleasure Ground

PARKEND ROAD

STROUD ROAD

A430 BRISTOL (Southbound)
To M5

Phillip Street
Theresa Street
Seymour Road
Robinson Road West

BRISTOL

B4072

STROUD

Montpelier Street

Falkner Street
Midland Road
Conduit Street
Howard Street
Sisney Street

STATION ROAD

PARK ROAD

GLOUCESTER STATION

Bus Sta

Station Road
Northcote Rd
Barton Street

Leisure Centre

Widden Street
All Saints Road
Dainty Street
Victoria Street
Blenheim Road
Vauxhall Road
Stratton Road
Hopewell Street
Ryecroft Street
Falkner Street
St James St
BARTON STREET
Upton Street

Millbrook Street
Jersey Road

DERBY ROAD

Windmill Parade
Alfred Street
India Road

Salisbury Road
B4073

Grove Street
High Street
Moor Street
Adelaide Street
Vicarage Road

EASTERN AVENUE
A38

To Fruit & Vegetable Market

Fire Station

Cemetery & Crematorium

Coney Hill

99

GUILDFORD

CENTRAL PLAN

C(4)   **Tourist Information Centre** — Civic Hall
ℹ️   London Road *tel 67314* (see also public
buildings and places of interest)

Public buildings and places of interest

G(1)   **Archbishop Abbot's (Trinity) Hospital**
A picturesque brick-built building
founded by George Abbot — a native of
Guildford and Archbishop of Canterbury
from 1611 to 1633 — in 1619 as an
almshouse for 12 men and 8 women.

J(2)   **Castle Keep and Gardens** A rectangular
Norman keep of three storeys, situated
in attractive gardens. Fine view from
the summit.

F(3)   **Citizens' Advice Bureau**

C(4)   **Civic Hall and Tourist Information Centre**
A modern building opened in 1962 and
home of the Guildford Philharmonic
Orchestra.

G(5)   **Guildford House** A fine town house of
1660, noted for its beautifully-
carved staircase and finely-decorated
plaster ceilings. Frequently changing
art exhibitions are held here.

F(6)   **Guildhall** The picturesque 17th-C
façade of this building which overlooks
the High Street, is noted for its
projecting clock.

G(7)   **Holy Trinity Church** A late 18th-C
red-bricked church standing at the top
of the High Street, which contains
the tomb of Archbishop Abbot.

G(8)   **Library**

G(9)   **Municipal Buildings**

J(10)   **Museum, Castle Arch** Contains
collections on local history, geology
and archaeology, including those of the
Surrey Archaeological Society.

G(11)   **Royal Grammar School** A 16th-C building
famous for its collection of chained
books in the library.

G(12)   **St Joseph's Church (RC)**

J(13)   **St Mary's Church** Guildford's oldest
and most interesting church which
preserves specimens of Saxon, Norman,
Early English and Transitional
architecture.

J(14)   **St Nicolas' Church** Rebuilt in the
late 19thC but preserving the
Perpendicular Loseley Chapel, with
interesting monuments of the Mores
of Loseley family.

B(15)   **St Saviour's Church** A late 19th-C
structure with a prominent tower

E(16)   **Sports Centre**

F(17)   **Treadwheel Crane** Restored 18th-C
treadwheel crane of the old town wharf.

G(18)   **Tunsgate** With its tall Tuscan columns
are all that remain of the old corn
exchange and law courts.

J(19)   **Yvonne Arnaud Theatre** Opened in 1965.

F/G/J   **High Street and Quarry Street** These
two streets, the former paved with

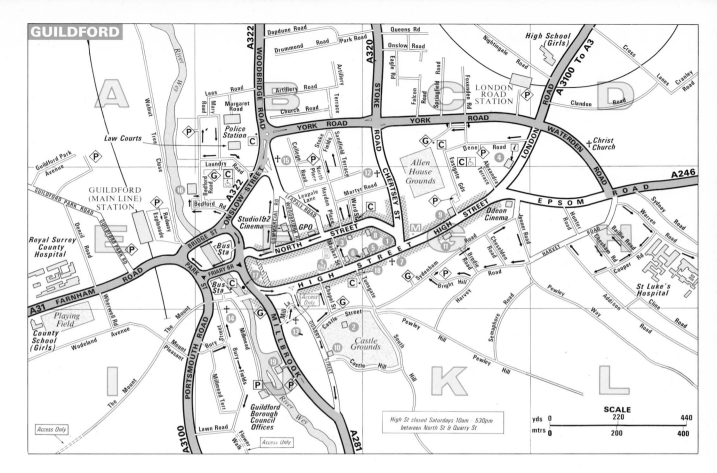

GUILDFORD

---

ranite setts, have been designated
Conservation Area. The elegant
Georgian fronts of many of the
buildings often hide far older backs.

Hospitals

Royal Surrey County Hospital, Farnham
Road *tel 71122*

St Luke's Hospital, Warren Road *tel
71122*

Sport and Recreation

(16) Sports Centre, Bedford Road — swimming
pools etc (see also public buildings
and places of interest)

Theatres and Cinemas

Odeon Cinema, Epsom Road *tel 504990*
Studio 1 & 2 Cinemas, Woodbridge Road
tel 64334

J(19) Yvonne Arnaud Theatre, Millbrook
tel 64571 (see also public buildings
and places of interest)

Department Stores

Debenhams Ltd, Millbrook
A & N Ltd, High Street
Marks and Spencer Ltd, High Street
Early closing day Wednesday

Markets

F Fruit and Vegetable Market, North
Street (Friday and Saturday)

Advertisers

F Berni Market Tavern
G Mercantile Credit
F THF Angel Hotel

DISTRICT PLAN

H AA Service Centre — Fanum House,
London Road *tel 72841*

Public buildings and places of interest

J(20) Cathedral On a magnificent site on
the summit of Stag Hill, overlooking
the town and surrounding countryside.
Designed by Sir Edward Maufe and
consecrated in 1961, it is a fine
example of modern materials and
methods of construction.

G(21) St John the Evangelist Church The
oldest parts, dating from the early
14thC, are the nave and south chapel.
The tower was added in the 15thC.

J(22) University of Surrey A modern university
which was granted its charter in 1966.

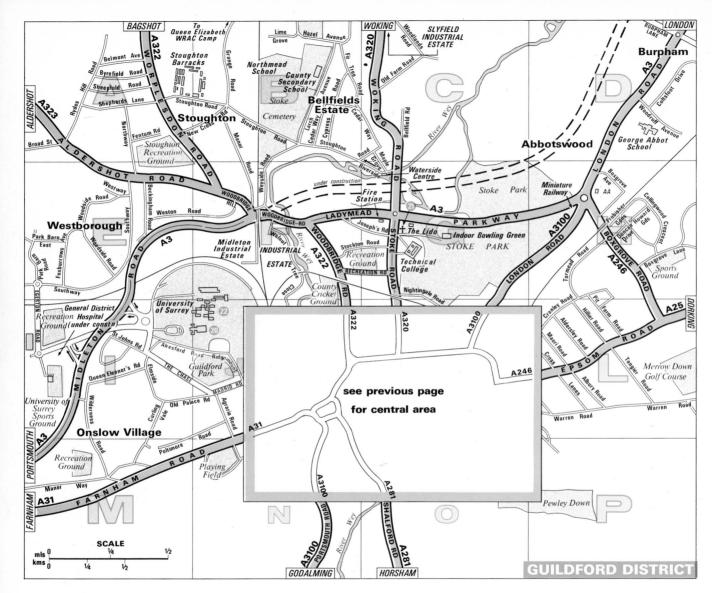

The main site is on Stag Hill, below the Cathedral.

Loseley House An Elizabethan house of 1562 with fine panelling, furniture, ceilings, fireplaces and tapestries. 3m S of Guildford via Portsmouth Road A3100 then B3000 (N)

St Catherine's Chapel A ruined chantry chapel built c1308 on top of a steep sandy hill, which affords a splendid view of Guildford and the Wey valley. ¾m S of Guildford via Portsmouth Road A3100 (N)

Sutton Place Gardens A beautiful 16th-C house in red brick and terracotta, situated in an extensive and picturesque garden layout. (Gardens only open to the public). 4m NE via London Road A3 (D)

Sport and Recreation

G   **Lido,** Stoke Park

L   **Merrow Downs Golf Course**

G   **Waterside Centre,** Riverside — boating, canoeing, kayak and sub-aqua activities.

HEREFORD

i **Tourist Information Centre** — Trinity Almshouses Car Park *tel 68430*

Public buildings and places of interest

H(1) **All Saints' Church** An Early English to Perpendicular church, noted for its library of 300 chained books, 14th-C carved stalls and twisted spire.

H(2) **Booth Hall** A hall of c1400 with an unusual restored timber roof, having tie-beams and hammer-beams.

D(3) **Bulmers Railway Centre**

H(4) **Castle Green** Once the site of the massive Norman castle keep.

H(5) **Cathedral** A Norman foundation with many later additions and alterations. Features of note are the 14th-C tower with ball-flower decoration, The Early English Lady Chapel of 1220 and the chained library of over 1,600 books. Nearby are some 15th-C houses, the College of Vicars Choral, Foundations of Chapter House gardens and the bishop's cloisters.

F(6) **Churchill Gardens Museum** Located in a Regency House with fine grounds and containing costumes, furniture, water-colours and paintings by local artists, in particular those of Brian Hatton.

H(7) **City Walls** The most extensive remains of the medieval walls, once over 1,900yd long, are the western section. Recently restored and incorporating two of the once 15 bastions.

E(8) **Coningsby Hospital and Black Friars Monastery Ruins.** The Hospital was founded as an almshouse in 1614 and incorporated earlier buildings, including a dining hall of c1170, of the Knights of St John of Jerusalem. The monastic ruins are of 14th-C date.

H(9) **Library, Museum and Art Gallery** Contains local natural history, archaeological, geological and folk life collections, English water colours, glass, silver, and ceramics.

H(10) **Old House, Butchers' Guild** A restored half-timbered building of 1621, preserved as a period house and furnished in the Jacobean style.

H(11) **St Peter's Church** A 12th- to 14th-C church with 15th- to 16th-C timber roofing and 15th-C canopied choir stalls.

H(12) **Shire Hall** A building of 1817-19 by Robert Smirke in the Grecian style.

H(13) **Town Hall**

H(14) **Wye Bridge** Dates back to 1490 and was widened in 1826. Four of the six arches are original. A new bridge has recently been built alongside.

Belmont Abbey The Abbey church in Victorian Gothic style was opened in 1859. Later additions include the 112ft tower of the 1880s. 2m SW via Belmont Road A465(J)

Herefordshire Waterworks Museum Broomy Hill. Housed in a Victorian pumping station of 1856 and containing two steam pumping engines of 1895 and 1906. ¾m W via Broomy Hill (G)

Hospitals

F	**County Hospital** *tel 68161*
L	**General Hospital** *tel 2561*
G	**Victoria Eye Hospital** *tel 65961*

Sport and Recreation

A	**Hereford Racecourse**
F	**Hereford Rugby Club**
E	**Hereford United Football Club**, Edgar Street
K	**Swimming Baths**

Wormsley Golf Course 8m NW via Whitecross Road A438 then A480 (D)

Cinemas

H	**Focus Cinema**, High Town *tel 2554*

Departme

M Black and Sons (Hereford) Ltd, 29 Widemarsh Street

Chadds of Hereford Ltd, 40/43 Commercial Street

Marks and Spencer Ltd, High Town

Early closing day Thursday

Markets

Main Market Day Wednesday

E	**Livestock Market** (Monday to Friday)
H	**Market** (indoor) (Monday to Saturday)

Advertisers

E	**Berni** The Imperial
H	**THF** Green Dragon Hotel

Hereford Cathedral

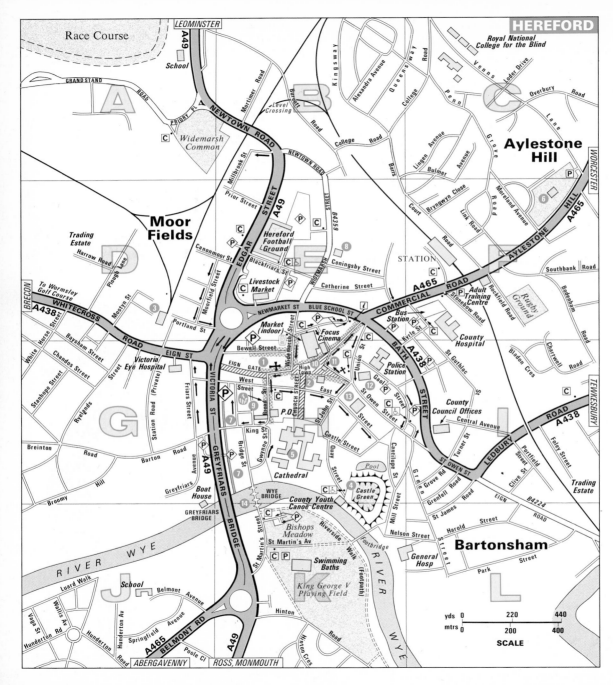

Race Course

Royal National College for the Blind

LEOMINSTER

A49

School

GRAND STAND

PRIORY RD

NEWTOWN ROAD

A49

Mortimer Road

Level Crossing

Burcott Road

NEWTOWN ROAD

B4359

Kingsway

Alexandra Avenue

College Avenue

Queens way

Queensway

College Road

Barrs Court Road

Lingen Avenue

Bulmer Avenue

Penn Grove

Venns

Loder Drive

Overbury Road

Lane

Aylestone Hill

Widemarsh Common

C

Moor Fields

Millbrook St.

Prior Street

EDGAR STREET

A49

Hereford Football Ground

P

WIDEMARSH STREET

Coningsby Street

Catherine Street

Moreland Avenue

Bryngwyn Close

Link Road

Court

Road

P

6

WORCESTER

AYLESTONE HILL

A465

Southbank Road

Bodenham Road

Trading Estate

Harrow Road

Canonmoor St.

Blackfriars St.

Livestock Market

8

STATION

A465

COMMERCIAL ROAD

Rockfield Road

Stonebow Road

Rugby Ground

Chartwell Road

Bladon Cres

BRECON

A438

WHITECROSS ROAD

Plough Lane

Mostyn St.

Moorfield Street

Portland St.

3

To Wormsley Golf Course

White Horse Street

Baysham Street

Chandos Street

Stanhope Street

Ryelands Street

EIGN ST.

NEWMARKET ST.

BLUE SCHOOL ST.

Market (indoor)

Bewell Street

EIGN GATE

1

Wide Marsh Street

Focus Cinema

High Town

10

11

2

East Street

St John St.

13

Union Street

St Owen Street

12

Gaol St.

Police Station

BATH STREET

A438

County Hospital

Adult Training Centre

St Guthlac St.

County Council Offices

Central Avenue

LEDBURY ROAD

A438

Portfield Street

Clive Ave

Foley Street

Trading Estate

B4224

TEWKESBURY

Victoria Eye Hospital

VICTORIA ST.

Friars Street

West Street

Broad St.

CHURCH STREET

P.O.

9

King St.

Gwynne St.

Bridge St.

7

7

Cathedral

5

Castle Street

Quay Street

Cantilupe St.

Pool

4

Castle Green

Mill Street

St Owen St.

Turner St.

Green

Grenfell Road

St James Street

EIGN ROAD

Breinton Road

Barton Road

Broomy Hill

GREYFRIARS

A49

Greyfriars Avenue

Boat House

GREYFRIARS BRIDGE

14

WYE BRIDGE

County Youth Canoe Centre

C

P

Bishops Meadow

St Martin's Av

St Martin's Street

Riverside Walk

RIVER WYE

Nelson Street

Harold Street

Grove Rd

Park Street

General Hosp

Bartonsham

RIVER WYE

Luard Walk

School

Belmont Avenue

Springfield Avenue

Vaga St.

Wallis Av

Hunderton Rd

Hunderton Av

Hunderton Road

Poole Cl

BELMONT RD

A49

A465

Hinton Road

Hinton Cres

Swimming Baths

King George V Playing Field

(footpath)

Footbridge

ABERGAVENNY

ROSS, MONMOUTH

yds 0 — 220 — 440
mtrs 0 — 200 — 400
SCALE

HULL

CENTRAL PLAN

F **AA Service Centre** — 27 Carr Lane *tel 28580*

B(1) ⓘ **Tourist Information Centre** — City Information Service, Central Library, Albion Street *tel 223344* (see also public buildings and places of interest)

Public buildings and places of interest

B(1) **Central Library, City Information Service and Film Theatre**
F(2) **City Hall**
C(3) **College of Further Education**
F(4) **Customs and Excise Buildings**
F(5) **Ferens Art Gallery** Contains a permanent collection of modern British paintings, 20th-C sculpture, 19th-C marine paintings and Old Masters, particularly of the English and Dutch schools. Also frequent temporary exhibitions.
G(6) **Guildhall and Law Courts**
G(7) **Holy Trinity Church** A 14th- and 15th-C structure and one of the largest parish churches in England. It is noted for its early brickwork, a fine font and a massive stone tower.
G(8) **Maister's House (NT)** A Georgian merchant's house of 1743 with an impressive staircase, and entrance hall with finely-carved doors.
F(9) **Municipal Offices**
E(10) **Regional College of Art**
G(11) **St Mary's Church** Early 14th-C, with a brick tower of 1697, later encased in stone.
F(12) **Telephone House** The only municipal telephone service in the United Kingdom operates from here.
F(13) **Town Docks Museum** The museum which was transferred to these premises during 1975, has a display on 'Whales and Whaling'. Other sections devoted to the history of shipping and fishing will be opened 1976-77.
G(14) **Transport and Archaeology Museum** Contains exhibits of transport through the ages, the Mortimer Archaeological Collection, and three 4th-C Roman pavements from a site at Rudston.

G(15) **Trinity House** Formerly the offices of a Guild of Humber pilotmen. It is now concerned with seamen's welfare. The building dates from 1753 and contains paintings associated with its history.
G(16) **Wilberforce House** An early 17th-C Elizabethan mansion where William Wilberforce, the slave emancipator was born in 1759. Now the Wilberforce Historical Museum exhibiting relics of the slave trade; many rooms in period styles from Stuart to Victorian; and personal items relating to William Wilberforce.
C(17) **Wilberforce Monument**

Theatres and Cinemas

E **ABC Cinema,** Fernsway *tel 23530*
F **Cecil Cinema,** Anlaby Road *tel 224981*
F(2) **City Hall,** Queen Victoria Square *tel 20123* (see also public buildings and places of interest)

B **Dorchester Cinema,** George Street *tel 29450*
B(1) **Film Theatre,** Central Library *tel 25017* (see also public buildings and places of interest)
A **Humberside Theatre,** Spring Street *tel 23638*
B **New Theatre** Kingston Square *tel 20463*
E **Regent Cinema,** Anlaby Road *tel 212433*
E **Tower Cinema,** Anlaby Road *tel 212356*

Department Stores

Binns Ltd, Paragon Square
Boyes W and Co Ltd, 226-232 Hessle Road
Boyes W and Co Ltd, 310a Holderness Road
Debenhams Ltd, Prospect Street
Dunn Clifford Ltd, Prospect Street
Hull and East Riding Co-operative Society, Jameson Street

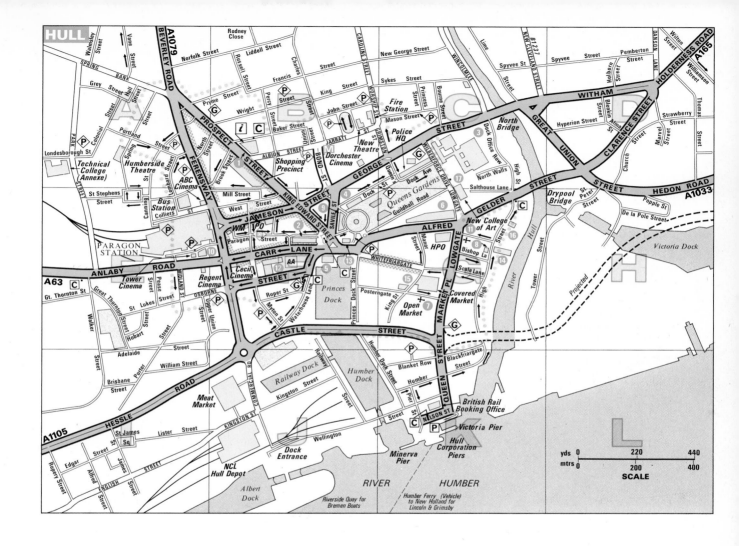

HULL

Marks and Spencer Ltd, 42-3 Whitefriargate
Willis Ludlow Ltd, Carr Lane
Early closing day Thursday. A few shops close all
day Monday

Markets

G	Covered Market (Daily except Sunday)
J	Meat Market, Commercial Road
G	Open Market, King Street (Tuesday, Friday and Saturday)

Advertisers

F	Berni White House Hotel
F	Centre Hull Centre Hotel
B	Mercantile Credit

DISTRICT PLAN

Public buildings and places of interest

B(18) **University of Hull** A modern university in a pleasant setting north-west of the City Centre. Most of the Halls of Residence are located in Cottingham.

Hospitals

B **Hull Hospital for Women,** Cottingham Road *tel 407899*

N **Hull Maternity Hospital,** Hedon Road *tel 76215*

L **Hull Royal Infirmary,** Anlaby Road *tel 28541*

E **Hull Royal Infirmary,** (Sutton Annexe) *tel 701151*

H **Kingston General Hospital,** Beverley Road *tel 28631*

B **Townend Maternity Home,** Cottingham Road *tel 42199*

Sport and Recreation

H **Beverley Road Swimming Baths**

I **East Park Lido,** (Open-air Swimming Pool)

N **East Hull Baths,** Holderness Road

K **Hull City Association Football Club,** Boothferry Park

L **Hull Cricket Club,** Anlaby Road

L **Hull and East Riding Rugby Union Football Club,** West Park, The Circle, Anlaby Road

I **Hull Kingston Greyhound Stadium,** Craven Park, Holderness Road

I **Hull Kingston Rovers Football Club,** Craven Park, Holderness Road

F **Hull Municipal Golf Course,** Springhead Park, Willerby Road

L **Hull Rugby League Football Club,** Boulevard Ground

L **Hull Vikings Speedway Club,** Boulevard Stadium

E **Sutton Park Golf Course,** Salthouse Road

Theatres and Cinemas

G **Open-air Theatre,** West Park, Anlaby Road

Hull Docks

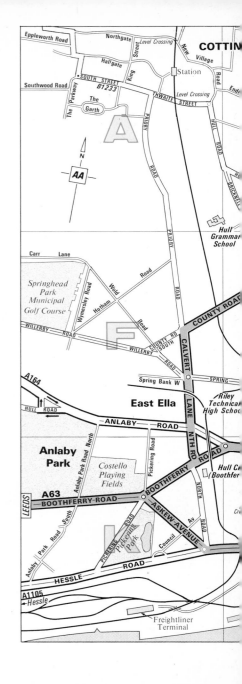

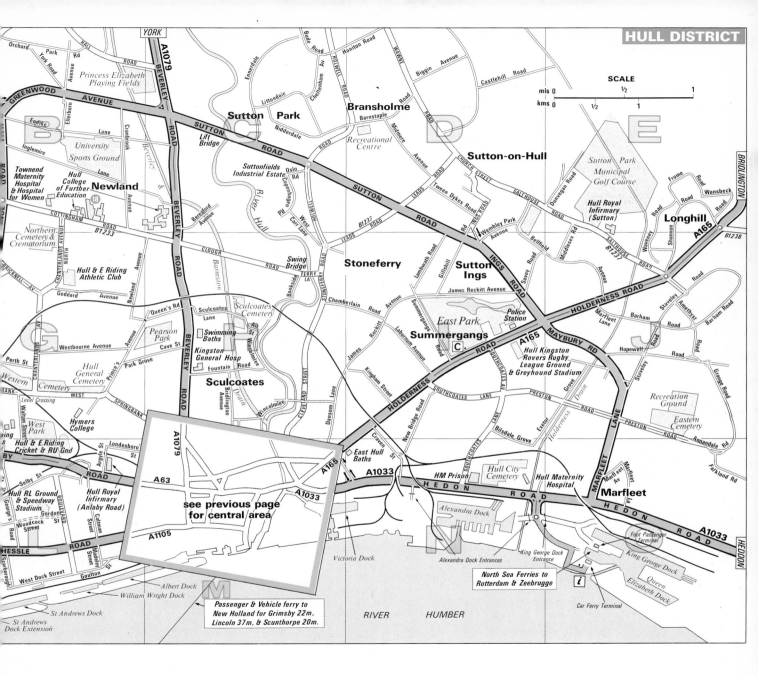

YORK

A1079

SCALE

mls 0 ½ 1

kms 0 ½ 1

Orchard
Park
York Road
HALL Rd

GREENWOOD
AVENUE

Princess Elizabeth Playing Fields

BEVERLEY
AVENUE

SUTTON ROAD

Sutton Park

Bransholme

Ennetdale
Littondale
Nidderdale
Barnstaple

Bude Road
Honiton Road
Biggin Avenue
Castlehill Road

Cheltenham Av
Midmere
Avenue

Recreational Centre

Sutton-on-Hull

Sutton Park Municipal Golf Course

Frome
Road
Wansbeck

BRIDLINGTON

Endike
Ellerburn
Lane
Inglemire
Cranbrook

University Sports Ground

Lift Bridge

Suttonfields Industrial Estate

Oslo Rd
Copenhagen Rd
West
Carr Lane

CHURCH STREET

Tween Dykes Road

Wembley Park Avenue

SALTHOUSE

Hull Royal Infirmary (Sutton)

Dunvegan Road

Middlesex Rd

Longhill

A165

B1238

Townend Maternity Hospital & Hospital for Women

Hull College of Further Education

Newland

18

COTTINGHAM ROAD

B1233

Beresford Avenue

River Hull

B1237

LEEDS ROAD

SUTTON ROAD

Lambworth Road

Gillbank

Bellfield

Shannon
Road
Waverley

Amethyst
Barham Road

Northern Cemetery & Crematorium

CHANTERLANDS AVENUE NORTH

CLOUGH ROAD

Barmston Drain

Swing Bridge

Stoneferry

FERRY LA

Sutton Ings

James Reckitt Avenue

HOLDERNESS ROAD

Staveley
Barham
Road

Marfleet Lane

Hopewell
Road

BICKNELL AV

Hull & E Riding Athletic Club

Goddard
Avenue

Newland
Avenue

Queen's Rd

Sculcoates Lane

Sculcoates Cemetery

Chamberlain Road

Avenue

Reckitt

James

Summergangs Road

Summergangs

C.

East Park

Police Station

A165

MAYBURY RD

Hull Kingston Rovers Rugby League Ground & Greyhound Stadium

Grove

Staveley Road

Grange Road

CHANTERLANDS AV

Westbourne Avenue

Pearson Park

Cave St
Park Grove

Swimming Baths

Alt St

Windmill

Sculcoates

Kingston General Hosp

Fountain Rd

Laburnum Avenue

Kingham Street

Southcoates

HOLDERNESS ROAD

Bilsdale Grove

PRESTON ROAD

Holderness Drain

LANE

Recreation Ground

Eastern Cemetery

Amandale Rd

Perth St

Hull General Cemetery

PRINCE'S AVE

WEST

SPRINGBANK

Bridlington Avenue

Drain

Wincolmlee

Dansom Lane

Cleveland Street

New Bridge Road

Exeter

PRESTON ROAD

MARFLEET LANE

Falkland Rd

BANK

Level Crossing

Walton Street

West Park

Hymers College

Londesboro St

Argyle St

ROAD

A1079

A63

A1105

see previous page for central area

A165

A1033

A1033

East Hull Baths

Craven St

HEDON ROAD

HM Prison

Hull City Cemetery

Hull Maternity Hospital

Marfleet Av

Marfleet

HEDON ROAD

A1033

HEDON

Hull & E.Riding Cricket & RU Gnd

Selby St

Hull RL Ground & Speedway Stadium

BOULEVARD

Gordon
Woodcock Street

ST GEORGE'S

Colman Street

Madeley Street

Hull Royal Infirmary (Anlaby Road)

HESSLE
ROAD

Scarborough

West Dock Street

Goulton Street

Albert Dock

William Wright Dock

Victoria Dock

Alexandra Dock

Alexandra Dock Entrances

King George Dock Entrance

North Sea Ferries to Rotterdam & Zeebrugge

i

Foot Passenger Terminal

King George Dock

Queen Elizabeth Dock

Car Ferry Terminal

St Andrews Dock

St Andrews Dock Extension

Passenger & Vehicle ferry to New Holland for Grimsby 22m, Lincoln 37m, & Scunthorpe 20m.

RIVER   HUMBER

INVERNESS

N AA Road Service Centre (80) — Bishops Road Car Park *tel 33213*

K [i] Tourist Information Centre — Inverness, Loch Ness and Nairn Tourist Organisation, 23 Church Street *tel 34353*

Public buildings and places of interest

J(1) **Abertarff House** Built c1592, it retains its old turnpike stair and now houses the headquarters of An Comunn Gaidhealach (Gaelic Association) and a Highland craft and information centre.

K(2) **Castle** The present castle built between 1834 and 1846, which replaced an earlier building destroyed by the Jacobite army in 1746, houses the Sheriff's Court House and administrative offices. In the courtyard is the old castle well, discovered and restored in 1909, and in the Castle esplanade is the Flora MacDonald Monument erected in 1899.

N(3) **Highland Regional Offices**

B(4) **Cromwell's Clock Tower** This is all that remains of the Citadel built by Cromwell between 1652 and 1657 for a garrison of 1,000 men. The Citadel was demolished in 1661.

F(5) **Dunbar's Hospital** An almshouse dating from 1688.

F(6) **High Parish Church** Largely rebuilt 1770-2 but retaining its 14th-C vaulted tower. The execution stone in the courtyard bears bullet marks recalling the spot where prisoners from the Battle of Culloden were executed.

K(7) **Library, Museum and Art Gallery** The museum contains many interesting Jacobite and Highland folklore relics. The art gallery has mainly temporary exhibitions.

J(8) **St Andrew's Cathedral** The Episcopal Cathedral of the Diocese of Moray, Ross and Caithness, completed in 1869. Of particular interest are the illuminated windows, carved pillars and the baptismal font which is a copy of Thorwalden's font in Copenhagen Cathedral.

K(9) **Tolbooth Steeple** A fine 130ft-high steeple of 1791, which was formerly used as a gaol.

M(10) **Tomnahurich Cemetery** A fine view of Inverness and its surroundings can be obtained from the 220ft summit of this cemetery, once claimed to be the most beautiful cemetery in the world.

K(11) **Town House** A Gothic-style town hall, completed in 1882, containing many fine paintings and stained glass. A framed document in the Council Chambers bears the signatures of the cabinet ministers who attended the first cabinet meeting held outside London, in 1921 under Lloyd George. In front is the Mercat Cross, surmounting the Clach-na-Cudaiann, or Stone of the Tubs, which recalls the spot where women rested when carrying home their tubs or pails of water.

Clava Cairns A group of burial cairns with three concentric rings of great stones, of late Neolithic or Early Bronze Age date. 5½m E via Millburn Road A9 and B9006 (H)

Culloden Battlefield The site of the battle, where the Jacobite army of Bonnie Prince Charlie was defeated by British forces under the Duke of Cumberland on April 16 1746. The old Leanach farmhouse around which the battle was fought is now a museum. Nearby are the Graves of the Clans, Wells of the Dead, and Cumberland Stone. 6m E via Millburn Road A9 and B9006 (H)

Ness Islands Situated in the River Ness, just south of the town. A series of islands linked by bridges in a wooded setting.

Hospitals

P **Hilton Hospital** (Geriatric) *tel 34151*
N **Royal Northern Infirmary**, Ness Walk *tel 34411*

Sport and Recreation

E **Caledonian Football Club Ground**, Telford Street

A **Clachnacuddin Football Club Ground**, Grant Street

F **Inverness Baths**, Riverside Street

P **Inverness Golf Club**, Culcabock Road

L **Inverness Thistle Football Club Ground**, Kingsmills Park

Inverness Ice Rink, Bught Park — skating and curling (September to April) 1m SW via Glenurquart Road A82 and Bught Drive (M)

Torvean Municipal Golf Course, Glenurquart Road. 1¼m SW via Glenurquart Road A82 (M)

Theatres and Cinemas

N **Eden Court Theatre**, Bishop's Road *tel 221719*

G **La Scala Cinema**, Academy Street *tel 33302*

G **Little Theatre**, Farraline Park

Department Stores

Alex Cameron & Co, High Street
Arnotts, 7 Union Street
F A Cameron, Church Street
Early closing day Wednesday

Advertisers

F **Mercantile Credit**
K **THF** Royal Hotel

Flora Macdonald's monument

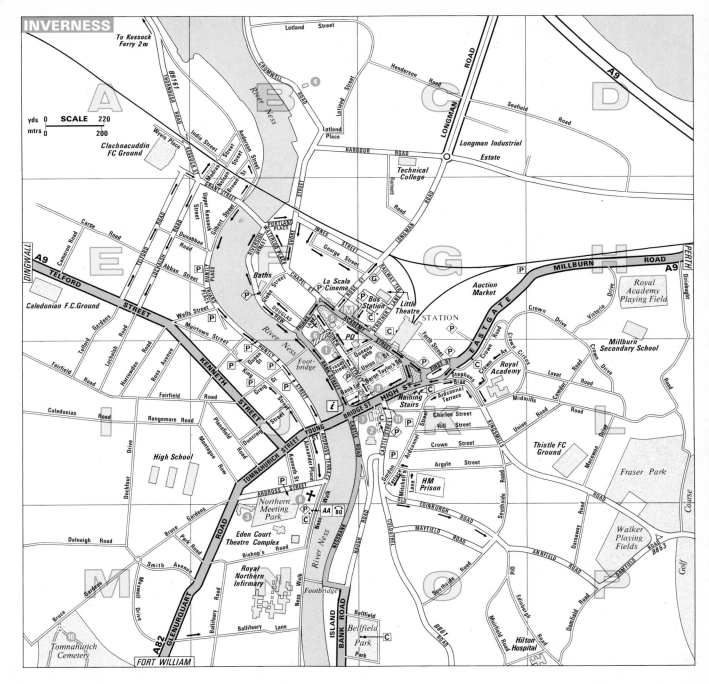

INVERNESS

To Kessock
Ferry 2m

SCALE
yds 0   220
mtrs 0   200

A9 DINGWALL

B9161 THORNBUSH ROAD

KESSOCK ST

TELFORD ROAD

LOCHALSH ROAD

Wyvis Place

India Street

Anderson Street

Nelson Street

Brown St

Madras Street

Grant Street

Upper Kessock Street

Gilbert Street

Carse Road

Cameron Road

Clachnacuddin
FC Ground

Dunabban Road

Abban Street

Ailinth Place

FRIARS PLACE

Lotland Street

CROMWELL ROAD

Lotland Street

Henderson Road

LONGMAN ROAD

Seafield Road

A9

Lotland
Place

HARBOUR ROAD

Burnett Road

Technical
College

Longman Industrial
Estate

SHORE STREET

WATERLOO PLACE

RIVERSIDE STREET

PORTLAND PLACE

George Street

INNES STREET

CHAPEL STREET

Grant Street

Douglas Row

HUNTLY STREET

River Ness

Baths

La Scala
Cinema

Bus
Station

Little
Theatre

Auction
Market

RAILWAY TERRACE

ROSE STREET

STROTHERS LANE

MILLBURN ROAD

P

A9 PERTH

Dinbught

Royal
Academy
Playing Field

Crown Drive

Victoria Drive

Millburn
Secondary School

EASTGATE

Crown Av.

Crown Circus

Crown Drive

Lovat Road

Cawdor Road

Crown Drive

Caledonian F.C.Ground

Wells Street

Muirtown Street

KENNETH STREET

Telford Gardens

Lochlash Road

Harrowden Road

Ross Avenue

Queens St

King Street

Greig Street

GILBERT STREET

CHURCH STREET

BANK STREET

FRASER LANE

ACADEMY ST

PO

Queensgate

Union Street

Baron Taylor's St

Fraser Street

Bank Lane

G

STATION

Forth Street

First St

Stephens Brae

Ardconnel Terrace

Royal
Academy

Midmills Road

Union Road

KINGSMILLS ROAD

Fairfield Road

Fairfield Road

Caledonian Road

Rangemore Road

Planefield Road

Duncraig Street

YOUNG STREET

TOMNAHURICH STREET

BRIDGE ST

HIGH ST

Raining
Stairs

CASTLE ROAD

Charles Street

Hill Street

Crown Street

Argyle Street

Lovat Road

Macewan Road

Thistle FC
Ground

Fraser
Park

L

Golf Course

High School

Montague Row

Kenneth St

Alexander Place

ARDROSS TERRACE

ARDROSS STREET

NESS WALK

Northern
Meeting
Park

AA 80

Eden Court
Theatre Complex

Bishop's Road

Royal
Northern
Infirmary

HM
Prison

Gordon Terrace

Mitchell's Lane

OLD EDINBURGH ROAD

Southside Road

MAYFIELD ROAD

ANNFIELD ROAD

Darnaway Road

Darnfield Road

Walker
Playing
Fields

B853

Duchour Drive

Dalneigh Road

Bruce Gardens

Park Road

Smith Avenue

Ballifeary Road

Ballifeary Lane

NESSBANK

River Ness

Footbridge

ISLAND BANK ROAD

Bellfield
Bellfield
Park
Park

C

Southside Road

B861

Old Edinburgh Road

Muirfield Road

Hilton
Hospital

Maxwell Drive

Bruce Gardens

A82 GLENURQUART ROAD

FORT WILLIAM

Tomnahurich
Cemetery

HAUGH ROAD

CUDUTHEL

B861

1 2 3 4 5 6 7 8 9 10 11

111

Breakdown and Information Service *tel Chelmsford 61711 or Norwich 29401*

J(11) **Tourist Information Centre** — Town Hall,
i Cornhill *tel 55851* (see also public
buildings and places of interest)

Public buildings and places of interest

G(1) **Central Library**
G(2) **Christchurch Mansion** A fine brick house
of 1548 now incorporating a museum of
domestic antiquities. The kitchen has
a 16th-C fireplace and domestic utensils.
The Wolsey Art Gallery is at the rear
of the house. Pictures displaying the
life of the town are on display in the
corridors.
L(3) **Suffolk College**
J(4) **Corn Exchange Entertainment, Conference
and Arts Centre**
B(5) **Ipswich School** Founded in 1400, the
school has occupied its present site
since 1852.
F(6) **Museum** Houses collections of natural
history, geology and archaeology showing
the history of Suffolk from earliest times
to the medieval period. There is also an
ethnographical collection and art gallery.
J(7) **St Lawrence's Church** The church has a
flint tower originally built in the
15thC then rebuilt in 1882, and a 15th-C
stone screen.
G(8) **St Margaret's Church** The church is noted
for the double hammer-beam roof in the
nave and has an exceptional example of
the Royal Arms of Charles II.
G(9) **St Mary-le-Tower Church** The civic
church of the town, with a tower 176ft
high and a pulpit carved by Grinling
Gibbons.
J(10) **Sparrowe's (or Ancient) House** A
picturesque, old pargetted house dating
back to 1567. Now a book shop.
J(11) **Town Hall and Tourist Information Centre**
J(12) **Unitarian Meeting House** A plaster and
timber building dating from c1700.
N(13) **Wolsey's Gateway and St Peter's Church**
The gateway, a fine example of medieval
brickwork, is a relic of a college
built by Cardinal Wolsey in 1536. St
Peter's Church contains one of the rare

examples of a 12th-C black marble
Tournai font.

Hospitals

B **Ipswich & East Suffolk Hospital,**
Anglesea Road Wing *tel 212477 or
51021*

Sport and Recreation

O **Fore Street Baths,** Fore Street
I **Ipswich Town FC,** Portman Road
E **St Matthews Baths,** St Matthews Street

Theatres and Cinemas

K **ABC Cinema,** Butter Market *tel 53353*
K **Gaumont Theatre,** St Helen's Street *tel
53641*
J(4) **Ipswich Film Theatre,** Corn Exchange,
King Street *tel 215544*
F **Odeon Cinema,** Lloyds Avenue *tel 52082*
E **Wolsey Theatre** (due to open late 1979)

Department Stores

Co-operative, Carr Street
Corders, Tavern Street
Debenhams Ltd, Waterloo House
Marks and Spencer Ltd, 16 Westgate Street
Early closing day — Monday and Wednesday, most
shops are open 6 days a week.

Markets

I **Livestock Market,** Portman Road (Tuesday)
F **Open Market,** Crown Street (Thursday and
Friday)

Advertisers

J **Berni** Limmers Tavern
J **Mercantile Credit**
J **THF** Crown and Anchor Hotel
K **THF** Great White Horse Hotel

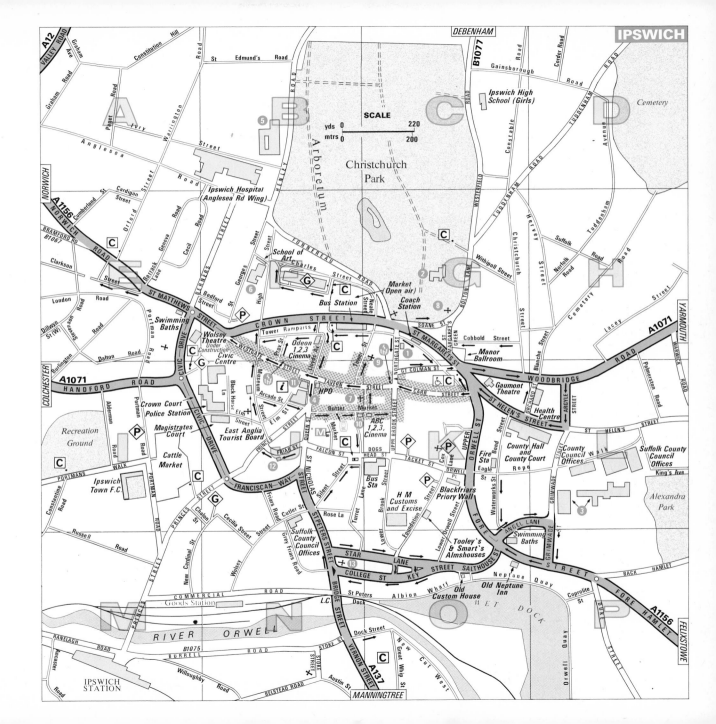

IPSWICH

A12
VALLEY ROAD
Graham Ave
Constitution Hill
St Edmund's Road
DEBENHAM
B1077
Gainsborough
Road
Corder Road
Road
Cemetery

Paget Road
Ivry Road
Warrington Road
Anglesea Street
Road
Arboretum
Christchurch Park
SCALE
yds 0 — 220
mtrs 0 — 200
Ipswich High School (Girls)
Constable Road
TUDDENHAM ROAD
Tuddenham Avenue

NORWICH
A1156
NORWICH ROAD
BRAMFORD RD B1067
Clarkson Street
London Road
Stewart Road
Dillwyn St (W)
Burlington Road
Dalton Road
Cumberland St
Cardigan Street
Orford Road
Geneva Road
Cecil Road
ELMERS
Bedford Street
Georges St
High Street
School of Art
Charles Street
FONNEREAU ROAD
HENLEY ROAD
Christchurch
Withipoll Street
WESTERFIELD ROAD
BOLTON LANE
Market (Open air)
Coach Station
Suffolk Road
Norfolk Road
Hervey Street
Cemetery Road
Tuddenham Road
Suffolk Road

COLCHESTER
A1071
HANDFORD ROAD
Portman Road
Alderman Road
CIVIC DRIVE
Swimming Baths
Wolsey Theatre Under Construction
Civic Centre
Tower Ramparts
CROWN STREET
Odeon 1,2,3 Cinema
WESTGATE STREET
Museum St
Black Horse Ln
Arcade St
Elm St
Butter Market
TAVERN STREET
HPO
NORTHGATE STREET
ST MARGARET'S ST
COLMAN'S ST
CARR STREET
SOANE ST
ST HELEN'S STREET
WOODBRIDGE ROAD
A1071
YARMOUTH
A1071
WARWICK ROAD
Palmerston Road
Manor Ballroom
Cobbold Street
Blanche St
Gaumont Theatre
Health Centre
Orchard St
Argyle Street
St Helen's Street

Recreation Ground
PORTMANS WALK
Crown Court Police Station
Magistrates Court
Cattle Market
East Anglia Tourist Board
PRINCES STREET
FRIAR ST
FALCON ST
ABC 1,2,3 Cinema
DOGS HEAD ST
TACKET ST
UPPER ORWELL ST
Fire Sta
Eagle St
County Hall and County Court
Bond St
Rope St
GRIMWADE STREET
County Council Offices
Suffolk County Council Offices
King's Ave
Alexandra Park

Constantine Road
Russell Road
Ipswich Town F.C.
PORTMAN ROAD
FRANCISCAN WAY
ST NICHOLAS STREET
Friars Road
Cecilia Street
Cutler St
Rose La
Silent Street
Turret Lane
Bus Sta
Brook Street
Foundation Street
Waterworks St
H M Customs and Excise
Blackfriars Priory Wall
Lower Orwell Street
ST PETERS STREET
Chalon St
New Cardinal St
Wolsey St
Grey Friars Road
Suffolk County Council Offices
STAR LANE
COLLEGE ST
KEY STREET
SALTHOUSE ST
Tooley's & Smart's Almshouses
Angel Lane
FORE STREET
Swimming Baths
GRIMWADE STREET
BACK HAMLET
A1156

IPSWICH STATION
Ancaster Road
Ranelagh Road
COMMERCIAL ROAD
Goods Station
RIVER ORWELL
B1075
BURRELL ROAD
Willoughby Road
BELSTEAD ROAD
BRIDGE STREET
STOKE STREET
VERNON STREET
A137
MANNINGTREE
St Peters Dock
Albion Wharf
Old Custom House
Dock Street
New Cut West
New Great Whip St
Austin St
Neptune Quay
Old Neptune Inn
WET DOCK
Coprolite St
Quay
Orwell Quay
FORE HAMLET
DUKE STREET
A1156
FELIXSTOWE

LEEDS

CENTRAL PLAN

P **AA Service Centre** — 95 The Headrow *tel 38161*

P(2) **Tourist Information Centre** — Central Library *tel 31301/34485*
i

Public buildings and places of interest

V(1) **Black Prince Statue**

P(2) **City Art Gallery, Library and Museum** The art gallery contains a large collection of old masters, 19th- and 20th-C British and French paintings, watercolours and contemporary British sculpture. The museum contains a world-wide archaeological collection but is chiefly concerned with Yorkshire.

P(3) **City Varieties Theatre** The only place in the world where real music hall is played today and best known for the BBC series 'The Good Old Days'.

I(4) **Civic Hall** A modern building with an imposing porticoed front, flanked by twin towers 170ft high topped by gilded owls each 8ft high.

J(5) **Civic Theatre and College of Art**

K(6) **College of Building**

W(7) **Corn Exchange** An unusual oval-shaped building with a domed interior dating from 1861.

B(8) **Grammar School** Founded in 1552.

Q(9) **Grand Theatre** A fine, late Victorian building dating from 1878.

V(10) **Holy Trinity Church** The only surviving 18th-C church in Leeds, built 1721-7 and a perfect example of its period.

I(11) **Leeds Polytechnic**

V(12) **Queen's Hall**

P(13) **St Anne's Cathedral (RC)** A Gothic-style church completed in 1904, possessing good timber tunnel vaulting and a reredos by Pugin in the south chancel chapel.

P(14) **St John's Church** Built 1631-4, it retains highly interesting woodwork, notably the screen, pulpit and panelled wainscoting.

W(15) **St Peter's Parish Church** The oldest foundation in Leeds. It was rebuilt in 1839-41 and retains a notable Saxon cross shaft discovered at that time.

O(16) **Town Hall** Designed by Cuthbert Broderick in 1858, it has an impressive colonnaded front and a massive clock-tower rising to 225ft. The triennial Leeds Music Festival is held here.

C(17) **University** The University, which received its charter in 1904.

Hospitals

I **Leeds General Infirmary,** Great George Street *tel 32799*

H **Maternity Hospital at Leeds,** Hyde Terrace *tel 459681*

Sport and Recreation

N **International Swimming Pool,** Westgate

Theatres and Cinemas

Q **ABC Cinemas 1 & 2,** Vicar Lane *tel 451013*

P(3) **City Varieties Music Hall,** The Headrow *tel 30808* (see also public buildings and places of interest)

J(5) **Civic Theatre** *tel 455505* (see also public buildings and places of interest)

Q(9) **Grand Theatre** *tel 40971/450891* (see also public buildings and places of interest)

I **Leeds Playhouse,** Calverley Street *tel 42111*

P **Odeon Film Centre,** The Headrow *tel 30031*

P **Plaza Cinema,** New Briggate *tel 456882*

Q **Tower Cinema,** 54 New Briggate *tel 458229*

Department Stores

Debenhams Ltd, 121 Briggate
Hemingways Department Store Ltd, 8 Harrison Street
Lewis's Ltd, The Headrow
Marks and Spencer Ltd, 46 Briggate
Schofields (Yorkshire) Ltd, 79 The Headrow
Willis Ludlow Ltd, Vicar Lane
Early closing day Wednesday (A few shops close Monday)

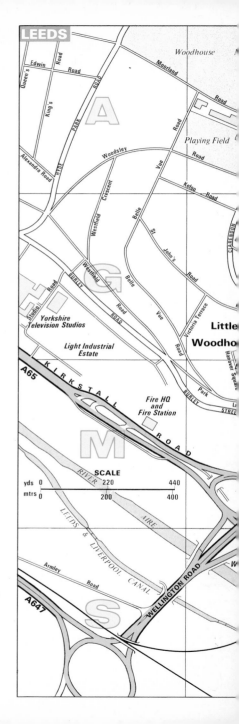

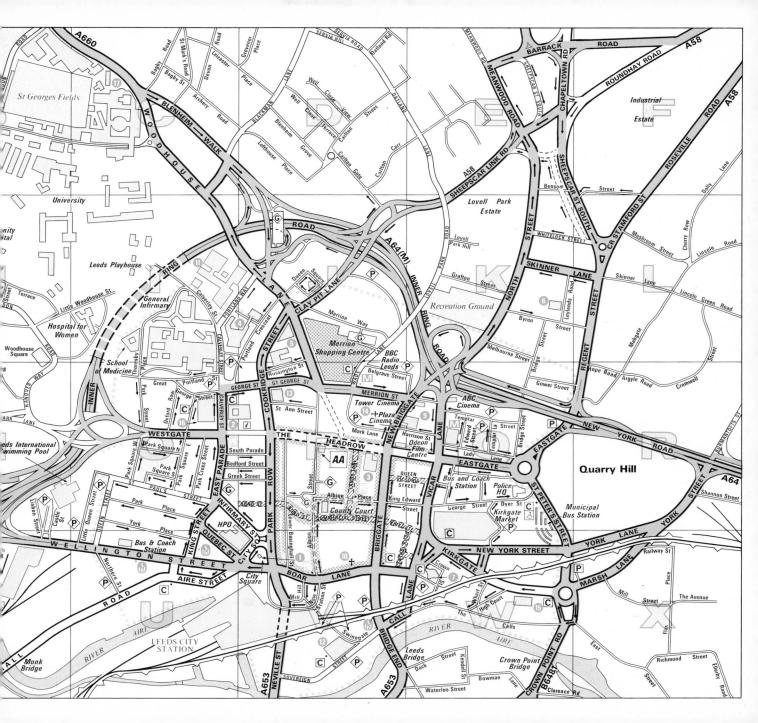

Markets

Q   **Kirkgate Market** (General — Tuesday, Friday, Saturday; Corn and Hay — Tuesday; Fruit and Vegetables — each weekday)

Advertisers

O   **Berni** Athenaeum Tavern
P   **Berni** The Albion
V   **Berni** Jacomelli's
V   **THF** Golden Lion Hotel
U   **THF** Hotel Metropole
U   **THF** Wellesley Hotel
Q   **Mercantile Credit** (branch office)
P   **Mercantile Credit** (area office)

DISTRICT PLAN
Public buildings and places of interest

G(18)   **Kirkstall Abbey and Abbey House Museum.** There are interesting remains of this 12th-C Cistercian Abbey set in a small park near the River Aire. The museum is housed in the abbey gatehouse and covers folk-life of Yorkshire of the last 300 years, including a full-scale model of streets and buildings connected with old trades in the Leeds area.

M(19)   **Middleton Colliery Railway** The first railway authorized by Act of Parliament in 1758. Industrial locomotives and rolling stock are in use. Trains, normally steam-hauled, are run on weekend afternoons during the summer months.

O(20)   **Temple Newsam House** A fine Tudor and Jacobean house set in a 935-acre park with woods, lakes and ornamental gardens. Lord Darnley (who married Mary, Queen of Scots) was born here in 1545. There are fine Georgian and Tudor rooms and a collection of English furniture, paintings, silver and ceramics.

Hospitals

D   **Chapel Allerton Hospital** *tel 623404*
B   **Cookridge Hospital** *tel 673411*
B   **Ida and Robert Arthington Hospital** *tel 677292*
J   **Killingbeck Hospital,** York Road *tel 648164*
C   **Meanwood Park Hospital** *tel 758721/783619*
N   **St George's Hospital,** Rothwell *tel 822211*
G   **St Mary's Hospital,** Green Hill Road *tel 638771*
I   **St James's Hospital,** Beckett Street *tel 33144*
J   **Seacroft Hospital,** York Road *tel 648164*

Sport and Recreation

G   **Bramley Rugby League Football Club,** The Ground, Town Street
D   **Cobble Hall Golf Course,** Elmete Lane
G   **Gotts Park Golf Course**
M   **Greyhound Racing,** Leeds Stadium, Elland Road
G   **Headingley Rugby Union Club,** Bridge Road
M   **Leeds United Association Football Club,** Elland Road
H   **Leeds Rugby League Football Club,** St Michael's Lane, Headingley
M   **Middleton Park Golf Course**
M   **New Hunslett Rugby League Football Club,** Leeds Stadium, Elland Road
D   **Roundhay Golf Course,** Park Lane
D   **Roundhay Park Open-air Swimming Pool,** Wetherby Road
M   **South Leeds Golf Course,** Dewsbury Road Car Terminus
O   **Temple Newsam Golf Course**
H   **Yorkshire County Cricket Club,** Headingley Cricket Ground

Markets

J   **Seacroft Town Centre** (Friday and Saturday)
I   **Wholesale Fish, Fruit and Vegetable Market,** Pontefract Lane
I   **Wholesale Meat Market and Abattoir,** Pontefract Lane

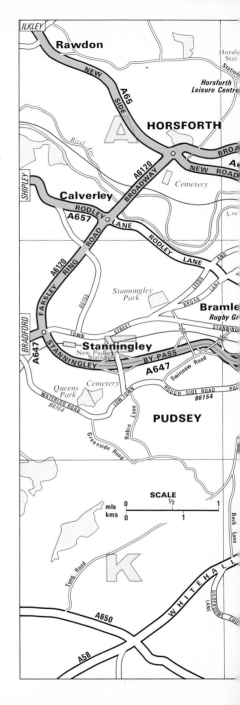

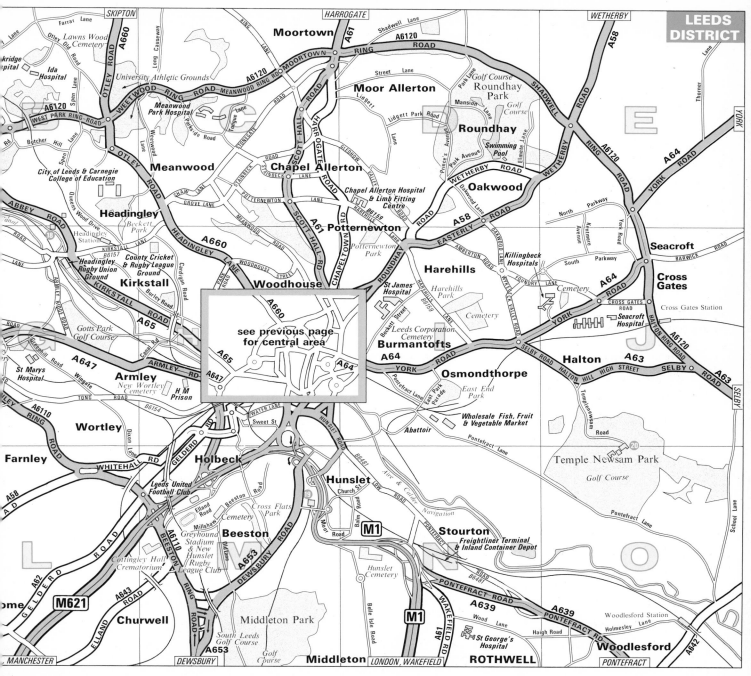

see previous page
for central area

117

LEICESTER

G   **AA Service Centre** — Fanum House, 132 Charles Street *tel 20491*

G ⓘ   **Tourist Information Centre** — 12 Bishop Street *tel 20644*

Public buildings and places of interest

F(1)   **Castle and County Magistrates Court** Little remains of the Norman Castle with the exception of the motte and Great Hall. The latter, preserved behind a façade of 1695, is now in use as a law court.
Access to the Castle Yard is through two gateways, of 15th- and 16th-C date.

G(2)   **Clock Tower** Dates from 1868 and commemorates four of Leicester's benefactors.

G(3)   **Corn Exchange** A 19th-C building situated in the Market Place. It has an unusual outside staircase.

P(4)   **De Montfort Hall** Built in 1913 with an impressive Tuscan-style colonnade, it is well-known as a venue for opera, ballet, dances, concerts and music festivals.

O(5)   **Granby Hall** A large centre for exhibitions and shows.

F(6)   **Guildhall (AM)** A magnificent timbered guildhall, dating in part from 1340, containing the ancient town library.

C(7)   **Haymarket Theatre** Opened in 1973, it is part of the Haymarket development project.

F(8)   **Jewry Wall Museum** (Situated beneath Vaughan College) Museum of Leicestershire archaeology from the earliest times to the Middle Ages, including the 2nd-C Roman Baths and Jewry Wall.

J(9)   **Leicester Polytechnic**

G(10)   **Municipal Buildings**

K(11)   **Museum and Art Gallery** Dates from 1849 with displays of geology, natural history, painting and sculpture.

F(12)   **Museum of Costume, Roger Wygston's House** The house dates from the 15thC and displays English costume from 1760 to 1920.

J(13)   **Museum of Royal Leicestershire Regiment** Housed in the early 15th-C Magazine Gateway (AM) of the Newarke.

F(14)   **Newarke Houses** Two buildings, Chantry House of 1511 and an adjacent house of c1600, together form a museum of the city's and county's social history from 1500 to the present day.

K(15)   **New Walk Centre** Leicester City Council offices

G(16)   **Reference Library and Tourist Information Centre**

F(17)   **St Martin's Cathedral** A 13th- to 15th-C structure preserving a carved chancel roof and showing good modern woodwork.

F(18)   **St Mary de Castro Church** A Norman and later church with a lofty crocketted 14th-C spire and notable Norman chancel sedilia.

F(19)   **St Nicholas Church** The Saxon to 13th-C church, the city's oldest, incorporates Roman materials and has a Norman south door.

G(20)   **Town Hall and Magistrates Court** The Town Hall dates from 1875.

J(21)   **Trinity Hospital Almshouses** Part of the original Newarke (a walled enclosure added to the castle in the 14th-C and surviving only in the street name); the almshouses date from 1331 and later. The chapel is of interest.

P(22)   **University** A University college since 1921, it received full university status in 1957 and has expanded considerably in recent years.

P(23)   **War Memorial, Arch of Remembrance** Designed by Sir Edwin Lutyens.

Hospitals

K   **Fielding Johnson Hospital**, Regent Road *tel 541414*

J   **Royal Infirmary**, Infirmary Square *tel 541414*

Sport and Recreation

O(5)   **Granby Halls** — roller skating (winter only) (see also public buildings and places of interest)

N   **Leicester City Football Club**, Filbert Street

O   **Rugby Football Club**, Welford Road

B   **St Margaret's Swimming Baths**, Vaughan Way

County Cricket Club, 1 m S via Aylestone Road A426 **(N)**

Speedway and Greyhound Stadium, Parker Road ½m N via North Gate Street A5125 **(A)**

Theatres and Cinemas

C   **ABC Cinemas 1 & 2**, Belgrave Gate *tel 24346*

C   **Cinecenta Cinemas**, Abbey Street *tel 25892*

C(7)   **Haymarket Theatre**, Belgrave Gate *tel 52521*

G   **Little Theatre**, Dover Street *tel 21945*

G   **Odeon Cinema**, Rutland Street *tel 22892*

J   **Phoenix Theatre**, Newarke Street *tel 58832*

Department Stores

Fenwicks Ltd, Market Street
Lewis's Ltd, Humberstone Gate
Marks and Spencer Ltd, 18 Gallowtree Gate
Rackmans Ltd, Hotel Street
Early closing day — some small shops close half day Thursday, a few large stores close all day Monday.

Markets

G   **Retail Market**, Market Place (general, meat, fish, poultry — Wednesday, Friday and Saturday)

Advertisers

C   **Berni** Steak Bar
B   **Berni** Fish and Quart
F   **Berni** Wolsey Tavern
G   **Mercantile Credit**
G   **Centre** Leicester Centre Hotel

Guildhall

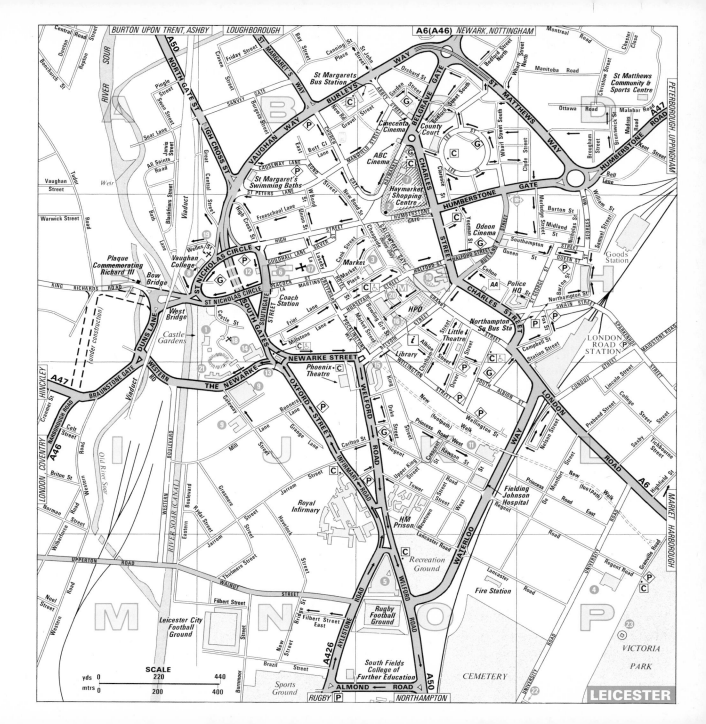

B(7) Tourist Information Centres — East
Midlands Tourist Board Offices,
90 Bailgate *tel 29828* (see also
public buildings and places of interest)

F(5) Information Centre City Hall, Beaumont
Fee *tel 32151* (see also public
buildings and places of interest)

Public buildings and places of interest

F(1) Aaron the Jew's House An important
example of 12th-C domestic architecture.

F(2) Cardinal's Hat A magnificent late 15th-C
timber-framed house, used as an inn in
the 16thC, and one of the many fine
timber buildings in the City Centre.

B(3) Castle (AM) 11th-C and later structure
retaining the Norman bailey and two
motte mounds. The 18th- and 19th-C
buildings within the walls are the
former prison (now the County Archives
Office) and the Crown Court.

C(4) Cathedral A splendid Norman and later
building dominating the City and
surrounding country. Of particular
note are the west front, the triple
towers, St Hugh's Choir and the
beautiful Angel Choir, the 13th-C
Chapter House, the Tournai
font and an original copy of Magna
Carta. Nearby are the fine buildings of
Cathedral Close and Minster Yard,
including the 13th-C Bishop's House
and 19th-C Palace and the 14th-C
Vicar's Court.

F(5) City Hall and Information Centre

C(6) East Gate A massive Roman tower dating
from the 3rdC.

B(7) East Midlands Tourist Board Offices

B(8) Exchequer Gate The west gatehouse of
the Close wall, dating from the 14thC.

J(9) Greyfriars City and County Museum and
City Library A former friary dating
from the 13thC with a fine barrel
roof. Now a museum of antiquities.
The library adjoins the museum.

J(10) High Bridge A Norman vaulted bridge
spanning the Witham River, with a
timber-framed 16th-C house on the
west side.

F(11) Jew's House Another Norman house of

c1170-80, and probably a better-known
example than Aaron the Jew's House (1).

A(12) Museum of Lincolnshire Life Exhibits
cover the period from Elizabethan times
to the present day.

B(13) Newport Arch (AM) Dating from the
2nd-C it is the last Roman arch in
England which still spans a road. To the
east is a fragment of the Colonia wall
and ditch — the latter was 30ft deep. To
the south is Bailgate with remnants of a
Roman colonnade.

G(14) Potter Gate Dates from the early 14thC.

C(15) Priory Gate

J(16) St Benedict's Church Preserves an 11th-C
tower.

J(17) St Mary-le-Wigford Church Mainly 13th-C
with a Norman tower and a Roman
memorial stone.

N(18) St Mary's Guildhall (or John of Gaunt's
stables) (AM) A fine Norman guildhall
dating from c1180.

N(19) St Peter-at-Gowt's Church The tower
also dates from the 11thC.

J(20) St Swithin's Church A modern church
with a Roman altar stone.

J(21) Stonebow and Guildhall The Stonebow
gateway is late 15th and early 16th-C.
Above it is the fine, partly timbered
Guildhall which contains the Civic
insignia and royal charters.

F(22) Theatre Royal

G(23) Usher Gallery Contains a fine
collection of miniatures, glass,
ceramics, coins, watches and water-colours.

High Bridge — Tudor House

Hospitals

H County Hospital, Sewell Road *tel 29921*
B Lawn Hospital, Union Road *tel 26226*
St George's Hospital, Long Lays Road *tel 29921*
1¼m NW via Yarborough Road A1102(A)
St John's Hospital, London Road, Bracebridge
Heath *tel 27401* 3m S via High Street and Cross
O'Cliffe Road A15 (N)

Sport and Recreation

C Lincolnshire County Cricket Club,
Lindum Sports Club, Wragby Road
C Lincoln Rugby Union Football Club,
Lindum Sports Club, Wragby Road
City Sports Centre (including swimming pool),
Skellingthorpe Road 2m S via High Street A15 (M)
the Dixon Street A1180
Lincoln City Football Club, Sincil Bank 1m S via
Canwick Road A158 (O) or High Street A15 (N)
Lincoln Racecourse (Point-to-point events 1½m
NW via Carholme Road A57 (E)
South Common Golf Course 1m S via Canwick
Road A158 (O)

Theatres and Cinemas

J ABC Cinema, Saltergate *tel 23062*
N Odeon Cinema, High Street *tel 20951*
F(22) Theatre Royal, Clasketgate *tel 25555*

Department Stores

Bainbridges (Lincoln) Ltd, 233 High Street
Marks and Spencer Ltd, 204 High Street
Mawer and Collingham, High Street and Mint St
Early closing day Wednesday

Markets

J Central Market, Sincil Street (Fruit
and Vegetables — Weekdays; General —
Thursday, Friday and Saturday)
J Corn Market, Corn Exchange (Friday)

Advertisers

J Berni The Falcon
F Mercantile Credit
C THF Eastgate Hotel

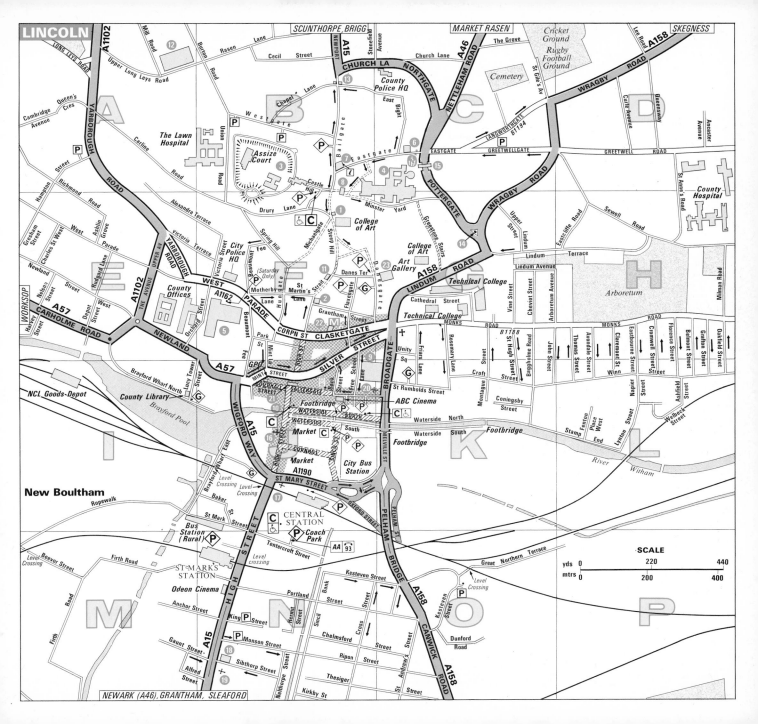

... try us!

If there is anything you ever want to know about the City, but don't know who to ask, try the City Information Offices. Whatever your query, we've got the answer, or will help you find it.

City Information Office,
St. John's Centre, 1st Floor, Liverpool L1 1NL.
Telephone: 709 3631 or 709 8681
8.45 a.m. - 5.30 p.m. Mon. - Sat.

The City Public Relations Office,
Municipal Buildings, Dale Street, Liverpool
L69 2DH. Telephone: 227 3911
8.30 a.m. - 4.45 p.m. Mon. - Fri.

Liverpool

LIVERPOOL

CENTRAL PLAN

J   **AA Service Centre** — Derby Square
tel 051-709 7252

G ⓘ   **Tourist Information Centre** — 187 St John's Precinct, 1st Floor, Elliot Street *tel 051-709 3631/8681*

Public buildings and places of interest

K(1)   **Anglican Cathedral** This notable red sandstone Cathedral with a 331ft tower was commenced in 1904. Its modern Gothic style is strongly marked by the individuality of its architect Sir Giles Gilbert Scott. ¼m S via Rodney Street.

J(2)   **Bluecoat Chambers** Well-restored Queen Anne-style buildings of 1716.

C(3)   **College of Technology**

F(4)   **Council Offices and Information Bureau**

I(5)   **Cunard Building** A well known waterfront landmark.

I(6)   **Dock Board Offices**

L(7)   **Metropolitan Cathedral (RC)** This very impressive modern cathedral of conical shape was designed by Sir Frederick Gibberd and constructed in 1967. It possesses a central pinnacled lantern tower with stained glass by John Piper and Patrick Reyntians.

L(8)   **Philharmonic Hall**

E(9)   **Royal Liver Building** Nearly 300ft high, surmounted by two examples of the 'liver' a mythical bird from which, by tradition, the city takes its name.

G(10)   **St George's Hall** A notable building of 1838-54, possibly the finest Greco-Roman style building in Europe, designed by H L Elmes and containing seven courts of law, a main hall with seating capacity for 1,750 and a small concert hall.

G(11)   **St John's Beacon** A 450ft-high tower, Liverpool's highest building, with a restaurant and observation platform.

F(12)   **Town Hall** Built 1749-54 to a design by John Wood the Elder, with enlargements of 1789-92 by James Wyatt and the addition of the portico and council chamber in 1811 and the large ballroom in 1820.

H(13)   **University** Many of the colleges date from the 19thC but the University became a separate institution in 1903. The main site of over thirty modern buildings close to the centre of the town dates from 1949.

G(14)   **Walker Art Gallery, Merseyside County Museum and the City Libraries** The art gallery contains the largest collection of European paintings in Britain outside London, with works dating from the 14thC to the present day. The museum houses archaeology, ethnography, ceramics and applied arts from the Mayer collection; a historic musical instruments collection, geological and shipping galleries, a natural history display based on the Ainsdale National Nature Reserve, an aquarium, a new gallery of transport of the Merseyside region, displays illustrating the history of timekeeping and space exploration, and a planetarium.
The Library is one of the oldest and largest public libraries in England with a bookstock of over two million including the Brown Library with commercial, technical, arts and recreation, philosophical and religious and local history collections; the Hornby Library of fine and rare books, manuscripts, prints and autograph letters; and International Library.

Hospitals

A   **David Lewis Northern Hospital**, Leeds Street *tel 051-236 6491*

L   **Hahnemann Hospital**, 42 Hope Street *tel 051-709 8474*

H   **Liverpool Dental Hospital**, Pembroke Place *tel 051-709 0281*

L   **Liverpool Ear, Nose and Throat Infirmary**, Myrtle Street *tel 051-709 0741*

L   **Liverpool Maternity Hospital**, Oxford Street *tel 051-709 5511*

H   **Liverpool Royal Infirmary**, Pembroke Place *tel 051-709 5511*

L   **Royal Liverpool Children's Hospital**, Myrtle Street *tel 051-709 0821*

E   **St Paul's Eye Hospital**, Old Hall Street *tel 051-236 7794*

Sport and Recreation

E   **Liverpool Stadium**, St Paul's Square

Theatres and Cinemas

G   **ABC Cinema**, Lime Street *tel 051-709 6277*

G   **Empire Theatre**, Lime Street *tel 051-709 1555*

L   **Everyman Theatre**, Hope Street *tel 051-709 4776*

G   **Futurist Cinema**, Lime Street *tel 051-709 3186*

K   **Neptune Theatre**, Hanover Street *tel 051-709 7844*

G   **Odeon 1, 2, 3 & 4**, London Road *tel 051-709 0717*

G   **Playhouse Theatre**, William Square *tel 051-709 8363*

G   **Royal Court Theatre**, Roe Street *tel 051-709 5163*

L(8)   **Royal Liverpool Philharmonic Society**, Philharmonic Hall, Hope Street *tel 051-709 3789* (see also public buildings and places of interest)

G   **Scala Cinema**, Lime Street *tel 051-709 1084*

K   **Studios 1, 2 & 3**, Mount Pleasant Brownlow Hill *tel 051-709 7847*

Department Stores

Army and Navy Stores, 47 Ranelagh Street
Binns Ltd, 9 Church Street
Blackler's Stores Ltd, Elliot Street
G & H Stores, 81 Kirkdale Road
Gimbles, Great Charlotte Street
Hughes T J and Co Ltd, Audley House, London Road
Lee George Henry and Co Ltd, 20 Basnett Street
Lewis's Ltd, Ranelagh Street
Marks and Spencer Ltd, Compton House, Church Street
Milletts Outfitters, Lord Street
Owen Owen Ltd, Clayton Square
Oxleys Department Store Ltd, 22 Fleet Street
Early closing day Wednesday

Markets

H **Monument Place Market** (Thursday and Saturday)

G **St John's Market**, St John's Centre (Daily)

Advertisers

J **Berni** Mersey Tavern

I **Berni** River Inn

F **Berni** The Albany

E **Mercantile Credit**

G **THF** St George's Hotel

G **Centre** Liverpool Centre Hotel

DISTRICT PLAN

P **AA Road Service Centre (44)** — Car Park, Gomer Street, Birkenhead *tel 051-647 7252*

P **Tourist Information Centre** — Reference Department, Central Wirral Area Library, Borough Road, Birkenhead *tel 051-652 6106*

Public buildings and places of interest

Q(15) **Birkenhead Town Hall and Information Bureau**

G(16) **Bootle Museum and Art Gallery** Small museum noted for its fine collection of English pottery and porcelain. Also monthly changing art exhibitions.

I(17) **Croxteth Hall** An 18th-C and later hall in a large park.

S(18) **Harthill Botanical Gardens,** Calderstones Park. A large and comprehensive collection of hardy and tropical plants. Noted for its hot houses, in particular its Orchid House.

J(19) **Knowsley Safari Park** Situated in the grounds of a 17th- to 19th-C mansion, with lions, cheetahs, elephants, zebra, etc, roaming freely in natural surroundings. Also dolphinarium.

V(20) **Lady Lever Art Gallery,** Port Sunlight. Displays pictures by famous English masters in addition to collections of sculpture, Chinese porcelain, Wedgwood wares and English furniture.

Q(21) **Priory Ruins,** Birkenhead. These remains date from the 12thC.

K(22) **St James' Church,** Birkenhead. A modern church with a richly-decorated lectern.

Q(23) **St Mary's Church,** Birkenhead. This was built in 1821.

X(24) **Speke Hall (NT)** A magnificent 'black and white' half-timbered hall, completed in 1610 with interior courtyard, Great Hall, 16th- and 17th-C plasterwork and the Mortlake tapestries.

R(25) **Sudley Art Gallery** An early 19th-C merchant's house containing a large collection of works including paintings by Reynolds, Gainsborough, Wilkie, Mulready, Romney, Holman Hunt, Turner and Bonington. Also some 19th-C French paintings, British sculpture, pottery and costume.

K(26) **Wallasey Town Hall and Information Bureau**

P(27) **Williamson Art Gallery and Museum,** Birkenhead. Collections include an important English water-colours section, sculpture, decorative arts, ceramics, glass, silver and furniture. A local history and maritime museum adjoins.

Hospitals

C **Aintree and Fazakerley Hospitals,** Longmoor Lane, Liverpool 9 *tel 051-525 5980*

N **Alder Hey Children's Hospital,** Eaton Road, Liverpool *tel 051-228 4811*

P **Ashton Hospital,** 26 Village Road, Oxton *tel 051-652 3143*

P **Birkenhead Children's Hospital,** Woodchurch Road, Birkenhead *tel 051-652 5401*

P **Birkenhead General Hospital,** Park Road North, Birkenhead *tel 051-652 66134*

G **Bootle Hospital,** Derby Road, Liverpool *tel 051-922 4541*

N **Broadgreen Hospital (General),** Thomas Drive, Liverpool 14 *tel 051-228 4878*

X **Garston Hospital,** Woolton Road

L **John Bagot Hospital,** Netherfield Road North

G **Liverpool Stanley Hospital,** Stanley Road *tel 051-922 2161*

M **Mill Road Maternity Hospital,** Mill Road *tel 051-263 2656*

R **Mossley Hill Hospital,** Park Avenue *tel 051-724 2335*

M **Newsham General Hospital,** Belmont Road *tel 051-263 7381*

N **Olive Mount Children's Hospital,** Mill Lane *tel 051-722 2261*

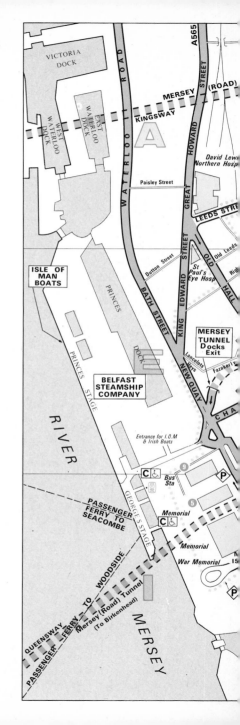

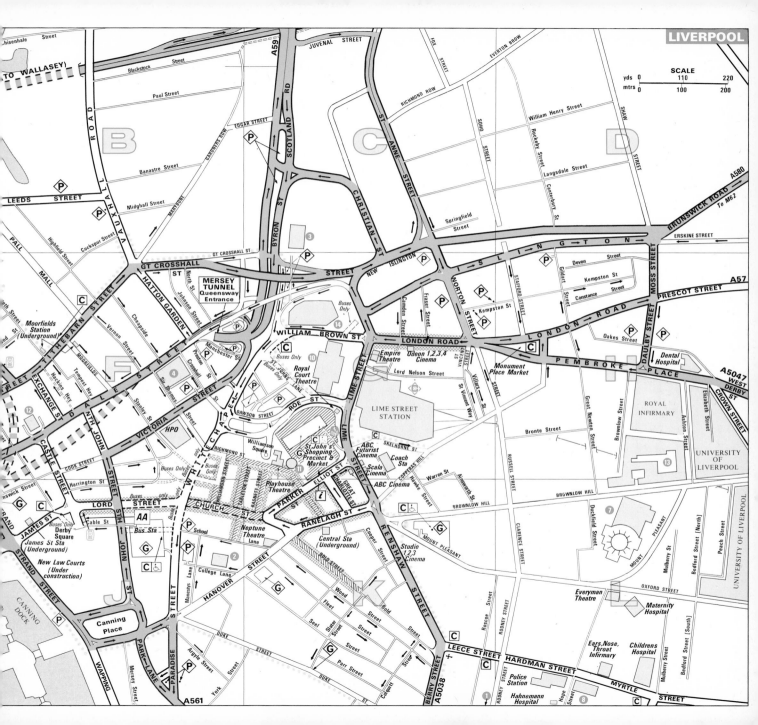

M	**Park Hospital**, Newsham Park *tel 051-263 9641*
R	**Princes Park Hospital**, 96 Upper Parliament Street *tel 051-709 7361*
N	**Rathbone Hospital**, Mill Lane *tel 051-228 4657*
Q	**Royal Southern Hospital**, Caryl Street *tel 051-709 6841*
P	**St Catherine's Hospital**, Church Road, Birkenhead *tel 051-652 2281*
K	**St James's Hospital**, Tollemache Road, Claughton *tel 051-652 3571*
R	**Sefton General Hospital**, Smithdown Road *tel 051-733 4020*
K	**Victoria Central Hospital**, Liscard Road, Wallasey *tel 051-638 7000*
K	**Wallasey Hospital for Women**, Claremount Road *tel 051-638 4224*
G	**Walton Hospital (General)**, Liverpool 9 *tel 051-525 3611*
M	**Women's Hospital**, Catherine Street *tel 051-709 5461*

Sport and Recreation

C	**Aintree Racecourse**
S	**Allerton Park Golf Course**, Allerton
P	**Birkenhead Park Rugby Union Football Club**, Park Road North
B	**Bootle Golf Club**, Dunnings Bridge Road
O	**Bowring Park Golf Course**, Roby Road
U	**Brackenwood Golf Club**, Brackenwood Park, Bracken Lane, Bebington
T	**Childwall Golf Club**, Naylors Road, Gateacre
H	**Everton Football Club**, Goodison Park
O	**Huyton Leisure Centre**, Roby Road, Huyton
O	**Huyton and Prescot Golf Club**, Hurst Park, Huyton Lane, Huyton
O	**Huyton Rugby League Football Club**, Endmoor Road, Huyton
D	**Kirkby Sports Centre**, Whitefield Road, Kirkby
D	**Kirkby Town Football Club**, Simonswood Lane, Kirkby
T	**Lee Park Golf Club**, Gateacre
W	**Liverpool Cricket Club**, Aigburth Road
H	**Liverpool Football Club**, Anfield Road
D	**Liverpool Municipal Golf Course**, Ingoe Lane, Kirkby, Liverpool
R	**Liverpool Rugby Union Football Club**, St Michael's, Church Road
V	**Oval Sports Centre**, Old Chester Road, Bebington

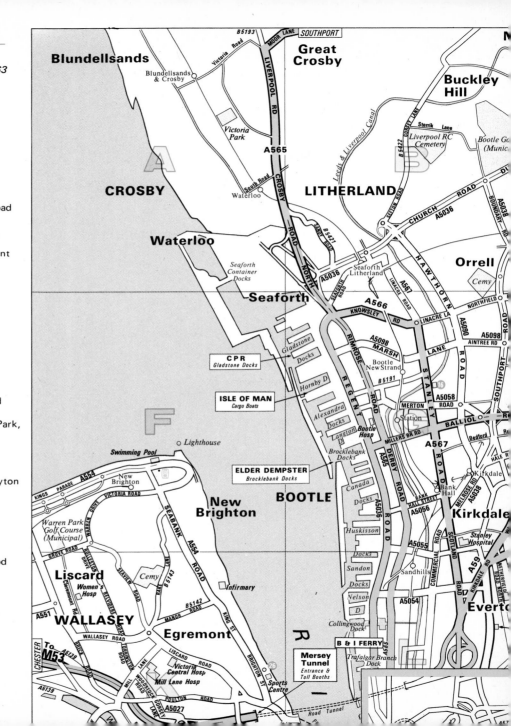

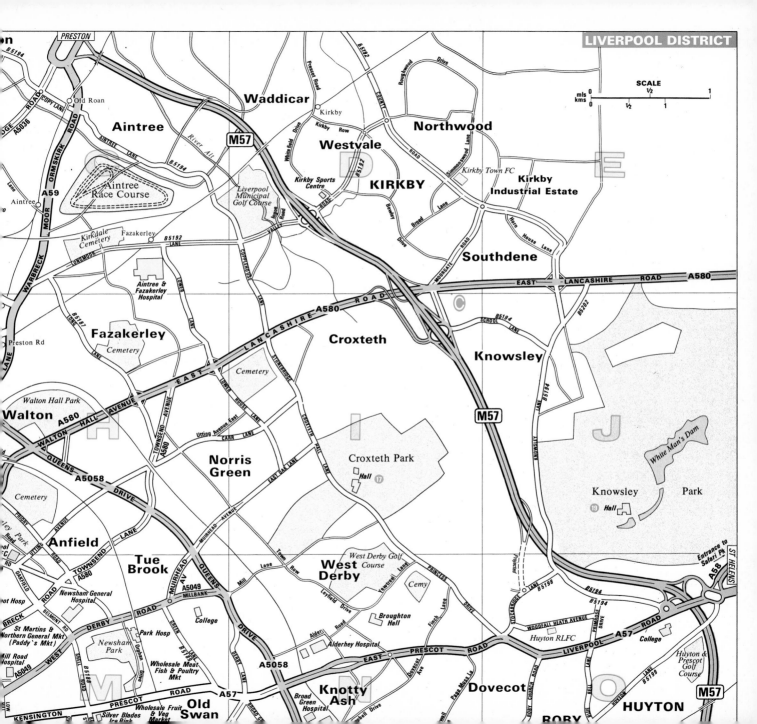

U	**Prenton Golf Club,** Golf Links Road, Prenton, Birkenhead
M	**Silver Blades Ice Rink,** Prescot Road
P	**Tranmere Rovers Football Club,** Prenton Park, Birkenhead
F	**Warren Park Golf Links,** Grove Road, Wallasey
N	**West Derby Golf Club,** Yew Tree Lane
P	**Wirral Ladies Golf Club,** Bidston Road, Oxton, Birkenhead
Y	**Woolton Golf Club,** Doe Park, Woolton, Liverpool

Department Stores

Army and Navy General Stores, 160 Linacre Road
Beatties of Birkenhead, 92 Grange Road
Hughes T J and Co Ltd, Grange Road, Birkenhead
Hughes T J and Co Ltd, New Strand, Bootle
Marks and Spencer Ltd, 212 Grange Road, Birkenhead
Marks and Spencer Ltd, 301 Liscard Road, Wallasey
Marks and Spencer Ltd, New Strand Shopping Precinct
Robb Brothers Ltd, Grange Road, Birkenhead
Rostance's Ltd, 13 Oxton Road, Claughton
Rostance's Ltd, 57 New Chester Road, New Ferry

Markets

L	**North General** (Saturday) and **St Martin's Market** (Daily), Great Homer Street
M	**Wholesale Fruit, Vegetable and Flowers Market,** Prescot Road (Daily)
M	**Wholesale Meat, Poultry and Fish Market,** Prescot Road (Monday to Friday)

Advertisers

F	**Berni** Queens Royal
P	**Mercantile Credit**
I	**Crest** Liverpool Crest Motel

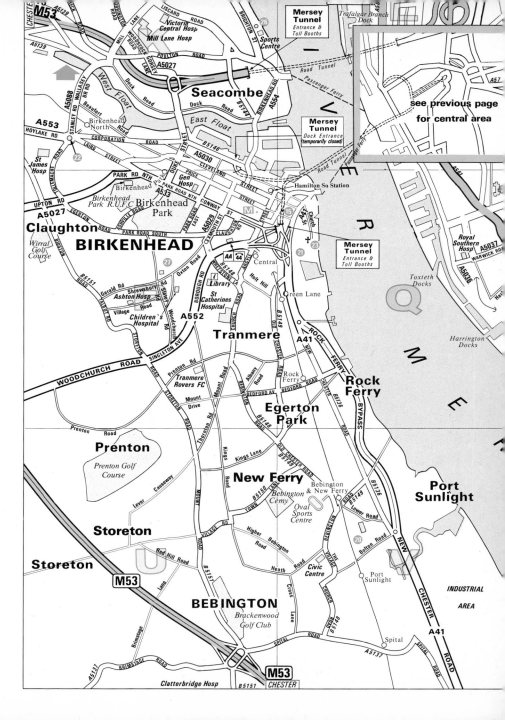

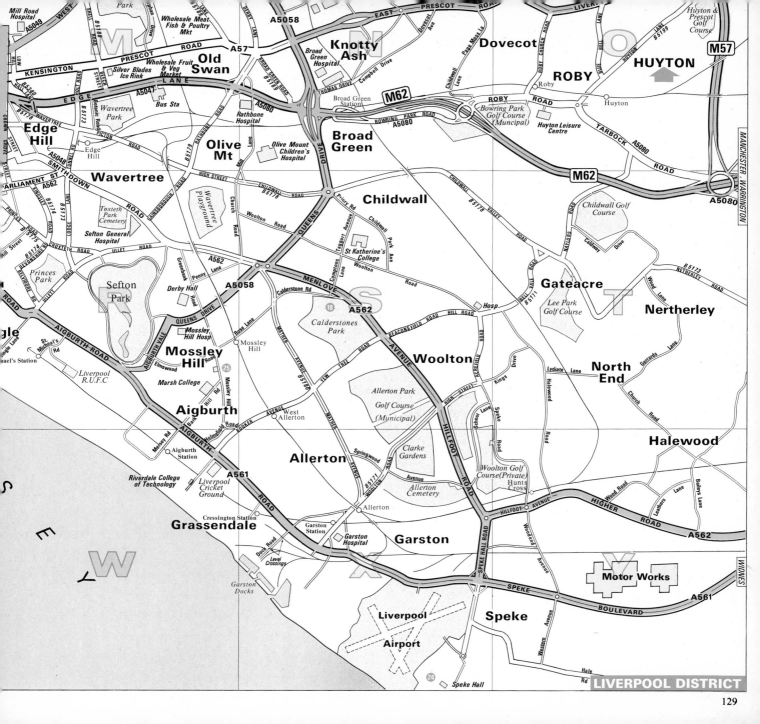

LLANDUDNO

E	**AA Road Service Centre (115)** — Car Park in Back Madoc Street *tel 79453*
E *i*	**Tourist Information Centres** — Chapel Street *tel 76413*
B *i*	**Opposite Pier Gates**, Promenade *tel 76572* (summer months only)

Public buildings and places of interest

E(1)	**Doll Museum and Model Railway**
B(2)	**Great Orme Cabin Lift** Longest passenger cable car in Britain, leading to Great Orme's Head.
A(3)	**Great Orme Tramway** Over 60 years old and nearly a mile in length, this cable railway carries passengers to the summit of Great Orme (679ft) which dominates Llandudno.
B(4)	**Happy Valley Rock Gardens**
D(5)	**Haulfre Gardens** Interesting terraced gardens and aquarium.
I(6)	**Rapallo House Museum and Art Gallery** A picture gallery and small museum with collection of china and glassware, an armoury, Roman relics and old Welsh kitchen. Also ornamental gardens.
E(7)	**Town Hall**

St Tudno's Church, Great Orme's Head (A) Preserves some 13th-C coffin lids.

Hospitals

H	**Llandudno General Hospital**, Maesdu, West Shore *tel 77471*

Sport and Recreation

D	**Llandudno Cricket Club**, The Oval
H	**Maesdu Golf Club**
G	**North Wales Golf Club**, West Shore
F	**Swimming Pool**, Mostyn Broadway

Theatres and Cinemas

F	**Arcadia Theatre** (summer shows) *tel 76570*
D	**Astra Entertainment Centre Cinema**, Gloddaeth Street *tel 76666*
F	**Grand Theatre**, Mostyn Broadway *tel 77327*
B	**Happy Valley Theatre**, (open-air summer shows) *tel 75649*
E	**Palladium Cinema**, Gloddaeth Street *tel 76244*
B	**Pier Pavilion Theatre** *tel 75259*
E	**Savoy Cinema**, Mostyn Street *tel 76394*

Department Stores

Asda Super Stores, Mostyn Broadway

Clares Department Store, 97 Mostyn Street
Marks and Spencer Ltd, 61 Mostyn Street
Early closing day Wednesday (except summer)

Markets

E	**Market Hall** (Daily except Wednesday afternoons)

Advertisers

B	**THF** Grand Hotel
E	**THF** Marine Hotel

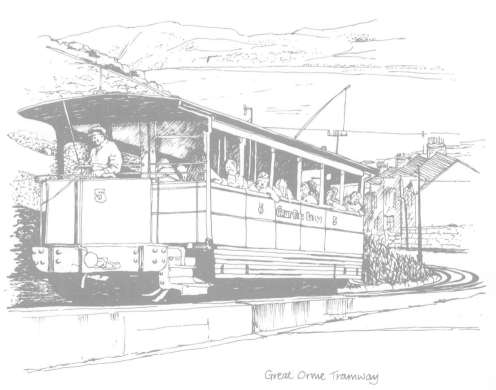

Great Orme Tramway

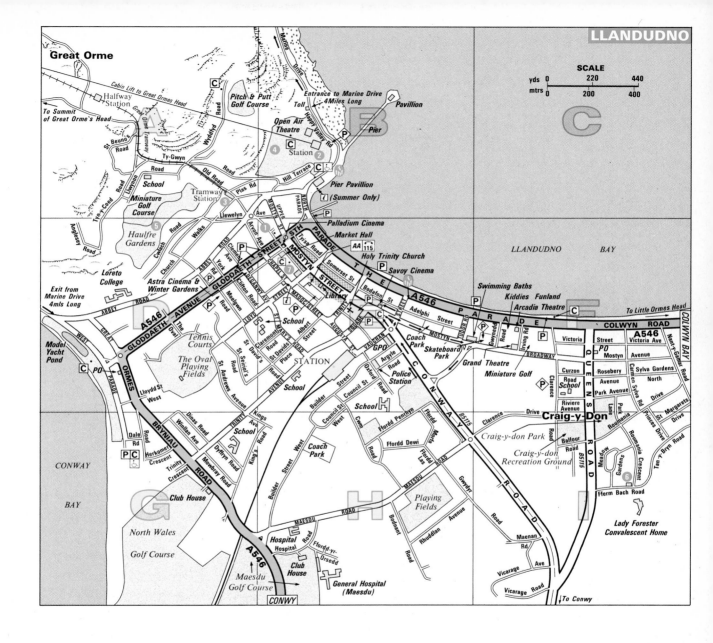

LLANDUDNO

Great Orme

SCALE
yds 0 — 220 — 440
mtrs 0 — 200 — 400

Cabin Lift to Great Ormes Head
Halfway Station
To Summit of Great Orme's Head
Pitch & Putt Golf Course
Entrance to Marine Drive 4 Miles Long
Toll
Pavillion
Pier
Open Air Theatre
Station
Happy Valley Rd
Pier Pavillion (Summer Only)

St Beuno Road
Ty-Gwyn
School
Tramway Station
Miniature Golf Course
Haulfre Gardens
Loreto College
Model Yacht Pond
Exit from Marine Drive 4mls Long

LLANDUDNO BAY

Palladium Cinema
Market Hall
Holy Trinity Church
Savoy Cinema
Astra Cinema & Winter Gardens
Library
GPO
Tennis Courts
The Oval Playing Fields
School
STATION
Police Station
School
Skateboard Park
Coach Park
Grand Theatre
Miniature Golf
Swimming Baths
Kiddies Funland
Arcadia Theatre

Victoria Ave
A546
COLWYN ROAD
To Little Ormes Head
Mostyn Avenue
Curzon Avenue
Roseberry Avenue
Park Avenue
Sylva Gardens
Road School
Riviere Avenue
Craig-y-Don
Craig-y-don Park
Clarence Drive
Craig-y-don Recreation Ground
Balfour Road
Roumania Crescent
Fern Bach Road
Lady Forester Convalescent Home

Model Yacht Pond
Dale Rd
Winllan Ave
Dinas Road
Dyffryn Road
Mowbray Road
Herkomer Crescent
Trinity Crescent
Kings Ave
School
Club House
North Wales Golf Course
CONWAY BAY
Maesdu Golf Course
Hospital
Club House
General Hospital (Maesdu)
Coach Park
Builder Street West
Council St West
Cwm
Ffordd Penrhyn
Ffordd Dewi
Maesdu Road
Ffordd Las
Playing Fields
Rhuddlan Avenue
Bodnant
Maenan Rd
Vicarage Ave
Vicarage Road
To Conwy
CONWY

131

LONDON (CENTRAL)

N   **AA Service Centre** — 5 New Coventry Street *tel 01-954 7355*

R *i*   **Tourist Information Centre** — The London Tourist Board, 26 Grosvenor Gardens *Tel 01-730 0791*

Public buildings and places of interest

N(1)   **Banqueting House** Built in 1619 to a design by Inigo Jones, it contains painted ceilings by Rubens.

I(2)   **British Crafts Centre** Designed to promote and sell work by British craftsmen, the exhibits are changed regularly and cover a wide variety of British crafts.

D(3)   **British Museum** Founded in 1753, this vast museum is famous for ancient sculpture, prints, drawings and books.

P(4)   **British Museum of Natural History** The Museum houses the national collection of animals and plants, both recent and fossil, and of rocks, minerals and meteorites.

P(5)   **Brompton Oratory** Roman Catholic Church in the Italian Renaissance style built in 1878 by Herbert Gribble.

R(6)   **Buckingham Palace** Built in 1703, it was remodelled by Nash in 1830 and the east front refaced in 1913 by Ashton Webb. A flag flies when the Queen is in residence. The Changing of the Guard takes place daily, outside.

D(7)   **Building Centre**

D(8)   **Courtauld Institute Galleries** Important collection of Impressionist and Old Master paintings.

N(9)   **Design Centre** Headquarters of the Design Council, the pictorial card index lists British quality goods, their price and where to buy them.

E(10)   **Dickens' House** Dickens lived here 1837-39. The house contains many personal relics along with manuscripts and first editions.

J(11)   **HMS Discovery** Built in 1901 for Captain Scott's first expedition to the Antarctic. *Discovery* is now used as a drill ship for the Royal Navy.

H(12)   **Embroiderers' Guild** A society to encourage the art of embroidery with a unique collection available for study.

E(13)   **Foundling Hospital** Pictures by Hogarth, Gainsborough and others, also sculpture and Handel relics.

P(14)   **Geological Museum** Exhibitions include The Story of the Earth, The Gemstone Collection, The Regional Geology of Great Britain and The Economic Minerals of the Earth.

S(15)   **Guards Museum** Small museum in Guards Chapel, Wellington Barracks.

N(16)   **Horse Guards** Built in 1753 from designs by William Kent. The ceremony of Mounting and Changing of the Guard takes place daily.

T(17)   **Houses of Parliament** A mid-19th-C Gothic building. The House of Lords lies to the south of a central hall and the House of Commons to the north.

X(18)   **Industrial Health Safety Centre**

J(19)   **Inns of Court and Chancery**

S(20)   **Jewel Tower** 14th-C tower of the old Palace of Westminster.

T(21)   **Lambeth Palace** Official home of the Archbishops of Canterbury. The buildings date mainly from the 15th and 16thCs.

M(22)   **Lancaster House** Built in the 19thC for the Duke of York, Lancaster House is now used as a centre for Government hospitality.

J(23)   **London Silver Vaults**

B(24)   **Madame Tussauds** The wax exhibition came to England from Paris and settled in London in 1835. Exhibits include the Chamber of Horrors, historical figures and many famous and infamous people.

N(25)   **Marlborough House** Built by Sir Christopher Wren for the Duke of Marlborough. Inside are magnificent wall paintings depicting the Duke's famous battles.

M(26)   **Museum of Mankind** Ethnological and archaeological collections of pre-industrial societies from most parts of the world excluding Western Europe.

N(28)   **National Gallery** A collection of the chief European schools of painting from the 13thC to 1900.

N(29)   **National Portrait Gallery** National collection of portraits of the famous and infamous in British history. Also sculptures, miniatures, engravings,

photographs and cartoons.

J(30)   **Old Curiosity Shop** Now an antique shop, this Tudor house, built in 1567, was immortalised by Dickens in *The Old Curiosity Shop.*

D(31)   **Percival David Foundation of Chinese Art** Displays Chinese ceramics from the 10th to the 18thCs.

N(32)   **Pipe Museum** Situated in Dunhill's tobacco shop.

B(33)   **Planetarium** The night skies are projected on to the inside of the dome to an accompanying commentary.

P(34)   **Polish Institute and Sikorski Museum**

D(35)   **Pollock's Toy Museum** Old toys, dolls and theatres are on display along with the oldest teddy bear in England.

C(36)   **Post Office Tower**

R(37)   **The Queen's Gallery** Changing exhibitions of pictures and works of art at Buckingham Palace.

J(38)   **Roman Bath** Restored in the 17thC.

M(39)   **Royal Academy of Arts** Founded by George III in 1768. The summer exhibition is of works by living artists, and loan exhibitions are held throughout the rest of the year.

J(40)   **Royal College of Surgeons**

V(41)   **Royal Hospital** Founded in 1682 by Charles II, the Royal Hospital houses the Chelsea Pensioners, veteran and invalid soldiers. The Chelsea Flower Show is held in the hospital grounds every year.

R(42)   **Royal Mews** Many state coaches and carriages are on display, including the Gold State Coach, the Irish State Coach and the Scottish State Coach.

N(43)   **St James's Palace** Built by Henry VIII in 1530-6, with later additions by Wren.

N(44)   **St Martin-in-the-Fields** The church was rebuilt in the early 18thC by Gibbs, a pupil of Wren. It has a fine steeple and a richly-decorated, galleried interior.

P(45)   **Science Museum** Many working models, actual locomotives, machinery, etc, cover all aspects of science and industrial and technological developments.

J(46)   **Sir John Soane's Museum** The home of Sir John Soane, built in 1812, contains his collections of antiques, sculpture, paintings, drawings and books.

K(47) **Tate Gallery** Collections of British paintings from the 16thC to the present day. Also collections of foreign paintings and sculpture from 1880 to the present day.

*(48) **Victoria and Albert Museum** Built as a result of the Great International Exhibition in 1851, the museum contains one of the world's greatest collections of fine and decorative arts.

G(49) **Wallace Collection** The collection of works of art bequeathed to the nation by Lady Wallace in 1895 includes pictures by Rubens and Gainsborough and 18th-C French art.

R(50) **Wellington Museum** The London home of the 1st Duke of Wellington from 1817, Apsley House was presented to the nation by the 7th Duke in 1947.

S(51) **Westminster Abbey** Founded in 1065 by Edward the Confessor, all the monarchs since William the Conqueror have been crowned here. The Statesmen's Aisle in the north transept commemorates the many English statesmen buried here.

R(52) **Westminster Cathedral** Founded in 1896 and completed in 1903, the most notable features include the mosaics in Blessed Sacrament Chapel and a bronze panel of St Teresa of Lisieux.

T(53) **Westminster Hall** Built 1097-99 by William Rufus, it is the oldest remaining part of Westminster Palace.

Exhibition and Concert Halls

S **Caxton Hall**
S **Central Hall**
E **Conway Hall**
H **Kingsway Hall**
O **Purcell Room** including Queen Elizabeth Hall
P **Royal Albert Hall**
P **Royal College of Music**
O **Royal Festival Hall**
K **Royal Horticultural Halls**
B **Rudolf Steiner Hall**
S **St John Church** (BBC Concerts)
B **Seymour Hall**
B **Wigmore Hall**

Hospitals

U **Brompton Hospital**, Fulham Road, SW3 tel 01-352 8121

U **Chelsea Hospital for Women**, Dovehouse Street, SW3 tel 01-352 6446

G **Fitzroy Nuffield Hospital**, 10-12 Bryanston Square, W1 tel 01-723 1288

S **Grey Coat Hospital**, Greycoat Place, SW1 tel 01-834 8380

E **Hospital for Sick Children**, Great Ormond Street, WC1 tel 01-405 9200

E **Italian Hospital**, Queen Square, WC1 tel 01-831 6961

C **London Foot Hospital**, 33 Fitzroy Square, W1 tel 01-636 0602

C/D **Middlesex Hospital**, Mortimer Street, W1 tel 01-636 8333

J **Moorfields Eye Hospital**, High Holborn, WC1 tel 01-836 6611

C **National Heart Hospital**, Westmoreland Street, W1 tel 01-486 0824

E **National Hospital for Nervous Diseases**, Queen Square, WC1 tel 01-837 3611

A **Paddington Green Children's Hospital**, Paddington Green, W2 tel 01-723 1081

N **Royal Dental Hospital**, 32 Leicester Square, WC2 tel 01-930 8381

E **Royal London Homoeopathic Hospital**, Gt Ormond Street, WC1 tel 01-837 3091

U **Royal Marsden Hospital**, Fulham Road, London SW3 tel 01-352 8171

C **Royal National Orthopaedic Hospital**, 234 Great Portland Street, W1 tel 01-387 5070

O **Royal Waterloo Hospital**, Waterloo Road, SE1 tel 01-928 7421

Q **St George's Hospital**, Hyde Park Corner, SW1 tel 01-235 4343

I **St John's Hospital for Diseases of the Skin**, Lisle Street, Leicester Square, WC2 tel 01-437 8383

F **St Mary's Hospital**, Praed Street, W2 tel 01-262 1280

J **St Paul's Hospital**, Endell Street, WC2 tel 01-836 9611

J **St Peter's Hospital**, Henrietta Street, WC2 tel 01-836 9347

T **St Thomas' Hospital**, Lambeth Palace Road, SE1 tel 01-928 9292

B **Samaritan Hospital for Women**, Marylebone Road, NW1 tel 01-402 4211

I **Shaftesbury Hospital**, Shaftesbury Avenue, WC2 tel 01-836 2711

D **University College Hospital**, Gower Street, WC1 tel 01-387 9300

University College Hospital Group:
D **Royal Ear Hospital**, Huntley Street, WC1 tel 01-387 9300

D **Dental Hospital**, Mortimer Market, WC1 tel 01-387 9300

D **Maternity Hospital**, Huntley Street, WC1 tel 01-387 9300

D **Private Wing**, Grafton Way, WC1 tel 01-387 9300

B **Western Opthalmic Hospital**, Marylebone Road, NW1 tel 01-402 5101

X **Westminster Children's Hospital**, Vincent Square, SW1 tel 01-828 9811

X **Westminster Hospital**, Dean Ryle Street, Horseferry Road, SW1 tel 01-828 9811

Cinemas

I **ABC 1 & 2**, Shaftesbury Avenue, WC2 tel 01-836 8861

I **Academy 1**, Oxford Street, W1 tel 01-437 2981

I **Academy 2**, Oxford Street, W1 tel 01-437 5129

I **Academy 3**, Oxford Street, W1 tel 01-437 8819

I **Astral 1 & 2**, Rupert Street, W1 tel 01-437 5359

W **Biograph**, Wilton Road, SW1 tel 01-834 1624

N **Centa**, Piccadilly, W1 tel 01-437 3561

N **Cinecenta**, Panton Street, SW1 tel 01-930 0631

I **Classic**, Charing Cross Road, WC2 tel 01-930 6915

I **Classic Moulin**, Great Windmill Street, tel 01-437 1653

I **Classic**, Oxford Street tel 01-636 0310

A **Classic**, Praed Street, SW1 tel 01-723 5716

R **Classic**, Victoria Street, SW1 tel 01-834 6588

I **Columbia**, Shaftesbury Avenue, W1 tel 01-734 5414

I **Compton**, Old Compton Street, W1 tel 01-437 4555

M **Curzon**, Curzon Street, W1 tel 01-499 3737

I **Dominion**, Tottenham Court Road, W1 tel 01-580 9562

I   **Empire,** Leicester Square, WC2
tel 01-437 1234

N   **Eros,** Piccadilly Circus, W1
tel 01-437 3839

I   **Film Centre,** Charing Cross Road, WC2
tel 01-437 4815

G   **Gala Royal,** Marble Arch, W2
tel 01-262 2345

E   **Gate 2,** Brunswick Square, WC1
tel 01-837 1177

N   **Institute of Contemporary Arts,** Carlton House Terrace, SW1 *tel 01-930 6393*

I   **Jacey,** Leicester Square, WC2
tel 01-437 2001

N   **Jacey,** Trafalgar Square, WC2
tel 01-930 1143

N   **Leicester Square Theatre,** Leicester Square, WC2 *tel 01-930 5252*

N   **London Pavilion,** Piccadilly Circus, W1
tel 01-437 2982

Q   **Minema,** Knightsbridge, SW7
tel 01-235 4225

O   **National Film Theatre 1 & 2,** South Bank, SE1 *tel 01-928 3232*

N   **Odeon,** Haymarket, SW1 *tel 01-930 2738*

N   **Odeon,** Leicester Square, WC2
tel 01-930 6111

G   **Odeon,** Marble Arch, W2 *tel 01-723 2011*

I   **Odeon,** St Martin's Lane, WC2
tel 01-836 0691

N   **Plaza 1, 2, 3 & 4,** Regent Street, W1
tel 01-437 1234

I   **Prince Charles,** Leicester Place, WC2
tel 01-437 8181

H   **Regent Theatre,** Regent Street, W1
tel 01-637 9863

I   **Rialto,** Coventry Street, W1
tel 01-437 3488

I   **Ritz,** Leicester Square, WC2
tel 01-437 1234

I   **Scene 1, 2, 3 & 4,** Swiss Centre, Leicester Square, WC2 *tel 01-439 4470*

I   **Soho,** Brewer Street, W1 *tel 01-734 4205*

M   **Starlight Cinema,** Mayfair Hotel, Stratton Street, W1 *tel 01-629 7777*

H   **Studio 1, 2, 3 & 4,** Oxford Street, W1
tel 01-437 3300

B   **Times Centa 1 & 2,** Chiltern Court, Baker Street, NW1 *tel 01-935 9772*

I   **Warner West End 1, 2, 3 & 4,** Cranbourn Street, WC2 *tel 01-439 0791*

Theatres

O   **Adelphi,** The Strand, WC2
tel 01-836 7611

I   **Albery,** St Martin's Lane, WC2
tel 01-836 3878

J   **Aldwych,** Aldwych, WC2 *tel 01-836 6404*

I   **Ambassadors,** West Street, WC2
tel 01-836 1171

I   **Apollo,** Shaftesbury Avenue, W1
tel 01-437 2663

I   **Arts** (Theatre Club), Gt Newport Street, WC2 *tel 01-836 2132*

I   **Astoria,** Charing Cross Road, WC2
tel 01-734 4291

I   **Cambridge,** Earlham Street, WC2
tel 01-836 6056

A   **Cockpit,** Gateforth Street, NW8
tel 01-402 5081

N   **Coliseum,** St Martin's Lane, WC2
tel 01-836 3161

N   **Comedy,** Panton Street, SW1
tel 01-930 2578

J   **Criterion,** Piccadilly, W1 *tel 01-930 3216*

J   **Drury Lane Theatre Royal,** Catherine Street, WC2 *tel 01-836 8108*

J   **Duchess,** Catherine Street, WC2
tel 01-836 8243

N   **Duke of York's,** St Martin's Lane, WC2
tel 01-836 5122

J   **Fortune,** Russell Street, WC2
tel 01-836 2238

N   **Garrick,** Charing Cross Road, WC2
tel 01-836 4601

I   **Globe,** Shaftesbury Avenue, W1
tel 01-437 1592

N   **Haymarket, Theatre Royal,** Haymarket, SW1 *tel 01-930 9832*

N   **Her Majesty's,** Haymarket, SW1
tel 01-930 6606

E   **Jeannetta Cochrane,** Theobalds Road, WC1 *tel 01-242 7040*

I   **Lyric,** Shaftesbury Avenue, W1
tel 01-437 3686

M   **Mayfair,** Stratton Street, W1
tel 01-629 3036

O   **National Theatre,** (Cottesloe, Lyttelton & Olivier Theatres), South Bank, SE1
tel 01-928 2252

J   **New London,** Parker Street, WC2
tel 01-405 0072

C   **Open Space Theatre,** 303/307 Euston Road, NW1 *tel 01-387 6969*

I   **Palace,** Shaftesbury Avenue, W1
tel 01-437 6834

H   **Palladium,** Argyll Street, W1
tel 01-437 7373

I   **Phoenix,** Charing Cross Road, WC2
tel 01-836 8611

I   **Piccadilly,** Denman Street, W1
tel 01-437 4506

I   **Prince Edward,** Old Compton Street, W1 *tel 01-437 6877*

N   **Prince of Wales,** Coventry Street, W1
tel 01-930 8681

I   **Queen's,** Shaftesbury Avenue, W1
tel 01-734 1166

H   **Regent Theatre,** Regent Street, W1
tel 01-637 9863

V   **Royal Court,** Sloane Square, SW1
tel 01-730 1745

J   **Royal Opera House,** Covent Garden, WC2 *tel 01-240 1066*

J   **Royalty,** Portugal Street, WC2
tel 01-405 8004

I   **St Martin's,** West Street, WC2
tel 01-836 1443

O   **Savoy,** Strand, WC2 *tel 01-836 8888*

I   **Shaftesbury,** Shaftesbury Avenue, WC2
tel 01-836 6596

J   **Strand,** Aldwych, WC2
tel 01-836 2660

D   **Vanbrugh,** Malet Street, WC1
tel 01-580 7982

J   **Vaudeville,** Strand, WC2
tel 01-836 9988

R   **Victoria Palace,** Victoria Street, SW1
tel 01-834 1317

I   **Warehouse (Donmar),** Earlham Street, WC2 *tel 01-836 6808*

R   **Westminster,** Palace Street, SW1
tel 01-834 0283

N   **Whitehall,** Whitehall, SW1
tel 01-930 6692

I   **Windmill,** Gt Windmill Street, W1
tel 01-437 6312

I   **Wyndham's,** Charing Cross Road, WC2
tel 01-836 3028

Department Stores

Army and Navy Stores Ltd, 105 Victoria Street, SW1

Bourne and Hollingsworth Ltd, 116-128 Oxford Street, W1

Civil Service Stores, 423-427 Strand

Debenhams Ltd, Oxford Street, W1

Dickins and Jones Ltd, 224-244 Regent Street, W1

Fortnum and Mason Ltd, 181 Piccadilly, W1

Harrods Ltd, 87-135 Brompton Road, Knightsbridge, SW1

Harvey Nichols and Co Ltd, 109-125 Sloane Street, Knightsbridge, SW1

John Lewis and Co, 278-306 Oxford Street, W1

Marks and Spencer Ltd, 173 Oxford Street, W1
Marks and Spencer Ltd, 458 Oxford Street, Marble Arch, W1
Peter Jones, Sloane Square, SW1
Selfridges, 400 Oxford Street, W1
Swan and Edgar, 49 Regent Street, W1
Early closing day — most large stores open six days a week. Shops in the West End are open until 7.30pm on Thursday; shops in Knightsbridge, Sloane Square and King's Road are open until 7.30pm on Wednesday. A few large stores do not open on Saturday afternoon.

Markets

I **Berwick Street,** Soho, W1 (fruit and vegetables) (Monday to Saturday, Thursday morning only)

I **Earlham Street,** Holborn, WC2 (general and antiques) (Monday to Saturday)

D **Goodge Place,** W1 (general) (Monday to Saturday)

J **Jubilee Market,** Covent Garden, WC2 (general, fruit and vegetables) (Monday to Friday)

T **Lower Marsh,** The Cut, SE1 (general) (Monday to Saturday, Thursday morning only)

I **Rupert Street,** W1 (fruit and vegetables) (Monday to Saturday)

S **Strutton Ground,** SW1 (general) (Monday to Friday, Saturday morning)

X **Tachbrook Street,** SW1 (general) (Monday to Saturday)

Advertisers

H **Berni** Steak Bar

Centre Hotels:

D **Bedford Corner Hotel,** Bayley Street WC1

D **Bloomsbury Centre Hotel,** Coram Street, WC1

I **Ivanhoe Hotel,** Bloomsbury Street, WC1

I **Kenilworth Hotel,** Great Russell Street, WC1

C **Regent Centre Hotel,** Carburton Street, W1

S **St James Hotel,** Buckingham Gate SW1

E **Mercantile Credit,** Burne House, High Holborn, WC1

Trust Houses Forte Hotels

M **Browns Hotel,** Dover Street, W1

N **Cavendish Hotel,** Jermyn Street, SW1

G **Cumberland Hotel,** Marble Arch, W1

L **Grosvenor House Hotel,** Park Lane, W1

Q **Hyde Park Hotel,** Knightsbridge, SW1

J **Kingsley Hotel,** Bloomsbury Way, WC1

N **Quaglino's,** Bury Street, W1

I **Regent Palace Hotel,** Piccadilly Circus, W1

E **Russell Hotel,** Russell Square, WC1

C **St Georges Hotel,** Langham Place, W1

J **Strand Palace Hotel,** Strand, WC2

J **Waldorf Hotel,** Aldwych, WC2

H **Westbury Hotel,** New Bond Street, W1

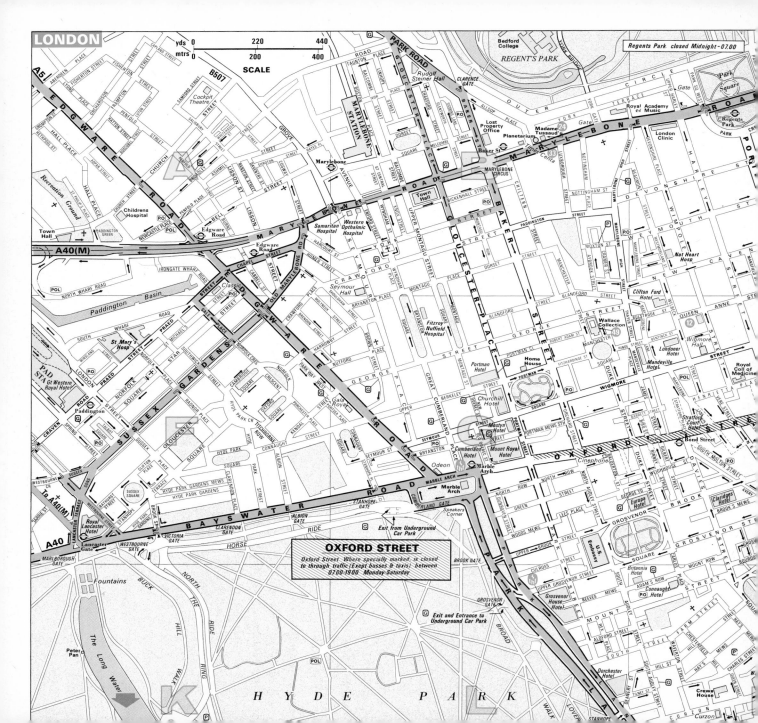

LONDON

yds 0   220   440
mtrs 0   200   400

SCALE

Regents Park closed Midnight–07.00

REGENT'S PARK

OXFORD STREET

Oxford Street. Where specially marked is closed
to through traffic (Exept busses & taxis) between
0700–1900 Monday Saturday

Exit from Underground
Car Park

Exit and Entrance to
Underground Car Park

Speakers
Corner

H Y D E   P A R K

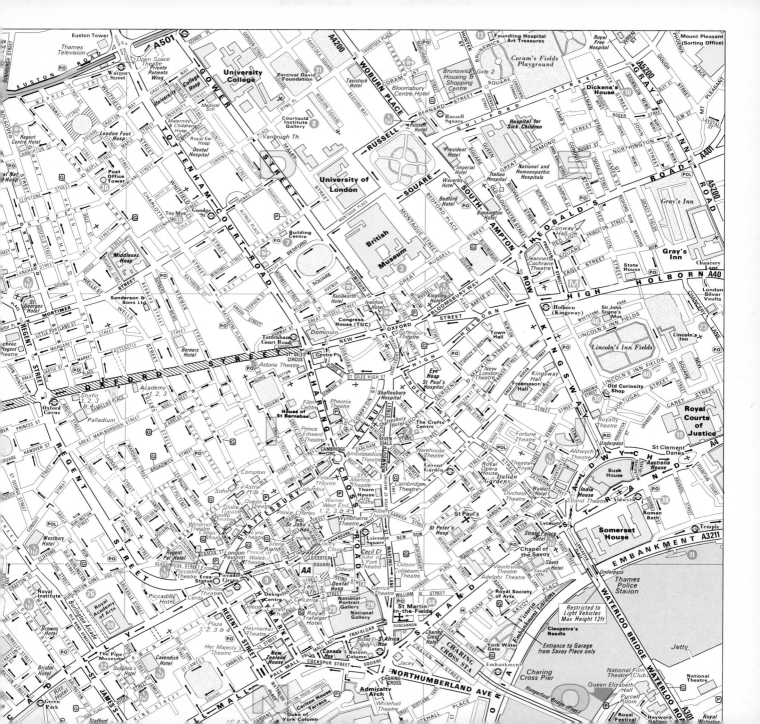

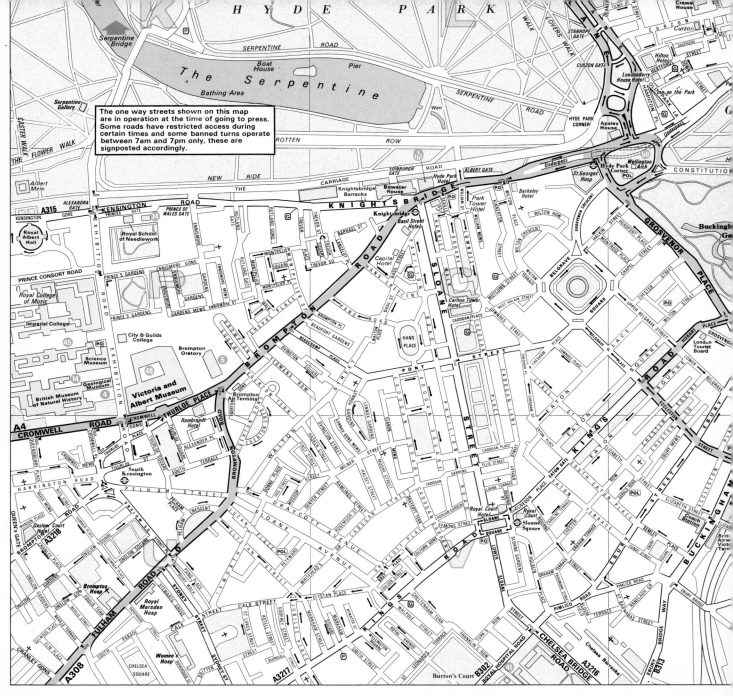

The one way streets shown on this map are in operation at the time of going to press. Some roads have restricted access during certain times and some banned turns operate between 7am and 7pm only, these are signposted accordingly.

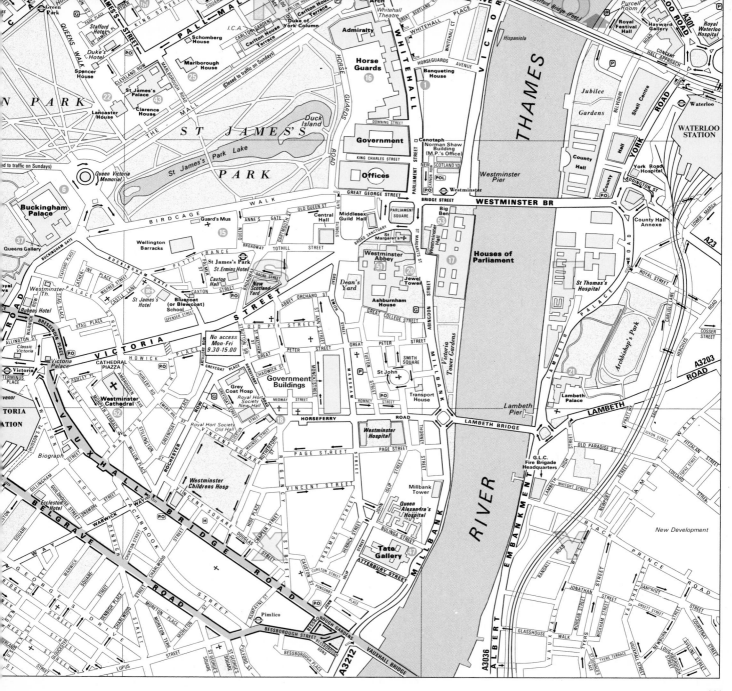

MANCHESTER

CENTRAL PLAN

F   **AA Service Centre** — St Ann's House, St Ann's Place *tel* **061-485 6155** 24-hour Breakdown Service *tel* **061-485 6299**

G *i*   **Tourist Information Centres** — County Hall Extension, Piccadilly Gardens *tel* **061-247 3111**

F(17) *i*   **Tourist Information Centre** — Town Hall *tel* **061-247 3111** (see also public buildings and places of interest)

Public buildings and places of interest

F(1)   **Art Gallery and Athenaeum** Housed in building of 1824 by Sir Charles Barry, and contains large collection of paintings, silver, ceramics etc.

B(2)   **Cathedral** Until 1847 the parish church, this chiefly 15th-C structure is in Perpendicular style. It features some outstanding woodwork, particularly in the Choir and is the widest medieval church in Britain.

F(3)   **Cenotaph and Garden of Remembrance**

F(4)   **Central Library** This was designed in 1934 in the form of a rotunda and is England's largest municipal library. In the basement is the Library Theatre.

B(5)   **Chetham's Hospital** A mainly 15th-C building, but parts date back to Norman times with modern additions. Now an independent grammar school. The free library founded 1653 claims to be the oldest in England.

E(6)   **City Exhibition Hall**

F(7)   **Cross Street Chapel** Originally built in 1697, this is the oldest nonconformist place of worship in Manchester.

F(8)   **Free Trade Hall** A fine building rebuilt in 1951 after severe bomb damage but retaining facade of 1856. This is the home of the Halle Orchestra.

F(9)   **John Ryland's University Library** Opened in 1899, the library houses a valuable collection of rare books, manuscripts and early bibles.

E(10)   **Liverpool Road Station (AM)** (not open). This was the Manchester terminus of the famous Liverpool and Manchester railway opened in 1830.

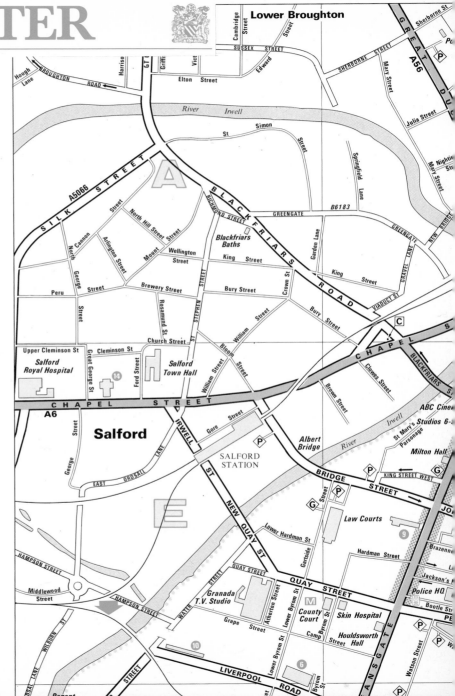

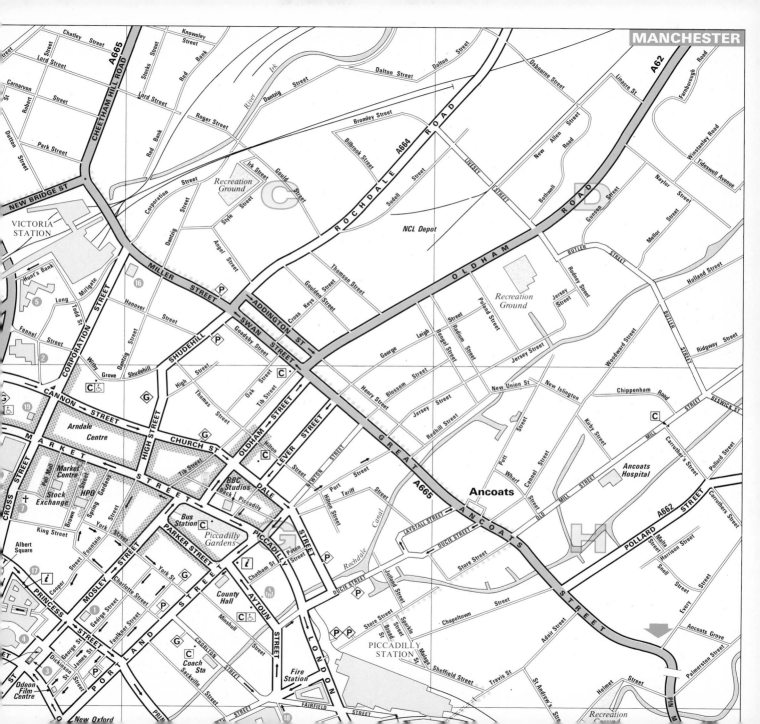

K(11) **North Western Museum of Science and Industry** Exhibits include steam and internal combustion engines, machine tools, electrical exhibits, paper-making, printing, and textile machinery.

F(12) **Royal Exchange** This includes the new Royal Exchange Theatre.

F(13) **St Anne's Church** An early 18th-C church in which de Quincey, the writer, was baptised. Notable items are a Queen Anne altar table and a fine oil painting of the *Descent from the Cross*.

E(14) **St John's Cathedral (RC)** Situated at Salford, this cathedral was rebuilt in 1848.

F(15) **St Mary's Church (RC)** Known as the 'Hidden Gem' because of its fine altar and hidden location.

C(16) **The New Century Hall**

F(17) **Town Hall** A building of 1877 in neo-Gothic style, with 280ft clock tower, on which the figures are represented by Lancashire roses and fleur-de-lis. The Council Chamber is housed in the Town Hall extension of 1938.

K(18) **University of Manchester Institute of Science and Technology**

F(19) **'Wellington' Inn** A picturesque half-timbered structure of the 14thC.

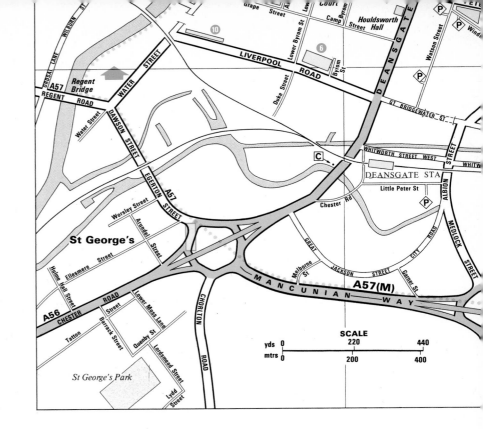

Hospitals

H **Ancoats Hospital,** Mill Street *tel 061-205 2204*

F **Manchester and Salford Skin Hospital,** Quay Street. *tel 061-834 4346*

E **Salford Royal Hospital,** Chapel Street *tel 061-834 8656*

Sport and Recreation

L **Ardwick Sports Centre,** Hyde Road

A **Blackfriars Baths,** Richmond Street

Theatres and Cinemas

L **ABC Cinema,** Ardwick Green *tel 061-237 1141*

F **ABC Cinema,** Deansgate *tel 061-832 2112*

F(4) **Library Theatre** *tel 061-236 7110* (see also public buildings and places of interest)

J **New Oxford Theatre,** Oxford Street *tel 061-236 8266*

F **Odeon Film Centre,** Oxford Street *tel 061-236 8264*

K **Royal Northern College of Music,** Oxford Road *tel 061-273 6283*

F(12) **Sixty-Nine Theatre Co Ltd,** Royal Exchange, St Ann's Square *tel 061-832 4877* (see also public buildings and places of interest)

J **Studios 1-5,** Oxford Road *tel 061-236 2437*

F **Studios 6-9,** Deansgate House, Deansgate *tel 061-834 3580*

Department Stores

Arndale Centre, Market Street and Corporation Street

Debenhams, Market Street

Kendal Milne, Deansgate

Lewis's, Mosley Street and Market Street

Marks and Spencer Ltd, Market Street and Corporation Street
Early closing day Wednesday

Markets

F **Market Centre,** Market Street

Advertisers

G **Berni** Hole in the Wall

F **Berni** Café Royal

E **Mercantile Credit**

G **THF** Grand Hotel

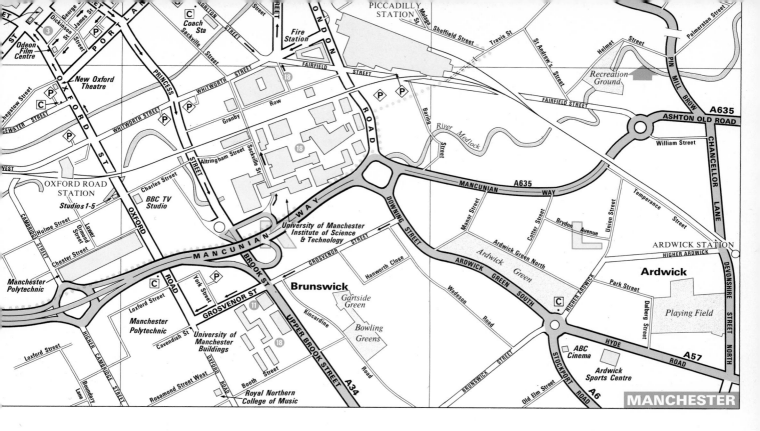

DISTRICT PLAN
Public buildings and places of interest

L(20) Belle Vue Leisure Park A banqueting, exhibition and entertainment centre.

K(21) Manchester Museum, The University. Contains exhibits of geology, natural history, archaeology, coins, stamps, aquarium and vivarium.

E(22) Monks Hall Museum 16th-C building with later additions, with permanent collection of Nasmyth machinery, paintings, ceramics and local bygones. Also temporary exhibitions.

(23) Ordsall Hall Museum Partly half-timbered manor house with later brick-built wing (1639), with Tudor Great Hall, Star Chamber with 14th-C features, Victorian farmhouse kitchen and social history displays.

K(24) Platt Hall Georgian Mansion of 1764, housing Gallery of English Costume.

C(25) Queen's Park Gallery Houses a permanent collection of pictures and sculpture and a museum of the Manchester Regiment and 14th/20th King's Hussars.

F(26) Salford Museum and Art Gallery Main features are a reproduction of a late 19th-C street, typical of a northern industrial town, and the L S Lowry collection of paintings.

E(27) Salford Science Museum Of greatest interest is the replica of a coal-mine.

F(28) Salford University

L(29) Slade Hall, Rusholme. A timber-framed house dating from the late 16thC with some 19th-C alterations.

K(30) Whitworth Art Gallery The collections include oil paintings, British and European water-colours, drawings, prints, textiles, tapestries and embroideries.

K(31) University

Foxdenton Hall, Chadderton. A 17th-C hall in Renaissance-style which was restored in 1965. 6m NE via Oldham Road A62 (D) and Rochdale Road A663.

Heaton Hall A Georgian house designed by James Wyatt in 1772 with contemporary furnishings, the Assheton Bennett Collection of 17th- and 18th-C Dutch and Flemish paintings and an organ of 1790. In Heaton Park 3½m N via Bury Road A665 (B).

Wythenshawe Hall A restored 16th- to 19th-C half-timbered manor house with 17th-C furniture, paintings, Royal Lancastrian pottery and prints. In Wythenshawe Park (Wythenshawe Road B5167), 5m S via Princess Road A5103 (N)

Hospitals

D   **Booth Hall Children's Hospital**, Charlestown Road, Manchester 9 *tel 061-740 8174*

O   **Christie Hospital and Holt Radium Institute**, Wilmslow Road, Manchester 20 *tel 061-445 8123*

K   **Dental Hospital of Manchester and Turner Dental School**, Bridgeford Street, Manchester 15 *tel 061-273 5252*

P   **Duchess of York Hospital for Babies**, Burnage Lane, Manchester 19 *tel 061-224 1427*

E   **Hope Hospital**, Eccles Old Road, Manchester 6 *tel 061-789 5252*

E   **Ladywell Hospital**, Eccles New Road, Manchester 5 *tel 061-789 2753*

K   **Manchester Royal Infirmary**, Oxford Road, Manchester 13 *tel 061-273 3300*

G   **Manchester Victoria Memorial Jewish Hospital**, Elizabeth Street, Manchester 8 *tel 061-834 0704*

D   **Monsall Hospital**, Monsall Road, Manchester 10 *tel 061-205 2393*

C   **North Manchester General Hospital, (Crumpsall)** Manchester 8 *tel 061-740 1444*

C   **North Manchester General Hospital, (Springfield)**, Crumpsall, Manchester 8 *tel 061-740 1444*

A   **Prestwich Mental Hospital**, Bury New Road, Manchester *tel 061-773 9121*

Wythenshawe Hall

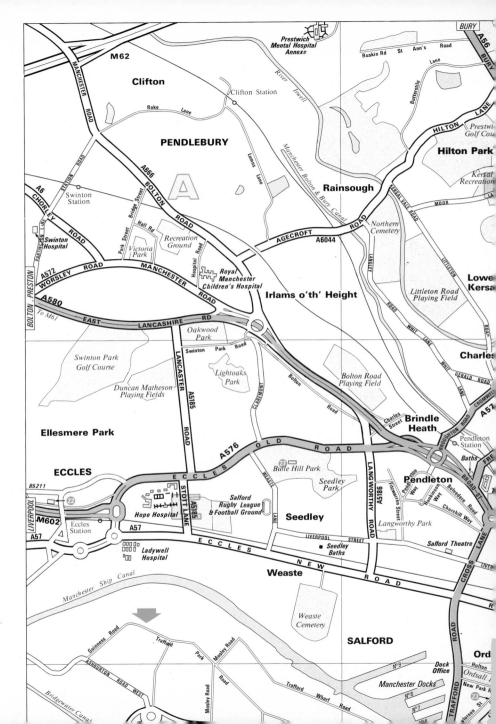

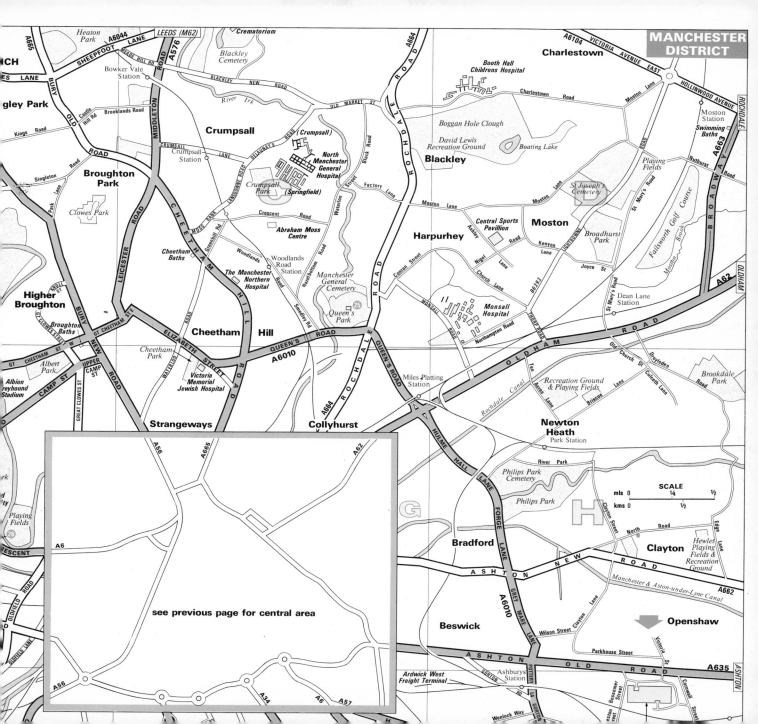

Heaton Park

A6044

SHEEPFOOT LANE

LEEDS (M62)

A576

Crematorium

Blackley Cemetery

A665

LANE

MEADE HILL RD

MIDDLETON ROAD

BLACKLEY NEW ROAD

River Irk

A6104 VICTORIA AVENUE EAST

Charlestown

HOLLINWOOD AVENUE

ROCHDALE

CH

A664

ROAD

Booth Hall Childrens Hospital

Charlestown Road

Moston Lane

Moston Station

Swimming Baths

A6663

Broughton Park

BURY

OLD

ROAD

Castle Hill Rd

Brooklands Road

Kings Road

Singleton Road

Park Lane

Clowes Park

Crumpsall

(Crumpsall)

Crumpsall Station

CRUMPSALL LANE

DELAUNAYS ROAD

OLD MARKET ST

Black Road

North Manchester General Hospital

Boggan Hole Clough

David Lewis Recreation Ground

Boating Lake

Blackley

Nuthurst Road

Playing Fields

St Joseph's Cemetery

BROADWAY

Falsworth Golf Course

CHEETHAM

HILL

ROAD

LEICESTER ROAD

MOSS BANK

Greenhill Rd

Crumpsall Park

(Springfield)

Crescent Road

Abraham Moss Centre

LANSDOWNE ROAD

Factory Lane

Waterloo Street

Moston Lane

Central Sports Pavillion

Moston

Broadhurst Park

St Mary's Road

Mostson Brook

A62

OLDHAM

Higher Broughton

KNOLL ST

BURY NEW ROAD

Cheetham Baths

Woodlands

The Manchester Northern Hospital

Woodlands Road Station

Hazelbottom Road

Smedley Rd

Manchester General Cemetery

Queen's Park

25

Harpurhey

Conran Street

Ashley Road

Kenyon Lane

B6393

Nigel Street

Church Lane

Joyce St

St Mary's Road

Dean Lane Station

OLDHAM ROAD

Monsall Hospital

MONSALL ROAD

THORP ROAD

Old Church St

Droylsden

Brookdale Park

GT CHEETHAM ST E

ELIZABETH STREET

GT CHEETHAM ST W

Broughton Baths

Cheetham Park

WATERLOO RD

Cheetham Hill

Victoria Memorial Jewish Hospital

QUEEN'S ROAD

A6010

A664

ROCHDALE ROAD

QUEEN'S ROAD

Miles Platting Station

Northampton Road

Ten Acres Lane

Recreation Ground & Playing Fields

Briscoe Lane

Coleshill Lane

Rochdale Canal

Edge Lane

Albion Greyhound Stadium

GT CLOWES ST

CAMP ST

GREAT CLOWES ST

UPPER CAMP ST

Albert Park

GT CHEETHAM ST

Strangeways

Collyhurst

Newton Heath

Park Station

Clayton

Hewlet Playing Fields & Recreation Ground

A662

GORTON

OLDFIELD

OLDFIELD RD

Playing Fields

26

CRESCENT

A6

A56

A665

A62

see previous page for central area

G

HULME HALL LANE

FORGE LANE

River Park

Philips Park Cemetery

Philips Park

Clayton Street

H

North Road

Clayton Lane

Edge Lane

SCALE

mls 0 ¼ ½

kms 0 ½

Bradford

ASHTON

NEW

ROAD

A6010

GREY MARE LANE

Beswick

Wilson Street

Clayton Lane

Manchester & Aston-under-Lyne Canal

A662

Openshaw

A56

A34

A6

A57

ASHTON

OLD

ROAD

A635

ASHTON

Ardwick West Freight Terminal

Ashburys Station

GORTON

POTTERY

LA GORTON

Parkhouse Street

Victoria St

Cornwall Street

Bessemer Street

Wenlock Way

A **Royal Manchester Children's Hospital,** Pendlebury, Manchester *tel* 061-794 4696

J **St Joseph's Hospital,** Carlton Road, Manchester 16 *tel* 061-226 2231

K **St Mary's Hospital,** Whitworth Park, Manchester 13 *tel* 061-224 9633

J **Stretford Memorial Hospital,** Seymour Grove, Manchester 16 *tel* 061-881 5353

A **Swinton Hospital,** 196 Partington Lane, Swinton *tel* 061-794 1284

C **The Manchester, Northern Hospital,** Cheetham Hill Road, Manchester 8 *tel* 061-740 2244

O **Withington Hospital,** Nell Lane, Manchester 20 *tel* 061-445 8111

Sport and Recreation

M **Ashton-on-Mersey Golf Course,** Church Lane, Sale

L **Belle Vue Greyhound Stadium**

L **Belle Vue Speedway**

D **Central Sports Pavilion,** Ashley Lane

N **Chorlton Golf Course,** Barlow Hall

D **Failsworth Golf Course,** Nuthurst Road, New Moston

P **Heaton Moor Golf Course,** Heaton Moor, Stockport

P **Houldsworth Golf Course,** Longford Road West

J **Lancashire County and Manchester Cricket Club,** Old Trafford

K **Manchester City Football Club,** Maine Road

J **Manchester United Football Club,** Old Trafford

B **Prestwich Golf Course,** Hilton Lane

N **Sale Golf Course,** Old Hall Road

E **Salford Football Club,** Willows Road

E **Salford Rugby Football Club,** Willows Road

J **Stretford Sports Centre,** Talbot Road

E **Swinton Park Golf Course,** East Lancashire Road

J **White City Greyhound Stadium**

Advertisers

P **Berni** The Kingsway

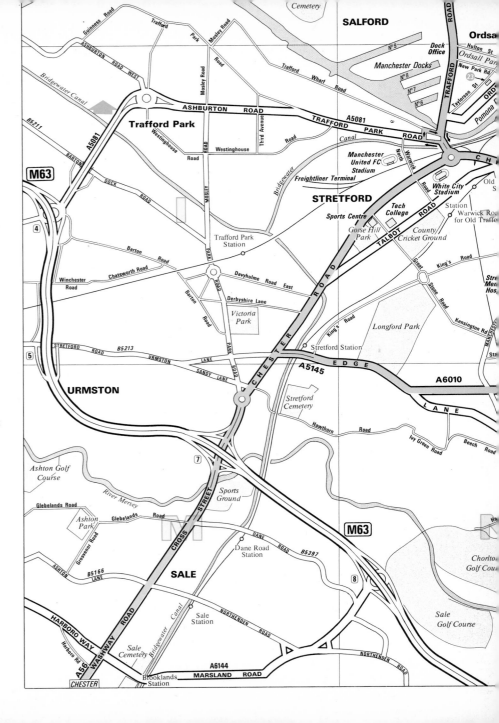

146

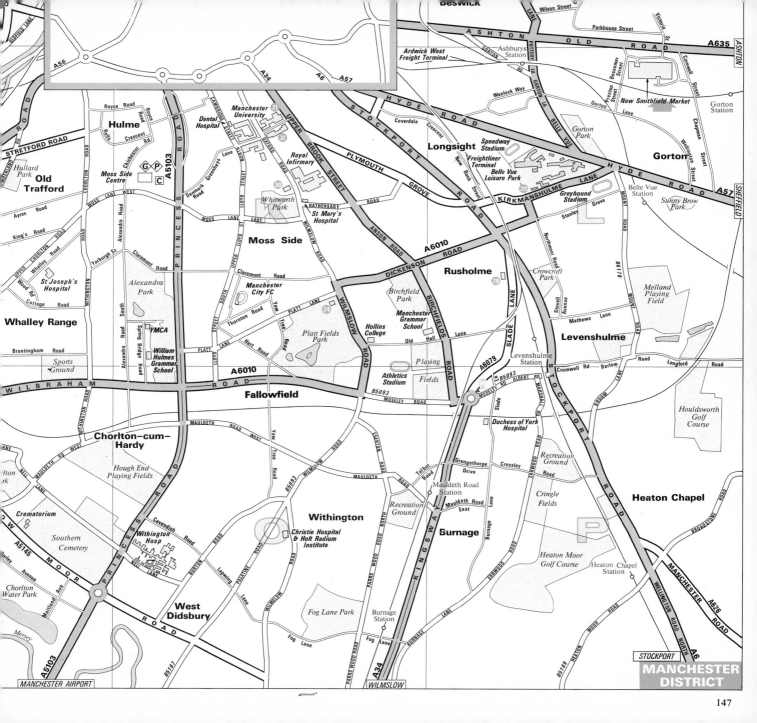

This is a map of the Manchester District showing streets, landmarks and areas.

Beswick

Wilson Street
Parkhouse Street
ASHTON OLD ROAD
A635
Victoria St
ASHTON
A56
A5103
A34
A6
A57

Hulme
Royce Road
Royce Road
Boyce Rd
Crescent
Chichester Rd

Dental Hospital
Manchester University

Ardwick West Freight Terminal
Ashburys Station
GORTON LA
GORTON LA
Wenlock Way
Bessemer Street
Preston Street
Cornwall Street
New Smithfield Market
Gorton Station
A635

HYDE ROAD
BELLE VUE STREET

Longsight
Gorton Park
Gorton
A57
SHEFFIELD

Old Trafford
Hullard Park
STRETFORD ROAD
BERTRAND RD

Moss Side Centre
G P
C

Royal Infirmary
Whitworth Park
St Mary's Hospital
HATHERSAGE

Speedway Stadium
Freightliner Terminal
Belle Vue Leisure Park
New Bank Street
KIRKMANSHULME LANE
20
Greyhound Stadium
Belle Vue Station
Sunny Brow Park
Stanley Grove

Ayres Road
King's Road
UPPER CHORLTON ROAD
Whalley

St Joseph's Hospital
Wood Road
College Road

Moss Side
Alexandra Park
Claremont Road
Yarburgh St
Claremont Road

Manchester City FC
Thornton Road
YMCA
William Hulmes Grammar School

Whalley Range
Brantingham Road

Alexandra Road
Spring Bridge Road
PLATT LANE
Platt Fields Park
Yew Tree Road
Hart Road
PLATT LANE
24

WILMSLOW ROAD
Hollins College
Birchfield Park
Manchester Grammar School
Old Hall
Lane

DICKENSON ROAD
A6010
ANSON ROAD
GROVE
STOCKPORT ROAD
PLYMOUTH GROVE
UPPER BROOK STREET

Rusholme
29
Crowcroft Park
Stovell Avenue
Mathews Lane
Northmoor Road
B6178
MOUNT ROAD
Melland Playing Field
Levenshulme
Houldsworth Golf Course

SLADE LANE

Sports Ground
WILBRAHAM ROAD
A6010
Fallowfield

Athletics Stadium
Playing Fields
B5093
MOSELEY ROAD

Levenshulme Station
Cromwell Rd
Barlow Road
Longford Road
BROOM LANE
STOCKPORT ROAD

A6079
B5093
Duchess of York Hospital
Slade Ln
MOSELEY RD
ALBERT RD
MARSHALL ROAD

Chorlton-cum-Hardy
MAULDETH ROAD WEST
Hough End Playing Fields
EGERTON ROAD
MAULDETH ROAD
WILMSLOW ROAD
Yew Tree Road
B5093

Crematorium
Southern Cemetery
A5145
Chorlton Water Park
Maitland Ave
Darley Avenue
PRINCESS ROAD
Cavendish Road
Withington Hosp
NELL LANE
BURTON ROAD
Lapwing Lane
PALATINE ROAD
WILMSLOW ROAD

Withington
Christie Hospital & Holt Radium Institute
Recreation Ground
Mauldeth Road Station
Mauldeth Road East
Grangethorpe Drive
Crossley Road
Recreation Ground
Cringle Fields
Talbot Road
Burnage
KINGSWAY
ERIWOOD ROAD
BURNAGE LANE

Heaton Chapel
P

West Didsbury
Fog Lane Park
Fog Lane
Burnage Station
Burnage Lane
Fog Lane
Heaton Moor Golf Course
Heaton Chapel Station
MANCHESTER ROAD
WELLINGTON ROAD NORTH
BROADSTONE ROAD
A626

A5103
MANCHESTER AIRPORT
B5167
Mersey
A34
WILMSLOW
PARRS WOOD ROAD
B5169
HEATON MOOR ROAD

STOCKPORT
A6
MANCHESTER DISTRICT

147

C	AA Road Service Centre (107) — Wilson Street *tel 246832*
G [i]	Tourist Information Centre — 125 Albert Road *tel 245750*

Public buildings and places of interest

J(1)	**Art Gallery** Contains a steadily growing collection of paintings including some good, contemporary British paintings. Also programme of monthly changing exhibitions.
C(2)	**Cathedral (RC)** The Cathedral is the see of a Roman Catholic bishop and contains a fine, canopied pulpit.
N(3)	**Dorman Museum** Recently extended to become a small arts centre and containing a permanent collection illustrating the geology, ecology and natural history of the region.
G(4)	**Teesside Polytechnic**
G(5)	**Town Hall and Municipal Buildings**

Hospitals

M	**Middlesbrough General Hospital,** Ayresome Green Lane *tel 83133*
K	**Middlesbrough Maternity Hospital,** Park Road North *tel 245156*
F	**North Riding Infirmary,** Newport Road *tel 246002*
M	**West Lane Hospital** *tel 87736*

Sport and Recreation

O	**Albert Park** — Bowling Greens, Tennis Courts and Skating Rink
G	**Central Baths,** Gilkes Street
P	**Clairville Stadium (Athletics)**
N	**Middlesbrough Football Club,** Ayresome Park

Cleveland Park Stadium Stockton Road (Greyhound Racing and Speedway) 1½m SW via Newport Road A66 (I) and Stockton Road

Prissick Outdoor Sports Centre, Marton Road 2½m S via Marton Road A172 (P)

Theatres and Cinemas

G	**ABC Cinema,** Linthorpe Road *tel 247400*
N	**Little Theatre,** The Avenue *tel 85181* ½m S via The Avenue
G	**Odeon Cinema,** Corporation Road *tel 242888*

Department Stores

Baums Department Store, 89 Newport Road
Binns Ltd, 37 Linthorpe Road
Debenhams, The Corner, 1 Newport Road
Marks and Spencer Ltd, 25 Linthorpe Road
Upton E and Sons Ltd, 32 Southfield Road
Wright and Co Ltd, Tower House
Early closing day Wednesday

Markets

G	**The Arcade,** Grange Road (Saturday)

Advertisers

C	**Mercantile Credit**

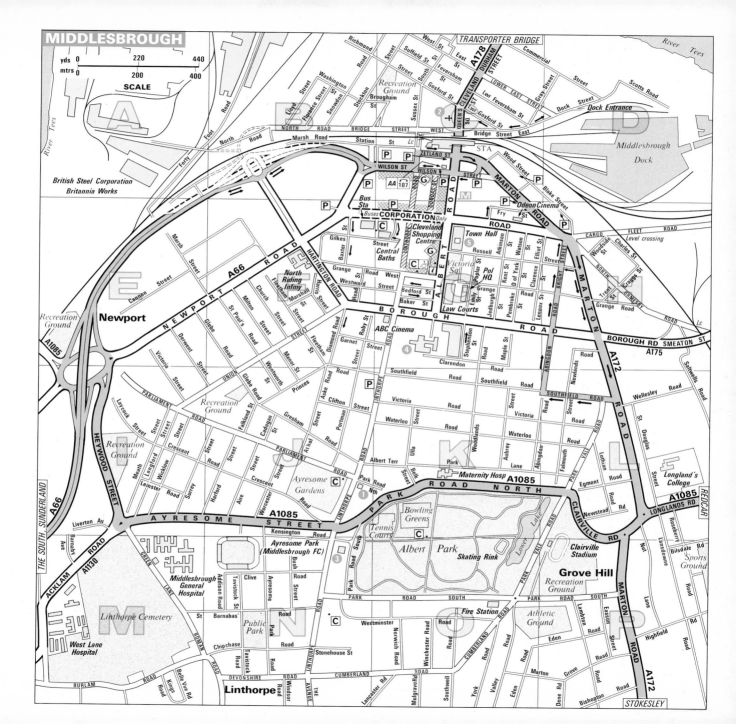

MIDDLESBROUGH

SCALE
yds 0 — 220 — 440
mtrs 0 — 200 — 400

River Tees

River Tees

TRANSPORTER BRIDGE

British Steel Corporation
Britannia Works

Middlesbrough Dock

Dock Entrance

Commercial Street
Scotts Road

West St
Richmond Street
Suffield St
East St
Feversham Street
South St
Gosford St
Sussex St
Lwr Feversham St
Lwr Gosford St
Gray Street
Dock Street
Blake Street

Recreation Ground
Brougham

Washington St
Florence Street
Snowdon
Stockton St
North Road
Marsh Road
Station St
Bridge Street West
Bridge Street East

A178
DURHAM STREET
QUEEN'S CLEVELAND ST
LOWER EAST STREET
Wood Street
MARTON ROAD

2

STA

ZETLAND ST
WILSON ST
WILSON ST

P P

AA 107

Bus Sta
Buses   CORPORATION   Only

Cleveland Shopping Centre
C

Odeon Cinema
Fry St

CARGO   FLEET   ROAD
Level crossing
Woodside St
Charles St
Krags St
NORTH ORMESBY ROAD

Newport

A66 NEWPORT ROAD

HARTINGTON ROAD

North Riding Infmy
Fleetham St
Marshall St
Harris Street

Gilkes Street
Baxter Street
Central Baths
Grange Road
Westward Road
Head St

BOROUGH

Town Hall
5
Russell St
Atkinson St
Watson St
Elliot St
Victoria Sq
Poplar St
Kent St
D of York
Clarence
Grange Road
Emily St
Jedburgh St
Pembroke St
Lennox St

ALBERT ROAD
BRIGHT STREET
Trent St
Grange Road

BOROUGH ROAD SMEATON ST
A175
A172

Recreation Ground
A1085

Cannon Street
Marsh Street

Victoria Street
Milton Street
Church Street
St Paul's Road
Derwent Street
Globe Road

UNION STREET
Wentworth Street
Manor St
Fleetham St
Princes

Diamond Road
Ruby St
ABC Cinema
4
Garnet Street
Stephenson St
Clarendon Rd
Maple St

Law Courts
Abingdon Road

Southfield Road
Newlands Road

PARLIAMENT ROAD

Recreation Ground

Laycock Street
Meath St
Longland St
Wicklow St
Leinster Road
Falkland Street
Cadogan St
Crescent
Surrey St
Harford St
Aire St
Worcester St
Aske Road
Clifton Street
Portman
Athol
Gresham Street

LINTHORPE ROAD
Park Road
P

Victoria Street
Waterloo Road
Albert Terr

Ulla St
Woodlands Rd
Aubrey St
Abingdon
Falmouth

Victoria
Waterloo
Park Lane

Wellesley Road
St Douglas
Iothian Road
Egmont Rd
Newstead Rd

Longland's College

A1085
REDCAR

HEYWOOD STREET

Recreation Ground

Ayresome Gardens
C
1
Nth

PARK ROAD NORTH

Maternity Hosp
A1085

LONGLANDS RD
CLAIRVILLE RD

THE SOUTH, SUNDERLAND
A66
A1130 ACKLAM ROAD

Liverton Av
Barnaby Ave

AYRESOME STREET
A1085

Kensington Road

Ayresome Park
(Middlesbrough FC)
3

Bowling Greens
C
Tennis Courts
Albert Park
Skating Rink
Lower Lake

Clairville Stadium

Grove Hill
Recreation Ground

Bilsdale Rd
Lansdowne Rd
Roseberry Rd
Sports Ground

Middlesbrough General Hospital

Linthorpe Cemetery

West Lane Hospital

GREEN LANE
Tavistock St
Clive St
Ayresome Street
Bush St
Addison Road

Barnabas' Rd
Chipchase Road
Public Park
Stonehouse St

ROMAN ROAD
Barnabas'

Westminster Road
Norwich Road
C

Fire Station

Athletic Ground

PARK ROAD SOUTH

PARK VALE ROAD
CUMBERLAND ROAD
Cumberland Rd

MARTON ROAD
A172

BURLAM ROAD
Kings Road
Belle Vue Rd
DEVONSHIRE ROAD
Windsor Road
LINTHORPE ROAD
CUMBERLAND ROAD
THE AVENUE
Lancaster Rd
Mulgrave Rd
Southwell Rd
York Rd
Valley Rd
Eden Rd
Marton Rd
Grove Rd
Dene Rd
Bishopton Rd

Linthorpe

Highfield Rd
Easson Rd
Lambton Rd

STOKESLEY
A172

| E | **AA Service Centre** — 13 Princess Square *tel 610111* |
| E(3) | **Tourist Information Centre** — City Information Service, Central Library, Princess Square *tel 610691* (see also public buildings and places of interest) |

Public buildings and places of interest

H(1)	**All Saints' Church** A rebuilt, 18th-C church.
H(2)	**Black Gate** The 13th-C gatehouse now houses the Bagpipe Museum which displays over 100 sets of English, Irish, Scottish, European and Egyptian pipes.
E(3)	**Central Library, Northern Arts Gallery and Tourist Information Centre**
G(4)	**City Walls** Slight remains of the 14th-C city walls are still to be seen.
E(5)	**Civic Centre**
D(6)	**Eldon Square Sports Centre and Shopping Precinct**
H(7)	**Guildhall and Merchants' Court** The Guildhall, dating from 1658, was recased in 1796. The adjoining Merchants' Court contains a 17th-C chimney piece.
B(8)	**Hancock Museum** One of the finest natural history museums in England. Other collections include geological specimens and insects.
H(9)	**John George Joicey Museum (Holy Jesus Hospital)** An almshouse founded in 1681 with displays of arms and armour, period rooms and local history.
E(10)	**Laing Art Gallery and Museum** Armour, costumes, local history etc on display with British oil paintings from the 17thC onwards.
B(11)	**Museum of Science and Engineering** Exhibits relate to the development of the transport, mining and ship-building industries in the north east.
H(12)	**Plummer Tower Museum** The restored tower, part of the ancient city walls, is now a museum.
B(13)	**Royal Grammar School**
D(14)	**St Andrew's Church** A 13th- to 14th-C church, the oldest in the city. The font is 15th-C.
G(15)	**St John's Church** This 13th- to 14th-C church has a fine 17th-C pulpit.

G(16)	**St Mary's RC Cathedral** Designed by Pugin in 1844.
H(17)	**St Nicholas' Cathedral** Dating mainly from the 14th and 15thCs, this former parish church gained cathedral status in 1882. The crown spire, 194ft high, is surmounted by an open lantern on flying buttresses. Inside, the knave and choir are 14th-C.
H(18)	**The Keep (Castle)** The 12th-C keep of the castle is now a museum.
H(19)	**Trinity House** An early 18th-C chapel and hall is the main feature of interest.
B(20)	**University** In the Quadrangle, the Museum of Antiquities displays Roman remains. The Hatton Gallery contains mainly 14th- to 18th-C European paintings. The Greek Museum contains a collection of pottery, painted vases, bronzes and armour and weapons. The Mining Museum has miscellaneous mining relics on display.

Hospitals

B	**Fleming Memorial Hospital,** Great North Road, Jesmond *tel 813257*
B	**Princess Mary Maternity Hospital,** Great North Road *tel 811312*
A	**Royal Victoria Infirmary,** Queen Victoria Road *tel 25131*

The Tyne bridges

Newcastle General Hospital, Westgate Road *tel 38811* 1¼m W via Westgate Road A6115 (D)

Sport and Recreation

D	**Newcastle United FC,** S James Park
E	**Northumberland Baths,** Northumberland Road
C	**Northumberland County Cricket Club,** Osborne Avenue

North Durham Cricket Ground, Prince Consort Road, Gateshead ¾m S via A6127 (H)

Theatres and Cinemas

E	**ABC Cinema,** Haymarket *tel 23345*
G	**ABC 1 & 2,** Westgate Road *tel 610618*
G	**New Tyne Theatre,** Westgate Street *tel 21551*
E	**Odeon Cinema,** Pilgrim Street *tel 23248*
E	**Queens Cinerama Theatre,** Northumberland Place *tel 24481*
G	**Studios 1, 2, 3 & 4,** Waterloo Street *tel 610151*
H	**Theatre Royal,** Grey Street *tel 22061*
E	**Tyneside Film Theatre,** Pilgrim Street *tel 21507*
E	**University Theatre,** Barras Bridge *tel 23421*

Department Stores

Bainbridges, Eldon Square Precinct
Binns Ltd, Market Street
Farnons Department Store, 12 Nun Street
Fenwick Ltd, Northumberland Street
Marks and Spencer Ltd, 83 Northumberland Street
Issac Walton, Grainger Street
S Wenger, 30 Grainger Street
Early closing day Monday and Wednesday

Markets

G	**Bigg Market** (Tuesday, Thursday and Saturday) (general)
D	**Grainger Market,** Grainger Street (Daily) (general)
D	**Clayton Street** (Daily) (fish, plants and vegetables)
H	**Quayside Market,** Quayside (Sunday mornings) (general)

Advertisers

| C | **Mercantile Credit** |
| E | **Centre** Newcastle Centre Hotel |

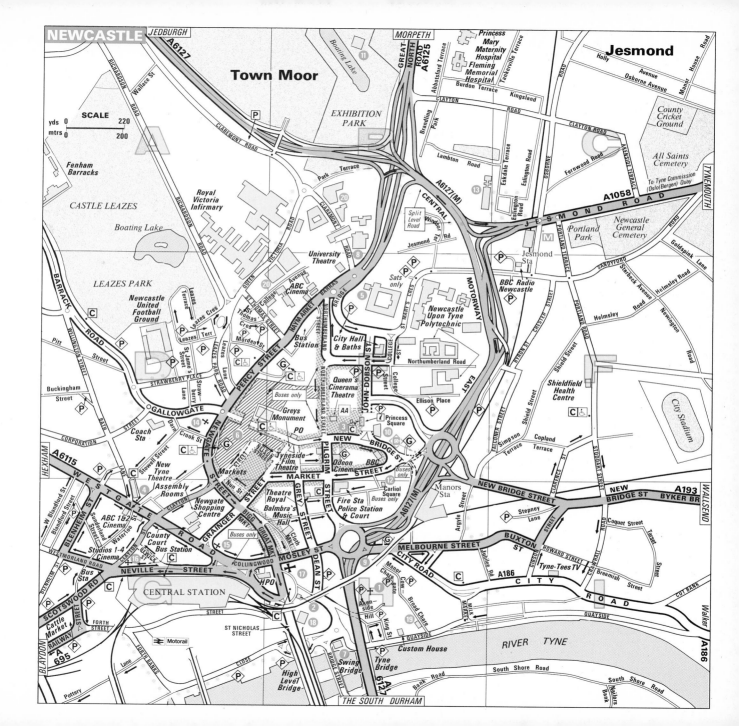

NEWQUAY

E ⓘ **Tourist Information Centre** — Morfa Hall, Cliff Road *tel 2119/2716*

Public buildings and places of interest

A(1) **Ancient Huer's Hut** Formerly used by fishermen watching for pilchard shoals.

E(2) **Municipal Offices and Public Library**

I(3) **Trenance Gardens, Zoo and Amusement Park** The gardens with their sheltered position are particularly favourable for the cultivation of uncommon flowers and shrubs and over 300 unusual varieties are contained here. The zoo, covering over eight acres of landscaped grounds, has an interesting selection of animals, birds and reptiles. The park also contains pitch and putt, driving range, boating lake and miniature railway.

Trerice Manor (NT) A small Cornish manor house, rebuilt 1571-73 with an elaborate facade, displaying unusual curly gables. The interior includes some fine plaster ceilings and fireplaces. 3m SE via Henver Road A392 and A3058 (F)

Hospitals

I **Newquay and District Hospital**, St Thomas Road *tel 3883*

E **Newquay Health Centre**, St Thomas Road *tel 3110*

Sport and Recreation

D **Dry Ice-Skate Rink**, Tower Road

I **Golf Driving Range and Toboggan Run**

H **Newquay Association Football Club**, Clevedon Road

D **Newquay Golf Club**

I **Pitch and Putt Golf Course**

F **Sports Centre** (Venue of Newquay Cricket Club and Newquay Hornets Rugby Football Club)

Theatres and Cinemas

F **Astor Cinema**, Narrowcliff *tel 2023*

E **Camelot Cinema**, The Crescent *tel 4222*

E **Cosy Nook Theatre**, Towan Parade *tel 3365*

E **Newquay Theatre** *tel 3379*

Department Stores

Dingle E and Co Ltd, 29 Bank Street
Early closing day Wednesday but most shops remain open during the summer months.

Trerice Manor

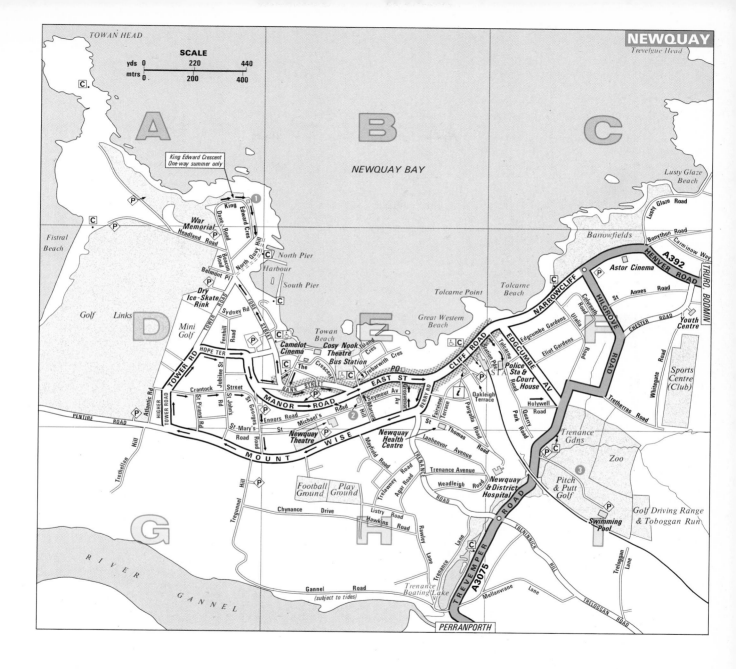

TOWAN HEAD

SCALE

yds 0   220   440
mtrs 0   200   400

A

B

C

NEWQUAY BAY

Lusty Glaze Beach

King Edward Crescent
One-way summer only

Fistral Beach

War Memorial

King Edward Cres

Headland Road

Dane Road

Beacon Road

North Quay Hill

Belmont Pl

North Pier

Harbour

South Pier

Tolcarne Point

Tolcarne Beach

Barrowfields

Lusty Glaze Road

Bonython Road

Carminow Way

A392

HENVER ROAD

TRURO
BODMIN

Astor Cinema

St Annes Road

NARROWCLIFF

Colvreath Road

Ulalia Road

Chester Road

Whitgate Road

Youth Centre

Dry Ice-Skate Rink

Sydney Rd

TOWER ROAD

TOLVE STREET

Golf Links

Mini Golf

Fernhill Road

HOPE TER

JS St

Crantock Street

Jubilee St

St Pirans Rd

St Georges

St Johns Rd

Camelot Cinema

BANK STREET

MANOR ROAD

The Crescent

Cosy Nook Theatre
Bus Station

Towan Beach

Island Cres

Treharwith Cres

Great Western Beach

EAST ST

CLIFF ROAD

STATION

Trebarwith Cres

PO

Station Rd

Edgcumbe Gardens

Eliot Gardens

EDGCUMBE AV

HILGROVE ROAD

SPORTS CENTRE (Club)

Tretherras Road

Police Sta & Court House

Holywell Road

Oakleigh Terrace

Trenance Gdns

Zoo

Seymour Av

Marcus Hill

Gover Hill

St Thomas Road

Fairview Terrace

St Michael's

Newquay Theatre

Ennors Road

St Marys Road

MOUNT WISE

Berry Rd

Pargolla Road

Quarry Park Road

Lanhenvor Avenue

Newquay Health Centre

Marfield Road

Trebarwey Road

Agar Road

TRENANCE ROAD

Trenance Avenue

Headleigh Road

Rawley Road

Pitch & Putt Golf

Newquay & District Hospital

Swimming Pool

Golf Driving Range & Toboggan Run

ATLANTIC Rd

HIGHER TOWER ROAD

PENTIRE ROAD

Trethellan Hill

Tregunnel Hill

Chynance Drive

Football Ground

Play Ground

Listry Road

Hawkins Road

Trenance Lane

Trevemper Road

A3075

Trenance Lane

Trelawney Lane

Trenance Boating Lake

Gannel Road
(subject to tides)

Mellanvrane Lane

Trethiggey Lane

TRELOGGAN ROAD

R I V E R   G A N N E L

PERRANPORTH

D

E

F

G

H

I

153

CENTRAL PLAN

G   **AA Service Centre** — 67 Abington Street *tel 37411*

K [i]   **Tourist Information Centre** — 21 St Giles Street *tel 34881*

Public buildings and places of interest

J(1)   **All Saints Church** Mainly a 17th-C classical building with portico of 1701 and decorated ceiling, and retaining its tower of the 14thC. It contains a statue of Charles II who provided timber for rebuilding.

J(2)   **Central Museum and Art Gallery** Contains fine collection of footwear through the ages with a reproduction of a cobbler's shop. Also local archaeological finds, English ceramics and fine arts.

J(3)   **County Hall** A fine building of 1682, displaying carved plaster ceilings.

I(4)   **Cromwell's House of Hazelrigg Mansion** A house dating from 1662.

K(5)   **Gramophone Record Library**

J(6)   **Guildhall** A Victorian Gothic building of 1861, decorated with figures from town history.

G(7)   **Library**

G(8)   **St Giles Church** The tower is Norman and 17th-C, the rest of the building being in Perpendicular style, enlarged in 1857.

J(9)   **St John Baptist Church (RC)** Part of the 12th-C Hospital of St John survives here.

I(10)   **St Peter's Church** Preserves fine and richly-carved Norman work, notably the tower arch and pier capitals. The exterior is largely 17th-C.

F(11)   **St Sepulchre's Church** One of England's four round churches, dating from the 12thC. It contains a 6ft-high brass of 1640.

K(12)   **St Thomas a Becket's Well** (site of).

F(13)   **Welsh House** This house dates back to 1595 and escaped the fire of 1675.

Hospitals

L   **General Hospital,** Billing Road *tel 34700*

D   **St Edmund's Hospital,** Wellingborough Road *tel 36125*

Sport and Recreation

P   **Midsummer Meadow Recreation Ground and Bathing Pool**

G   **Swimming Baths,** Upper Mounts

Theatres and Cinemas

G   **ABC Cinema,** Abington Square *tel 35839*

H   **Arts Theatre,** Pytchley Street *tel 401056*
     Masque Theatre, *tel 711284* (performances normally at Art Theatre)

K   **Repertory Theatre,** Guildhall Road *tel 32533*

Department Stores

Debenhams Ltd, The Drapery
Marks and Spencer Ltd, Abington Street
Rayboulds, 89 Kettering Road
Early closing day Thursday

Markets

J   **Cattle Market,** Victoria Promenade (Saturday)

F   **Open Market,** Market Square (Wednesday, Friday and Saturday)

Advertisers

G   **Berni** The Wedgwood

G   **Mercantile Credit**

DISTRICT PLAN
Public buildings and places of interest

G(14)   **Abington Park — Museum, Church of St Peter and St Paul and Museum of the Northamptonshire Regiment** The former 15th- to 18th-C manor house, where Shakespeare's grand-daughter lived, contains collections of domestic items, toys, local history, pottery and porcelain.
The nearby Church of St Peter and St Paul contains the grave of Shakespeare's grand-daughter Elisabeth.
The Museum of the Northamptonshire Regiment displays a pictorial history of the regiment from 1741 to 1960.

F(15)   **Cathedral of Our Lady and St Thomas (RC)** This is the centre of the largest Roman Catholic Diocese in England.

G(16)   **County Cricket and Football Ground**

J(17)   **Delapre Abbey** Mainly a 17th-C house on site of former abbey, with a south facade of the mid 18thC and a library added c1820. It now contains the Northamptonshire Record Office.

G(18)   **District Council and Development Offices, Cliftonville House**

J(19)   **Queen Eleanor Cross** This is one of the three surviving 13th-C crosses erected by Edward I in 1290 in memory of Eleanor, his queen.

G(20)   **St Matthew's Church** A notable modern structure containing a Madonna and Child by Henry Moore and a Crucifixion by Graham Sutherland.

H   **Billing Mill Museum** Billing Aquadrome. A 19th-C watermill with a photographic gallery of all the well-known mills of the Nene Valley.

Hospitals

B   **Harborough Road Hospital,** *tel 845509*

C   **Manfield Orthopaedic Hospital,** Kettering Road *tel 491121*

F   **Margaret Spencer Hospital,** Dallington *tel 51125*

E   **Princess Marina Hospital,** Weedon Road, Upton *tel 52323*

G   **St Andrew's Mental Hospital,** Billing Road *tel 21311*

E   **St Crispin Hospital,** Duston *tel 52323*

G   **St John's Hospital,** Weston Favell *tel 401243*

Sport and Recreation

H   **Billing Aquadrome** — water skiing, boating marina, swimming, fishing

K   **Casuals Rugby Football Club,** Rushmill's House, Bedford Road

G(16)   **Northampton County Cricket and Football Club** (see also public buildings and places of interest)

J   **Delapre Golf Complex**

B   **Kingsthorpe Golf Course**

D   **Lings Forum,** Weston Favell Centre — swimming pool etc.

C   **Northampton Golf Course**

A   **Northamptonshire County Golf Club,** Church Brampton

G   **Saints Cricket and Hockey Club,** Birchfield Road East

F   **Saints Rugby Club,** Sturtridge Pavilion, Franklin Gardens

Overstone Solarium — swimming pool, fishing, park etc. 5m NE via A43 (C)

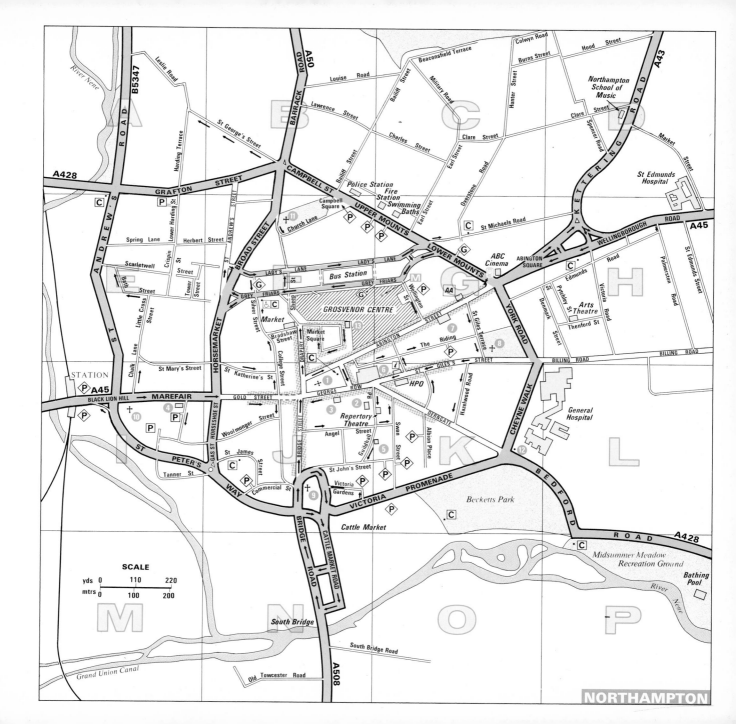

NORTHAMPTON

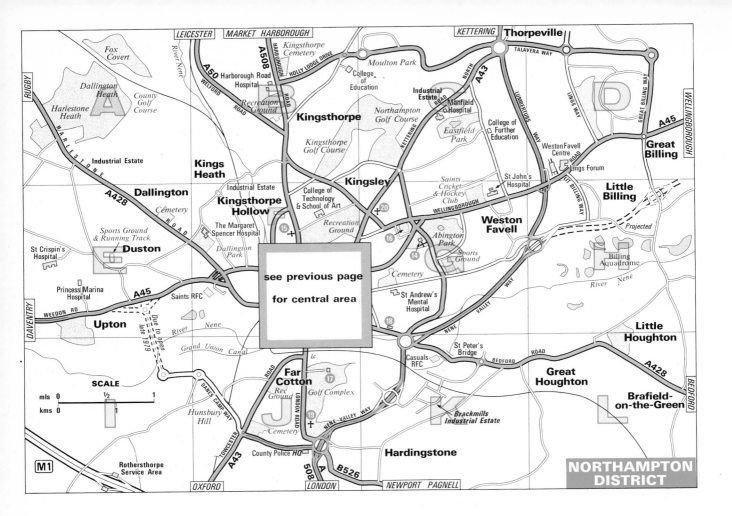

NORTHAMPTON DISTRICT

see previous page for central area

LEICESTER MARKET HARBOROUGH KETTERING

Thorpeville

A50 A508 HOLLY LODGE DRIVE TALAVERA WAY

River Nene

Kingsthorpe Cemetery

Fox Covert

Moulton Park

GREAT BILLING WAY WELLINGBOROUGH

Dallington Heath

County Golf Course

Harborough Road Hospital

College of Education

Industrial Estate

Manfield Hospital

A43 NORTH ROAD

LINGS WAY

A45

Harlestone Heath

Recreation Ground

Kingsthorpe

Northampton Golf Course

Eastfield Park

College of Further Education

Weston Favell Centre

Great Billing

Industrial Estate

Kingsthorpe Golf Course

KETTERING ROAD

Lings Forum

LIT BILLING WAY

Little Billing

HARLESTONE ROAD

Kings Heath

A428

Dallington

Industrial Estate

Kingsley

Saints Cricket & Hockey Club

St John's Hospital

WELLINGBOROUGH ROAD

Projected

Cemetery

College of Technology & School of Art

20

Weston Favell

River Nene

Sports Ground & Running Track

Kingsthorpe Hollow

15

16

Abington Park

Billing Aquadrome

The Margaret Spencer Hospital

Recreation Ground

St Crispin's Hospital

Dallington Park

14

Sports Ground

Duston

Princess Marina Hospital

A45

WEEDON RD

Saints RFC

18

St Andrew's Mental Hospital

NENE

VALLEY WAY

Little Houghton

Upton

Due to open late 1979

River Nene

Grand Union Canal

St Peter's Bridge

BEDFORD ROAD

Great Houghton

A428

BEDFORD

DAVENTRY

SCALE

mls 0 ½ 1
kms 0 1

lc

Casuals RFC

Brafield-on-the-Green

Far Cotton

17

Golf Complex

Rec Ground

LONDON ROAD

DANES CAMP WAY

Hunsbury Hill

19

Cemetery

NENE VALLEY WAY

Brackmills Industrial Estate

M1

Rothersthorpe Service Area

TOWCESTER

A43

County Police HQ

508

A

B526

Hardingstone

OXFORD LONDON NEWPORT PAGNELL

RUGBY

156

NORWICH

CENTRAL PLAN

G 🛈   **Tourist Information Centre** — Augustine Steward House, 14 Tombland *tel 20679*

Public buildings and places of interest

J(1)   **Assembly House** A restored Georgian building, now a centre for many of the City's arts and cultural societies, and including the Noverre cinema.

H(2)   **Bishop Bridge** This 13th-C bridge is the oldest in Norwich and one of the oldest in Britain. Visible upstream is the Cow Tower, a northern remnant of the city walls.

G(3)   **Bishop's Palace** A 12th- to 15th-C house.

P(4)   **Boom Towers** These are relics of the former city walls, and nearby on Carrow Hill are some more substantial remains of the 14th-C walls and Black Tower.

F(5)   **Bridewell Museum** Local industries and rural crafts contained in a 14th-C flint-faced house.

J(6)   **Castle and Gardens** The massive Norman castle keep, much restored, contains a museum and art gallery.

G(7)   **Cathedral** A norman and later building, with a lofty, decorated spire. The Norman nave, Saxon Bishop's throne, 15th-C choir stalls, beautiful cloisters and a wealth of carved roof bosses are all notable. In Life's Green is the grave of Nurse Edith Cavell, killed by the Germans in 1915.

J(8)   **Central Library and American War Memorial**

J(9)   **City Hall** An imposing edifice built in 1938 and considered to be one of the best designed municipal buildings in England.

F(10)   **Elm Hill** Perhaps the most picturesque street of old houses in the city. Includes the thatched 15th-C Briton's Arms.

G(11)   **Erpingham Gate** An old gateway of 1420, leading to the Cathedral precincts.

G(12)   **Ethelbert Gate** Built in 1272, with a chapel above the archway.

G(13)   **Great Hospital** Founded in 1249 and incorporating the parish church of St Helen. Other buildings include the cloister and a house of 1752 by Thomas Ivory.

J(14)   **Guildhall** A picturesque structure of chequered flints dating from 1407.

G(15)   **King Edward VI Grammar School** Established in 1553. Among its most famous pupils was Admiral Lord Nelson.

F(16)   **Maddermarket Theatre** A well-known reconstruction of an Elizabethan-style theatre housed in a former Roman Catholic church.

G(17)   **Maid's Head** A hotel, dating back in part to the 15thC, which has an interesting interior including Norman, Tudor, Jacobean and Georgian work.

O(18)   **Music House** The oldest dwelling-house in Norwich, part of which dates from the 12thC.

F(19)   **Octagon Chapel** A fine building of 1756.

H(20)   **Pull's Ferry** This is the former water-gate of the Cathedral precincts, but no ferry now operates.

F(21)   **St Andrew's and Blackfriars' Hall** St Andrew's Hall dates from 1449 and is the finest surviving example of a former Dominican Friary in England. Used as a civic hall.

I(22)   **St Giles' Church** An early-Perpendicular church showing a lofty tower.

I(23)   **St John Baptist Cathedral (RC)** A large, late-Victorian edifice, designed by the Brothers Scott, with some notable stained glass.

F(24)   **St Peter Hungate Church** Carries the date of 1460 and has a hammer-beam roof. It is now a museum of church art and craftsmanship.

J(25)   **St Peter Mancroft Church** The largest of the city churches, with a fine 15th-C tower and much old glass.

J(26)   **Shire Hall and Crown Court**

F(27)   **Stranges' Hall** A notable 15th-C building, now used as a folk museum.

Assembly House

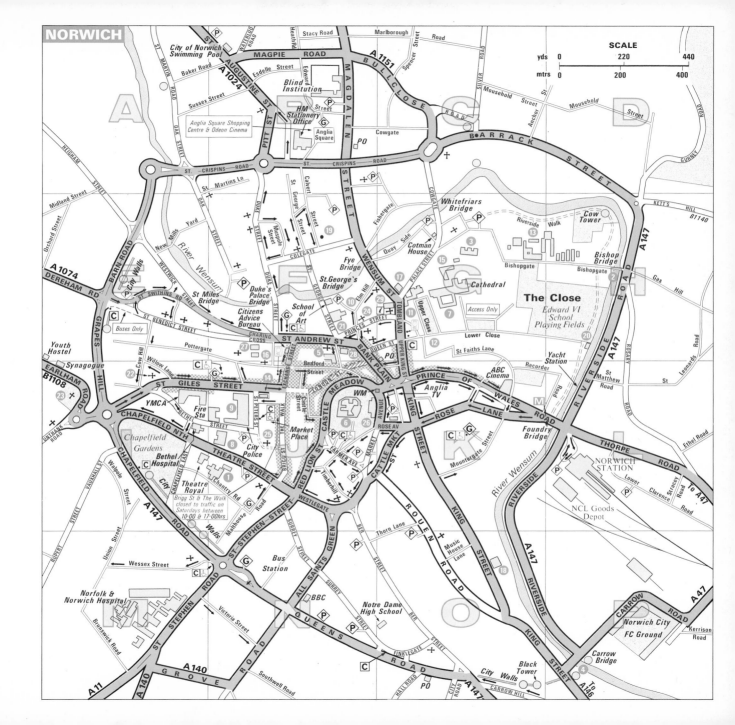

F(28) **Suckling House and Stuart Hall** A 15th- to 16th-C merchant's house with a fine banqueting hall. The adjoining Stuart Hall is a modern assembly room.

G(29) **Tombland Alley and Samson and Hercules House** The house displays quaint figures of 1549. Nearby stands the 16th-C house of Augustine Steward, who was a notable citizen of that time. The house now contains the Tourist Information Centre.

Hospitals

I **Bethel Hospital,** Bethel Street *tel 613411*
M **Norfolk and Norwich Hospital,** St Stephens Road *tel 28377*

Sport and Recreation

B **City of Norwich Baths,** St Augustines
P **Norwich City Football Club,** Carrow Road

Theatres and Cinemas

K **ABC Cinema,** Prince of Wales Road *tel 23312*
F(16) **Maddermarket Theatre,** St John's Alley *tel 20917* (see also public buildings and places of interest)
J(1) **Noverre Cinema,** Assembly House, Theatre Street *tel 26402* (see also Assembly House under public buildings and places of interest)
B **Odeon Cinema,** Anglia Square *tel 21903*
I **Theatre Royal,** Theatre Street *tel 28205*

Department Stores

Bonds (Norwich) Ltd, All Saints Green
G F Butcher (Draper) Ltd, Swan Lane
Debenhams Ltd, Orford Place
Garlands, London Street
Jarrold and Sons Ltd, London Street
Marks and Spencer Ltd, Rampant Horse Street
Peter Robinson Shopping Centre, 15 The Haymarket
Early closing day Thursday. A few shops close all day.

Markets

Market Days Wednesday and Saturday
J **The Provision Market,** Gentlemen's Walk (daily)

Advertisers

G **Berni** Steak Bar
J **Berni** Norfolk Tavern
K **Mercantile Credit**

DISTRICT PLAN

K **AA Service Centre** — Fanum House, 126 Thorpe Road *tel 29401*

Public buildings and places of interest

G(30) **Royal Norfolk Regiment Museum** Arms, armour, uniforms, medals etc of the Royal Norfolk Regiment from 1685 to the present day.
I **University of East Anglia** Founded 1963

Hospitals

A **Hellesdon Hospital,** Drayton Road *tel 44222*
J **Colman Hospital,** Department of Continuing Care, Unthank Road *tel 28377*
L **St Andrew's Hospital,** Thorpe St Andrew *tel 31122*
E **West Norwich Hospital,** Bowthorpe Road *tel 28377*
L' **Whitlingham Hospital,** Whitlingham *tel 28521*

Sport and Recreation

N **Eaton Golf Club,** Newmarket Road
O **Lakenham Baths,** Martineau Lane
K **Lakenham Cricket Ground**
A **Royal Norwich Golf Club,** Hellesdon

Markets

Market days Wednesday and Saturday
N **The Livestock Market,** Hall Road

Advertisers

N **THF** The Post House

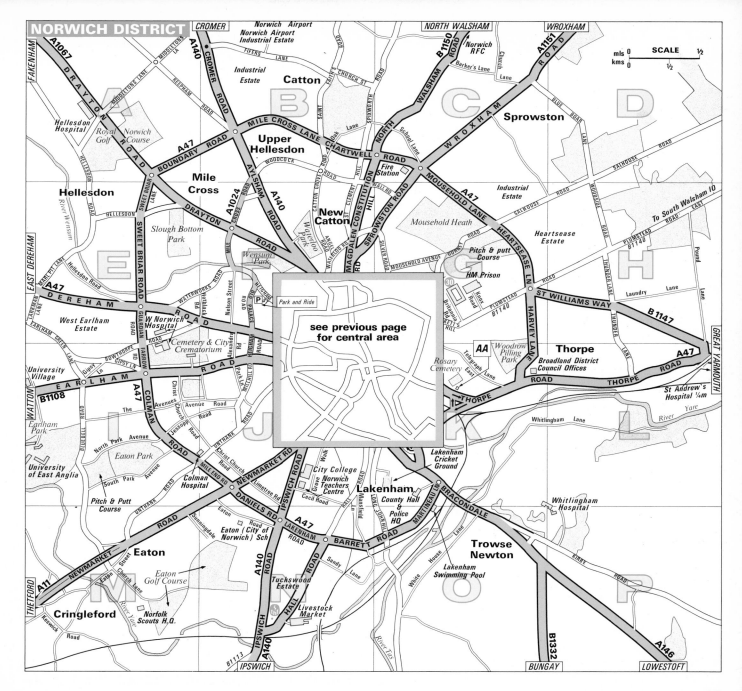

CROMER NORTH WALSHAM WROXHAM

Norwich Airport
Norwich Airport
Industrial Estate

Catton

Norwich
RFC

Barker's Lane

Sprowston

A1067 FAKENHAM

DRAYTON ROAD

Hellesdon
Hospital

Royal
Norwich
Golf Course

MILE CROSS LANE CHARTWELL

Upper
Hellesdon

A47

BOUNDARY ROAD

Fire
Station

Mousehold Heath

Industrial
Estate

Mile
Cross

AYLSHAM ROAD

MOUSEHOLD LANE

A47

Heartsease
Estate

Hellesdon

A1024

New
Catton

HEARTSEASE LN

River Wensum

Slough Bottom
Park

DRAYTON ROAD

MILE CROSS ROAD

Waterloo
Park

Pitch & putt
Course

HM Prison

Wensum
Park

MAGDALEN CONSTITUTION HILL

SPROWSTON ROAD

30

St Williams Way

Industrial
Estate

EAST DEREHAM

A47

DEREHAM ROAD

West Earlham
Estate

Marl Pit Lane

Hellesdon Road

W Norwich
Hospital

WATERWORKS

P

Park and Ride

see previous page
for central area

AA

Woodrow
Pilling
Park

Thorpe

Broadland District
Council Offices

Rosary
Cemetery

HARVEY LANE

B 1147

A47

THORPE ROAD

GREAT YARMOUTH

University
Village

EARLHAM ROAD

Cemetery & City
Crematorium

COLMAN ROAD

B1108 WATTON

Earlham
Park

Eaton Park

North Park Avenue

Christ
Church
Road

NEWMARKET RD

IPSWICH ROAD

City College

Norwich
Teachers
Centre

Cecil Road

Lakenham

County Hall
& Police
HQ

Lakenham
Cricket
Ground

St Williams Way

BRACONDALE

Whitlingham Lane

River Yare

St Andrew's
Hospital ¼m

Whitlingham
Hospital

University
of East Anglia

Pitch & Putt
Course

South Park Avenue

Colman
Hospital

Eaton

MILE END RD

DANIELS RD

A47

Eaton (City of
Norwich) Sch

BARRETT ROAD

Sandy Lane

MARTINEAU LN

White House Lane

Lakenham
Swimming Pool

Trowse
Newton

KIRBY ROAD

A11 THETFORD

NEWMARKET ROAD

Eaton

Eaton
Golf Course

River Yare

Norfolk
Scouts H.Q.

Cringleford

Keswick Road

IPSWICH ROAD

A140

LAKENHAM ROAD

Tuckswood
Estate

Livestock
Market

A47

HALL ROAD

B1113 IPSWICH

A140

B1332 BUNGAY

A146 LOWESTOFT

mls 0 ⋯ ½
kms 0 ⋯ ½

SCALE

To South Walsham 10

B 1150 Road

A1151 ROAD

NORTH WALSHAM ROAD

WROXHAM ROAD

Blue Boar Lane

Salhouse Road

B 1140 PLUMSTEAD ROAD

Pound Lane

Laundry Lane

THUNDER LANE

161

CENTRAL PLAN

G 🛈 **Tourist Information Centre** — 54 Milton Street *tel 40661*

Public buildings and places of interest

J(1) **Albert Hall**

J(2) **Albert Hall Institute**

B(3) **Arboretum Park and Aviaries** Renowned for its dahlia border and other flowers in season.

N(4) **Castle** The present castle consists of a 17th-C Italianate-style mansion, which forms a fine viewpoint, and houses a museum and art gallery. Displays include ceramics, silver, textiles, ethnography, archaeology, 17th- to 20th-C English and Dutch paintings, medieval alabasters, and modern paintings and sculpture. Also Regimental Museum of the Sherwood Foresters. Of the medieval castle only the late 13th-C gatehouse remains, which has been restored. Near the gateway is a group of statues representing Robin Hood and his Merry Men.

N(5) **Castlegate Museum** An elegant row of Georgian, terraced houses displaying costumes from 17thC to the present day, textiles, in particular lace (for which Nottingham is famed) and dolls.

J(6) **Cathedral (RC)** This is an early work by Pugin, dating from 1842-44.

F(7) **College of Art and Design**

K(8) **Council House** A fine building of 1927-29, in Portland stone with facade displaying Greek and Roman influence and domed clock tower housing a loud bell known locally as 'Little John'.

A(9) **Forest Recreation Ground** The Annual Goose Fair (amusements) is held here in the first week in October.

F(10) **Guildhall**

G(11) **Mechanics Institute**

G(12) **Midland Design Centre**

J(13) **Midland Group Gallery** Exhibitions of contemporary paintings, sculpture, pottery and mixed media.

N(14) **People's College**

J(15) **Playhouse Theatre** A large modern theatre opened in 1963.

L(16) **St Mary's Church** A large 15th-C structure, with a massive tower, Royal Arms of 1710 and some monuments.

N(17) **St Nicholas' Church** A church of 1678 with additions of the 18thC.

K(18) **St Peter's Church** A mainly 15th-C structure, retaining 13th-C work in the nave, and with rebuilt chancel of 1870. It features an organ of 1812.

K(19) **Shire Hall** The central block was built to a design by James Gordon of 1770.

F(20) **Theatre Royal**

J(21) **The Royal Children Inn** The sign is made from the shoulder bone of a whale.

F(22) **Trent Polytechnic (Newton Buildings)**

L(23) **Victoria Leisure Centre**

K(24) **Willoughby House** A house built c1730

J(25) **Ye Olde Salutation Inn** A well-preserved and picturesque building of the 13thC.

N(26) **Ye Olde Trip to Jerusalem Inn** This inn bears the date 1189 and is claimed to be the oldest inn in the country.

Hospitals

J **Eye Hospital**, The Ropewalk *tel 46161*

J **General Hospital**, Park Row *tel 46161*

B **Women's Hospital**, Peel Street *tel 40591*

Sport and Recreation

L **Humber Tenpin Bowling Alley**, Barker Gate

L **Ice Stadium**, Lower Parliament Street

L(23) **Victoria Baths**, Victoria Leisure Centre, Sneinton (see also public buildings and places of interest)

Theatres and Cinemas

J **ABC Cinema**, Chapel Bar *tel 45260/46894*

J **Classic Cinema**, Market Street *tel 44749*

K **Co-operative Arts Theatre**, George Street *tel 46096*

K **Nottingham Film Theatre**, Broad Street *tel 46095*

J **Odeon Film Centre**, Angel Row *tel 47766*

J(15) **Playhouse Theatre**, Wellington Circus *tel 45671* (see also public buildings and places of interest)

F(20) **Theatre Royal** *tel 42328* (see also public buildings and places of interest)

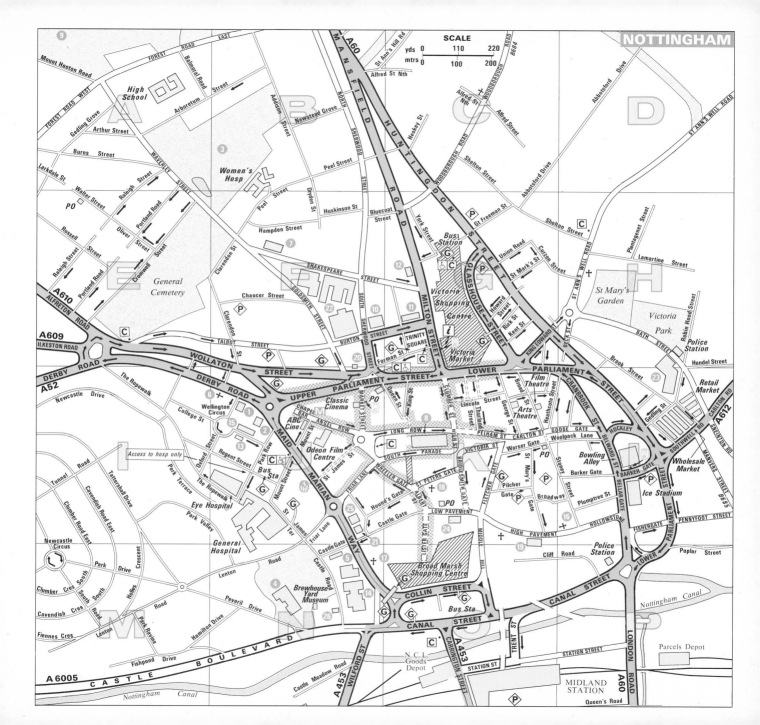

Department Stores

Debenhams Ltd, Long Row and Market Street
Farmer Henry and Co Ltd, Music House, 57 Long Row
Greater Nottingham Co-operative Society Ltd, Arndale Centre, Broad Marsh
Jessop and Son Ltd, Victoria Centre
Marks and Spencer Ltd, 5 Albert Street
Pearson Brothers (Nottingham) Ltd, Long Row
Tobys J H Ltd, 12 Friar Lane
Early closing day Thursday

Markets

L   **Sneinton Open-air Retail Market,** Bath Street (Monday and Saturday mornings)
L   **Sneinton Wholesale Markets,** Bath Street (Monday to Friday 05.00-13.00hrs; Saturday 05.00-13.30hrs)
G   **Victoria Market,** Victoria Centre (Daily-but main market days Monday, Wednesday Friday and Saturday)

Advertisers

J   **Berni** Black Bay Inn
G   **Berni** New Welbeck
L   **Berni** Old Cricket Players
J   **Mercantile Credit**
J   **THF** Albany Hotel

DISTRICT PLAN

J   **AA Service Centre** — Fanum House, 484 Derby Road *tel 77751*

Public buildings and places of interest

I(27)   **Wollaton Hall** An imposing Elizabethan mansion dating from 1580-88, situated in a large park and housing a natural history museum. The courtyard buildings house a museum of Nottingham's industries, in particular lace-making, hosiery, pharmacy and printing.

J(28)   **University** Founded in 1881 it moved to its present site in 1928 and was granted its own charter in 1948. Many impressive new buildings have been added in recent years.

Hospitals

C   **Basford Hospital,** Hucknall Road *tel 607161*
C   **Cedars Hospital,** Woodthorpe *tel 63343*
C   **City Hospital,** Hucknall Road *tel 608111*
H   **Coppice Hospital,** Mapperley *tel 608144*
C   **Firs Maternity Hospital,** Mansfield Road *tel 623271*
B   **Highbury Hospital,** Highbury Road, Bulwell *tel 271275*
D   **Mapperley Hospital** *tel 608144*
J   **Queen's Medical Centre** *tel 700111* Includes University of Nottingham Medical School, Nottingham School of Nursing, Children's Dept, University Hospital and Nottingham Area School of Radiography (Radio-diagnosis)
H   **St Ann's Hospital,** Thorneywood Mount *tel 608144*

Sport and Recreation

C   **Carrington Lido,** Mansfield Road, Sherwood
J   **Highfields Open-air Swimming Pool,** University Boulevard
K   **Lenton Baths,** Willoughby Street
D   **Mapperley Golf Course**
G   **Noel Street Baths**
B   **Northern Baths,** Basford
L   **Nottingham Forest Football Club,** City Ground, Trent Bridge
L   **Nottingham Racecourse**
L   **Notts County Cricket Club,** Trent Bridge Ground
L   **Notts County Football Club,** Meadow Lane Ground
M   **Notts Rugby Football Club Ground,** Ireland Avenue, Beeston
G   **Radford Baths,** Boden Street
J   **Wollaton Park Golf Course**
Holme Pierrepont National Water Sports Centre, Adbolton Lane, Holme Pierrepont 3½m E via Radcliffe Road A52 (P)

Cinemas

K   **Savoy Cinema,** Derby Road *tel 42580*

Markets

L   **Cattle Market,** London Road (Monday to Saturday)

Advertisers

O   **Berni** The Château
G   **Berni** The Grosvenor

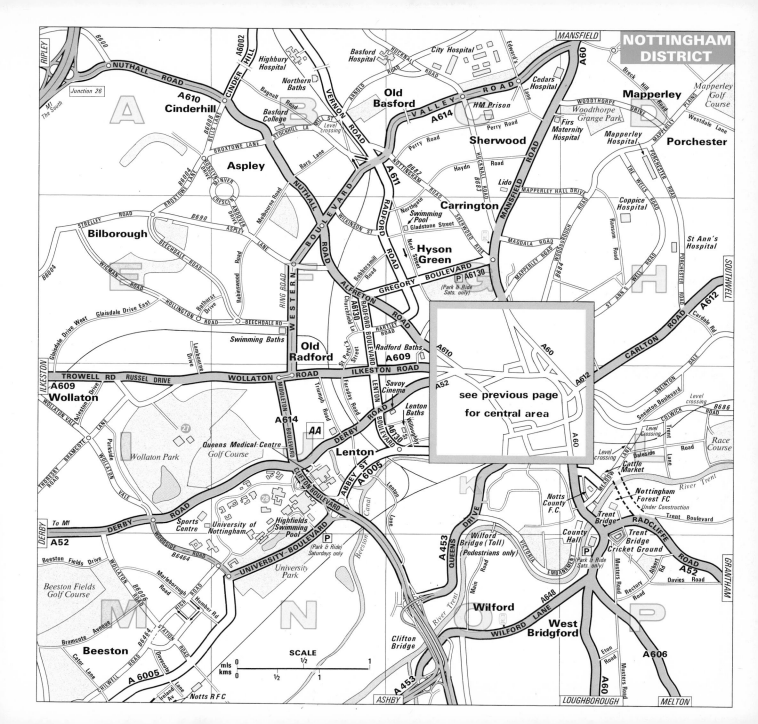

NOTTINGHAM DISTRICT

OXFORD

CENTRAL PLAN

K   **AA Service Centre** — 133-4 High Street
tel 40286

J ⓘ   **Tourist Information Centre** — St Aldates
tel 48707

Public buildings and places of interest

COLLEGES

K(1)   **All Souls College** (1437)
J(2)   **Balliol College** (1260-66)
K(3)   **Brasenose College** (1509)
O(4)   **Christ Church** (1525)
K(5)   **Corpus Christi College** (1516)
K(6)   **Exeter College** (1314)
K(7)   **Hertford College** (1874)
J(8)   **Jesus College** (1571)
F(9)   **Keble College** (1870)
C(10)   **Linacre College** (1962)
K(11)   **Lincoln College** (1427)
L(12)   **Magdalen College** (1448)
G(13)   **Manchester College** (1888)
G(14)   **Mansfield College** (1889)
K(15)   **Merton College** (1264)
K(16)   **New College** (1379)
J(17)   **Nuffield College** (1937)
K(18)   **Oriel College** (1324-26)
N(19)   **Pembroke College** (1624)
K(20)   **Queen's College** (1340)
F(21)   **Regents Park College** (1957)
F(22)   **Ruskin College** (1899)
B(23)   **St Anne's College** (1952)
B(24)   **St Antony's College** (1948)
H(25)   **St Catherine's College** (1962)
L(26)   **St Edmund Hall** (c1220)
P(27)   **St Hilda's College** (1893)
F(28)   **St John's College** (1555)
J(29)   **St Peter's College** (1929)
F(30)   **Somerville** (1879)
F(31)   **Trinity College** (1554-5)
K(32)   **University College** (1249)
G(33)   **Wadham College** (1610-13)
I(34)   **Worcester College** (1714)

Churches

K(35)   **All Saints Church** An imposing 18th-C structure noted for its panelled ceiling and fine tower.

O(36)   **Christ Church Cathedral** A Norman cathedral with later additions including the 13th-C Cathedral spire. The Cathedral was restored in the 1870s by Sir Giles Gilbert Scott and the east wall was rebuilt.

K(37)   **St Mary's Church** The University Church of St Mary the Virgin has a fine spired 13th- to 14th-C tower and a porch of 1637 displaying twisted pillars. This has been the University Church since the 14thC.

OTHER PLACES OF INTEREST

F(38)   **Ashmolean Museum** One of the oldest museums in Europe, its treasures include Old Master and modern drawings, water-colours, prints and miniatures and an extensive collection of coins.

K(39)   **Bodleian Library** Second only to the British Museum in the Commonwealth.

J(40)   **Carfax Tower** The 13th-C tower is all that remains from the former St Martin's Church.

J(41)   **City Library** Westgate Shopping Centre

J(42)   **County Hall**

K(43)   **Divinity School** Displays fine Perpendicular work, notably the arched roof with pendant bosses.

K(44)   **Indian Institute**

F(45)   **Martyrs' Memorial** Erected in 1841 by Sir Giles Gilbert Scott in memory of Cranmer, Ridley and Latimer, burnt at the stake.

K(46)   **Museum of the History of Science** Collection of early scientific instruments etc.

J(47)   **Museum of Modern Art** Temporary exhibitions of contemporary British and international Art.

G(48)   **New Bodleian Library**

J(49)   **Oxford Castle** The Tower is all that remains of the chapel of the Norman Castle built in 1071.

K(50)   **Radcliffe Camera** Built by James Gibbs in 1739-49, with a remarkable view from the dome. It is now part of the Bodleian Library.

G(51)   **Rhodes House** Founded in 1926 for Rhodes Scholars from overseas.

K(52)   **Sheldonian Theatre** Designed by Wren and presented to the University in 1669. The Annual Commemoration is held here in late June. Opposite is the early 18th-C Clarendon building by Hawksmoor.

K(53)   **Town Hall,** Museum of Oxford. Main displays tell the story of Oxford through objects, photographs, models and sound.

G(54)   **University Museum** Built 1855-60 to house the natural science collections. The Pitt-Rivers anthropological collection is notable.

Hospitals

A   **The Oxford Eye Hospital,** Walton Street
tel 49891

B   **The Radcliffe Infirmary,** Woodstock Road
tel 49891

Sport and Recreation

C   **Oxford University Cricket Ground,** University Parks, Parks Road

Oriel College

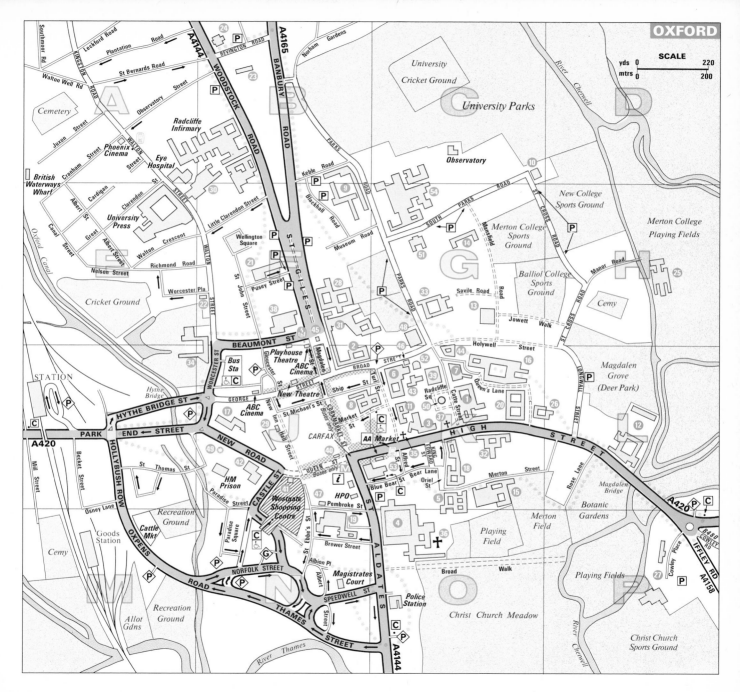

SCALE

yds 0   220
mtrs 0   200

University Cricket Ground

University Parks

New College Sports Ground

Merton College Playing Fields

Southmoor Rd

Leckford Road

Plantation   Road

St Bernards Road

Walton Well Rd

KINGSTON   ROAD

Observatory   Street

Cemetery

Juxon   Street

Cranham   Street

Phoenix Cinema

Radcliffe Infirmary

Eye Hospital

British Waterways Wharf

Cardigan   Street

Albert St

Great   Clarendon   Street

University Press

Canal   Street

Albert Street

Walton   Crescent

Nelson Street

Richmond Road

Oxford Canal

Cricket Ground

Worcester Pla

WALTON   STREET

WOODSTOCK   ROAD

BEVINGTON   ROAD

BANBURY   ROAD

Norham Gardens

Keble   Road

Blackhall   Road

Museum   Road

Little Clarendon Street

Wellington Square

Pusey Street

St John   Street

Worcester St

BEAUMONT   ST

Observatory

SOUTH   PARKS   ROAD

Mansfield   Road

PARKS   ROAD

ST   GILES

Magdalen

Playhouse Theatre

ABC Cinema

New Theatre

Ship   St

BROAD   STREET

Turl   St

Cornmarket St

St Michael's St

Gloucester   STREET

GEORGE   STREET

New Inn   Hall   Street

ABC Cinema

CARFAX

AA   Market

Market   St

Radcliffe Sq

Brasenose

Catte Street

Queen's Lane

Holywell   Street

Savile   Road

Jowett   Walk

Merton College Sports Ground

Balliol College Sports Ground

Cemy

Magdalen Grove (Deer Park)

ST   CROSS   ROAD

LONGWALL   STREET

Manor   Road

STATION

Hythe Bridge

HYTHE BRIDGE ST

PARK   END   STREET

A420

Becket   Street

Mill   Street

HOLLYBUSH ROW

NEW   ROAD

CASTLE ST

St Thomas   St

HM Prison

Paradise   Street

Paradise   Square

Osney Lane

OXPENS   ROAD

Goods Station

Cattle Mkt

Recreation Ground

Cemy

Recreation Ground

Allot Gdns

NORFOLK   STREET

THAMES   STREET

Albion Pl

Albert

Westgate Shopping Centre

St Ebbe's St

Brewer Street

HPO

Pembroke St

SPEEDWELL ST

Magistrates Court

Police Station

ST   ALDATES

QUEEN   ST
Buses only

Blue Boar   St

Bear Lane

Oriel St

Merton   Street

Rose Lane

Christ Church Meadow

Playing Field

Merton Field

Botanic Gardens

Magdalen Bridge

Broad   Walk

Playing Fields

Christ Church Sports Ground

River   Chenwell

River Thames

HIGH   STREET

A420

IFFLEY   RD

A4158

B480 COWLEY RD

Cowley Place

A4144

River Chenwell

Theatres and Cinemas

J   **ABC 1, 2 and 3 Cinema,** George Street *tel 44607*

J   **ABC Cinema,** Magdalen Street *tel 43067*

J   **New Theatre,** George Street *tel 44544*

A   **Phoenix,** Walton Street *tel 54909*

J   **The Playhouse Theatre,** Beaumont Street *tel 47133*

Department Stores

H Boswell and Co Ltd, 1 Broad Street

Co-operative, 18 Cornmarket Street

Debenhams, Magdalen Street

Fenwicks of Bond Street, St Ebbes Westgate

Marks and Spencer Ltd, Queen Street

Selfridges Ltd, Westgate

Early closing day Thursday

Markets

M   **Cattle Market,** Oxpens Road, Wednesday (Cattle)

K   **Covered Market,** High Street, open every day except Thursday

Advertisers

A   **Berni** Jericho House

K   **Berni** The Mitre

J   **Mercantile Credit**

F   **THF** Randolph Hotel

DISTRICT PLAN
Public buildings and places of interest

COLLEGES

J(55)   **Lady Margaret Hall** (1878)

J(56)   **St Hugh's College** (1886)

J(57)   **University Department of Education**

M(58)   **Westminster College** (1899)

F(59)   **Wolfson College** (1966)

Hospitals

P   **The Churchill Hospital,** Headington *tel 64841*

O   **The Cowley Road Hospital,** Cowley Road *tel 64841*

K   **The John Radcliffe Hospital,** Nuffield Maternity Department *tel 64711*

S   **Littlemore Hospital (including Ashurst and Ley Clinics),** Littlemore *tel 778911*

L   **The Nuffield Orthopaedic Centre (including Mary Marlborough Lodge),** Headington *tel 64841*

L   **The Park Hospital for Children,** Headington *tel 45651*

O   **Rivermead Hospital,** Abingdon Road *tel 40321*

P   **The Slade Hospital,** Headington *tel 64841*

K   **The Warneford Hospital,** Headington *tel 45651*

Sport and Recreation

N   **Hinksey Pools,** Lake Street

O   **Long Bridges Bathing Place,** Thames tow-path from Folley Bridge.

B   **North Oxford Golf Club,** Banbury Road

N   **Oxford City FC,** White House Road, Abingdon Road

N   **Oxford RFC,** Oxford Sports Club, Southern-by-pass

T   **Oxford Stadium,** Cowley — greyhound racing and speedway racing

K   **Oxford United FC,** Manor Ground, Osler Road, Headington

O   **Oxford University Association FC,** Iffley Road

O   **Oxford University RFC,** Iffley Road

O   **Oxford University Running Ground,** Iffley Road

P   **Southfield Golf Club,** Hill Top Road, Southfield

P   **Temple Cowley Swimming Baths,** Temple Road, Cowley

J   **Tumbling Bay Bathing Place,** Thames tow-path, Botley Road

E   **Wolvercote Bathing Place,** Port Meadow, Godstow Road, Wolvercote

Markets

T   **Open Market,** Oxford Stadium, Cowley (Sunday)

Advertisers

A   **THF** Travelodge

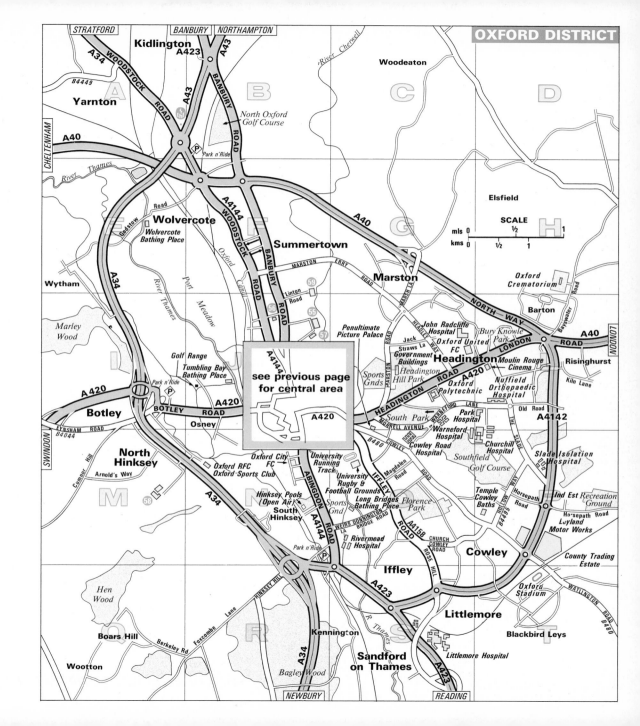

STRATFORD
BANBURY NORTHAMPTON

Kidlington
A423 A43

A34
B4449
WOODSTOCK ROAD
A43

A

Yarnton

B

River Cherwell
Woodeaton

C

D

A40
CHELTENHAM
River Thames

A43
BANBURY ROAD

North Oxford Golf Course

Park n' Ride

Elsfield

SCALE
mls 0 ½ 1
kms 0 ½ 1

Road
Wolvercote
Gosdow
Wolvercote Bathing Place

A4144
WOODSTOCK ROAD

E

F

Summertown

A40

Marston

MARSTON FERRY ROAD
MARSTON LA

G

H

Oxford Crematorium

Barton

A40
LONDON

Wytham

A34

Oxford Canal
BANBURY ROAD

Linton Road

59

50

55

57

Penultimate Picture Palace

John Radcliffe Hospital
Oxford United FC
Straws La
Jack
Headington
Government Buildings
Headington Hill Park

Bury Knowle Park

Moulin Rouge Cinema

NORTH WAY

ROAD

A40

LONDON

Risinghurst

Kiln Lane

Port Meadow

River Thames

Marley Wood

I

J

Golf Range
Tumbling Bay Bathing Place

Park n' Ride

A420

BOTLEY

see previous page for central area

A4144

A420

A420

HEADINGTON ROAD
HEARNE WAY

Sports Gnds

Headington Hill Park

Oxford Polytechnic
A420
Nuffield Orthopaedic Hospital

Old Road
Park Hospital

THE SLADE

A4142

Botley
ROAD

Osney

North Hinksey

EYNSHAM ROAD
B4044
SWINDON

Cumnor Hill
Arnold's Way

58
M

Oxford RFC
Oxford Sports Club

Oxford City FC

Hinksey Pools (Open Air)

South Hinksey

ABINGDON ROAD

University Running Track

University Rugby & Football Grounds

Sports Gnd
Long Bridges Bathing Place

Magdalen Road
IFFLEY ROAD

South Park
MORRELL AVENUE
COWLEY
B480

Cowley Road Hospital

Warneford Hospital

Southfield Golf Course

Churchill Hospital

Slade Isolation Hospital

Temple Cowley Baths

Horsepath Road
BOULTON ROAD
B4495

Ind Est
Recreation Ground

Horsepath Road
Leyland Motor Works

A34

WEIRS DONNINGTON LA
BRIDGE ROAD

Rivermead Hospital

Florence Park

RADLEY ROAD
A4158

CHURCH COWLEY ROAD
ROSE HILL

Cowley

Oxford Stadium

County Trading Estate

WATLINGTON ROAD
B480

Park n' Ride

A423

Iffley

A423

Littlemore

Blackbird Leys

Hen Wood

Q

R

S

T

Boars Hill

Berkeley Rd
Foxcombe Lane

HINKSEY HILL

Kennington

A34

Bagley Wood

Sandford on Thames

A423

R Thames

Littlemore Hospital

Wootton

NEWBURY

READING

Perth

N   AA Road Service Centre (83), Car Park in Canal Street *tel 23551*

N   Tourist Information Centre — Perth Tourist Association, Marshall Place *tel 22900/27108*

Public buildings and places of interest

C(1)   **Balhousie Castle** Originally built in 1478 but restored in Scottish Baronial style in the 17thC and extensively added to in 1862. It now contains the headquarters and regimental museum of the famous Black Watch (The Royal Highland Regiment).

T(2)   **Branklyn Gardens (NTS)** Although only two acres in area, it is considered to be the finest garden of its size in Britain, with a notable collection of rhododendrons, shrubs and alpine plants.

I(3)   **City Hall**

I(4)   **Fair Maid's House** The home, during the 14thC, of Simon Glover, a noted glovemaker whose daughter Catherine was the heroine of Sir Walter Scott's *Fair Maid of Perth.* Now a centre for Scottish crafts and antiques.

I(5)   **Museum and Art Gallery** The building has a fine classical portico. The art collection is mainly of the Scottish school. The museum houses a fine regional natural history collection, and a guide to the City's life and culture throughout history, including early equipment used in the whisky industry.

C(6)   **Old Academy** It has a façade of 1807.

I(7)   **Perth and Kinross District Council Offices.**

I(8)   **St John's Church** A restored church in Gothic style, dating from the mid 15thC, with a fine carillon of bells which chime every 15 minutes. John Knox delivered a famous sermon here in 1559, and several kings have attended services. The north transept contains Sir Robert Lorimer's War Memorial Chapel.

H(9)   **St Ninian's Episcopal Cathedral**

I(10)   **Sandeman Public Library**

I(11)   **Sheriff Courts** These stand on the site of the former 16th-C Gowrie House where the conspiracy took place in 1660.

M(12)   **Sir Walter Scott's Statue**

I(13)   **Theatre**

Scone Palace and site of Royal City of Scone Famous in Scottish history as a seat of Government in Pictish times; home of the Stone of Destiny until 1296, when it was removed to Westminster Abbey; and crowning place of Scottish kings until 1651. The present palace, home of the Earl of Mansfield, was largely rebuilt in 1803, and incorporates part of an earlier palace of 1580. It contains a fine collection of French furniture, porcelain, 16th-C needlework, ivories and objets d'art. 2m N via Isla Road A93 (D).

Hospitals

O   Hillside Hospital, Barnhill *tel 22266*

E   Murray Royal Hospital, Muirhall Road *tel 24282*

F   Perth Royal Infirmary, Tullylumb *tel 23311*

Sport and Recreation

C   Bell's Sports Centre, Hay Street

P   Craigie Hill Golf Course

T   King James VI Golf Course, Moncrieffe Island

D   Perth Corporation Golf Course, North Inch

C   Perth Corporation Swimming Baths, Dunkeld Road

B   Perth Ice Rink, Indoor Bowling and Squash Courts Dunkeld Road

C   Perthshire Cricket Club, North Inch (pitch adjacent to Bell's Sports Centre)

B   St Johnstone Football Club Ground, Muirton Park

Perth Hunt Racecourse, Scone Park 2m N via Isla Road A93 (D)

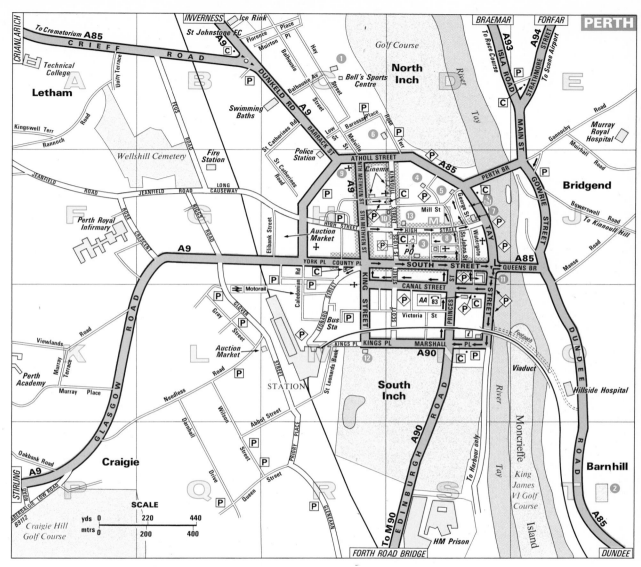

Theatres and Cinemas

Odeon Cinema, Kinnoull Street
tel 24265

(13) **Perth Theatre**, High Street *tel 21031*
(see also public buildings and places
of interest)

Playhouse Cinema, Murray Street
tel 23126

Department Stores

Caird A and Sons Ltd, 21 High Street
Co-operative, Scott Street
Lawsons Ltd, 198 South Street
McEwens of Perth, St John Street
Marks and Spencer Ltd, High Street
Wallace, High Street/King Edward Street
Early closing day Wednesday but some shops and
stores remain open during the summer months.

Markets

Market Days Monday and Friday
H   **Auction Market**, Elibank Street
M   **Auction Market**, Glover Street

Advertisers

I   **Mercantile Credit**
I   **THF** Royal George Hotel

PLYMOUTH

G   **AA Service Centre** — 10 Old Town Street
         tel 69989
J(7)   **Tourist Information Centre** — Civic
ⓘ   Centre *tel 68000 ext 2309/2409* (see
         also public buildings and places of
         interest)

Public buildings and places of interest

O(1)   **Aquarium and Marine Laboratory**
P(2)   **Barbican and Mayflower Memorial** The
         quay, known as the Barbican, in Sutton
         Harbour has inscribed tablets, one
         recalling the departure of the
         Mayflower in 1620.
E(3)   **Cathedral (RC)** A 19th-C building with
         a tall spire.
G(4)   **Central Library, City Museum and Art
         Gallery** Contains collections of
         paintings, including the Reynolds'
         family portraits and the Cottonian
         collection, ceramics, drawings, local
         and natural history, archaeology and
         model ships.
G(5)   **Charles Church** Dating from 1640-58,
         it was gutted during the last war and
         has been retained as a memorial to the
         City's civilian dead.
O(6)   **Citadel (AM)** Built by Charles II in
         1666, it commands the old town and the
         approaches to the harbour. It is
         considered to be one of the finest
         fortifications of its kind in Britain.
         There is a magnificent entrance gateway
         dated 1670, and the remaining buildings
         include the Guard House, the
         Governor's House and St Katherine's
         Chapel.
J(7)   **Civic Centre** An impressive building
         200ft-high with a public viewing
         gallery giving excellent views across the
         City and Plymouth Sound. Regular art
         exhibitions are held here.
O(8)   **Elizabethan House** Located in the
         Elizabethan district of the old port
         (Sutton Harbour and the Barbican). This
         late 16th-C house retains most of its original
         architectural features.
K(9)   **Guildhall** Built 1870-74, and re-opened
         in 1959 after extensive war damage.
         It has a very prominent square tower

and historical windows by F H Coventry.

K(10)   **Merchant's House** The finest merchant's
         house of the 16th and 17thC left in the
         City. Open as a museum of early Plymouth,
         it is a guide to the ancient town which grew
         up during the Middle Ages between St
         Andrews Church and Sutton Pool, which
         now survives in part in the Barbican area.
G(11)   **Plymouth Polytechnic**
K(12)   **St Andrew's Church and Prysten House**
         The fine 15th-C tower of the church
         escaped bomb damage during the last
         war. Nearby is Prysten (or the Priest's)
         house dating from 1490. It is the oldest
         house in the City.
N(13)   **Sir Francis Drake Statue**
N(14)   **Smeaton's Tower** The upper part of the
         lighthouse that once stood on the
         Eddystone Rock, 14 miles out to sea.
         The architect was the famous engineer
         Thomas Smeaton.
K(15)   **Wall Mural,** The Parade. A huge,
         colourful wall mural painted on the side
         of a house by a local artist.

Hospitals

D   **Plymouth General Hospital** (Freedom
         Fields) *tel 68080*
D   **Plymouth General Hospital** (Greenbank)
         tel 68080

Sport and Recreation

F   **Tenpin Bowling Club,** Mayflower Street
P   **Mayflower Sailing Club,** Phoenix Wharf
N   **Tinside Open-air Swimming Pool,** Hoe
         Road

Theatres and Cinemas

J   **ABC 1, 2 & 3 Cinema** *tel 63300*
J   **Drake Cinema,** Derry's Cross *tel 68825*
N   **Hoe Theatre** *tel 68000*
I   **Odeon Cinema** *tel 68825*
J   **Athenaeum Theatre** *tel 266104*
L   **Plaza Cinema,** 36 Bretonside *tel 64450*

Plymouth Sound

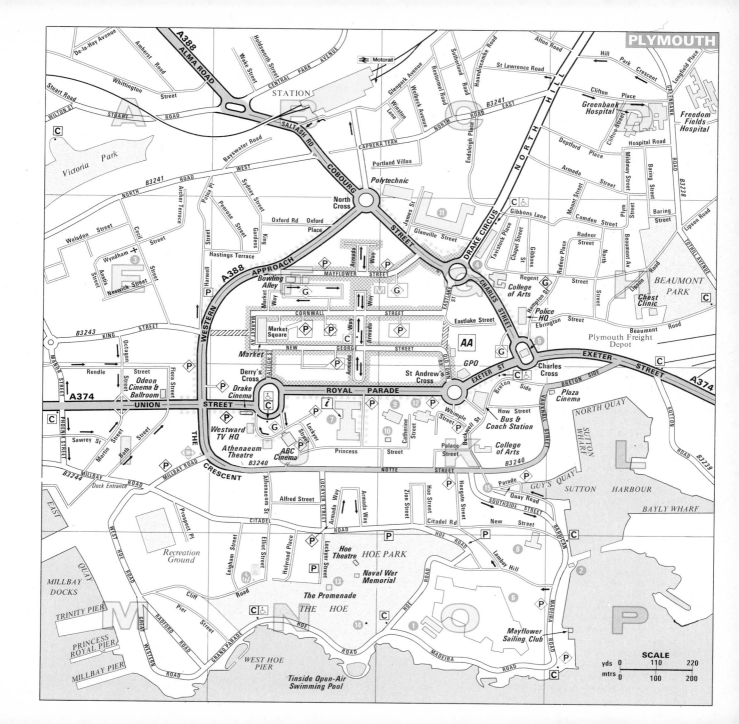

Department Stores

Co-operative, Derry's Cross
Costers Ltd, New George Street
Debenhams, Royal Parade
Dingle E and Co Ltd, 40 Royal Parade
Marks and Spencer Ltd, Old Town Street
Early closing day Wednesday but most shops remain open 6 days a week.

Markets

F   **Covered Market,** Market Avenue

Advertisers

I   **Centrelink** Continental Hotel
N   **Berni** Grand
F   **Mercantile Credit**
N   **THF** Mayflower Post House

DISTRICT PLAN

Public buildings and places of interest

N(16)   **Admiral's Hard,** Stonehouse. A landing place in the Stonehouse Pool for the passenger ferry to Cremyll (for Mount Edgcumbe).

N(17)   **Drake's Island (NT)** A 7-acre island in Plymouth Sound fortified for 500 years. Defences strengthened by Drake, and garrisoned up to the end of the Second World War. Now developed as an adventure training centre.

M(18)   **Mount Edgcumbe Park** A fine 16th-C mansion, restored after bomb damage in 1941. It is set in a large deer park with fine avenues and shrubberies overlooking the Sound.

A(19)   **Royal Albert Bridge** Completed in 1859, this railway bridge 110ft above river level is probably the most famous of all Brunel's works. It can be examined closely from the adjacent road bridge opened in 1961.

N(20)   **Royal William Victualling Yard** These buildings at East Stonehouse are mainly the work of John Rennie and incorporate a statue of William IV.

L(21)   **Saltram House (NT)** A mid-18th-C mansion incorporating the remains of a Tudor house. The interior contains two rooms designed by Robert Adam,

much fine period furniture and many portraits by Sir Joshua Reynolds. It is surrounded by a landscaped park.

Hospitals

K   **Mount Gould Hospital** *tel 266286*
I   **Devonport Hospital,** Devonport *tel 53533*
J   **Royal Naval Hospital,** Stonehouse *tel 53740*
F   **Scott Hospital** *tel 51363*

Sport and Recreation

J   **Central Park Swimming Pool**
J   **Devonport Services Rugby Football**

F   **Club,** Rectory Ground, Devonport
F   **Kitto Sports Centre,** Honicknowle Lane, Honicknowle
F   **Mayflower Sports Centre,** Central Park
N   **Mount Wise Swimming Baths,** Mutton Cove, Devonport
F   **Plymouth Albion Rugby Football Club,** Beacon Park
F   **Plymouth Argyle Football Club,** Home Park, Central Park
F   **Plymouth Cricket Club,** Peverell Park
F   **Skateboard Park,** Central Park

Cinemas

K   **Belgrave Cinema,** Belgrave Road, Mutley *tel 62423*

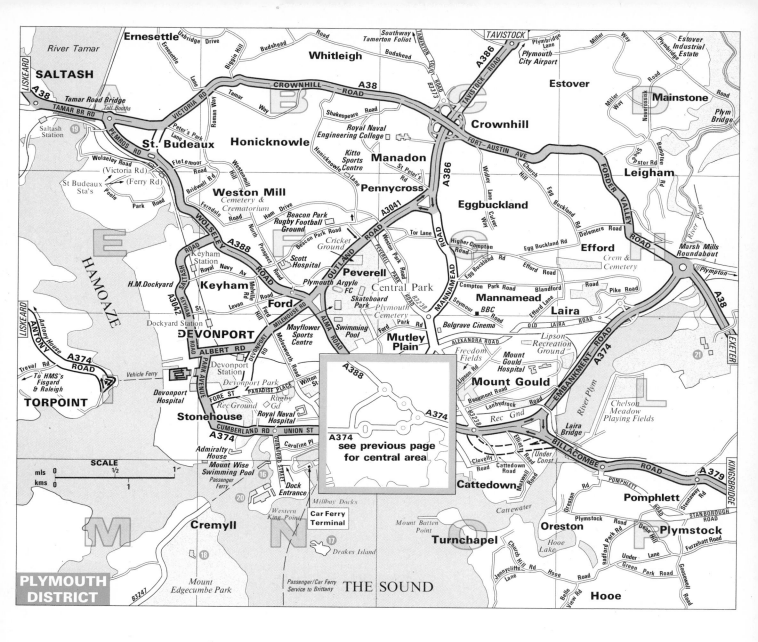

PLYMOUTH DISTRICT

175

PORTSMOUTH

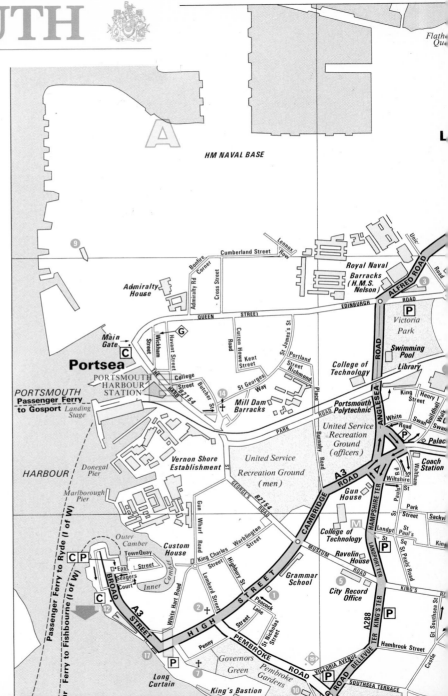

AA Road Service Centre (43) — *tel 67012*
At Portsbridge 3¾m N on A3 (B)

N ⓘ   **Tourist Information Centres** — Castle
     Buildings, Clarence Esplanade
     tel 26722 (Regional)

F ⓘ   **Tourist Information Centre** — Civic
     Offices *tel 834092*

Public buildings and places of interest

I(1)   **Buckingham House** The Duke of
     Buckingham was murdered here in 1628.

I(2)   **Cathedral** Incorporating the former
     Parish Church of St Thomas of
     Canterbury, founded in 1180 and still
     incomplete. The transepts and chancel
     are 12thC and the nave and tower were
     rebuilt in 1693.

F(3)   **Cathedral (RC)**

B(4)   **Charles Dickens' Birthplace Museum** The
     house where Charles Dickens was born
     in 1812, now displayed as a Georgian
     period house and containing many
     interesting Dickensian relics.

J(5)   **City Museum and Art Gallery** Contains
     collections of English pottery, glass,
     furniture, sculpture and paintings.
     Also local history galleries and monthly
     temporary exhibitions.

O(6)   **Cumberland House Museum** Exhibits
     include local natural history and
     geology and an aquarium of marine and
     freshwater fish.

I(7)   **Garrison Church** A restored, partly-
     13th-C church.

F(8)   **Guildhall** This imposing structure was
     burnt out during the Second World War,
     but was rebuilt in 1959.

A(9)   **HMS Victory and Portsmouth Royal
     Naval Museum** Admiral Lord Nelson's
     famous flagship in the Battle of
     Trafalgar (1805), now preserved in dry
     dock. The adjacent museum contains
     many fine exhibits connected with
     Nelson, his officers and men; ship models,
     including the *Victory*, figureheads and
     a huge panorama of the Battle of
     Trafalgar.

I(10)   **Lord Nelson Statue**

N(11)   **Naval Memorial**

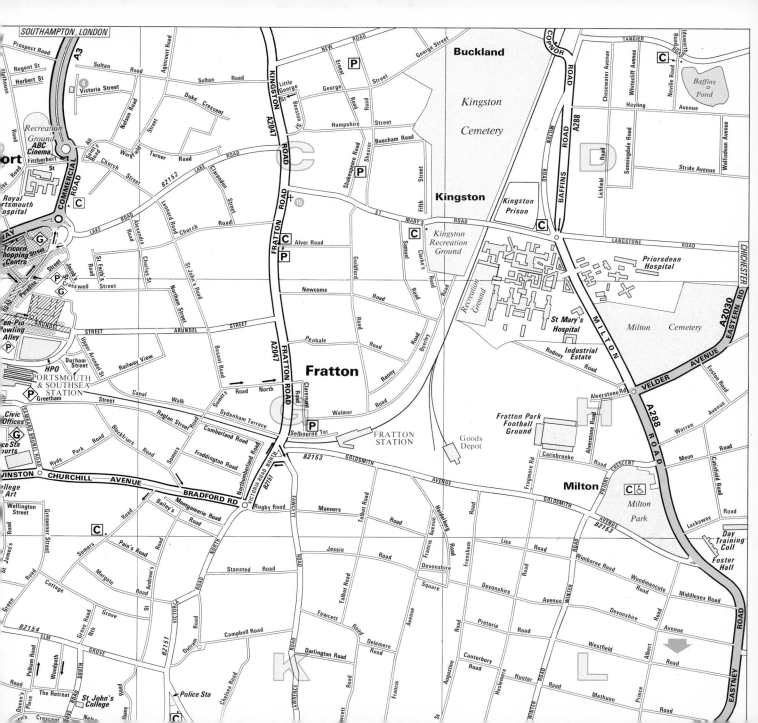

I(12) Round Tower and Point Battery An old
tower dating back to 1417, and once
part of an 18-gun battery defending the
harbour.

L(13) Royal Marines Museums, Eastney
Barracks. Displays the chronological
history of the Royal Marines from 1644
to the present day and includes
uniforms, badges and medals.

E(14) St George's Church A Georgian church
erected in 1754.

C(15) St Mary's Church In the churchyard is
the 'Royal George' memorial of 1782.

N(16) Southsea Castle Museum A military and
naval history museum housed within
Henry VIII's castle of 1539, including
items salvaged from the wreck of
Henry VIII's ship the *Mary Rose,*
which sank in 1453.

I(17) Square Tower Dates from the time of
Henry VIII and is surmounted by a bust
of Charles I.

Eastney Beam Engine House Fine building housing
Boulton and Watt reciprocal steam pumps
installed 1887. Adjacent building of 1904
contains Crossley gas engines. 2½m E via
Henderson Road (L)

Hospitals

B Royal Portsmouth Hospital *tel 22281*

H St Mary's Hospital, Milton Road —
Artificial Limb and Appliance Centre
tel 29571; General Practitioner
Maternity Unit *tel 29695*

Sport and Recreation

F **Ambassador Tenpin Bowling Alley,**
Arundel Street

H **Portsmouth Football Club,** Fratton Park,
Southsea

E **United Services Sports Ground,** Burnaby
Road (Cricket and Rugby)

F **Victoria Park Swimming Pool**
Portsmouth City Golf Course, Crookhorn Lane
4m E via Eastern Road A2030 (H)
Portsmouth Stadium, Target Road, Tipner
(Greyhound Racing) 2¼m N via A3 (B)

Theatres and Cinemas

B **ABC Cinema,** Commercial Road
tel 23538

K **Kings Theatre,** Albert Road, Southsea
tel 28282

F(8) **Guildhall Concert Hall** *tel 83472* (see
also public buildings and places of
interest)

K **Odeon Cinema,** Festing Road, Southsea
tel 32163

F **Palace Cinema,** Guildhall Walk *tel 25029*

Department Stores

Debenhams, Palmerston Road, Southsea
Knight and Lee, Palmerston Road, Southsea
Landports Department Store, 134 Commercial
Road

Marks and Spencer Ltd, 163 Commercial Road
Marks and Spencer Ltd, 41 London Road
Portsea Mutual Co-operative Society Ltd,
Fratton Road
Early closing day Wednesday. Some shops in the
Southsea area close all day Monday. Many stores
remain open 6 days a week from May to
September.

Advertisers

J **Mercantile Credit**
I **Centre** Portsmouth Centre Hotel

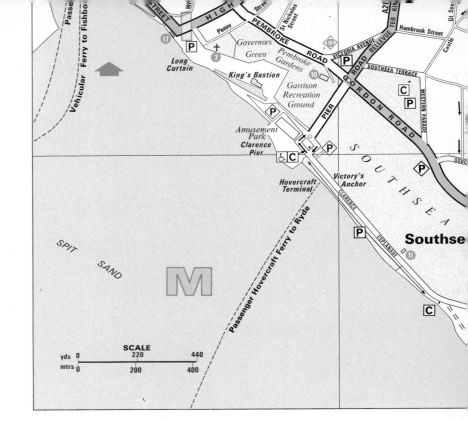

SCALE

| yds | 0 | 220 | 440 |
| mtrs | 0 | 200 | 400 |

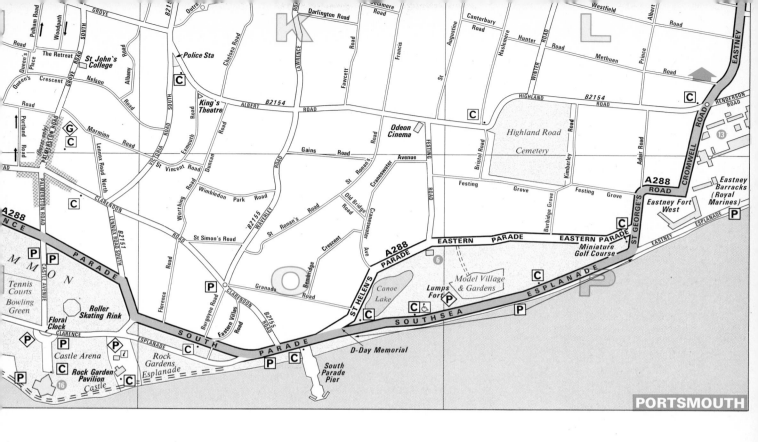

PORTSMOUTH

READING

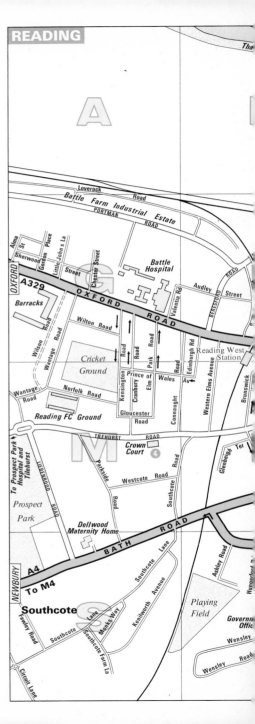

I   **AA Service Centre** — 45 Oxford Road *tel 581122*

O(2)   **Tourist Information Centre** — Civic
i   Offices, Civic Centre *tel 55911*

Public buildings and places of interest

J(1)   **Abbey Remains (AM)** The Benedictine abbey was founded in 1121 by Henry I, who was buried here in 1136. The Abbey was one of the most important in the Kingdom in medieval times. After the dissolution in 1539 the Abbey became a quarry for building materials.

O(2)   **Civic Offices and Tourist Information Centre** Adjacent to the Butts Shopping Centre.

Q(3)   **College of Technology**

M(4)   **Crown Court**

I(5)   **Greyfriars Church** A flint church of the 14thC, with a fine west window.

O(6)   **Hexagon,** multi-purpose entertainments centre.

J(7)   **Museum, Art Gallery and Library** Collections of exhibits from the Roman town of Silchester. Also displays of the development of the Thames Valley.

X(8)   **Museum of English Rural Life, Whiteknights Park** A collection of highly interesting agricultural, domestic and craft exhibits, under the auspices of Reading University.

Q(9)   **Reading School**

J(10)   **St Laurence's Church** Dating from the 12thC, this church has a 111ft-high tower, a 16th-C font and interesting monuments.

I(11)   **St Mary's Church** Rebuilt in 1551, it contains a carved-oak gallery (1631) and a rebuilt organ which was at the Great London Exhibition of 1851.

J(12)   **Shire Hall, County Council Offices, Crown Court**

X(13)   **University** A modern university widely known for its Agricultural Faculty, situated in the 600-acre Whiteknights Park. The old buildings in London Road are still in use.

Hospitals

G   **Battle Hospital,** 344 Oxford Road *tel 583666*

S   **Dellwood Maternity Home,** Leibenrood Road *tel 54266*

M   **Prospect Park Hospital,** Tilehurst *tel 54826*

Q   **Royal Berkshire Hospital,** 3 Craven Road *tel 85111*

Sport and Recreation

Q   **Arthur Hill Memorial Baths,** King's Road

H   **Central Swimming Baths,** Battle Street

M   **Reading Football Club,** Elm Park, Norfolk Road

Calcot Park Golf Course, Calcot 3m W via Bath Road A4 (S)

Meadway Sports Centre, Dunsfold Road 3m W via Tilehurst Road and The Meadway (M)

Reading RUFC, Holme Park, Sonning 3m E via London Road then B4446 (L)

Reading Stadium, Smallmead Road, 2m S via Basingstoke Road A33 (V)

Sonning Golf Course, Sonning 3½m E via London Road A4 (L)

Theatres and Cinemas

I   **ABC Cinema,** 25 Friar Street *tel 53931*

R   **ABC Cinema,** London Road, *tel 61465*

O   **Gaumont Cinema,** Oxford Road *tel 57887*

I   **Odeon Theatre,** Cheapside *tel 57887*

Department Stores

The Co-operative, 18 Cheapside
Debenhams, Broad Street
Heelas, Broad Street
Knights, 100 Broad Street
Marks and Spencer Ltd, Broad Street
Early closing day — Some large stores close all day Monday, some small shops close half day Wednesday.

Markets

I   **Great Knollys Street,** cattle (Monday)

O   **St Mary's Butts,** general (Wednesday, Friday and Saturday)

Advertisers

Q   **Mercantile Credit**

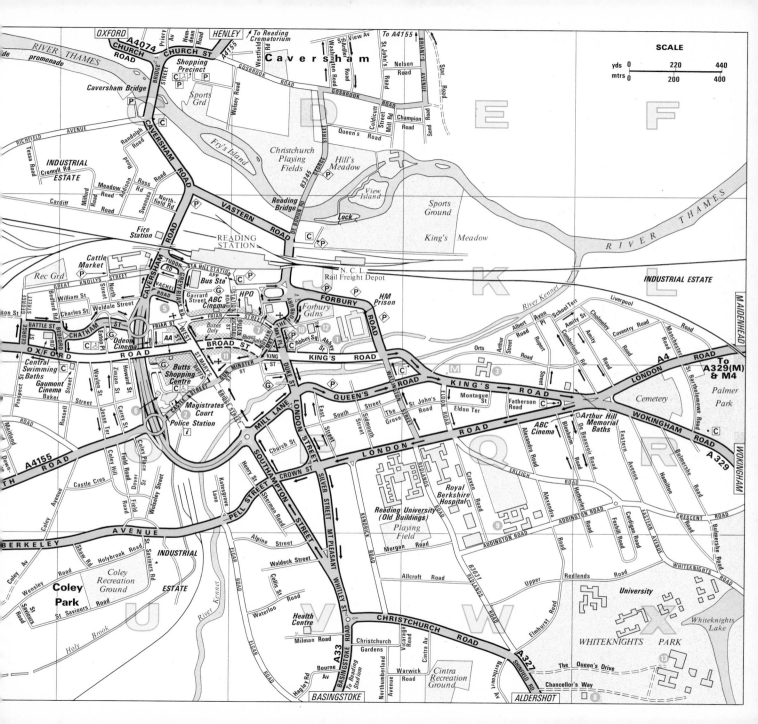

A 🛈   **Tourist Information Centre** — 85 High Street (adjacent to Watts Charity) *tel Medway 43666*

Public buildings and places of interest

ROCHESTER

A(1)   **Castle (AM)** The massive 104ft-high keep with its thick Kentish ragstone walls is one of the finest Norman military ruins in the country.

A(2)   **Cathedral** Founded in 604, the present building dates from 1080. Among its notable features are the Norman West door, the 14th-C Decorated Chapter Room doorway, the large Early English crypt, and the 14th-C paintings on the choir walls.

E(3)   **College of Design**

D(4)   **Eastgate Museum** An Elizabethan house portrayed in Charles Dickens' *Edwin Drood* as the 'Nuns' House'. It now houses a museum of local and natural history including Dickensian items and relics of the Roman occupation. A portion of the Roman and medieval walls stands nearby.

A(5)   **Guildhall** An impressive red-brick building of 1687 standing on a series of Doric columns and surmounted by a copper weather vane of 1780 in the form of a full-rigged ship. The interior hall has fine panelling, an outstanding plaster ceiling and several interesting portraits.

D(6)   **King's School** One of the oldest schools in England, founded in 604 and refounded by Henry VIII in 1542.

G(7)   **Mid Kent College of Technology**

A(8)   **Old Corn Exchange** The unusual clock which projects from the 18th-C façade is referred to in two of Dickens' novels.

A(9)   **Public Library and Corn Exchange**

D(10)   **Restoration House** Built 1587, and by tradition the place where Charles II stayed on his return to England for the Restoration in 1660. It houses some scale model steam locomotives.

D(11)   **St Margaret's Church** Dates mainly from a rebuilding of 1823 but retains its fine 15th-C castellated tower.

A(12)   **St Nicholas' Church** Dates originally from 1423 but rebuilt in 1624 and restored in 1862. Now partly used as Diocesan offices. It contains a curious octagonal font.

A(14)   **Watts Charity (Six Poor Travellers' House)** This building has Dickensian associations as the 'Seven Poor Travellers' Hostel'. Its foundation by Richard Watts dates from 1579, but the present building was erected in 1771.

CHATHAM

B(15)   **HM Naval Dockyard** Guided tours are available, starting from the Pembroke Gate.

E(16)   **St Bartholomew's Chapel** This is the chapel of the leper hospital founded in 1078, and is the oldest surviving building in the locality.

E(17)   **St Mary's Parish Church** Parts of this church date from 1120.

E(18)   **Sir John Hawkins' Hospital** Founded in 1592 and rebuilt in 1722.

F(19)   **Gillingham Public Library and Information Bureau.**

Old Corn Exchange

C(20)   **Royal Engineers' Museum** Royal School of Military Engineering. The Museum contains many general exhibits and a collection of relics associated with General Gordon.

Hospitals

I   **All Saints Hospital,** Magpie Hall Road *tel Medway 41212*

I   **Medway Hospital,** Windmill Road *tel Medway 46111*

E   **St Bartholomew's Hospital,** New Road *tel Medway 41511*

G   **St William's Hospital,** St William's Way *tel Medway 44622*

Sport and Recreation

C   **Black Lion Sports Centre and Swimming Pool,** Brompton Road

H   **Casino Sports Hall,** Maidstone Road

C   **County Cricket Ground,** Brompton Road

C   **Rugby Football,** United Services Ground, Brompton

Chatham Town Football Club, The Sports Ground, Maidstone Road 1*m* S via Maidstone Road A230 (H)

Greyhound Racing, Rochester Stadium, City Way 1¾*m* S via City Way A229 (G)

Theatres and Cinemas

F   **ABC Cinema,** 385 High Street, Chatham *tel Medway 46756*

E   **Central Hall,** High Street, Chatham *tel Medway 48584*

D   **Odeon Cinema,** High Street, Rochester *tel Medway 43272*

Department Stores

ROCHESTER

Featherstone's Ltd, 375 High Street

CHATHAM

Edward Bates, 125 High Street
Harwood T C Ltd, 108 High Street
Marks and Spencer Ltd, 154 High Street
Early closing day Wednesday

Markets

A   **Market,** Corporation Street, Rochester (Friday)

Note
The High Street Chatham, between Church Street and Railway Street, and between Railway Street and Manor Road is closed to traffic on Saturdays between 10.00 and 17.00hrs.

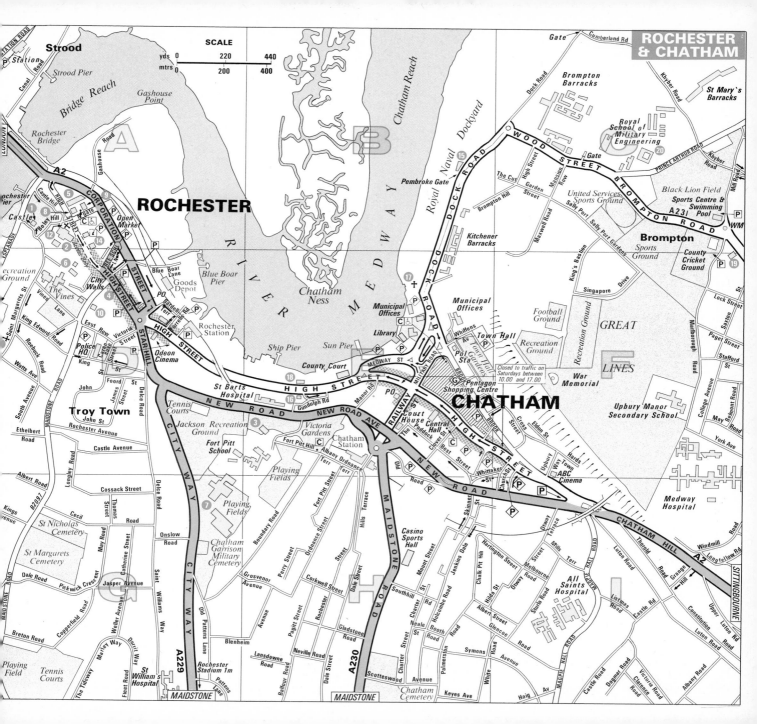

SALISBURY

G   **AA Road Service Centre (101)** — Central Car Park *tel 22246*

G [i] **Tourist Information Centre** — 10 Endless Street *tel 4956*

F(4) **Tourist Information Centre** — City Hall
[i] *tel 27676*

Public buildings and places of interest

K(1) **Bishop's Palace** An old House, part of which dates back to the 13thC, which now houses the Cathedral Preparatory School.

K(2) **Cathedral** Built over a period of 38 years from 1220, this Gothic-style Cathedral preserves a striking unity of design which was enhanced by the addition in 1334 of the decorated tower and spire (404ft). Also notable are the Cathedral cloisters (the largest in England), the chapter house, the medieval clock, and one of the three originals of the Magna Carta contained in the Cathedral Library.

K(3) **Church House** A 15th-C house in Perpendicular style with garden frontage on the River Avon.

F(4) **City Hall and Tourist Information Centre**

G(5) **City Library** On the site of and retaining the façade of the Victorian corn exchange. Also housed here, on the first floor, are the Edwin Young Art Gallery and John Creasey Literary Museum.

G(6) **Council House** A fine 18th-C building.

G(7) **Guildhall** This dates back to 1795 and contains two courts of justice and a banqueting room.

K(8) **Harnham Gate** One of the Cathedral Close gateways.

K(9) **High Street Gate** A picturesque old gateway leading to the Cathedral precincts.

G(10) **House of John A'Port and William Russell House** The former, built in 1425, is a fine example of 15th-C timber work both inside and out, and contains a 17th-C Jacobean oak-panelled room and fireplace. The latter, dating from 1306-1314, exposes two examples of wattle and daub infill. Today the two houses are the premises of Watson & Co's china shop.

G(11) **John Halle's Hall** Preserved in the façade and foyer of the Odeon Film Centre is this 15th-C banqueting hall, a splendid example of black and white timbering.

K(12) **Joiners' Hall (NT)** Displays a timbered 16th-C façade

K(13) **King's Arms** An old inn with Civil War associations.

J(14) **King's House** A late 14th-C house, one of the finest in the Cathedral Close, which is part of the College of Sarum St Michael.

K(15) **Malmesbury House** A Queen Anne house dating in part from the 14thC, famous for its baroque and rococo plasterwork.

K(16) **Mompesson House (NT)** A notable house of 1701 in the Cathedral Close, with splendid panelling, woodwork and plasterwork. Nearby is the old College of Matrons.

J(17) **North Canonry** A 17th-C flint and stone house.

G(18) **Poultry Cross** A cross dating from the 14thC.

K(19) **St Ann's Gate** One of the Cathedral Close gateways.

G(20) **St Edmund's Church** A Perpendicular structure, with a later tower of 1655, which is now used as an Arts Centre.

L(21) **St Martin's Church** An Early English to Perpendicular church, noted for its ribbed-timber roof, plaster panels and modern, painted glass.

K(22) **St Nicholas Hospital** An old building, situated near Harnham Bridge and the River Avon.

G(23) **St Thomas' Church** Early English to Perpendicular building, which is well known for its 15th-C 'doom' painting above the chancel arch.

K(24) **Salisbury and South Wilts Museum** An exceptionally interesting museum of Wiltshire natural and social history and archaeology, including models of Old Sarum and Stonehenge, pottery, costumes and crafts.

Old Sarum (AM) Originally an Iron Age camp, later a Roman fortress, and finally the site of a Norman castle and cathedral town. Foundations of the cathedral and castle can still be seen. 2m N via Castle Road A345 (C).

Wilton House A magnificent 16th- to 19th-C house, with 17th-C state apartments by Inigo Jones, including the famous 'Double Cube' Room, a world famous collection of paintings, furniture and sculpture, and an exhibition of 7,000 miniature model soldiers. The grounds are noted for their giant cedars of Lebanon and the Palladian bridge of 1737. 3m W via Wilton Road and A36 (A)

Hospitals

N   **Harnwood Hospital,** Old Blandford Road *tel 6212*

O   **Newbridge Hospital,** Odstock Road *tel 6262*

O   **Odstock Hospital,** Odstock Road *tel 6262*

E   **Old Manor Hospital,** Wilton Road *tel 3216*

F   **Salisbury General Hospital,** Fisherton Street *tel 6212*

Sport and Recreation

C   **Salisbury Football Club,** Victoria Park, Castle Road

G   **Swimming Pool,** College Street
Salisbury Racecourse, Netherhampton 4¼m W via Netherhampton Road A3094 and Netherhampton (I)

Theatres and Cinemas

G(11) **Odeon Film Centre,** New Canal *tel 22080* (see also John Halle's Hall under public buildings and places of interest)

F   **Playhouse Theatre,** Central Car Park, Fisherton Street/Malthouse Lane *tel 20333*

Department Stores

Debenhams, Blue Boar Row
Dingles, New Canal
Marks and Spencer Ltd, New Canal
Woodrows of Salisbury Ltd, 9 Queens Street
Wessex Co-operative, 7-15 Winchester Street
Early closing day Wednesday

Markets

B   **Cattle Market** (Tuesday)
G   **Market Place** (Tuesday and Saturday)

Advertisers

G   **Berni** County Hotel
K · **THF** White Hart Hotel

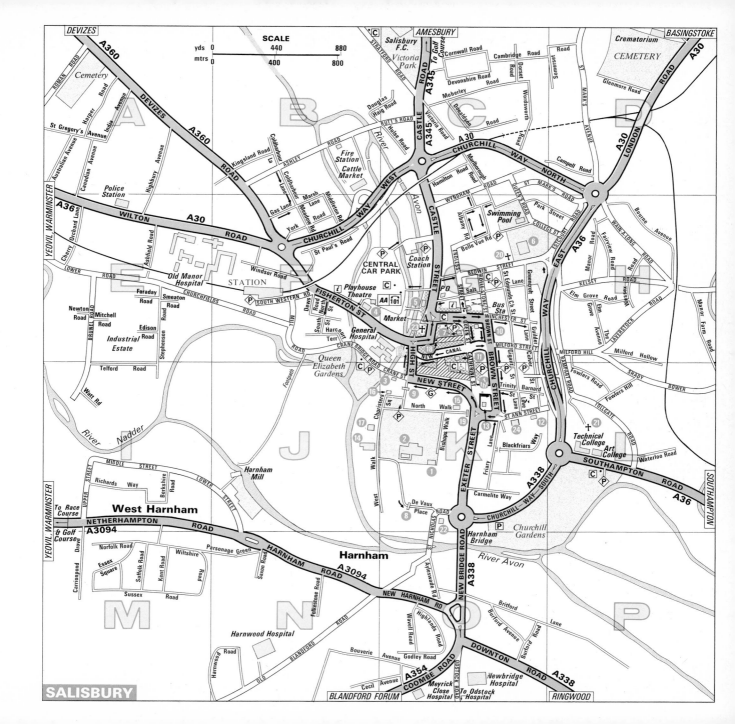

M   **AA Road Service Centre (74)** — *tel 60344*, 1mS on Seamer Road A64

K ⓘ   **Tourist Information Centre** — St Nicholas Cliff *tel 72261*

Public buildings and places of interest

K(1)   **Art Gallery** Contains a permanent collection by local artists and the Laughton collection (English school). Also frequent loan exhibitions.

H(2)   **Castle** Situated on a headland dividing the North and South Bays, the castle is notable for its 12th-C keep, the 13th-C barbican, and the long, curtain walls. In the castleyard are the remains of a 4th-C Roman signal station.

O(3)   **Italian and Holbeck Gardens**

K(4)   **Londesborough Lodge** A museum of bygones and Scarborough history.

B(5)   **Northstead Manor Gardens** Contain the Scarborough Zoo and Marineland, miniature railway (longest of its kind in Britain), an adventure playground and Open Air Theatre. Among the zoo's attractions are performing dolphins and sea lions and a display entitled 'Land of the Dinosaurs' with life-size models.

B(6)   **Planetarium** Housed in an interesting octagonal-shaped building with a hemispherical dome 17ft in diameter, on to which the night sky is projected.

K(7)   **Public Library**

K(8)   **Rotunda Museum** Regional archaeology.

H(9)   **St Mary's Church** A Transitional-Norman and Early English church with old chantry chapels, and in the churchyard the grave of Anne Brontë.

H(10)   **Three Mariners** Once an inn, this old house dates from 1300. It now houses a fishermen's craft centre and museum.

K(11)   **Town Hall**

K(12)   **Wood End** A former home of the Sitwell family situated in charming gardens, with a collection of first editions and portraits of this literary family. Also contained here are a natural history museum, a Yorkshire geological collection and an aquarium.

Hospitals

I   **Scarborough Hospital**, Scalby Road *tel 68111*

F   **St Mary's Hospital** *tel 76111*

G   **St Thomas Hospital**, Foreshore *tel 74347*

Sport and Recreation

B   **North Bay Swimming Pool**

A   **Northstead Indoor Swimming Pool**

B   **Scarborough Cricket Club Ground**, North Marine Road

L   **Scarborough Yacht Club**, Lighthouse Pier

P   **South Bay Swimming Pool**

Motor Cycle Racing, Olivers Mount Circuit 1¾m S via Filey Road A165 (O)

North Cliff Golf Club, 1¾m N via Columbus Ravine and Burniston Road A165 (A)

Scarborough Football Club, Athletic Ground, Seamer Road 1¼m SW via Westborough and Seamer Road A64 (M)

Scarborough Sports Centre, Filey Road 1m S via Filey Road A165 (O)

South Cliff Golf Club 1¾m S via Filey Road A165 (O)

Theatres and Cinemas

B   **Floral Hall**, Alexandra Gardens *tel 72185*

K   **Futurist Cinema and Theatre**, Foreshore Road *tel 60644*

J   **Odeon Cinema**, Westborough *tel 61725*

B(5)   **Open Air Theatre**, Northstead Manor Gardens (see also public buildings and places of interest)

G   **Opera House**, St Thomas Street *tel 69999*

J   **Theatre in the Round**, Valley Bridge *tel 70541*

O   **The Spa Theatre**, Spa Gardens *tel 65068*

Department Stores

Boyes W and Co Ltd, Queen Street
Debenhams Ltd, 31 Westborough
Marks and Spencer Ltd, 7 Newborough
Early closing day Monday or Wednesday

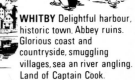

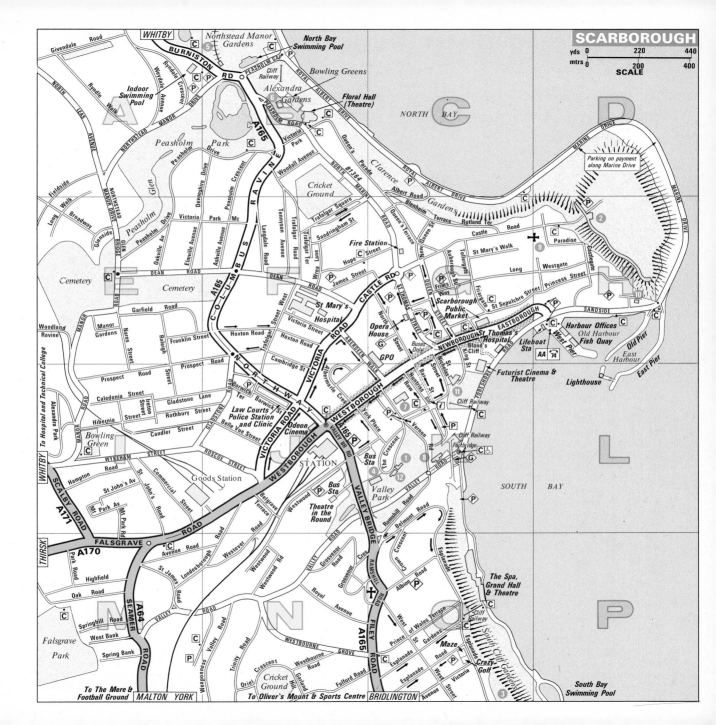

SCARBOROUGH

yds 0   220   440
mtrs 0   200   400
SCALE

WHITBY
BURNISTON RD
Northstead Manor Gardens
North Bay Swimming Pool
Bowling Greens
Peasholm Gap
Cliff Railway
Alexandra Gardens
Floral Hall (Theatre)

NORTH BAY

Givendale Road
Ryndle Crescent
Weydale Avenue
NORTH LEAS AVENUE
Indoor Swimming Pool
NORTHSTEAD MANOR DRIVE
Peasholm Park
Peasholm Glen
GLEN BRIDGE
Peasholm Drive
Fieldside
Long Walk
Broadway
Glenside
A165 BUS VINE
Peasholm Crescent
Devonshire Drive
Oakville Av
Elmville Avenue
Ashville Avenue
Victoria Park Mt
Tennyson Avenue
Langdale Road
Trafalgar Road
Trafalgar Ter
Sandringham St
Trafalgar Square
Woodall Avenue
Cricket Ground
Queen's Parade
NORTH MARINE ROAD
B1364
Clarence Gardens
ROYAL ALBERT DRIVE
Albert Road
Blenheim Terrace
Rutland Ter
Castle Road
MARINE DRIVE
Parking on payment along Marine Drive

Manor Gardens
Nares Street
Raleigh Street
Garfield Road
Franklin Street
Woodland Ravine
To Hospital and Technical College
Cemetery
Cemetery
DEAN ROAD
A165
COLUMBUS RAVINE
Victoria Street
Street West
Hoxton Road
DEAN ROAD
Fire Station
Hope Street
James Street
St Mary's Hospital
CASTLE RD
St Thomas Street
QUEEN STREET
New Queen St
Queen's Terrace
Ashborough St
Tollergate
St Mary's Walk
Long
Westgate
Princess Street
Friargate
St Sepulchre Street
SANDSIDE
Scarborough Public Market
Paradise
Eastgate
Harbour Offices
Old Harbour
Fish Quay
Lighthouse
Old Pier
East Harbour
East Pier

ALEXANDRA PARK
Prospect Road
Caledonia Street
Gladstone Lane
Ireton Street
Rothbury Street
Candler Street
Hibernia Street
Barwick Ter
Barwick St
Belle Vue Street
Law Courts Police Station and Clinic
Odeon Cinema
NORTHWAY
VICTORIA ROAD
Albemarle Cres
Aberdeen Walk
WESTBOROUGH
A165
York Place
Huntriss Row
Vernon Rd
The Crescent
Bland's Cliff
St Nicholas St
Barwick St
Newborough
EASTBOROUGH
St Thomas's Hospital
King St
Lifeboat Sta
West Pier
AA 74
Futurist Cinema & Theatre
Opera House
Narrow
GPO
Buses Only
FORESHORE ROAD
Cliff Railway

Alexandra Park
Bowling Green
WYKEHAM STREET
Commercial Street
St John's Road
St John's Av
Hampton Road
Roscoe Street
Goods Station
STATION
Belgrave Terrace
Westwood
Bus Sta
Valley Park
Theatre in the Round
Bus Sta
VALLEY BR RD
Valley Rd
South Cliff Gardens
Footbridge
Cliff Railway

SOUTH BAY

WHITBY
SCALBY ROAD
A171
THIRSK
FALSGRAVE
A170
Park Road
Highfield Road
Oak Road
Springhill
West Bank
Spring Bank
Falsgrave Park
SEAMER ROAD
A64
Avenue Road
St James Road
Londesborough Road
Westwood Rd
Westwood
Westover Road
VALLEY ROAD
Weaponness Valley Road
Trinity Road
Oriel Crescent
Crescent
Cricket Ground
Garland Road
Westbourne Road
WESTBOURNE GROVE
Fulford Road
FILEY ROAD
A165
Royal Avenue
Grosvenor Road
Grosvenor Cres
Ramshill Road
Crown Crescent
Albion Road
RAMSHILL ROAD
West Street
Prince of Wales Terrace
Gardens
Esplanade
Belmont Road
Esplanade
The Spa, Grand Hall & Theatre
Cliff Railway
Maze
Crazy Golf
Esplanade
Victoria Street
Avenue
South Cliff Gardens
South Bay Swimming Pool

To The Mere & Football Ground
MALTON YORK
To Oliver's Mount & Sports Centre
BRIDLINGTON

SHEFFIELD

CENTRAL PLAN

B   **AA Service Centre** — Fanum House, 2 Fargate *tel 28861*

G(7)   **Tourist Information Centre** — Central Library, Surrey St *tel 734760* (see also public buildings and places of interest)

Public buildings and places of interest

B(1)   **Cathedral** The cathedral church of Saint Peter and Saint Paul was formerly the parish church and dates from the 14th and 15thCs. The 16th-C Shrewsbury Chapel contains fine monuments. A new chapel was consecrated in 1948.

B(2)   **City Hall** Built from Darley Dale stone in 1932 it has six halls for meetings and concerts. Of note are the Oval Hall, seating over 2,600 people and the Memorial Hall, a memorial to the fallen of the First World War.

C(3)   **Crucible Theatre** A modern theatre built in 1971.

B(4)   **Cutlers' Hall** A Grecian-style building dating from 1832. It contains the Cutlers' Company collection of silver plate, with examples of craftsmanship dating from 1773. The historic Cutlers' Feast, dating from the early 17thC, is held here annually.

B(5)   **Former Girls' Charity School** An attractive pedimented house built in 1786.

B(6)   **Georgian houses in Paradise Square**

G(7)   **Graves Art Gallery, Central Library and Tourist Information Centre** The Central Library, dating from 1934, is one of the finest in the country and is officially approved as a repository for manorial records and other historical documents. The Graves Art Gallery, in the same building, has examples of Italian, English, and French painting, and collections of Chinese, Indian, Islamic and African Art.

G(8)   **Sheffield Polytechnic**

F(9)   **Town Hall** Contains the Lord Mayor's Parlour, the Council Chamber, and administrative offices. It dates from 1897 and has a tower 193ft high.

A(10)   **University** Dating from 1905, the University has nine faculties. Recent development includes a 19-storey Arts Tower.

Hospitals

A   **Jessop Hospital**, Leavygreave Road *tel 29291*

F   **Royal Hospital**, West Street *tel 20063*

Sport and Recreation

D   **Hyde Park Stadium**, Manor Oaks Road — greyhound racing

G   **Sheaf Valley Indoor Swimming Baths**

J   **Sheffield United Association Football Club**, Bramall Lane

K   **Silver Blades Ice Rink**, Queens Road

Theatres and Cinemas

C   **ABC Cinema**, Angel Street *tel 24620*

C   **Cinecenta**, Pond Street *tel 77939*

F   **Cineplex**, Charter Square *tel 70778*

C   **Classic Cinema**, Fitzalan Square *tel 25624*

C(3)   **The Crucible Theatre**, Norfolk Street *tel 79922*

F   **Gaumont Twin Cinemas**, Barkers Pool *tel 77962*

G(7)   **Library Theatre**, Tudor Place *tel 734716*

Department Stores

John Atkinson, The Moor
Cole Brothers Ltd, Barkers Pool
Marks and Spencer Ltd, Fargate
Marks and Spencer Ltd, 76 The Moor
Debenhams Ltd, 2 The Moor
Schofields (Yorkshire) Ltd, Angel Street
Rackmans of Sheffield, 50 High Street
Woolco, Haymarket
Early closing day — markets and small shops close on Thursday

Markets

C   **Castle Market**, Exchange Street, general (each weekday except Thursday)

J   **Open Markets**, The Setts and Moorfoot, general (Tuesday, Friday and Saturday)

C   **Sheaf Market**, Dixon Lane, general (each weekday except Thursday)

Advertisers

B   **Berni** Steak Bar

C   **Berni** Old No 12

F   **Mercantile Credit**

F   **THF** Grosvenor House

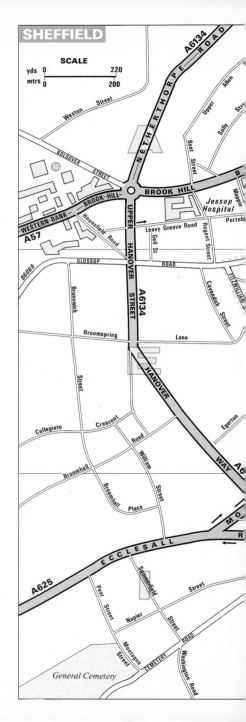

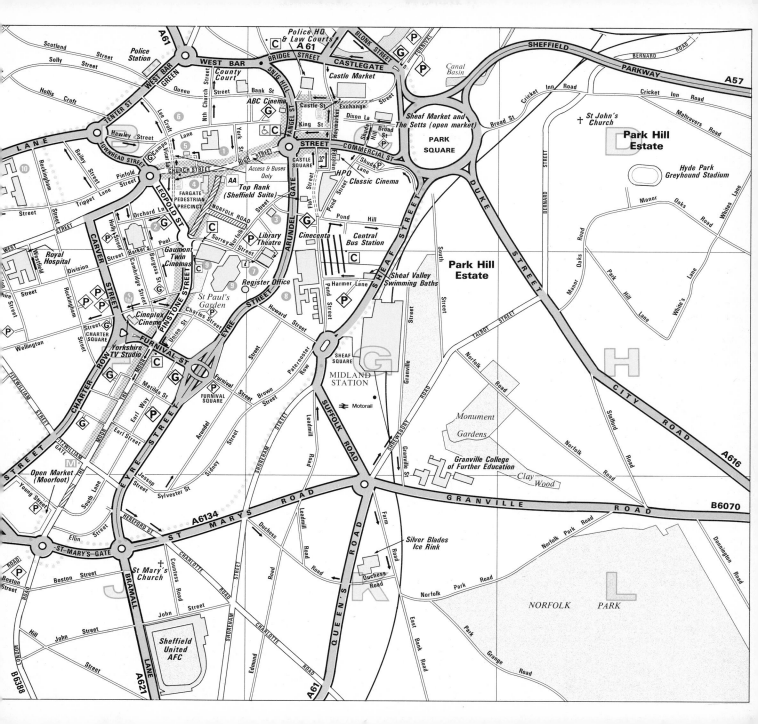

DISTRICT PLAN

Public Buildings and places of interest

N(11) Bishops House A picturesque, restored, timber-framed yeoman's house of c1500.

I(12) Botanical Gardens The well laid out gardens cover an area of 18 acres. There is also an aviary and an aquarium.

I(13) City Museum A regional museum of geology, natural history, archaeology, and Sheffield-area trades. The cutlery section is famous, including European and Sheffield work from the 16thC and the world's largest collection of Sheffield plate. Associated with the City Museum is Shepherd Wheel at Whiteley Wood, a preserved example of a Sheffield 'little mester's water-powered grinding shop. Adjacent is the Mappin Art Gallery which contains British paintings and sculpture from the 18th to 20thCs.

K(14) Manor Lodge Part of Sheffield Castle, the Turret House was thought to have been built to house Mary, Queen of Scots in the 14 years she was imprisoned in the Castle.

Abbeydale Industrial Hamlet 4m SW via Abbeydale Road A621. Sited at Abbeydale is the Abbeydale Industrial Hamlet, an 18th- and early 19th-C steel and scythe works now open to the public and one of the first examples of industrial archaeology preservation. Nearby in Abbey Lane stand the ruins of Beauchief Abbey, founded in 1175. (M)

Hospitals

I	**Charles Clifford Dental Hospital,** Wellesley Road *tel 663251*
I	**Children's Hospital,** Western Bank *tel 71111*
E	**Commonside Hospital,** Commonside *tel 662557*
I	**Hallamshire Hospital,** Glossop Road *tel 26484*
A	**Middlewood Hospital** *tel 349491*
M	**Nether Edge Hospital** *tel 56371*
B	**Northern General Hospital** *tel 387009*
F	**Royal Infirmary,** Infirmary Road *tel 20977*
I	**Weston Park Hospital,** Whitham Road *tel 686071*
I	**St George's Hospital,** Winter Street *tel 28881*

Sport and Recreation

C	**Concord Sports Centre,** Shire Green Lane
A	**Hillsborough Golf Club,** Worrall Road
N	**Lees Hall Golf Club,** Hemsworth Road, Norton
B	**Open Air Swimming Pool,** Longley Park, Crowder Road
E	**Owlerton Stadium,** Penistone Road — greyhound racing and speedway racing
A	**Sheffield Wednesday Football Club,** Hillsborough
H	**Tinsley Park Municipal Golf Course,** Tinsley

Markets

K	**Abbatoir and Meat Market,** Cricket Inn Road
K	**Parkway Wholesale Fruit and Vegetable Market,** Markets Road

Advertisers

I	**THF** Hallam Tower Hotel

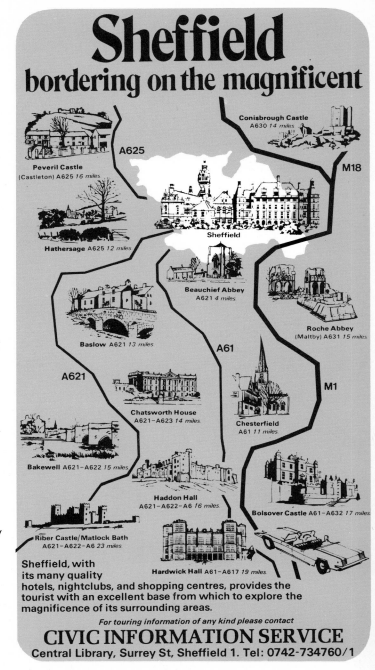

Sheffield
bordering on the magnificent

Sheffield, with its many quality hotels, nightclubs, and shopping centres, provides the tourist with an excellent base from which to explore the magnificence of its surrounding areas.

For touring information of any kind please contact

CIVIC INFORMATION SERVICE
Central Library, Surrey St, Sheffield 1. Tel: 0742-734760/1

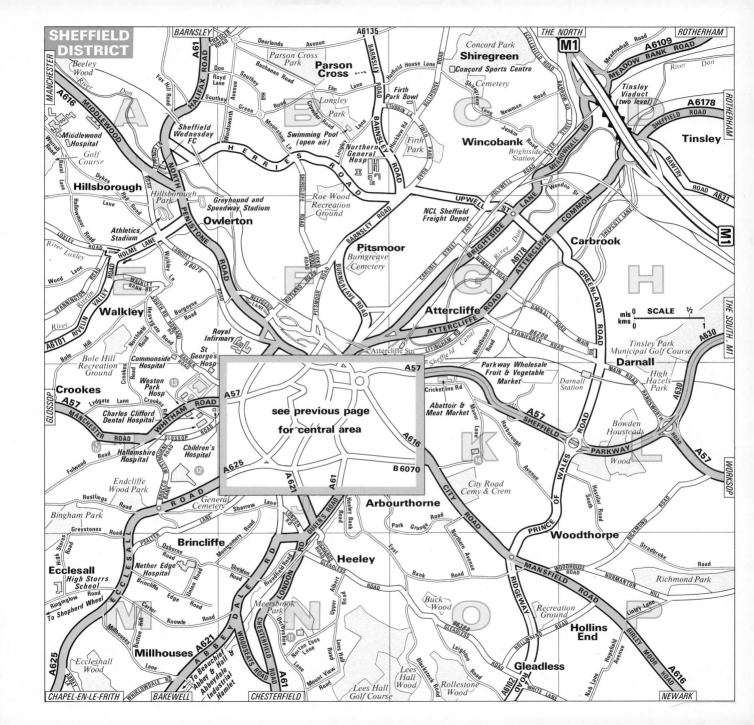

AA Road Service Centre (53) — Oteley Road
tel 53003. 1¾m SE via A458 (O)

M(15) **Tourist Information Centre** — The
 Square *tel 52019* (see also public
 buildings and places of interest)

Public buildings and places of interest

O(1) **Abbey Church** A fine Norman and
 Perpendicular church containing
 monuments of interest including an
 effigy of the founder, Roger de
 Montgomery.

H(2) **Abbot's House** One of the finest of
 the old houses in the town.

H(3) **Bear Steps** Recently-restored, timber-
 framed, 14th-C cottages with shops
 and a meeting hall. The Hall has a
 mid-14th-C crown-post roof.

H(4) **Butcher Row** An attractive street of
 old houses continued in Fish Street.

D(5) **Castle** Partly 13th-C but converted
 during the 18thC into a house and now
 used as a Council Chamber.

B(6) **Charles Darwin's Birthplace** A house
 known as the Mount, where Darwin was
 born in 1809.

M(7) **Clive House (Museum)** A Georgian house
 of architectural interest, once occupied
 by Clive of India and now housing a
 collection of pottery and porcelain.

O(8) **Coleham Pumping Station** The building
 and its two beam engines are now
 preserved as a museum.

I(9) **Draper's Hall** One of Shrewsbury's old
 half-timbered houses.

H(10) **Grope Lane** A picturesque and
 particularly narrow little alley.

N(11) **Guildhall**

H(12) **Ireland's Mansion** A fine, half-
 timbered house of the late 16thC.

D(13) **Library**

B(14) **Millington Hospital** A range of fine
 brick-built almshouses dating from
 1748.

M(15) **Music Hall and Tourist Information
 Centre**

D(16) **Old Council House Gateway** A fine,
 17th-C, half-timbered gateway.

M(17) **Old Market Hall** A splendid Elizabethan
 structure of 1595.

G(18) **Rowley's House** A notable, restored,
 half-timbered house, now a museum of
 Roman remains excavated from Wroxeter.

H(19) **St Alkmund's Church** A church of 1795
 with an earlier spire, 174ft high.

G(20) **St Chad's Church** Dates from 1792, the
 nave being in the form of a rotunda.

M(21) **St Julian's Church** Preserves an old
 tower, the remainder of the church
 dating mainly from 1750.

I(22) **St Mary's Church** A fine 12th- to
 17th-C church, noted for its old
 Herkenrode glass and a Jesse window.

The well-known annual floral fête is held
in the Quarry Grounds near the River

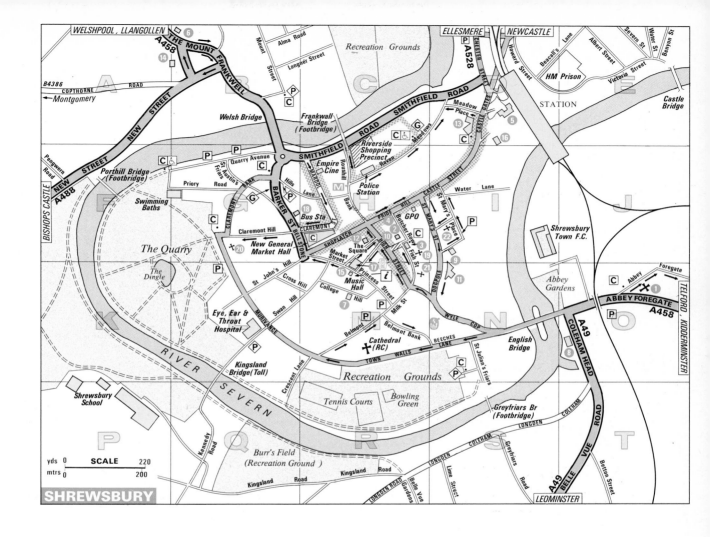

Severn. The modern buildings of Shrewsbury School lie across the river to the south (P).

Hospitals

L   **Eye, Ear and Throat Hospital** *tel 55771*

Sports and Recreation

G   **Shrewsbury Swimming Baths,** Priory Road
I   **Shrewsbury Town Football Club,** The Gay Meadow

Theatres and Cinemas

H   **Empire Cinema,** Mardol *tel 62257*
M(15) **Music Hall** The Square *tel 52019*
         (see also public buildings and places of interest)

Department Stores

Marks and Spencer Ltd, 5 Castle Street
Owen Owen Ltd, Pride Hill
Rackhams (Harrods) Ltd, 37 High Street
Wades, Mardol Block, Market Hall

Markets

H   **General Market** (Monday to Saturday, but main market days Wednesday and Saturday)

Advertisers

M   **Berni** The Criterion
H   **Mercantile Credit**
N   **THF** Lion Hotel

SOUTHAMPTON

CENTRAL PLAN

B   **AA Service Centre** — Fanum House, 11 The Avenue *tel 36811*

S   **AA Port Service Centre** — No 9 Berth (entrance via no 2 Gate, Canute Road), Southampton Docks *tel 28304*

S [i]   **Tourist Information Centres** — Canute Road (opposite Dock Gate 3) *tel 20438* (National)

J [i]   **The Precinct**, Above Bar Street *tel 23855 ext 615* (Local)

Public buildings and places of interest

N(1)   **Arundel or Wind Whistle Tower (AM)** One of the towers of the City Walls which dates from the Norman period.

N(2)   **Bargate (AM)** Originally a Norman construction but with later additions including the Edwardian drum towers. The upper-storey contains the former Guildhall, now a museum of local interest which includes a fine D-Day embroidery recording Southampton's involvement in the Second World War.

N(3)   **Catchcold Tower (AM)** At the North-West corner of the City Walls.

J(4)   **Cenotaph**

J(5)   **Civic Centre, Guildhall, Library and Art Gallery** A modern group of buildings in Portland stone, built 1932-39 and surmounted by a very prominent clock-tower. The Art Gallery includes 18th-to 20th-C British paintings, Continental Old Masters and modern French paintings. Also temporary exhibitions.

J(6)   **College of Art**

J(7)   **College of Technology** Contains the Mountbatten Theatre.

R(8)   **God's House and God's Gate** God's House, or Hospital, was founded in 1185 and contains the restored Norman chapel of St Julian. God's Gate c1300 adjoins the God's House Tower.

R(9)   **God's House Tower** Dating from the early 15thC and part of the ancient city walls, this tower now houses an archaeological museum containing local prehistoric, Roman, Saxon and medieval finds.

N(10)   **Holy Rood Church** Only the 14h-C tower of this church survived intact the bombing of 1940. The ruins are now preserved as a memorial to men of the Merchant Navy who lost their lives during the Second World War.

R(11)   **Mayflower Park with Memorials** The Pilgrim Fathers' Memorial, which stands opposite the park on the Western Esplanade, recalls the sailing of the *Mayflower* from the West Quay on 15 August 1620.

N(12)   **Polymond Tower** One of the towers of the City Walls which stands at the north-east corner.

J(13)   **R J Mitchell Museum** Dedicated to the designer of the *Spitfire* fighter plane.

O(14)   **St Mary's Church** Restored and re-dedicated in 1956. It was the origin of the song *'The Bells of St. Mary's'*.

N(15)   **St Michael's Church** The oldest church in the City, with parts dating back to 1070. The tall, slender spire was added in the 19thC and serves as a landmark for ships in Southampton Water. Preserved here is a rare 12th-C black marble Tournai font.

F(16)   **Titanic Memorial** A memorial to the engineers of the famous liner which struck an iceberg in 1912.

N(17)   **Tudor House Museum** A restored, half-timbered, 16th-C mansion containing a fine oak-panelled banqueting hall with minstrel's gallery, and exhibits of antiquarian and historical interest including furniture, decorative arts, paintings of Southampton and musical instruments. There is access through the garden to a Norman merchant's house dating from c1175.

N(18)   **West Gate** Dating from the 13thC, it led to the old West Quay from where the *Mayflower* sailed.

R(19)   **Wool House Maritime Museum** A fine example of a 14th-C warehouse, with buttressed stone walls and old roof timbering, containing an impressive maritime museum including models of great ships.

City Walls These date back to the 12thC but have more recent additions. The best preserved sections extend from the Arundel Tower southwards to the Town Quay. The notable arcaded sections of the wall are best seen near the southern part of the Esplanade.

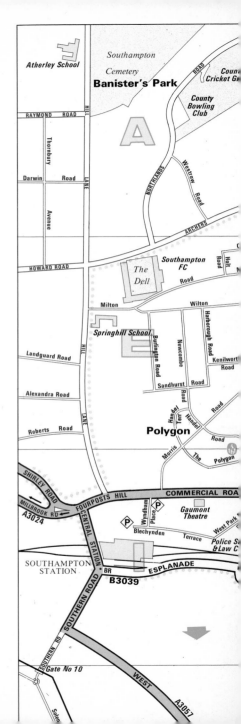

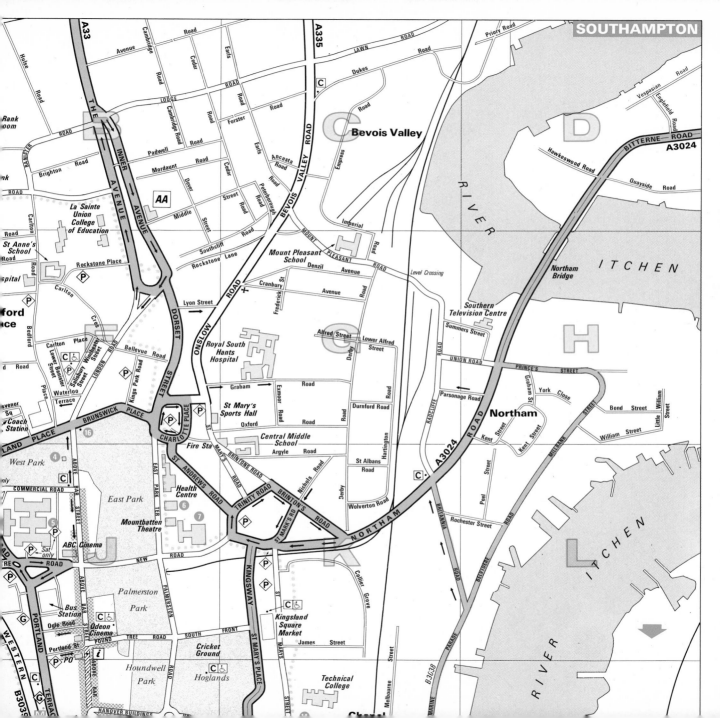

SOUTHAMPTON

Bevois Valley

RIVER

ITCHEN

Northam

RIVER

ITCHEN

195

Hospitals

G   **Royal South Hants Hospital,** Fanshawe Street *tel 34288*
F   **Southampton Eye Hospital,** Wilton Avenue *tel 22208*

Sport and Recreation

N   **Central Baths,** Western Esplanade
A   **Hampshire County Cricket Club,** Northlands Road
F   **St Mary's Sports Hall,** St Mary's Road
E   **Southampton Football Club,** The Dell, Milton Road
A   **Top Rank Ice Skating,** Banister Road

Theatres and Cinemas

J   **ABC Cinemas 1 and 2,** Forum Buildings, Above Bar Street *tel 23536*
I   **Gaumont Theatre/Cinema,** Commercial Road *tel 29772*
J(5)   **Guildhall,** Civic Centre *tel 32601* (see also public buildings and places of interest)
J(7)   **Mountbatten Theatre,** College of Technology (see also public buildings and places of interest)
J   **Odeon Cinema,** Above Bar Street *tel 22243*

Department Stores

Co-operative Retail Services, Above Bar Street
Debenhams, Queens Buildings, Queensway
Marks and Spencer Ltd, Above Bar Street
Owen Owen Ltd, 173 High Street
Plummers, Above Bar Street
Tyrrell and Green Ltd, 138 Above Bar Street
Early closing day Wednesday, or all day closing Monday, but many shops remain open six days a week

Markets

K   **St Mary's Street Market,** Kingsland Square — mainly fruit and vegetables (Friday and Saturday)

Advertisers

S   **Berni** The Oriental
N   **Mercantile Credit**
N   **THF** Dolphin Hotel
E   **THF** Polygon Hotel
R   **THF** Post House

Civic Centre

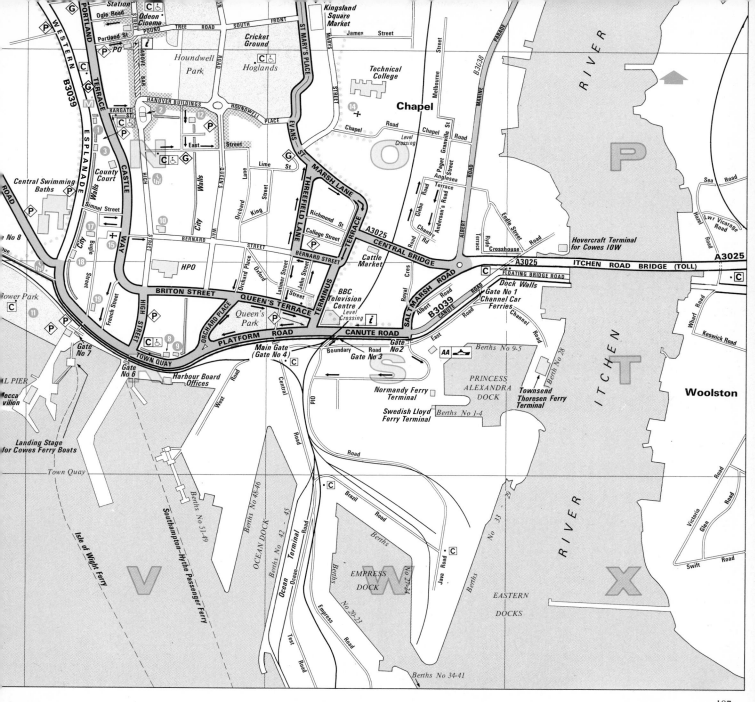

DISTRICT PLAN
Public buildings and places of interest

H(20) **Nuffield Theatre,** University of Southampton. This building was designed by Sir Basil Spence.

B(21) **Sports Centre** Covers approximately 270 acres and caters for a wide range of outdoor sports. It is considered to be one of the finest of its kind in the Commonwealth.

H(22) **University of Southampton** Dates from 1902 when it was the Hartley University College. It became a university by Royal Charter in 1952. Recent expansion includes many fine buildings designed by Sir Basil Spence.

H(23) **Zoological Gardens** Southampton Common. Small but attractively laid-out zoo, with comprehensive collection of animals and birds.

Hospitals

C **Fred Wooley House** (Royal South Hants Hospital Annexe), Winchester Road, Chilworth *tel 68524*

J **Moorgreen Hospital,** West End *tel West End 2258*

G **Southampton General Hospital,** Tremona Road *tel 777222*

G **Southampton Western Hospital,** Oakley Road, Millbrook *tel 771042*

Sports and Recreation

N **Bitterne Tenpin Bowling Alley,** Bitterne Road

C **Southampton Corporation Golf Course**

B(21) **Sports Centre** (see also public buildings and places of interest)

C **Stoneham Golf Club,** Bassett Green Road

N **Weston Cricket Ground,** Weston Lane, Woolston

Theatres and Cinemas

H(20) **Nuffield Theatre,** University Road *tel 555028* (see also public buildings and places of interest)

Advertisers

H **Berni** The Belmont

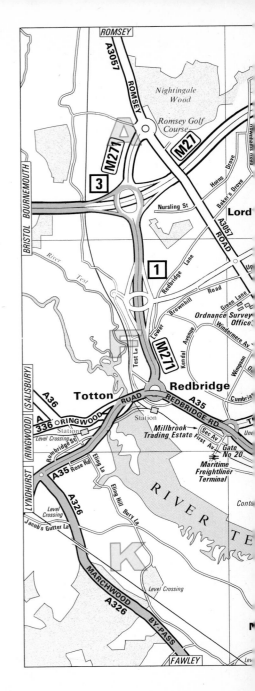

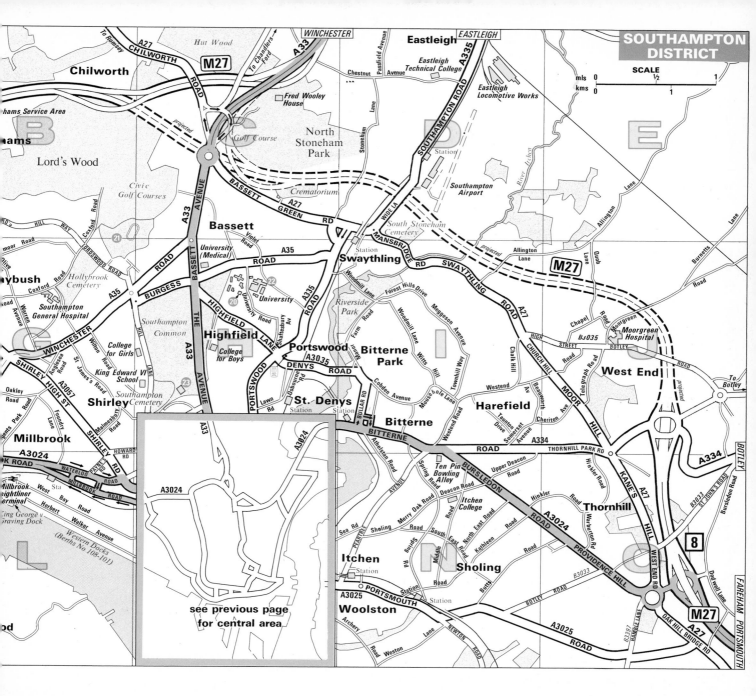

SCALE

mls
kms

Chilworth

To Romsey
CHILWORTH
A27

M27

Hut Wood

To Chandlers Ford

WINCHESTER

A33

EASTLEIGH

Eastleigh

Eastleigh
Technical College
A335

Chestnut

Passfield Avenue

Avenue

Eastleigh
Locomotive Works

*Fred Wooley
House*

North
Stoneham
Park

Stoneham

Lane

Road

Station

River Itchen

hams Service Area

B

Lord's Wood

Golf Course

projected

Crematorium

A27

Southampton
Airport

D

E

*Civic
Golf Courses*

A33
AVENUE

BASSETT
GREEN
RD

SOUTHAMPTON ROAD

*Allington
Lane*

Quob

Burnetts

oor

Road

HILL
WAY

21

BASSETT

ROAD

Bassett

*Violet
Road*

A35

South Stoneham
Cemetery

WIDE LA

MANSBRIDGE

A335

RD

Station

SWAYTHLING

A27

ROAD

Allington
Lane

M27

Road

Road

moor

Road

aybush

Coxford

BURGESS

*Hollybrook
Cemetery*

A35

*Coxford
Road*

*Warren
Avenue*

University
(Medical)

20

University
Road

22

University

A335
ROAD

Station

Swaythling

Woodmill Lane

Forest Hills Drive

SWAYTHLING

*High
Street*

Chapel

B3035

*Moorgreen
Hospital*

BOTLEY

Road

G

*Southampton
General Hospital*

THE

HIGHFIELD

*Southampton
Common*

Shaftesbury
Av

Highfield

LANE

A33

College
for Girls

College
for Boys

Portswood

A3035

PORTSWOOD

DENYS
Rd

ROAD

*Riverside
Park*

Bitterne
Park

*Farm
Road*

Woodmill Lane

*Meggeson
Avenue*

*Witts
Hill*

Townhill Way

H

I

Chalk Hill

CHURCH HILL

MOOR
HILL

*High
Street*

Telegraph Road

West End

To
Botley

J

A334
AVENUE

*Anglesea
Road*

A3057

St. James's Road

*Wilton
Road*

King Edward VI
School

Southampton
Cemetery

23

*Lawn
Rd*

*Osborne
Rd*

St. Denys

Station

BULLAR RD

A3024

Cobden Avenue

Mousehole Lane

*Westend
Road*

*Westend
Road*

Harefield

*Taunton
Drive*

Av

*Somerset
Avenue*

*Beaworth
Av*

*Cheriton
Road*

MOOR
HILL

A27

KANE'S

A334

B3033

ST. JOHN'S ROAD

BOTLEY

FAREHAM

PORTSMOUTH

*Oakley
Road*

SHIRLEY HIGH ST

*Malmesbury
Road*

Shirley

SHIRLEY
RD

Bitterne

Station

BITTERNE

Atheltston Road

ROAD

A334

THORNHILL PARK RD

HILL

PROVIDENCE HILL

WEST END RD

8

Millbrook

A3024

HOWARD
RD

PAYNES
RD

Ten Pin
Bowling
Alley

BURSLEDON

*Upper Deacon
Road*

*Hinkler
Road*

H. Walter Road

Warburton Rd

Thornhill

A27

B3033

St. John's Road

Burstedon Road

*Millbrook
Freightliner
Terminal*

*West
Bay
Road*

WATERLOO

Sta

MILLBROOK

ROAD

ROAD

A33

A3024

A3024

Itchen
College

Deacon Road

Merry Oak Road

Spring Road

North East Road

*Kathleen
Road*

Road

A3024

ROAD

OAK HILL BRIDGE RD

Dodwell Lane

*King George V
Graving Dock*

*Herbert
Road*

*Walker
Avenue*

see previous page
for central area

PEARTREE
AVENUE

Sea Rd

*Sheling
Road*

South East Road

*Bridds
Road*

*Middle
Road*

N

Sholing

*Butts
Road*

BOTLEY
ROAD

B3033

C

M27

A27

*Western Docks
(Berths No 108-101)*

L

Itchen

Station

A3025

PORTSMOUTH

Station

Woolston

*Archery
Road*

*Weston
Lane*

NEWTON
ROAD

A3025

B3397

HAMBLE LANE

OAK HILL BRIDGE RD

od

A3025
ROAD

199

E(7) *[i]* **Tourist Information Centre** — Judith Shakespeare House, 1 High Street *tel 3127/66185/66175* (see also public buildings and places of interest)

Public buildings and places of interest

F(1) **Gower Memorial Statue** A statue of Shakespeare flanked by four of his characters.

E(2) **Grammar School and Guildhall** A 15th-C half-timbered range of buildings. The original Guildhall occupies the ground floor and the upper hall has been used by the Grammar School since the Guild was suppressed.

E(3) **Guild Chapel** A 13th- to 15th-C chapel built for the Guild of the Holy Cross which contains the remains of a series of wall paintings.

H(4) **Hall's Croft** A Tudor house with a walled garden, this was the former home of Shakespeare's daughter Susanna and her husband Dr John Hall.

E(5) **Harvard House** A half-timbered house dating from 1596, the former home of the mother of the founder of Harvard University in the USA, John Harvard.

H(6) **Holy Trinity Church** The Church contains the tomb of, and a monument to, Shakespeare. The Church itself has a number of interesting features.

E(7) **Judith Shakespeare House and Tourist Information Centre** The former home of Shakespeare's daughter, Judith Quiney.

E(8) **Louis Tussaud's** Shakespearian play scenes in wax.

E(9) **Mason Croft, Shakespeare Institute** An early 18th-C brick building which was the home of the novelist Marie Corelli and is now a study and lecture centre for the University of Birmingham.

E(10) **Model Car Museum**

E(11) **New Place Estate** Foundations of Shakespeare's house and a replica of an Elizabethan garden. Furniture and local history exhibits are displayed in the adjacent Nash's House.

E(12) **Royal Shakespeare Theatre**

E(13) **Royal Shakespeare Theatre Picture Gallery and Museum** The gallery contains portraits of Shakespeare and famous Shakespearian actors and actresses, in addition to other theatrical relics.

B(14) **Shakespeare Centre** The headquarters of the Shakespeare Birthplace Trust which contains a specialised library and study centre.

E(15) **Shakespeare's Birthplace** A 16th-C half-timbered building which contains many relics connected with the poet's life, time and works.

B(16) **Stratford Motor Museum** A former Victorian church and school which displays cars and relics in period settings. The museum specialises in exotic sports and grand touring cars.

E(17) **Town Hall** A dignified building dedicated to the memory of Shakespeare by the famous actor David Garrick in 1769.

Anne Hathaway's Cottage, Shottery. The thatched and timbered Elizabethan cottage where Anne

Hall's Croft

Hathaway, who became Shakespeare's wife, was born. 1½m W via Shottery Road or Footpath (D)

Mary Arden's House A picturesque half-timbered Tudor building which was the birthplace of Shakespeare's mother. A farming museum is housed in the barns. 3¾m NW via Birmingham Road A34 (A)

Hospitals

A **Stratford-upon-Avon General Hospital,** Alcester Road *tel 5831*

Sport and Recreation

F **Stratford-upon-Avon Boat Club,** The Boat House

I **Stratford-upon-Avon Cricket, Hockey and Squash Club**

C **Stratford-upon-Avon Swimming Pool**

D **Stratford-upon-Avon Town Football Club,** Alcester Road

Stratford-upon-Avon Golf Club. 1m NE via Tiddington Road B4086 (F)

Stratford-upon-Avon Racecourse, Luddington Road. ½m SW via Evesham Road A439 (G)

Stratford-upon-Avon Rugby Club, Pearcecroft, Loxley Road (F)

Theatres and Cinemas

E(12) **Royal Shakespeare Theatre** *tel 2271* (see also public buildings and places of interest)

D **Stratford-upon-Avon Picture House,** Greenhill Street *tel 2622*

H **The Other Place,** Southern Lane *tel 2565*

Department Stores

Debenhams, Wood Street
Winters, High Street
Early closing day Thursday

Markets

D **Cattle Market** (Tuesday and Friday)
E **General Market,** Rother Street (Friday)

Advertisers

E **THF** White Swan Hotel
E **THF** Shakespeare Hotel
F **THF** Alveston Manor
F **THF** Swan's Nest Hotel

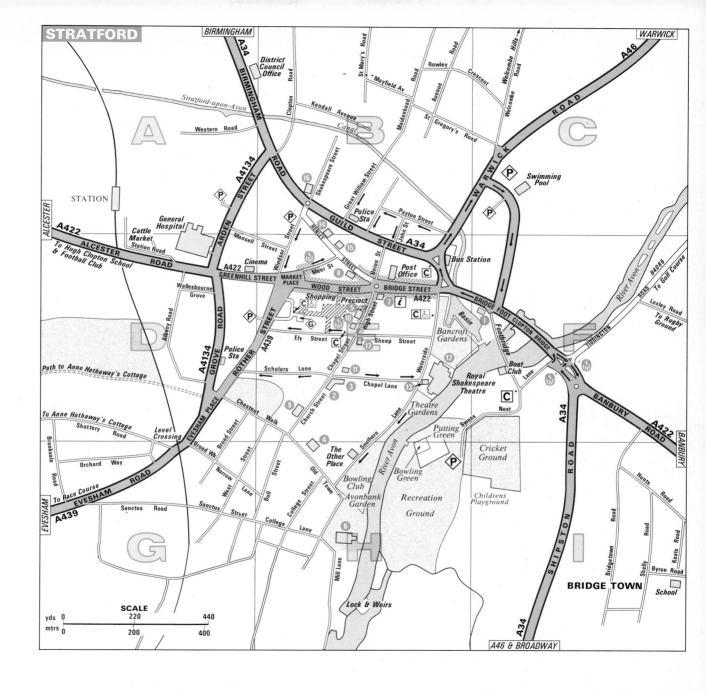

STRATFORD

BIRMINGHAM

WARWICK

STATION

ALCESTER

EVESHAM

A46 & BROADWAY

BANBURY

BRIDGE TOWN

District Council Office

Stratford-upon-Avon Canal

Western Road

St Mary's Road

Rowley

Mayfield Av

Welcombe Hills Road

Crescent

Avenue

Maidenhead

St Gregory's Road

Welcombe Road

Clopton Road

Kendall Avenue

A4134

BIRMINGHAM ROAD

A34

ARDEN STREET

Shakespeare Street

Great William Street

GUILD STREET

John St

Payton Street

WARWICK ROAD

A46

Swimming Pool

General Hospital

Cattle Market

Station Road

ALCESTER ROAD

A422

To Hugh Clopton School & Football Club

Mansell Street

Windsor Street

HENLEY STREET

Police Sta

A34

Bus Station

Cinema

A422

GREENHILL STREET

MARKET PLACE

Meer St

WOOD STREET

Union St

BRIDGE STREET

Post Office

A422

Basin

River Avon

B4086

To Golf Course

Loxley Road

To Rugby Ground

Wellesbourne Grove

Shopping Precinct

BRIDGE FOOT

CLOPTON BRIDGE

Footbridge

Albany Road

GROVE ROAD

A4134

ROTHER STREET

A439

High Street

Ely Street

Chapel Street

Sheep Street

Bancroft Gardens

Boat Club

TIDDINGTON

A34

Police Sta

Scholars Lane

Chapel Lane

Waterside

Royal Shakespeare Theatre

Nest

BANBURY ROAD

A422

Path to Anne Hathaway's Cottage

Church Street

Theatre Gardens

To Anne Hathaway's Cottage

EVESHAM PLACE

Chestnut Walk

Broad Street

Old Town

Southern Lane

River Avon

Putting Green

Swans

Cricket Ground

Hunts Road

Level Crossing

Shottery Road

Broad Wk

Narrow Lane

Bull Street

College Street

The Other Place

Bowling Green

Bowling Club

Recreation Ground

Childrens Playground

SHIPSTON ROAD

Shelly Road

Keats Road

Byron Road

Brookvale Road

Orchard Way

To Race Course

EVESHAM ROAD

A439

West Lane

Sanctus Road

Sanctus Street

College Lane

Mill Lane

Avonbank Garden

A34

School

Lock & Weirs

SCALE

yds 0 — 220 — 440

mtrs 0 — 200 — 400

201

B(8) **Tourist Information Centre** St Peter's Church, St Peter's Way (see also public buildings and places of interest)

Public buildings and places of interest

E(1) **Central Library, Art Gallery and Museum** Contains examples of local lustre-ware, pottery, glassware, a collection of 15th- to 19th-C silver, models of Sunderland-built ships, archaeology, natural history, local history, period rooms and 19th- to 20th-C paintings.

H(2) **Civic Centre and Town Hall** A modern building of interesting design, opened in 1970.

D(3) **Crowther Leisure Centre** Features of this new building include an ice rink, indoor bowling green and fun pool with artificial waves.

D(4) **Empire Theatre**

F(5) **Holy Trinity Church** This church dates from the 18thC.

A(6) **Monkwearmouth Station Museum** One of the best examples of Victorian railway architecture, designed by Thomas Moore of Sunderland in 1848. Re-opened as a land transport museum in 1971, it contains a restored Victorian booking office complete with figures of clerks and passengers, and a collection relating to the social and industrial history of Sunderland.

D(7) **St Michael's Church** Largely a rebuilding of the 19th and 20thCs in a modified Perpendicular style but preserves fragments of stonework, dating back to the 13thC including an effigy in the south aisle.

B(8) **St Peter's Church, Monkwearmouth and Tourist Information Centre** Originally part of a monastic foundation of 674, of which only the Saxon tower (60ft) and West Wall remain. The remainder of the church was rebuilt in the 19thC. The octagonal chapter house was built in 1974 to mark the 13th centenary and contains tourist information and a display illustrating the history of the church.

Fulwell Windmill This famous landmark, now fully restored, is the only complete windmill in the North East, 1¾m N via Newcastle Road A1018 (A)

Grindon Library Museum Grindon Lane. Edwardian period rooms and shop interiors. 2¾m W via Chester Road A183 (D)

Hylton Castle (AM) The well-preserved shell of a 15th-C tower-house castle. 2½m W via Southwick Road B1289 (A) then the Sunderland Airport Road

Ryhope Engines Museum Housed in the Ryhope Pumping Station, one of the finest industrial monuments of mid-Victorian times, are two restored beam engines and a museum illustrating varied aspects of water supply and use. Open weekends only. 3mS via Ryhope Road A1018 (H)

Seaburn Ocean Park and Amusement Centre 2m NE via Dame Dorothy Street and Whitburn Road A183 (B)

Fulwell Windmill

Hospitals

G **Royal Infirmary,** New Durham Road *tel 56256*

Children's Hospital, New Durham Road *tel 56256* 1½m SW via New Durham Road A690 (G)

Eye Infirmary, Queen Alexandra Road *tel 283616* 1½m S via Ryhope Road A1018 (H) then Sea View Road and Queen Alexandra Road

Accident and General Hospital, Chester Road *tel 56256* 1¼m W via Chester Road A183 (D)

Orthopaedic Hospital, Newcastle Road *tel 70031* 1m N via Newcastle Road A1018 (A)

Sport and Recreation

D(3) **Crowther Leisure Centre,** (see also public buildings and places of interest)

D **Swimming Pool,** High Street West

Mecca Bowling Centre, Newcastle Road ¾m N via Newcastle Road A1018 (A)

Sunderland Association Football Club, Roker Park Ground 1¼m N via Roker Avenue (B) Glandstone Street and Roker Park Road

Sunderland Cricket and Rugby Football Club, Ashbrooke Ground 1¼m S via Tunstall Road (G)

Swimming Pool, Newcastle Road ¾m N via Newcastle Road A1018 (A)

Theatres and Cinemas

D **ABC Cinema,** Holmeside *tel 74148*

D(4) **Empire (Civic) Theatre,** High Street West *tel 73274* (see also public buildings and places of interest)

D **Odeon Theatre (Cinema),** Holmeside *tel 74881*

E **Fairworld Cinema 1 & 2,** High Street West *tel 76317*

Department Stores

Binns Ltd, Fawcett Street
Joplings Ltd, John Street
Marks and Spencer Ltd, 77 High Street West
Thompson W C Ltd, Liverpool House, High Street West
Early closing day Wednesday

Markets

D **Covered Market,** Shopping Centre (daily)

Advertisers

E **Mercantile Credit**

SWANSEA

AA Road Service Centre (111) —
Junction Rutland Street/Oystermouth
Road *tel 55598*

J(3) **Tourist Information Centre** — Civic
ⓘ   Centre *tel 50821* (see also public
buildings and places of interest)

Public buildings and places of interest

H(1) **Castle** There are slight remains of this
14th-C castle or fortified manor house.
H(2) **Central Library**
J(3) **Civic Centre** A handsome white building
housing the Guildhall, Law Courts and
Brangwyn Hall used for concerts and
dances, and noted for the 20-ft high
British Empire Panels painted by the
Welsh artist Frank Brangwyn RA.
H(4) **Glynn Vivian Art Gallery** Contains
notable collections of Continental and
local Swansea and Nantgarw pottery
and porcelain, Old masters of the British,
French and Italian schools, and
contemporary British works of art.
L(5) **Leisure Centre** A major feature is the
indoor pool with a beach and
wave-making machine.
L(6) **Maritime and Industrial Museum**
J(7) **Patti Pavilion** Dances and varied
seasonal entertainments take place here.
L(8) **Royal Institution of South Wales Museum**
Founded in 1875 with exhibits including
local antiquarian and archaeological
finds, Swansea and Nantgarw china, a
reconstruction of a 19th-C Gower
kitchen, and industrial exhibits
including machinery from local steel,
copper and aluminium plants and a
small steam locomotive.
K(9) **St Mary's Church** The largest church in
Swansea, rebuilt in 1847 and restored
again after severe war damage in 1941.
It possesses unique carvings and some
fine stained glass.
I   **University College of Swansea**

Hospitals

A   Hill House Hospital *tel 23551*
C   Mount Pleasant Hospital *tel 55882*

204

Sport and Recreation

L(5) **Leisure Centre**, Oystermouth Road (see
also public building and places of
interest)
K   **Swansea City Association Football Club**,
Vetch Field
I   **Swansea Rugby Football and County
Cricket Club**, St Helen's Ground
J   **Victoria Swimming Baths**
Blackpill Municipal Golf Course. 2¼m W via
Mumbles Road A4067 (I)
Swansea Greyhound Stadium, Ystrad Road,
Fforestfach, 3¾m NW via Carmarthen Road A483
(D) and Ystrad Road A470

Theatres and Cinemas

H   **Castle Cinema**, Worcester Place *tel 53433*
K   **Grand Theatre**, Singleton Street
tel 55141
G   **Odeon Cinema**, The Kingsway *tel 52351*

Department Stores

Co-operative, Oxford Street
David Evans and Co (Swansea) Ltd, Princess Way
Debenhams, The Quadrant Shopping Area
Marks and Spencer Ltd, Oxford Street
Early closing day Thursday

Markets

G   **Covered Market**, Oxford Street
(Monday–Saturday, early closing
Thursday)

Advertisers

H   **Berni** Grand Hotel
H   **Berni** The Bush
H   **Berni** Three Lamps
G   **Mercantile Credit**
G   **THF** Dragon Hotel

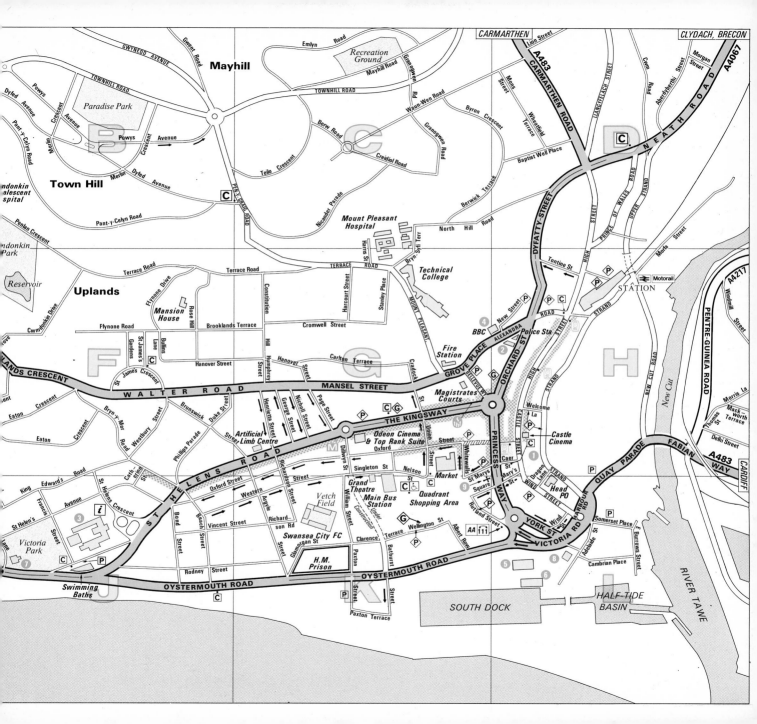

AA Road Service Centre (106) — Drakes Way *tel 21446* 1¼m NE via Drakes Way A420 (H)

F [i] **Tourist Information Centre** — David Murray John Tower, Brunel Centre *tel 30328*

Public buildings and places of interest

K(1) **Christ Church** This church, situated in the old town, dates from the 19thC.

G(2) **Civic Offices** Thamesdown Borough Council.

F(3) **Great Western Railway Museum and Railway Village** Opened in 1962, the museum contains the famous *City of Truro, Lode Star* and *North Star* and exhibits a wide range of nameplates, models, illustrations, posters and tickets. The Railway Village adjacent to the locomotive works has survived and is being restored.

O(4) **Museum and Art Gallery** Housed in the 19th-C Apsley House, the museum contains collections of items of local interest. The Art Gallery exhibits pictures by 20th-C artists including Moore, Piper, Sutherland, Grant, Bevan and Lowry.

B(5) **Oasis Leisure Centre**

B/K(6) **Technical College** and new extension.

K(7) **Town Hall and Public Library**

K(8) **Wyvern Theatre and Regional Film Centre** Opened in 1971, the Wyvern Theatre and Film Centre houses a fully-equipped theatre and an auditorium seating over 600 people.

Hospitals

M **Princess Margaret Hospital,** Okus Road *tel 36231*

N **Seymour Clinic,** Kinghill Street *tel 35193*

N **Victoria Hospital,** Okus Road *tel 36231*

Sport and Recreation

H **County Cricket Ground,** County Road

F **Milton Road Swimming Baths**

B(5) **Oasis Leisure Centre** (see also public buildings and places of interest)

H **Swindon Town Football Club,** Shrivenham Road

Blunsdon Greyhound and Speedway Stadium, 3½m N via Cricklade Road A345 (C)

Theatres and Cinemas

ABC Cinema, Regent Street *tel 22838*

O **Arts Centre,** Devizes Road *tel 26161 ext 561*

K(8) **The Wyvern Theatre and Regional Film Centre,** Theatre Square *tel 24481* (see also public buildings and places of interest)

Department Stores

Bon Marché, Regent Street
Co-operative, Fleetway House, Fleet Street
Debenhams Ltd, The Parade
McIlroy, Regent Street
Marks and Spencer Ltd, 81 Regent Street
Early closing day Wednesday

Markets

F **Market Hall,** David Murray John Tower, Brunel Centre (Tuesday to Saturday)

Advertisers

K **Berni** The Rifleman

K **Mercantile Credit**

Great Western Railway Museum

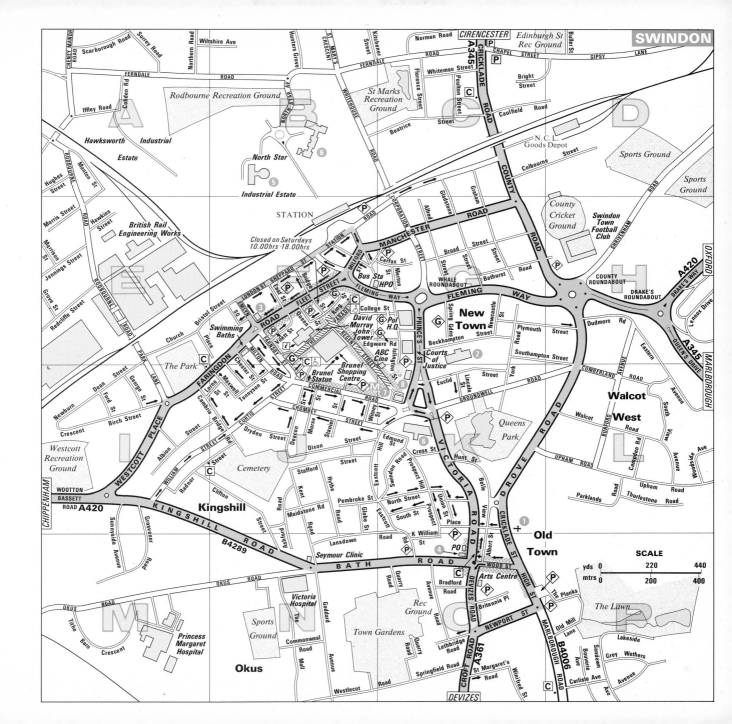

L AA Road Service Centre (89) — Victoria Parade *tel 25903*
G *i* Tourist Information Centre — Vaughan Parade *tel 27428*

Public buildings and places of interest

L(1) Aqualand Aquarium, Beacon Quay
H(2) Natural History Museum Contains items on local archaeology, natural history and the folk life of Devon.
J(3) Torre Abbey and Gardens An 18th-C house which contains the Corporation Art Gallery and interesting furniture. In the grounds are a 12th-C tithe barn and ruins of the Abbey.
F(4) Town Hall and Library
Kents Cavern Prehistoric stalactite and stalagmite caves of interest and natural beauty. At Wellswood 1m NE via Babbacombe Road B3199 (H)

Hospitals

C Rosehill Children's Hospital, Lower Warberry Road *tel 22570*
Torbay Hospital Lawes Bridge *tel 64567* 2m NW via Newton Road A380 (A)

Sport and Recreation

L Coral Island Leisure Complex
J Torquay Athletic Rugby Football Club, Recreation Ground
J Torquay Cricket Club, Recreation Ground
B Torquay Indoor Swimming Pool, St Marychurch Road
F Torquay Lawn Tennis Club, Belgrave Road
B Torquay Tenpin Bowling, Higher Union Street
L Royal Torbay Yacht Club, Beacon Hill
Torquay United Association Football Club, Plainmoor 1¼m N via Bronshill Road (B)

Theatres and Cinemas

G Colony Cinema, Union Street *tel 22146*
G Odeon Film Centre, Abbey Road *tel 22324*
K Princess Theatre *tel 27527*

Department Stores

Debenhams, 14 The Strand
Dingles of Torquay, Fleet Street
Early closing day Wednesday (higher part of town) and Saturday

Markets

G Market Hall, Market Street

Advertisers

L Berni Berni Inn
H Mercantile Credit
L THF Imperial Hotel

Inner harbour

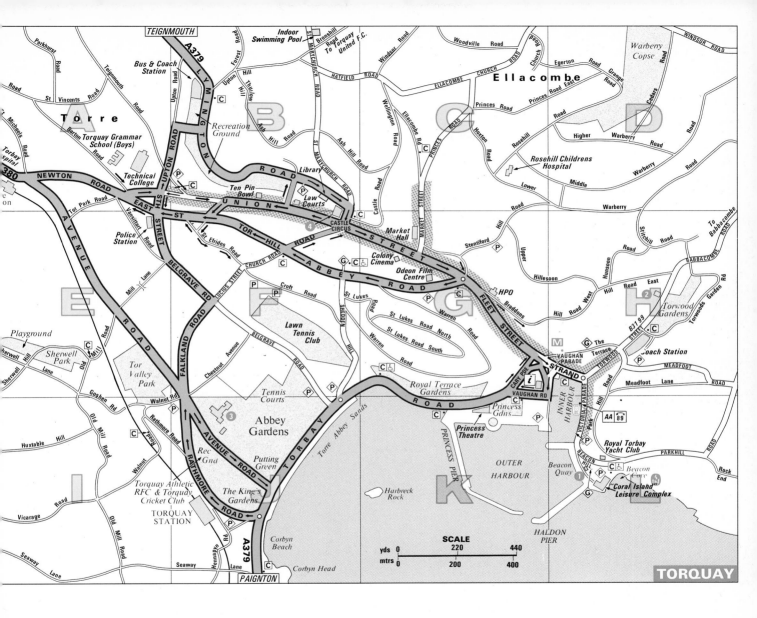

TEIGNMOUTH

Indoor Swimming Pool
Bronshill
To Torquay United F.C.

Warberry Copse
WINDSOR ROAD
Woodville Road
Egerton Road
Grange Road
Cedars Road

Parkhurst Road
Teignmouth Road
St Vincents Road

Bus & Coach Station
Upton Road
Forest Road
Upton Hill
Thurlow Hill

HATFIELD ROAD
Windsor Road
Church

ELLACOMBE CHURCH ROAD
Ellacombe

Torre
Barton Road
Torquay Grammar School (Boys)

Recreation Ground

St MARYCHURCH ROAD
Ash Hill Road
Ash Hill

Wellington Road

Princes Road East
Princes Road
Hoxton Street
Rosehill

Higher Warberry Road
Warberry

A380
St Michaels Road
Torbay Hospital

NEWTON ROAD
Technical College

UPTON ROAD
Library

UNION
Ten Pin Bowl

ROAD
Law Courts

Castle Road

Market Hall

Rosehill Childrens Hospital

Lower Warberry Road
Middle Warberry Road
Warberry Road

Tor Park Road
EAST STREET
Vansittart Road

St Efrides Road

TOR HILL ROAD
CASTLE CIRCUS

STREET

MARKET STREET

Stentiford Hill
Upper

Lincombe
To Babbacombe

AVENUE
Police Station

BELGRAVE RD
Mill Lane

CHURCH ROAD
LUCIUS STREET

ABBEY ROAD

Colony Cinema
Odeon Film Centre

HPO

FLEET STREET

B3199 Street

Playground

Sherwell Hill
Sherwell Park
Old Mill

Tor Valley Park

FALKLAND ROAD

Chestnut Avenue
Croft Road
BELGRAVE ROAD
SHEDDON HILL

Lawn Tennis Club

St Lukes Road
St Lukes Road North
Warren Road
St Lukes Road South
Warren Road

Braddons Hill Road West

Torwood Gardens

Coach Station
MEADFOOT ROAD

Huxtable Hill
Goshen Rd
Rathmore Road
Walnut Rd

Tennis Courts

ROYAL TERRACE
Royal Terrace Gardens

VAUGHAN PARADE

VAUGHAN RD
STRAND

Meadfoot Lane

Vicarage Road
Old Mill Road

RATHMORE ROAD

AVENUE ROAD

TORBAY ROAD

Abbey Gardens

Rec Gnd
Putting Green

The King's Gardens

Torre Abbey Sands

Harbreck Rock

ROAD

PRINCESS PIER

Princess Theatre
Princess Gdns

OUTER HARBOUR

INNER HARBOUR

AA 89

Royal Torbay Yacht Club
PARKHILL ROAD
Rock End

Seaway Lane

Torquay Athletic RFC & Torquay Cricket Club

TORQUAY STATION

A379
PAIGNTON

Corbyn Beach
Seaway Lane
Corbyn Head

Beacon Quay
Beacon Cove
Coral Island Leisure Complex

HALDON PIER

SCALE
yds 0 ... 220 ... 440
mtrs 0 ... 200 ... 400

TORQUAY

WEMBLEY COMPLEX

Wembley lies six miles north west of central London and close to the North Circular Road and the southern terminal of the M1 Motorway. The main buildings in the 73-acre complex consist of the Empire Stadium, the Wembley Arena and the new Conference Centre. Adjacent to the complex is the Eurocrest Hotel. The site was formerly a golf course before it was transformed to house the British Empire Exhibition in 1924. Many of the exhibition halls can still be seen (particularly along Olympic Way) and are now used for industrial and commercial purposes.

Wembley Stadium

The first event to be held in the world famous stadium was the 1923 FA Cup Final when the official attendance was recorded at 126,047 — although many more thousands managed to gain access. Since that date the capacity has been restricted to 100,000, of which 45,000 can be seated. Although renowned as the venue for major football matches, including the 1966 World Cup Final, the Stadium stages a variety of sporting events such as Rugby League, Gaelic football and hurling, hockey,

speedway and regular greyhound racing meetings. Other events have included religious crusades and pop concerts. The first post-war Olympic Games in 1948 were also held in the Stadium.

The public may see behind the scenes of Wembley Stadium on special tours which take in the dressing rooms, the players' tunnel and the Royal Box. For information on times and dates telephone 01-902 8833.

Wembley Arena

The Wembley Arena, previously named the Empire Pool, is an indoor building with 8,000 permanent seats and was first opened in 1934. Originally constructed as a swimming pool, it was soon converted to an ice rink — although it was used for swimming events in the 1948 Olympic Games. Nowadays the Arena regularly stages all manner of events including horse shows, basketball, five-a-side football, tennis, boxing promotions and concerts. Each Christmas during the pantomime season, spectacular ice shows are normally presented. Close by the Arena is a well equipped Squash Centre containing 14 courts and a glass-backed Championship Arena.

Conference Centre

The £18-million Conference Centre was opened in 1977 and is considered to be one of Europe's finest conference and exhibition buildings. The main auditorium can accommodate 2,500 people and is equipped with the latest audio and visual facilities. Lecture theatres, spacious display areas and well-appointed bars and restaurants all combine to provide excellent facilities for delegates, exhibitors and trade visitors. The Centre's facilities are not, however, restricted to business activities; concerts and sporting events are also regularly featured.

Parking

The extensive parking facilities, which include a multi-storey car park, can accommodate 5,000 cars or 1,000 coaches. The main open-space parking area is divided into numbered segments in order to aid vehicle location after events. Parking charges can vary according to the size and nature of events.

An open-air market, with accommodation for over 600 stalls, is held in an area of the car park each Sunday between 9am and 2pm. Parking on these occasions is free.

Public Transport

By rail —
Wembley Park Station (Metropolitan and Bakerloo Lines)
Wembley Complex Station (British Rail from Marylebone)
Within ¾ mile — Wembley Central Station (British Rail from Euston/Broad Street. Also Bakerloo Line during peak hours)
By bus —
London Transport 83, 92 and 182 routes all pass the complex.
Other useful buses that pass nearby are the 245 and 297.
By taxi —
Taxi ranks are situated outside the Conference Centre and Wembley Park Station. For further information contact Wembley Stadium Ltd, The Empire Stadium, Wembley, HA9 0DW. *tel 01-902 8833.*

Wembley Stadium

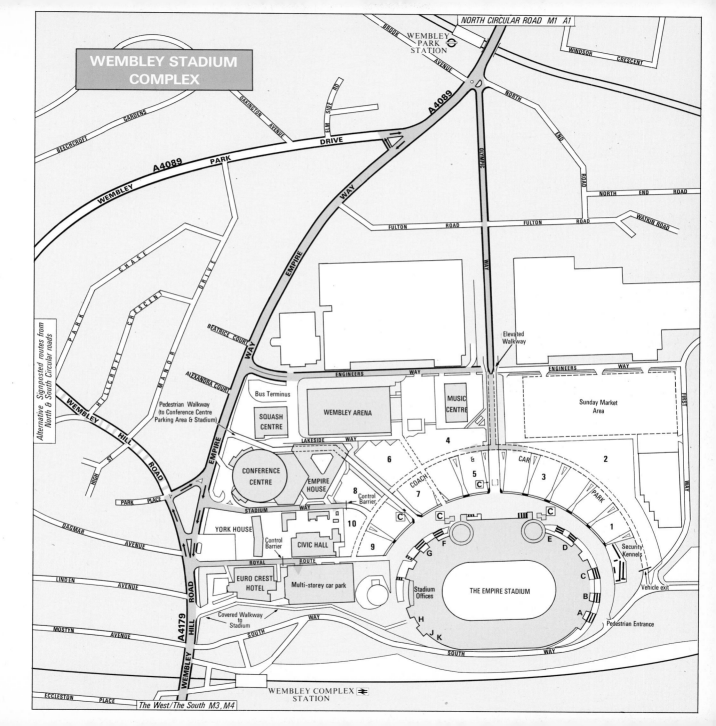

Breakdown Service *tel Southampton 36811*

K(9) **Tourist Information Centre** — Guildhall,
The Broadway *tel 68166* weekdays,
65406 weekends (see also public
buildings and places of interest)

Public buildings and places of interest

K(1) **Abbey House and Gardens** The public
gardens occupy the site of St Mary's
Abbey, a Benedictine nunnery founded
by Alfred the Great's wife in the latter
part of the 9thC. The Abbey House,
built about 1748, has been used since
1892 as the official residence of the
Mayors of Winchester.

F(2) **Castle Hall** At present used as law
courts, the 13th-C Aisled Hall is all
that remains of the castle. The 14th-C
Round Table associated with the legend
of King Arthur hangs on the west wall.

K(3) **Cathedral and Close** The second longest
cathedral in Europe, it was begun in
1079 and finished in 1404. The many
notable features include the splendid
nave, the chantry chapels, carved 14th-C
stalls, the 15th-C reredos and a 12th-C
black-marble Tournai font. The tombs
of Izaak Walton and Jane Austen lie in
the Cathedral. In the Close are many old
buildings, notably the Pilgrims' School
with a 13th-C Hall, and the Tudor
Cheyney Court.

G(4) **City Cross** Known locally as 'Butter
Cross', this 15th-C High Cross was
partially restored in 1865.

L(5) **City Mill (NT)** Built in 1774 this
watermill is now occupied by the Youth
Hostels' Association.

K(6) **City Museum** Contains displays relating
to the archaeology and history of the
City and central Hampshire.

K(7) **The Deanery,** Cathedral Close. A 13th-C
and later house.

G(8) **Godbegot House** A picturesque, restored
half-timbered building of Tudor date.

K(9) **Guildhall, Picture Gallery and Tourist
Information Centre** Built in 1873, the
Picture Gallery in the west wing of the
Guildhall displays local prints, drawings
and loan exhibitions.

C(10) **Hyde Abbey Gatehouse (AM)** The 15th-C
gatehouse is all that remains of Hyde
Abbey.

K(11) **King Alfred Statue** The bronze statue
of Alfred the Great, who held his court
at Winchester, was erected in 1901.

G(12) **Old Guildhall** An 18th-C building with
a projecting clock. Now used as a bank.

F(13) **Plague Monument** Erected in memory of
the plague of 1666, the monument dates
from 1759.

F(14) **Royal Greenjackets Regimental Museum**
Displays relating to the history of the
Regiment, including weapons, regimental
silver, colours and banners.

J(15) **Royal Hampshire Regimental Museum,**
Serle's House. The museum is housed in
the reception hall on the ground floor
of this 18th-C house.

H(16) **St John the Baptist Church** A 12th-C
church with a 15th-C tower and old
screenwork.

K(17) **St John's Hospital and Chapel** Founded
in the 13thC, the buildings are now
mainly 18th- and 19th-C with some traces
of the medieval building in the chapel.

F(18) **Westgate Museum** Small, civic museum
housed above the Westgate.

K(19) **Winchester College** Founded in 1382 by
William of Wykeham, this is one of
England's oldest public schools. The
Chapel and Tower, the Old School and
the Fromond Chantry Chapel are all of
interest.

K(20) **Wolvesey Castle** Remains of the mid-
12th-C castle of Bishop Henry de Blois.
Nearby stands the surviving wing of the
present 17th-C Bishop's Palace, built
by Wren with a late Tudor chapel.

St Cross Hospital 1¼m S via St Cross Road A333.
Founded in 1136 by Bishop Henry de Blois,
little remains of the original structure as most
of the hospital was rebuilt by Cardinal Beaufort
in the 15thC (N).

Hospitals

I **Royal Hampshire County Hospital,** Romsey
Road *tel 63535*

F **St Paul's Hospital,** St Paul's Hill *tel
3288*

Victoria Hospital, Alresford Road *tel 2048* 1¼m E
via Magdalen Hill B3404 (H)

Sport and Recreation

I **Winchester City Football Club,** Airlie Road
C **Winchester Recreation Centre,** North
Walls Recreation Ground — swimming,
bowls, cricket, football, putting
green, tennis
A **Winchester Tennis and Squash Club,**
Bereweeke Road
Royal Winchester Golf Club, Sarum Road 1½m W
via Romsey Road A3090 then Sarum Road (I)

Theatres and Cinemas

G **Studios 1, 2 and 3** North Walls *tel 2592*

Department Stores

The Co-operative, 8 High Street
Debenhams Ltd, 12/15 and 103/104 High Street
Marks and Spencer Ltd, 138 High Street
Early closing day Thursday

Markets

G **Antique Market,** Kings Walk
(Monday to Saturday)
G **Friarsgate,** general (Wednesday and Friday)
F **Stockbridge Road,** general (Saturday)
B **Worthy Lane,** cattle (Monday)

Advertisers

F **Berni** The Castle
K **THF** Wessex Hotel

Godbegot House

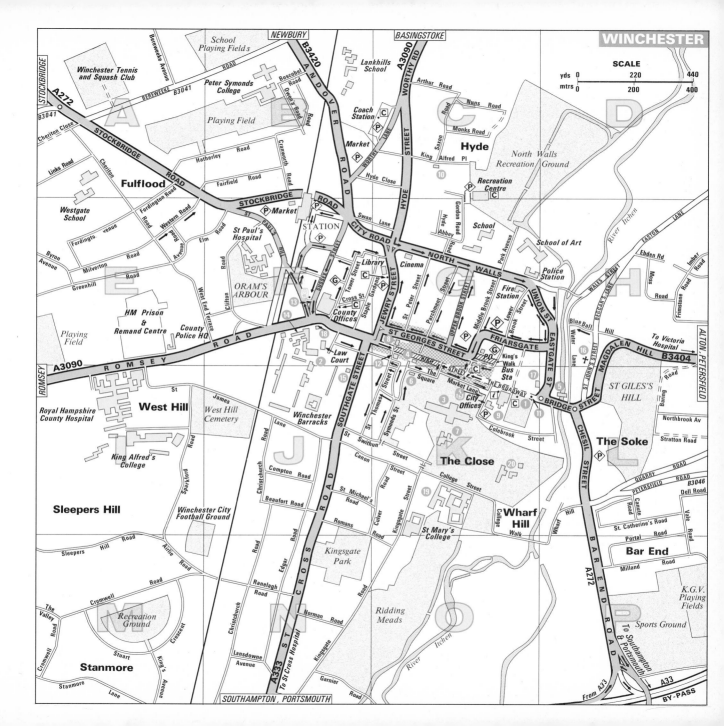

WINCHESTER

SCALE

yds 0 — 220 — 440
mtrs 0 — 200 — 400

STOCKBRIDGE

A272
B3041

NEWBURY
B3420

BASINGSTOKE
A3090
WORTHY RD

School Playing Fields
Lankhills School

Bereweeke Avenue
Winchester Tennis and Squash Club
Peter Symonds College
Boscobel Rd
Owen's Road
Playing Field
BEREWEKE
B3041

Cheriton Close
Cheriton Road
Links Road
Hatherley Road
Cranworth Road
Fairfield Road

Market
Coach Station
Arthur Road
Nuns Road
Monks Road
King Alfred Pl
Saxon Road

Hyde

North Walls Recreation Ground
River Itchen
EASTON LANE

STOCKBRIDGE ROAD

Fulflood

Westgate School
Fordington Avenue
Western Road
St Paul's Hill
Elm Road
WORTHY LANE

STOCKBRIDGE ROAD
Market
STATION
Swan Lane
CITY ROAD
Hyde Close
Hyde Abbey Road
Gordon Road
School
Park Avenue
School of Art
Ebden Rd
Moss Road
Imber Road
Frimstone Road

Byron Avenue
Milverton Road
Greenhill Road
West End Terrace
Clifton Road

St Paul's Hospital
ORAM'S ARBOUR
Library
Tower Street
Cross St
Staple Gardens
Cinema
NORTH WALLS
Fire Station
Police Station
Lower Brook Street
UNION ST
WALES STREET
BEGGAR'S LANE
Blue Ball Hill
Water Lane

HM Prison & Remand Centre
County Police HQ
County Offices
Sussex Street
JEWRY STREET
St Peter St
Parchment St
Middle Brook Street
Upper Brook Street
FRIARSGATE
EASTGATE ST
ST JOHN'S STREET
To Victoria Hospital
ALTON, PETERSFIELD
B3404

ROMSEY
A3090
ROMSEY ROAD
Law Court
SOUTHGATE STREET
ST GEORGES STREET
HIGH STREET
The Square
PO
King's Walk Bus Sta
THE BROADWAY
Market Lane
City Offices
BRIDGE STREET
St Giles's Hill
Baring Road

Playing Field

West Hill
West Hill Cemetery
Winchester Barracks
St James Lane
St Thomas St
Symonds St
Colebrook Street
Northbrook Av
Stratton Road

Royal Hampshire County Hospital
King Alfred's College
St Swithun St
Canon Street
Culver Road
Kingsgate Street
College Street
St Michael's Road
The Close
Wharf Hill
College Walk
Wharf Hill

The Soke

Sleepers Hill
Winchester City Football Ground
Christchurch Road
Compton Road
Beaufort Road
Romans Road
St Mary's College
CHESIL STREET
BARTEND ROAD
A272
Petersfield Road
B3046
Canute Road
Dell Road
Vale Road
St. Catherine's Road
Portal Road
Bar End
Milland Road

Airlie Road
Recreation Ground
Edgar Road
Ranelagh Road
Kingsgate Park
Ridding Meads
River Itchen
K.G.V. Playing Fields
Sports Ground

The Valley
Cromwell Road
Stuart Crescent
King's Avenue
Sleepers Hill Road
Christchurch Road
Norman Road
Kingsgate Road
Garnier Road

Stanmore
Stanmore Lane
Lansdowne Avenue
To St Cross Hospital
SOUTHAMPTON, PORTSMOUTH
A333
ST CROSS ROAD
To Southampton & Portsmouth
From A33
A33
BY-PASS

WINDSOR AND ETON

Public buildings and places of interest

F(1)   **Clewer Parish Church** Completed c1100, with the exception of the Chantry Chapel which was added c1380 by Sir Bernard Brocas.

K(2)   **East Berkshire College of Further Education**

C(3)   **Eton College** This famous Public School, second oldest in the country, was founded in 1440 by Henry VI, a statue of whom stands in the cobbled School Yard. Buildings of particular interest are the chapel, an impressive example of Perpendicular architecture, and Lupton's Tower of c1517. The Library of 1729 includes the original of Gray's *Elegy Written in a Country Churchyard* and a copy of the Guttenberg Bible.

C(4)   **Eton Parish Church** The present building dates from the mid-19thC and contains a handsome corona of Italian style in the chancel and parish registers dating back to 1594.

N(5)   **Household Cavalry Museum,** Combermere Barracks. One of the finest military museums in Britain, with exhibits dating from the Monmouth Rebellion (1685) to the present day.

G(6)   **King George V Memorial**

K(7)   **Nell Gwynne's House** Dates from c1670.

G(8)   **Old House Hotel** Dates from the late 17thC.

G(9)   **Our Lady of Sorrows Church (RC)** This church in Italian Renaissance style is a perfect miniature of a Roman basilica.

G(10)   **Queen Victoria Statue**

G(11)   **Theatre Royal** This playhouse dates from 1793.

G(12)   **The Cock Pit** A half-timbered building probably dating from 1420, now used as a restaurant. Inside are a knucklebone cockpit floor, and spurs and hood used in this sport. Outside are the parish stocks, whipping post and a mid-19th-C pillar box, one of the three surviving originals.

G(13)   **The Guildhall** A classical building of c1689 designed by Sir Thomas Fitz, and completed by Sir Christopher Wren.

It contains a museum of local historical and archaeological items, and a collection of Royal portraits.

H(14)   **Windsor Castle** This famous Royal castle was built by William the Conqueror, and restored with large 19th-C additions for George IV by Wyatville. There are fine State Apartments and Queen Mary's Doll's House is of interest. St George's Chapel is a splendid fan-vaulted Perpendicular building containing Royal tombs; in the choir are the

Eton College

stalls and brasses of the Garter Knights. The restored Albert Memorial Chapel was erected originally by Henry VII. The Home Park contains the Frogmore Mausoleum, with Queen Victoria's tomb.

G(15)   **Windsor Parish Church**
Windsor Great Park Beautifully wooded and covering some 4,800 acres. The eastern fringe of the park contains the beautiful woodland Savill Gardens and nearby Valley Gardens is Virginia Water, one of the largest artificial lakes in England, reached by way of Englefield Green. 4m SE via Albert Road A308 (P)
Windsor Safari Park Once a royal hunting ground and now a drive-in zoo with lion and cheetah reserves and dolphinarium. 3m SW via Winkfield Road B3022 (M)

Sport and Recreation

D   **Old Windsorians Rugby Football Club,** Home Park, Datchet Road

A   **Royal Windsor Racecourse**

F   **Swimming Pool,** Stovell Road

D   **Windsor and Eton Cricket Club,** Home Park

N   **Windsor and Eton Football Club,** St Leonard's Road

D   **Windsor Rovers Football Club,** Home Park

D   **Windsor Rugby Football Club,** Home Park

D   **Windsor Victoria Cricket Club,** Home Park

Theatres and Cinemas

G   **ABC Cinema,** 59 Thames Street *tel 63888*

G(11)   **Theatre Royal** *tel 53888* (see also public buildings and places of interest)

Department Stores

Caleys, 19 High Street
Daniel W J & Co Ltd, 120 Peascod Street
Early closing day Wednesday

Advertisers

G   **Berni** The Berni Inn

K   **Crest** Royal Adelaide Hotel

G   **THF** Castle Hotel

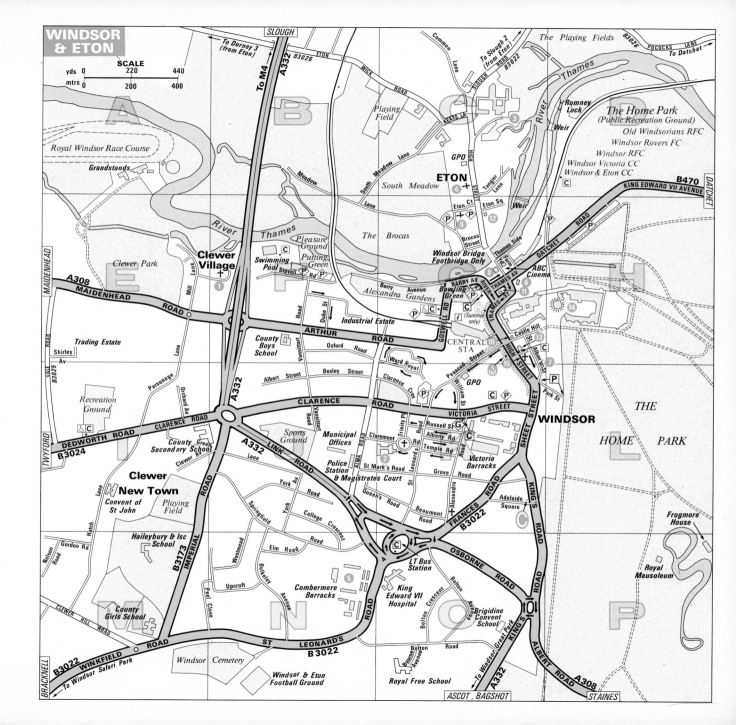

K   AA Service Centre — 19 The Gallery, Mander Square *tel 021-550 4858*

Public buildings and places of interest

K(1)   **Art Gallery** Contains a comprehensive collection including 18th- and 19th-C watercolours and oil paintings, modern prints, paintings and drawings, sculpture, Oriental art and antiquities.

J(2)   **Civic Hall** A fine, modern building opened in 1938, containing a concert hall with seating capacity for over 1,750.

O(3)   **St George's Church** This church was rebuilt in 1830.

O(4)   **St John's Church** An 18th-C church with fine 17th-C organ.

K(5)   **St Peter's Church** A fine, mainly 15th-C church with a tall, panelled tower, an octagonal font and notable carved pulpit. In the churchyard are the so-called 'Bargaining' stones and a very early carved cross-shaft.

J(6)   **Town Hall; Information Bureau**
Bantock House Museum Contains an important collection of English painted enamels and early Worcestershire porcelain, local japanned ware and cut steel work, pottery, local history and English and foreign dolls. 1¼m SW in Bantock Park via Merridale Road (I).

Hospitals

K   **Chest Clinic**, Bell Street *tel 21180*
P   **Royal Hospital**, Cleveland Road *tel 51532*
I   **Wolverhampton and Midland Counties Eye Infirmary**, Compton Road *tel 26731*
E   **West Park Hospital**, Park Road West *tel 26731*

Sport and Recreation

O   **Ambassador Bowling Centre**, Birmingham Road
F   **Central Swimming Baths**, Bath Avenue
E   **West Park** (Boating, tennis etc). The annual Wolverhampton Fiesta is held here
F   **Wolverhampton Wanderer's Football Club**, Molineux Ground

Theatres and Cinemas

K   **ABC Cinema**, Garrick Street *tel 22917*
K   **Grand Theatre**, Lichfield Street *tel 25244*
J   **Odeon Cinema**, Skinner Street *tel 20364*

Department Stores

James Beattie Ltd, Victoria Street
Bedford Williams Ltd, 11 Mander Square
Marks and Spencer Ltd, 19 Dudley Street
Owen Owen Ltd, Mander Centre
Rackmans, Snow Hill

Markets

N   **Open Market** (Tuesday, Wednesday, Friday and Saturday)
J   **Retail Market Hall** (Daily)

Advertisers

J   Berni Town Hall Tavern
J   Mercantile Credit

Bantock House

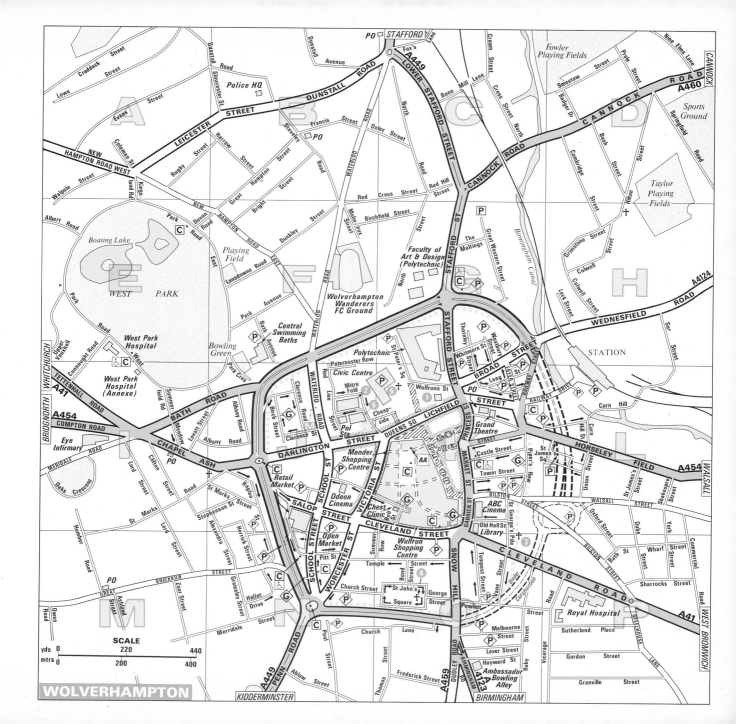

WOLVERHAMPTON

WORCESTER

B   **AA Road Service Centre (23)** — on A449 3m N of City Centre *tel 51070*

J(8)   **Tourist Information Centre** — Guildhall *tel 23471* (see also public buildings and places of interest)

Public buildings and places of interest

J(1)   **All Saints Church** A beautiful Georgian church of 1742 containing a rare chained bible of 1608.

F(2)   **Britannia House** An 18th-C building now used as a school.

N(3)   **Cathedral** A 13th- to 15th-C building preserving its original 11th-C crypt. Of special interest are the restored 14th-C tower, the choir stalls of 1379, Prince Arthur's Chantry, the effigy of King John — the earliest of its kind in England — and the Crypt Exhibition illustrating the history of the Cathedral from monastic times.

F(4)   **City Museum, Art Gallery and Library** (Victoria Institute). Exhibits cover local history, archaeology, geology and natural history. Also collections of the Worcestershire Regiment and the Worcestershire Yeomanry Cavalry.

O(5)   **Commandery** Noted for its 15th-C Great Hall and interesting mural paintings. It was the headquarters of King Charles II at the Battle of Worcester in 1651.

O(6)   **Edgar Tower** A 14th-C gateway.

K(7)   **Greyfriars (NT)** A half-timbered house dating from c1480 with early fireplaces, panelling and other features of its period.

J(8)   **Guildhall and Tourist Information Centre** A notable, restored 18th-C building in Georgian style with wings added later. Paintings and armour on show.

K(9)   **King Charles House** A timber-framed house from whence Charles II escaped from his enemies after the Battle of Worcester on 3 September 1651.

N(10)   **King's School** A foundation of 1541 housed in buildings dating from the 14th-C.

O(11)   **Royal Porcelain Works Museum** Contains the world's finest collection of Worcester china. Tours of the factory can be arranged.

J(12)   **St Andrew's Church** A 12th- and 15th-C church of which only the tower and spire (245ft high) now remain.

K(13)   **St Swithun's Church** A fine Georgian church of 1736, features of which are the woodwork, the three-decker pulpit surmounted by a carved and gilded pelican, with the Mayor's chair built in beneath, wrought iron altar, and 17th-C organ.

F(14)   **Shire Hall** A Classical style building of the Ionic order, with statue of Queen Victoria in the courtyard. The County Council meetings and courts are held here.

K(15)   **Tudor House** A 500-year-old timber-framed house, now a museum of local domestic life from Tudor to Victorian times.

Spetchley Park Fine gardens and park, with red and fallow deer, surrounding early 19th-C mansion. 3m E via London Road A44 and A422 (P)

Hospitals

L   **Ronkswood Hospital** *tel 356123*

L   **Shrub Hill Hospital** *tel 27122,* Maternity Unit *tel 22660*

B   **Worcester Eye Hospital,** Barbourne Road *tel 24017*

F   **Worcester Royal Infirmary,** Castle Street *tel 27122*

Sport and Recreation

F   **Sansome Walk Baths**

B   **Worcester City Football Ground,** St George's Lane North, Barbourne

J   **Worcester County Cricket Club,** County Ground, New Road

E   **Worcester Racecourse,** Pitchcroft

Worcester Citizens' Swimming Pool, Weir Lane, 1m S via Bromwich Road A449 (M)

Worcester Golf and Country Club, Boughton Park, St John's. 1m W via Bransford Road A4103 (M)

Theatres and Cinemas

F   **Odeon Cinema,** Foregate Street *tel 24733*

F   **Swan Theatre,** The Moors *tel 27322*

Department Stores

Co-operative, Trinity House, St Nicholas Street

Debenhams, 69 High Street
Marks and Spencer Ltd, 39 High Street
Russell and Dorrell Ltd, 15 High Street
Early closing day Thursday

Markets

J   **Blackfriars Market** (Wednesday, Friday and Saturday)

I   **Fruit and Vegetable Market,** Hylton Road (Daily except Sunday)

K   **General Market,** Market Hall, The Shambles (Monday to Saturday, except Thursday afternoon)

J   **Livestock Market,** The Butts (Monday)

J   **Old 'Sheep' Market,** Angel Street (Saturday)

Advertisers

K   **Berni** Pack Horse

F   **Mercantile Credit**

K   **THF** Giffard Hotel

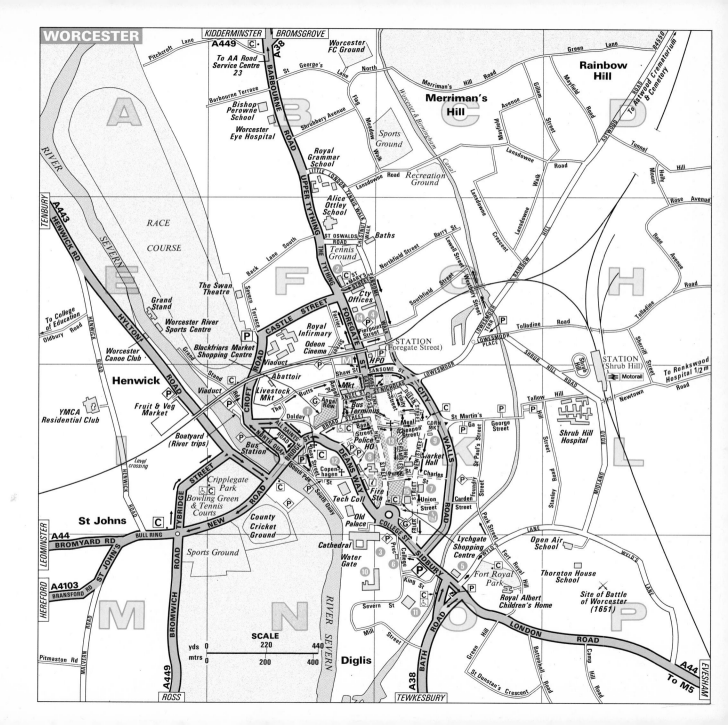

YORK

G   **AA Service Centre** — 6 Church Street *tel 27698*

B(51) **Tourist Information Centre** — De Grey
i   Rooms, Exhibition Square *tel 21756*
     (see also public buildings and places
     of interest)

Public buildings and places of interest

F(1) **All Saints Church** A late-Norman
church noted for its slender 120ft
spire and exceptional stained glass
of the 14th and 15thCs.

G(2) **All Saints Church,** Pavement. This
church has a fine octagonal lantern
tower and a 15th-C lectern with a
rare chained book.

B(3) **Art Gallery** Contains an interesting
collection of English and European
paintings from the 14th to 20th-Cs,
in particular the Lycett Green
collection of old masters.

F(4) **Arts Centre** Formerly St John the
Evangelist church.

B(5) **Assembly Rooms** An impressive
colonnaded ballroom of 1732-36.

H(6) **Black Swan Inn** A 15th-C merchant's
house, now an inn, preserving an
interesting room with medieval painted
panels and Delft tile fireplace.

B(7) **Bootham Bar** One of the medieval city
gates, built on the site of a former
Roman gate, which preserves its
portcullis.

B(8) **Bootham School** The finest of the
Georgian houses in Bootham.

H(9) **Borthwick Institute of Historical
Research** Part of the University of
York housed in St Anthony's Hall, a
guild hall of the 15th-C. There is an
exhibition of documents.

K(10) **Castle Museums and Assize Courts**
The former Debtor's Prison of 1705 and
the Female Prison of 1780 have been
expertly converted to house one of the
most impressive folk museums in the
world. Adjacent are the Assize Courts
of 1777.

B(11) **Central Library and City Information
Bureau**

G(12) **Clifford's Tower** A 13th-C quatrefoil
keep, the largest single remnant of
York Castle. The mound, together with

Baile Hill, its twin across the river,
was constructed by William the
Conqueror.

L(13) **Fishergate Bar** One of the smaller
city gates.

K(14) **Fishergate Postern Tower** Built c1505
this tower originally stood on the
banks of the River Foss. It affords
good views of the Minster.

F(15) **Guildhall** The mid-15th-C Commonhall,
completely restored after severe war
damage.

G(16) **Herbert House** A picturesque, half-
timbered Jacobean structure of 1557.

C(17) **Holy Trinity Church,** Goodramgate. This
13th- to 15th-C church, has a saddle-
back tower and 18th-C box pews.

F(18) **Holy Trinity Church,** Micklegate. A
fragment of a large Norman Priory
church with ancient stocks in the
churchyard.

B(19) **Hospitium** The 15th-C guesthouse of
St Mary's Abbey, now a museum of Roman
antiquities.

G(20) **Impressions Gallery of Photography,**
The Shambles. Displays of photographic
equipment and photographs.

F(21) **Judges' Lodging** A fine Georgian house
of c1720 (not open).

B(22) **King's Manor** A Tudor and later house,
with numerous royal connections. Now
part of York University.

F(23) **Lendal Tower** A riverside tower rebuilt
in the 19thC.

F(24) **Mansion House** The private residence of
the Lord Mayor, this fine Georgian
building of 1725-30 contains the City's
insignia, regalia and civic plate.

G(25) **Merchant Adventurers' Hall** A superb
14th- to 15th-C timbered hall of the
town's wealthiest and most influential
medieval guild.

C(26) **Merchant Taylors' Hall** A restored
medieval guild hall with a fine 14th-C
timbered roof.

F(27) **Micklegate Bar** The most important of
the city gates upon which the severed
heads of traitors were once displayed.

C(28) **Minster** A magnificent structure in the
Early English to Perpendicular styles,
built between c1220 and c1470, famous
for the twin-towered west façade, its

wealth of medieval stained glass, the
octagonal chapter house and 15th-C
choir screen. In the undercroft, where
traces of earlier Roman and Norman
buildings can be seen, is a museum
illustrating the history of the Minster.

C(29) **Minster Library** A large collection
of ancient books and manuscripts housed
in the 13th-C chapel of the former
Archbishop's Palace.

C(30) **Monk Bar** The finest of the City's
gates, vaulted on three floors, and
with its portcullis still in working
order.

B(31) **Multangular Tower,** Yorkshire Museum
Gardens. The west corner tower of the
Roman city, it was rebuilt c300. The
top section is medieval. Part of the
Roman wall extends north-east from
here to the Anglian tower of c600-700.

E(32) **National Railway Museum** The largest
static collection of historic railway
exhibits in Britain, comprising some 25
locomotives, over 20 items of rolling-
stock and many smaller relics.

C(33) **Old Starre Inn** The City's oldest pub,
in use as such from at least 1644. It
displays a rare beam or gallows sign.

H(34) **Red Tower** Dating from 1490, it is the
only substantial brick-built section of
the wall.

G(35) **Roman Baths Inn** A modern pub which has
extensive remains of a Roman steam bath.

H(36) **St Cuthbert's Church** After the Minster
this is York's oldest church, founded
in 687.

H(37) **St Deny's Church** Noted for its richly-
carved Norman doorway and 12th-C
glass, some of the oldest in York.

G(38) **St Helen's Church** Dating from the
14th-C, it is the civic church of York.
It contains 15th-C glass.

B(39) **St Leonard's Hospital** Remains of an
11th-C and later building, founded
by Canons from York Minster.

H(40) **St Margaret's Church** Although rebuilt
in 1852, this church retains a
magnificent Norman porch.

F(41) **St Martin-cum-Gregory's Church** Now
used as the Anglican Youth Centre, this
church dates from the early 13thC.

continued on page 224

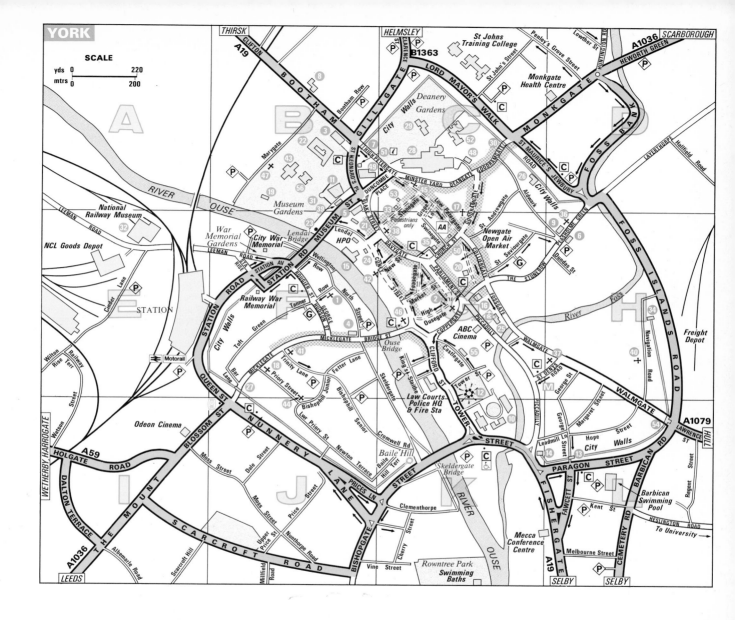

F(42) St Martin-le-Grand's Church Mainly 15thC, but severely damaged during the war, it has been partly rebuilt in a modern style. The remainder is used as a shrine of remembrance.

B(43) St Mary's Abbey, Yorkshire Museum Gardens. Medieval remains of this important Benedictine monastery stand on the foundations of a Norman building founded c1080.

J(44) St Mary's Church, Bishophill Junior. An ancient church with typical Saxon windows and herringbone work in the tower.

C(45) St Michael-le-Belfry's Church A fine Tudor church of c1536. Guy Fawkes was christened here.

G(46) St Michael's Church, Spurriegate. This ancient church has a beautiful interior with 12th-C arcades.

B(47) St Olave's Church The original church, founded in the 11thC, was used as a gun emplacement in the Civil War. The present building is mainly 18thC.

C(48) St William's College A fine building with timbered façade dating from 1453. Behind is a picturesque Georgian quadrangle.

B(49) Theatre Royal Although extensively rebuilt in Victorian times, parts of the original building of 1740 survive.

G(50) The Shambles One of the finest preserved medieval streets in Europe.

B(51) Tourist Information Centre, De Grey Rooms A magnificent Regency building of the 1830s with facilities for meetings and conferences.

C(52) Treasurer's House (NT) A 17th-C house, with a fine collection of furniture and works of art.

C(53) Twelfth Century House The restored remnant of a Norman dwelling house situated behind Stonegate.

L(54) Walmgate Bar The only town gate in England to retain its barbican. Also preserved intact are the wooden doors and portcullis.

G(55) York Heritage Centre Formerly the church of St Mary, Castlegate, the centre displays the architectural development of York from past to present.

B(56) Yorkshire Museum, Botanical Gardens and Tempest Anderson Hall The neo-classical building of 1827 contains important archaeological, natural history, geological and Yorkshire pottery collections. Adjacent is the Tempest Anderson lecture hall of 1912. Both are set in the beautiful gardens of the former abbey.

St Peter's School One of the earliest foundations in England, dating back to 718. ¾m NW via Bootham A19 (B)

University of York An attractive, modern university, opened 1963, which is centred around an artificial lake. Incorporated within the buildings is the Elizabethan Heslington Hall. 1½m SE via Heslington Road (L)

York Tyburn Site of the gallows where John Palmer (alias Dick Turpin) was hanged in 1739. 1¼m SW via The Mount A1036 (I)

St Martin-le-Grand

Hospitals

York District Hospital, Wigginton Road *tel 31313* ½m N via Gillygate B1363 (C)

Sport and Recreation

L   **Barbican Swimming Pool,** Paragon Street

K   **Rowntree Park Swimming Baths,** Terry Avenue (open air) (summer only)

Fulford (York) Golf Club, Heslington Lane 2m SE via Fishergate and Fulford Road A19 (L)

Heworth Golf Club, Muncaster House, Malton Road 1m NE via Heworth Green A1036 (D), then Burton Stone Lane

York City Football and Athletic Club, Bootham Crescent Stadium ¾m NW via Bootham A19 (B) then Bootham Crescent

York Cricket Club, Clifton Park, Shipton Road 1¼m NW via Bootham A19 (B)

York Race Course 1½m SW via The Mount A1036 (I)

York Rugby League Football Club, Wigginton Road ¾m N via Gillygate and Clarence Street B1363 (C)

York Rugby Union Football Club, Clifton Park, Shipton Road 1¼m NW via Bootham A19 (B)

Theatres and Cinemas

G   **ABC Cinema,** Piccadilly *tel 24356*

F(4)   **Arts Centre,** Micklegate *tel 27129* (see also public buildings and places of interest)

I   **Odeon Cinema,** Blossom Street *tel 23040*

B(49) **Theatre Royal,** St Leonard's Place *tel 23568* (see also public buildings and places of interest)

Department Stores

Boyes W and Co Ltd, Ousebridge
Debenhams Ltd, 5 Coney Street
Leak and Thorpe, 19 Coney Street
Marks and Spencer Ltd, 9 Pavement
Early closing day Wednesday

Markets

G   **Newgate** — open air (Monday to Saturday)

Advertisers

J   **Berni** The Windmill
G   **Mercantile Credit**
G   **Centre** White Swan Hotel